**SAP Business Intelligence**

 PRESS

SAP PRESS is a joint initiative of SAP and Galileo Press. The know-how offered by SAP specialists combined with the expertise of the publishing house Galileo Press offers the reader expert books in the field. SAP PRESS features first-hand information and expert advice, and provides useful skills for professional decision-making.

SAP PRESS offers a variety of books on technical and business related topics for the SAP user. For further information, please visit our website: *www.sap-press.com*.

Egger, Fiechter, Rohlf
SAP BW Data Modeling
2005, 437 pp., ISBN 978-1-59229-043-7

Egger, Fiechter, Salzmann, Sawicki, Thielen
SAP BW Data Retrieval
2006, 552 pp., ISBN 978-1-59229-044-4

Egger, Fiechter, Rohlf, Rose, Schrüffer
SAP BW Reporting and Analysis
2006, 578 pp., ISBN 978-1-59229-045-1

Forndron, Liebermann, Thurner, Widmayer
mySAP ERP Roadmap
2006, 293 pp., ISBN 978-1-59229-071-0

Karch, Heilig et al.
SAP NetWeaver Roadmap
2005, 312 pp., ISBN 978-1-59229-041-3

Egger, Fiechter, Kramer,
Sawicki, Straub, Weber

# SAP Business Intelligence

Galileo Press

Bonn • Boston

**ISBN    978-1-59229-082-6**

1st edition 2007, 1st reprint 2007

**Translation** Lemoine International, Inc., Salt Lake City, UT
**Copy Editor** Nancy Etscovitz, UCG, Inc., Boston, MA
**Cover Design** Silke Braun
**Layout Design** Vera Brauner
**Production** Vera Brauner
**Typesetting** Typographie & Computer, Krefeld
**Printed and bound in** the Netherlands

# Contents at a Glance

# Contents

## 3 Data Modeling in the Data Warehousing Workbench of SAP NetWeaver 2004s BI ............... 155

## 4    Data Retrieval ............................................... 213

## 5    Performance Optimization with Aggregates and BI Accelerator ............................................... 263

# Preface

I am very pleased to take the opportunity to address the readers of this book with a few words from SAP product development, especially since after SAP BW 3.5, SAP NetWeaver 2004s BI is a release whose functional width and depth marks the greatest step forward since SAP entered the business intelligence and data warehousing markets.

The most significant change is doubtlessly the new name—*SAP NetWeaver Business Intelligence*. The SAP BW 3.5 Release was already part of SAP NetWeaver 2004 and achieved significant synergies with other NetWeaver components, in particular, with SAP Enterprise Portal. Just think of the information broadcasting function that enables you to distribute reports via email or the portal.

With SAP NetWeaver 2004s, SAP has now managed to comprehensively integrate business intelligence into an integration platform for business processes. The resulting benefits are reflected in numerous areas. All applications that are based on SAP NetWeaver—whether they are SAP-proprietary applications, partner solutions, or customer-specific solutions—can now build on a standard portfolio of BI functions and tools. The coherence of user interfaces, interaction options, metadata, master data, and the general request processing is therefore guaranteed.

But, even as a standalone solution, BI benefits from the integration into SAP NetWeaver. Today, business intelligence can no longer be considered an isolated task. On the contrary, increasingly more, sometimes almost existential, interdependencies are being created with other software components. Consequently, no web-browser-based BI solution can exist today if it isn't integrated into a portal or intranet. The same holds true for document management: context-specific comments, descriptions, remarks, and so on, are critical if you want to communicate insights based on reports or analyses between different users. Other areas of integration include data quality (master data management), the tracking of tasks (collaboration), and business process management.

All those interdependencies are mapped in the NetWeaver platform; the BI component in SAP NetWeaver 2004s is virtually able to delegate the relevant tasks to the responsible special components. This ensures that BI-specific solutions (e. g., for the portal) don't make the system landscape more complex than it already is.

In the planning phase of BI in SAP NetWeaver 2004s, we had four strategic goals. You can determine how far we managed to set the right priorities and to attain the planned goals as outlined below. In any case, this book should prove invaluable to you.

### 1st Objective: Extending the Range of BI to Masses of End Users

In this age of the so-called *information democracy*, each employee of a company has the right to an appropriate supply of information. This alone (and there are many other reasons) turns the entire company staff into a potential business intelligence user base. SAP NetWeaver 2004s meets this requirement because of massive investments in two key areas: user friendliness and query performance. The new Business Explorer (web, Excel, and design tools), the integration into SAP NetWeaver Visual Composer, and the BI Accelerator as a performance turbo engine are the outstanding technology innovations in this respect.

### 2nd Objective: Real Integration of Planning and BI

Today, planning and budgeting are regarded as natural extensions to business intelligence. From the user departments' viewpoint, that is certainly not a new outlook as there is no strict separation between these areas that closely interact with each other in daily business processes. But, on the software side, reality looks different. BI and planning tasks are usually carried out using different tools, even though the same vendor provides these tools. With NetWeaver BI, we want to provide a realistic combination of BI and planning: identical user interfaces, the same design tools, identical master and metadata, common hierarchies, authorizations, processors, and so on. Therefore, each report has the potential to become a planning template.

### 3rd Objective: Assuming the Role of a Companywide Data Warehouse

A modern data warehouse must ensure that the stored information is as up-to-date, consistent, and complete as possible. A companywide view of the entire organization should ensure that correct strategic decisions can be made in real time and based on a consistent data basis. SAP NetWeaver 2004s addresses the requirements with a strategic implementation as a corporate data warehouse: simplified administration, reduced efforts during operation, improved data transfer processes, fewer implications of changes to the modeling, increased loading throughput, management of very large data quantities, and so on.

### 4th Objective: Service-Oriented Basis for All Kinds of Analytical Applications

The Enterprise Services Architecture (ESA) is the prerequisite for increased flexibility and agility in times of constantly changing requirements to IT and to the user departments. ESA is also the basis for a closer interaction of strategic and operational decision-making processes. The focus of service orientation in SAP NetWeaver 2004s BI is based on an improved support of *operational reporting* and *embedded analytics*. In other words, the BI functions are exposed as services and integrated into a model-driven application development using the Visual Composer.

Once again, Norbert Egger and his team of authors have found the right point in time to capture their rich project experience and excellent knowledge of the product in a book that reconciles theoretical concepts and practical use in a highly useful manner.

I hope that you enjoy reading this book and will have great success with your SAP NetWeaver 2004s Business Intelligence projects.

Walldorf, December 2006
**Stefan Sigg**
Vice President SAP NetWeaver BI
SAP AG

# Foreword

In recent years, the ability to adequately acquire and use information has increasingly become the driving force for many developments. A growing number of companies are currently realizing the outstanding importance of this ability and are therefore beginning to implement and operate the necessary organization, processes, and IT tools. In light of this development, the new positioning, comprehensive extension, and revision of the necessary tools performed by SAP AG are taking place at the right time.

The first collaboration with SAP PRESS that resulted in the *SAP BW Professional* book and into which I had entered very reluctantly became a surprising success story. Thanks to a very good partnership in which everyone who was involved in the project did an outstanding job, this first common publication was made possible in a relatively short timeframe.

*Beginning of the collaboration between SAP PRESS and CubeServ*

Due to the surprisingly strong demand and the very positive feedback for *SAP BW Professional*, we then created the (first) volumes of the SAP BW Library with the goal of presenting the basic principles of this product to the reader in a systematic way: Volume 1, *Data Modeling*, Volume 2, *Data Retrieval*, Volume 3, *Reporting and Analysis*, and Volume 4, *Planning and Simulation* (available only in German under the title *Planung und Simulation*), provide a comprehensive overview of SAP Business Information Warehouse and contain many sample implementations, most of which can be used across several software releases. The creation of these four volumes would not have been possible without the great commitment of a large number of CubeServ employees.

*The SAP BW Library*

At this time, we would like to express our thanks for the interest shown in the BW Library and the highly positive feedback we received from you.

*Thanks to readers*

The driving force behind the creation of these (and subsequent) books has been and still is the need to enable better business intelligence solutions on the basis of SAP BW or SAP NetWeaver, respec-

*Background and objective*

tively. To me, as one of those responsible for establishing this objective at the BI consulting firm CubeServ, this means that I have to try and nail down the knowledge for "What is possible?" and "How can it be implemented?" as well as throw in some caveats ("Don'ts") among the steadily growing SAP BI community.

Despite all the sometimes justified criticism regarding SAP BW software issues, I still consider it rather annoying to hear that "SAP BW is too slow" or "SAP BW can't do this and that," particularly when I have to review implementations that use inappropriate modeling, or when I discover that the application problems are caused by insufficient knowledge of those responsible for the available scope of functions.

**SAP NetWeaver 2004s BI** Now that SAP NetWeaver 2004s will soon be generally available, we're happy that we can already provide you with an overview of this new version. Don't be intimidated by the new terminology! The core of the functionality described here refers to changes and enhancements of the component that was previously called SAP BW. The new name, SAP NetWeaver 2004s BI, clearly signifies the central position that SAP assigns to business intelligence and how closely BI is interwoven with other processes and components.

SAP NetWeaver 2004s contains many new and revised functions for business intelligence and analytical applications. Having provided a best practice solution with Release SAP BW 3.5, SAP now closes existing gaps seamlessly, and simultaneously increases its lead over the competition in other areas. A first look at enhancements, for instance in the Business Explorer (BEx) Analyzer and BEx Web Application Designer, and at new developments such as the BEx Report Designer, BI-integrated planning, the BI Accelerator, or the Visual Composer, will already demonstrate this functional quantum leap to you in an impressive way.

**Have fun!** With regard to such a comprehensive advancement, it is, of course, a great pleasure for us, the authors, to provide you with an overview of this powerful, greatly extended tool, including numerous sample implementations. On behalf of all the authors of this book, I hope you, the readers, will have a lot of success when using your new BI version, as well as a lot of fun reading through these pages.

Jona (Switzerland), December 2006
**Norbert Egger**

# Introductory Notes

## Working with This Book

This book is intended to facilitate your work with the new *SAP NetWeaver 2004s BI* Release and to broaden your understanding of this application.

To make it easy for you to use this book, we have adopted special symbols to indicate information that might be particularly important to you.

▶ **Step by step**
An important component of this book is to introduce complex work with SAP BW step by step and explain it to you precisely. This icon points to the beginning of a step-by-step explanation.

▶ **Note**
Sections of text with this icon offer you helpful hints and detailed information in order to accelerate and simplify your work.

▶ **Recommendation**
This book offers tips and recommendations that have been proven in our daily consulting work. This icon indicates our practical suggestions.

▶ **Caution**
This icon indicates tasks or steps that require particular attention. The accompanying text indicates when you should exercise particular caution.

Special symbols

[.]

[«]

[+]

[!]

## Comprehensive Case Study

To enable easy access to the complex subject matter of SAP NetWeaver 2004s, we'll use a uniform case study in all the chapters of this book: a virtual company (CubeServ Engines). This case study will be used to present and communicate all the important require-

Model company "CubeServ Engines"

ments of business intelligence applications in a manner that reflects real life experience.

Company structure ► The model company, CubeServ Engines, operates internationally. It includes various subsidiaries as legal units. Subgroups combine the subsidiaries, and CubeServ Engines (Holding) AG runs the subgroups (see Figure 0.1).

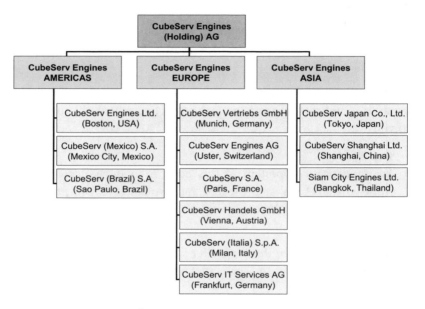

**Figure 0.1** The Structure of the Model Company: "CubeServ Engines"

Infrastructure ► The various elements of the company are specialized. Some of them are involved only in sales, some are production companies that also perform sales tasks, and a third group of businesses provides shared services.

Currencies ► The Euro is the group currency. In addition, the various company codes also use local currencies (US dollar, Mexican peso, Brazilian real, Euro, Swiss franc, Japanese yen, Chinese renminbi yuan, Thai baht).

Fiscal year variant ► The model company's fiscal year corresponds to the calendar year with four special periods.

IT systems ► CubeServ Engines uses four different operational systems. It uses SAP R/3 and the products of other software manufacturers for IT support of its transactional processes.

All additional requirements will be described in the individual chapters of this book.

## After You've Read the Book ...

Even after you've read the book, we'd like to continue to assist you if you need advice or help.

We offer the following options:

▶ **SAP BW Forum**
Under the motto of "Meet the Experts!" you can use an Internet forum to send additional questions to the authors and share them with the business intelligence community. Stop by for a visit at the following website: *www.bw-forum.com*. You will find exclusive materials for download here.

▶ **E-Mail to CubeServ**
If you have additional questions, you're invited to send them to the authors directly by email. See Appendix E, *Authors*, for their e-mail addresses.

## Acknowledgements

Books are never produced without the support and collaboration of many. That's why we'd like to express our special thanks to the following people for their collaboration, help, and patience:

CubeServ Group would like to express particular thanks to Dr. Heinz Häfner (Senior Vice President NetWeaver Operations) and Dr. Stefan Sigg (Vice President SAP NetWeaver BI, SAP AG) as well as to other employees at SAP. The publication of this book would not have been possible on this early date without their readiness to enter into a constructive and critical dialog and to provide us with such great support.    SAP

We would also like to thank the publishing company for the collaboration and great flexibility in accelerating the publication of this work.    The publisher

Furthermore, we would like to express our personal thanks to the following people:

### Norbert Egger

Because various members of our team have created this book, I'd like to thank all the authors sincerely for their participation. Without them, work on this book would have been impossible, because it requires comprehensive and specialized knowledge. Acknowledgement is also due to all other colleagues in the CubeServ Group, especially since I had less time than usual for them and my own work as well, while working on this volume. I would especially like to thank Wiebke Hübner for her great dedication and flexibility in managing this project, which has become yet another success. Above all, I thank my family, especially my beloved wife. She once again supported me by managing the entire family business and showing an endless amount of patience and care, although the additional burden was predictable upfront after the five books that we have already published. With love, I dedicate this book to her.

### Dr. Jean-Marie R. Fiechter

This book would not have been possible without various sources of help. Thanks are due to all those who helped me. Once again, I'd especially like to thank my wife, Karin, and my two children, Patrick and Olivier, for the patience and understanding they showed me as I wrote my sections of this book. I dedicate this book especially to my mother and my brother, Claude-Nicolas.

### Sebastian Kramer

I'd like to sincerely thank all those who supported me with new ideas and comments. Special thanks go to my partner Silke, who showed a great deal of understanding and patience for all those hours of our free time which I had to invest in the work for this book.

### Ralf Patrick Sawicki

I would like to thank the entire team at CubeServ Group for their support and feedback, especially Wiebke Hübner, who was always at my side to provide advice and help. I would also like to thank all my colleagues for their patience and their understanding that while I was writing the book I didn't always have time for them. I would like to dedicate this book to my parents Luzian and Karin Sawicki.

**Peter Straub**

A most sincere and loving thank you goes to my wife, Carole, and our kids, Ivo, Zoe, Luc, and Fiona for the many weekends and nights they had to spend without their father. Many new features and tools had to be provided to my co-authors at short notice and we often put a lot of strain on SAP NetWeaver 2004s BI that went beyond the limits and possibilities of the application.

**Stephan Weber**

I'd like to sincerely thank all colleagues at CubeServ Group. This book wouldn't have been possible without their participation. Norbert Egger and Peter Straub, in particular, have been tireless in providing me with their support at any time, day and night. First and foremost, I'd like to express my most heartfelt thanks to my wife, Eliane, who never ceased to encourage me to write my contribution to this book and who supported me in every respect.

Jona (Switzerland) and Flörsheim am Main (Germany), December 2006
**Norbert Egger**
**Dr. Jean-Marie R. Fiechter**
**Sebastian Kramer**
**Ralf Patrick Sawicki**
**Peter Straub**
**Stephan Weber**

*In recent years, technological innovations have catapulted the concept of a companywide, consistent information landscape from its academic ivory tower into the coarse reality of everyday work. This chapter provides an overview of the basic concepts and technologies required for a companywide information landscape.*

# 1 Business Intelligence Concepts— Innovations

## 1.1 The Closed-Loop Business Analytics Process

*"For many years, the computer profession and business have formed a partnership that has operated under what can be termed an open-loop architecture. But with recent advances in data-warehouse technology and the possibilities of the Internet, there is the prospect of what can be termed a closed-loop architecture for the marriage of business and computers. With a closed-loop business/computer architecture, new business opportunities and possibilities arise that were never before imaginable."*[1]

When Bill Inmon, president of Inmon Data Systems, introduced his vision of a *closed-loop analytical process* under the name of *Corporate Information Factory* (CIF) in 1998, people sneered at him. Today, things have substantially changed. The "screwballs" of the past are the innovative pioneers of today, and those who haven't yet implemented such a landscape run the risk of sooner or later losing their competitiveness.

The term *Corporate Information Factory* describes an information landscape that collects, transforms, standardizes, and stores data from the most disparate operational applications in a company in order to provide this information for analysis and reporting purposes. During this process, the data runs through different layers,

Companywide information landscape

---

1  Inmon, 1998.

after which this meaningful information can be used to influence the operational systems.

You can easily recognize those layers by taking a close look at Figure 1.1. The different layers are: the staging area, extract-transform-load (ETL), enterprise data warehouse, data marts (respectively data mining), and the decision-support system (DSS) applications. Each of these layers fulfills a specific purpose (standardization of data in the ETL, "Corporate Memory" in the EDW, user-friendly data staging in the data marts, and so on) so that all the individual parts of the jigsaw puzzle fit together to form a single picture.

But what you can clearly see already is that building up such an information landscape can be a very complex undertaking, which is often doomed to failure without the support of appropriate software tools.

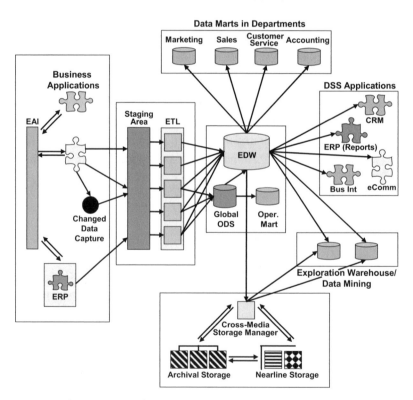

**Figure 1.1** The Corporate Information Factory According to Bill Inmon

Let us now return to the closed-loop business analytics process.[2] We will use it as a central thread throughout this chapter to better position the conceptual innovations in SAP NetWeaver 2004s Business Intelligence.

Closed-loop business analytics process

The primary goal of the closed-loop business analytics process is to enable you to convert operational data into analyzable information from which you can then generate *actionable knowledge*, to be used to influence the operational systems.

As you can easily see in Figure 1.1, this is only possible on the basis of a companywide, consistent information landscape.

For this reason, we'd first like to describe the five steps that form the closed-loop business analytics process and discuss their meaning for implementing a companywide, consistent information landscape (see Figure 1.2). This will make it much easier for you to understand SAP's priorities for the new SAP NetWeaver 2004s BI release.

Five process steps

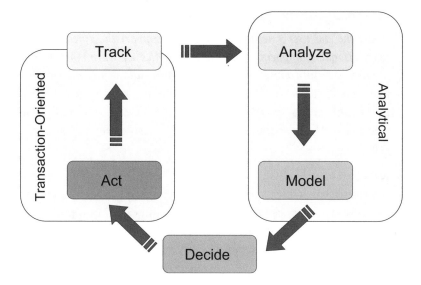

**Figure 1.2** Closed-Loop Business Analytics Process (Source: IDC, 2003)

1. **Track**

    The first step of the closed-loop business analytics process focuses on data acquisition and data storage.

---

2 Vesset, 2003.

First, the data is extracted from all relevant operational systems. Depending on the requirements, this happens either at set times (recurring regularly: daily, weekly, monthly, and so on) or almost in real time.

The data must then be cleansed, transformed, enriched, and standardized.

After that, the cleansed data can be imported and stored in the "basic layer: the enterprise data-warehouse layer of the data warehouse.

This layer serves as the basis for filling the upstream data marts with data as well as for forwarding the data to the DSS applications. Once the data has been staged sufficiently, the process enters the data-retrieval phase.

The following quote by Dan Vesset, Research Director for IDC's Analytics and Data Warehousing Software service, also emphasizes the importance of creating a clean foundation for the data warehouse, particularly regarding data retrieval:

*While the end user's needs and tools that support these needs differ, foundational components of business analytics software must be able to provide a unified architecture that supports all the user groups. End users should be able to view summary information and then drill down into detail that is specific to their business process. The underlying measures that enable this analysis must be consistent across the enterprise.[3]*

2. **Analyze**

Data retrieval, which consists of analyzing and modeling (as the primary activities) as well as presenting and distributing information (as secondary activities), represents the second and third steps in the *closed-loop business analytics process.*

Once the data has been stored in the data warehouse, it is finally available for analysis using business intelligence tools, for query, reporting, and multidimensional analysis.

Traditional business intelligence tools enable decision-makers and information users to answer the following questions. What hap-

---

3 Vesset, 2003.

pened? How did it happen? When did it happen? And if one additional aspect could be added, it might be: Why did it happen?

On the other hand, the following questions are not taken into account: Which alternate decisions are available? Which one is the ideal decision? What are the implications and possible consequences of this decision? What is going to happen?

To run a company with just those traditional BI tools would be like driving a car and looking only into the rear-view mirror. Although you can see everything that happens, you don't see it until it has happened, which might be too late.

[«]

3. **Model**

At this stage, the *advanced analytics tools* come into play. These tools are used to create rules, classifications, and additional models to support the decision-making process. In this context, the following methods are used: decision modeling, forecasting, simulation, optimization, and risk analysis.

Even though the diagram in Figure 1.2 gives you the impression that analyzing and modeling are sequential steps, real life is different. It often happens that the results of an Online Analytical Processing (OLAP) analysis serves as the basis for the creation of a model. Conversely, forecasts and simulations often result in profound analyses, or the modeling results must be presented and distributed. For that reason, it is clear that both steps are closely interrelated.

4. **Decide**

The fourth step of the closed-loop process involves making decisions based on solid information that has been presented in a user-friendly manner. The results obtained in the *Analyze* and *Model* steps represent the basis for those decisions.

The ability to access all types of information consistently and in an integrated way lays the foundation for making solid decisions.

5. **Act**

When the decisions have been made, the corresponding actions must be taken in the fifth step. This step can involve, for instance, the start of a new marketing campaign based on the results of previous campaigns. In another scenario, it may be necessary to automatically lock a credit card based on a transaction analysis and in order to prevent a fraudulent use. Still, another action might consist of granting or refusing a loan on the basis of specific customer profiles.

This step represents the necessary feedback to the operational processes in companies.

In some cases, the feedback occurs automatically. If that happens, we speak of a *retraction*. In other cases, a decision-maker (or end user) obtains actionable knowledge, and then we speak of a *manual feedback*.

To benefit significantly from the use of a data warehouse, the closed-loop process must in no way end with the modeling step. It is vital that this step is followed by the additional steps, *decide* and *act*.

[»]    It is the objective of each organization to accelerate the process of "track, analyze, model, decide, and act" to attain a competitive advantage. Speed without understanding, however, can also result in faster but wrong decisions. Therefore speed and precision must merge with understanding in order to produce a real competitive advantage.

## 1.2    Implementation in Modern Data-Warehousing Systems

Benefits of modern data warehouse systems

When it comes to a comprehensive utilization of the closed-loop process, modern data-warehousing systems come into play. Only this kind of business intelligence, which has been made possible with the introduction of today's data-warehousing tools, can maximize the business value and improve the competitive advantage for the company.

Technology vs. business processes

But those who consider the integration of such heterogeneous system landscapes to be a mere technological challenge are completely mistaken. Companies are experiencing a significantly higher need for flexibility, mobility, and innovation, especially in the area of business processes. Consequently, a competitive advantage can be attained only if the companies focus on their core business processes and tasks. On the other hand, IT departments must provide a high degree of flexibility and mobility to master these challenges quickly and efficiently.

The closed-loop technologies used should help you perform the following tasks:

▶ Make the complexity of systems and applications invisible to the user and reduce this complexity via standardization and integration, wherever possible.

▶ Optimize the interoperability between applications and systems, based on application and process integration.

▶ Provide consistent, intuitive access to all relevant information and to the actionable knowledge at any time and anywhere, using any frontend device.

▶ Achieve an increase in the productivity of end users by standardizing the user interfaces of all relevant applications.

▶ Ensure optimal system stability and data security as well as access control for sensitive information.

To master all those tasks successfully, the motto "think big; start small" should be observed more than ever before. In this context, an approach that is based on a *service-oriented architecture* (SOA) can help to build a landscape that's made up of reusable application components with the objective of saving time and money.

Please allow us now a slight digression in order to demonstrate the importance—or rather the inevitability—of such an approach.

Today, companies have to face numerous challenges:

▶ Markets and consumer behavior change ever more rapidly and require a high degree of flexibility and reactivity from successful companies.

▶ Companies are forced to implement new strategies faster and to shorten the development cycles for products and services. Only in this way can they attain a long-term advantage over their competitors.

▶ In order to cope with those increasingly tight innovation cycles, existing business processes must be constantly optimized, transformed, or even replaced by more efficient processes.

▶ To meet such challenges quickly and efficiently in terms of costs and resources, companies need dynamic and business-oriented IT departments that can react rapidly and flexibly to changing conditions and requirements.

▸ In recent years, IT has become a strategic tool that businesses need to secure competitive advantage and even to survive.

**Future-oriented IT landscape** To meet all those demands, the following requirements, which must be regarded as indispensable for a future-oriented IT landscape, have emerged in recent years:

▸ Technological openness

▸ Functional modularity

▸ Integrated technologies and components

▸ Reusable technologies and components

▸ Powerful development tools

The approach of a service-oriented architecture (SOA) aims to meet just those requirements. Openness, modularity, and integrated and reusable components form the basis for application development.

**Service-oriented architecture** A service-oriented architecture is based on an application platform that provides business functions as reusable, self-contained components. Working from that platform, different services are combined to map entire business processes, such as an ordering transaction. These services are managed centrally and "published" in directories where they can be found and used. Analysis functions are directly integrated in those operational services and no longer treated as separate processes. Finally, the whole structure is rounded off by lifecycle-management services. The objective of all those efforts is to increase the user productivity.

Thus, a companywide vision can grow via projects that are well managed in terms of time and resources.

Each subproject runs through a complete development cycle that consists of specifying and prioritizing the requirements, modeling, and implementation, as well as introduction and review (see Figure 1.3). The reuse of existing services and components therefore helps to consistently create a service-oriented IT landscape step by step.

**Advantages** This brings us back to our data-warehousing systems. The consistent integration of data-warehousing systems into a service-oriented architecture has two main advantages. First, projects can be run much faster and more cost-efficiently. Second, the data-warehousing systems allow for faster, more precise, and more accurate decisions because they base the closed-loop process on a solid, uniform, consistent service-oriented architecture and thereby ensure competitive advantage for the organization.

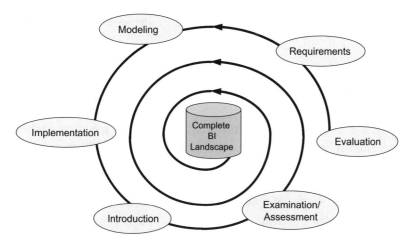

**Figure 1.3** Iterative Implementation of Projects in a Service-Oriented Architecture

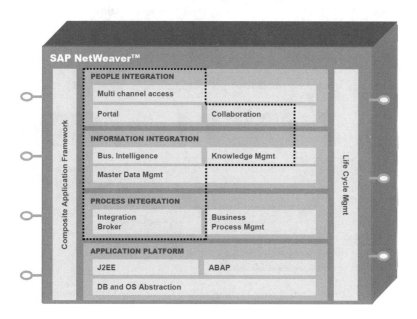

**Figure 1.4** SAP NetWeaver Architecture Components Relevant to SAP BI

35

Figure 1.4 shows such a structure by depicting SAP NetWeaver 2004s Business Intelligence. Not only does SAP NetWeaver 2004s BI contain all aspects of a service-oriented architecture—including an application platform, processes and services, the integration of operational and analytical functions, component lifecycle management, and the focus on the integration and standardization of user functions—but, it also provides the benefits of a closed-loop process by integrating the BI results into the operational processes.

## 1.3    New Features in SAP NetWeaver 2004s

With the new NetWeaver 2004s release, SAP pursued the goal of consistently implementing a closed-loop process architecture in its software application. Figure 1.5 shows that this goal has been impressively attained. As you can see, the most important new features of SAP NetWeaver 2004s have been smoothly integrated into the five steps of the closed-loop process:

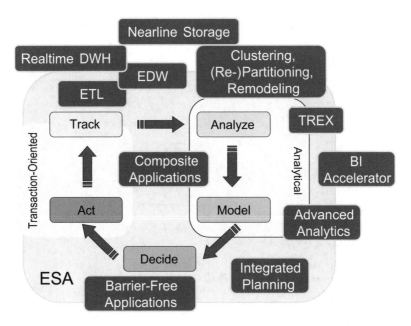

**Figure 1.5** Most Important New Features of SAP NetWeaver 2004s Business Intelligence

The most important new features in SAP NetWeaver 2004s BI are as follows:

Important new features

- ▶ The Enterprise Services Architecture (ESA)
- ▶ The Enterprise Data Warehouse (EDW)
- ▶ Real-time data warehousing (DWH)
- ▶ Information lifecycle management and the use of nearline storage
- ▶ Clustering, partitioning (repartitioning), and remodeling functions
- ▶ The new extraction, transformation, and loading (ETL) process including transformation rules and data-transfer process (DTP)
- ▶ The Business Intelligence Accelerator (BIA) including its search and classification functions (TREX)
- ▶ Advanced analytics applications
- ▶ BI-integrated planning
- ▶ Composite Application Framework (CAF) and barrier-free applications including
  - ▷ Visual Composer
  - ▷ Data Warehousing Workbench (DWB)

The following sections of this chapter provide a brief description of these new features and position them both within the SAP NetWeaver architecture and within the closed-loop process.

## 1.3.1 Enterprise Services Architecture (ESA)

By enhancing the approach of a *service-oriented architecture*, SAP has developed its *Enterprise Services Architecture* (ESA). For SAP, ESA is the future-oriented, modular architecture that builds completely on service-based, reusable application components (enterprise services). In this context, SAP NetWeaver 2004s provides the technological platform for implementing this SOA.

The greatest benefit of SAP ESA is the consistent support of the innovation and standardization cycle within a single environment.

Innovation and standardization cycle

Another fundamental advantage of ESA is that it focuses primarily on individual business processes such as purchasing, production, marketing, sales, accounting, and so on, instead of the technology. This

Focus

enables companies to rapidly adapt applications to new or modified processes and business procedures and even to develop new applications based on existing applications and systems. This, in turn, reduces complexity and increases efficiency and effectiveness of IT, which contributes to a lower total cost of ownership (TCO).

In summary, you can say that, by using ESA and NetWeaver, SAP provides a software architecture that has the following advantages:

▶ Increased productivity through standardization and full control of the business processes while outsourcing non-strategic tasks at the same time

▶ Increased degree of differentiation through the development of new business processes based on the existing infrastructure and the use of existing functions

▶ Increased degree of flexibility in the implementation and adaptation of processes in order to be able to keep pace with business changes

IT Practices
To facilitate the transition from the architecture to the actual implementation, SAP has sliced NetWeaver in layers. In this way, IT Practices came into being (see Figure 1.6).

Think big; start small
In other words, we can revert to the BI project motto mentioned earlier in this chapter: "Think big; start small." Whereas ESA does help to structure the companywide vision in this context (think big), it needs another component to master the iterative projects (start small). And it is exactly at this point that SAP's IT Practices concept comes into play.

Each of these IT Practices directly addresses one of the most important challenges of an organization and is therefore supposed to help companies find the right "starting point" for an iterative project implementation.

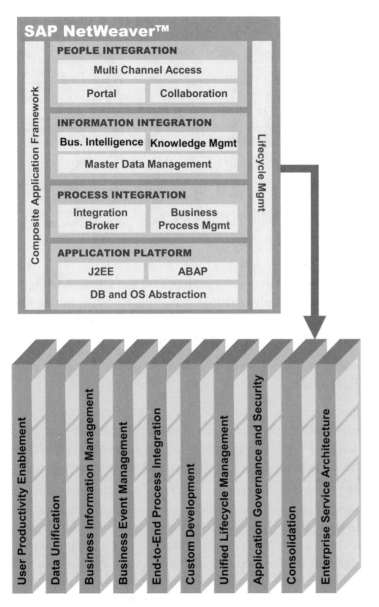

**Figure 1.6** IT Practices Emerged from SAP NetWeaver (Source: SAP)

## IT Practices and IT Scenarios

With its IT Practices, SAP has managed to provide a concept that is specifically tailored to meet the requirements of companies (see the overview in Figure 1.7). IT Practices consist of integrated and pre-defined IT Scenarios, which also are available for further use.

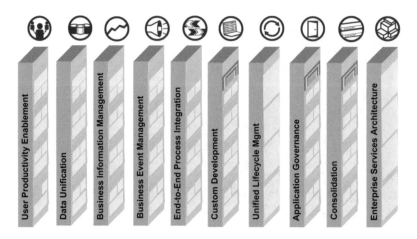

**Figure 1.7** Overview of IT Practices

IT Practices

IT Practices work across several components and enable a stringent orientation towards individual business processes such as purchasing, sales and marketing, or accounting. It is no longer the technology that is in the foreground, but the processes.

The use of IT Practices enables companies to realize significant competitive advantages:

▶ It is possible to map more profitable and efficient processes consistently and flexibly. Proprietary applications can be developed and integrated into a company portal, and companies can guarantee interoperability, a uniform layout, and consistency.

▶ IT Practices use the integrating features of SAP NetWeaver 2004s and define consistent user-oriented process flows that use the entire integration potential of this technology platform. You can create particularly far-reaching synergies by combining several SAP NetWeaver functions with each other. IT Practices such as user productivity, consolidation, or consistent process integration are leading the way to an overall strategy that supports business process management at strategic, operational, and individual levels.

▶ Different integration technologies are combined in such a way that new applications can be developed quickly, the potential of existing systems can be tapped in the best possible way, and new business processes can be created and extended quickly and flexibly.

As mentioned, each IT Practice consists of at least one or several IT    IT Scenarios
Scenarios. An IT Scenario contains a set of clearly structured components used to attain a defined business objective (see Figure 1.8).

## IT Practices                                        IT Scenarios

| IT Practices | IT Scenarios | | | | |
|---|---|---|---|---|---|
| User Productivity Enablement | Running an Enterprise Portal | Enabling User Collaboration | Business Task Management | Mobilizing Business Processes | Enterprise Knowledge Management |
| Data Unification | Master Data Harmonization | Master Data Consolidation | Central Master Data Management | | Enterprise Data Warehousing |
| Business Information Management | Enterprise Reporting, Query, and Analysis | Business Planning and Analytical Services | | Enterprise Data Warehousing | |
| Business Event Management | Business Event Resolution | | | Business Task Management | |
| End-to-End Process Integration | Enabling Application-to-Application Processes | Enabling Business-to-Business Processes | Business Process Management | Enabling Platform Interoperability | Business Task Management |
| Custom Development | Developing, Configuring, and Adapting Applications | | Enabling Platform Interoperability | | |
| Unified Life-Cycle Management | Software Lifecycle Management | | SAP NetWeaver Operations | | |
| Application Governance & Security | Authentication and Single Sign-On | | Integrated User and Access Management | | |
| Consolidation | Enabling Platform Interoperability | SAP NetWeaver Operations | Master Data Consolidation | Enterprise Knowledge Management | |
| Enterprise Service Architecture | Enabling Enterprise Services | | | | |

Figure 1.8 IT Practices Are Based on Reusable IT Scenarios (Source: SAP AG)

IT Scenarios use Web services and SAP NetWeaver functions (and
sometimes even non-SAP software) and usually consist of several
integrated and reusable software components. The scenarios may
exist as different variants.

Because IT Scenarios are not designed for a strictly defined company
size, they are infinitely scalable. They represent a functionality that is
self-contained and therefore cannot be integrated or included in
other IT Scenarios; however, they can be used, in different IT Practices.

In summary, the IT Scenarios represent the implementation of the
ESA concept of modular, self-contained, and reusable services.

### 1.3.2 The Enterprise Data Warehouse (EDW)

In the new NetWeaver 2004s release, SAP for the first time developed a complete business intelligence landscape that is strongly oriented towards Inmon's Corporate Information Factory (see Figure 1.1). When comparing the characteristics of Inmon's concept with SAP's implementation, there are several parallels that are readily apparent:

▶ Both landscapes have a modular structure (layers).

▶ The individual modules can be developed independently of each other.

▶ In both landscapes, the enterprise data warehouse is the central, indispensable object.

The EDW corresponds to an extensively enhanced data-storage layer of a traditional data warehouse and is rightfully regarded as the core of the business intelligence landscape. In a closed-loop-process architecture, the EDW forms the bridge between *Track* and *Analyze*. Without an EDW, analyses would be impossible, and the track results (ETL) have to be imported in the EDW.

EDW layer The business intelligence implementation of the EDW layer (see Figure 1.9) is based on layers and is completely integrated, despite its strong modularization.

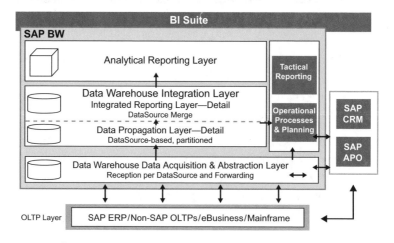

**Figure 1.9** BI Implementation of the EDW Concept

The consistent use of the layer structure by the SAP EDW implementation provides the following advantages:

▶ Fast data acquisition while at the same time unnecessary redundancies are being avoided

▶ Abstraction of the operational data acquisition process from the BI applications (application-independent and flexible)

▶ Basis for an open scalability in terms of both quantity and the number and type of data sources

▶ Use of the best performing data-storage technology for each layer

▶ Securing the "Corporate Memory" (historicized, comprehensive, and granular)

▶ Integration of processes and systems

In the end, the consistent implementation of the EDW concept results in the representation of the entire data warehousing structure as a layer model (see Figure 1.10):

**Layer Model**

▶ Data acquisition layer (ETL)

▶ Data storage layer including

  ▶ Detail level consisting of

    ▶ Data abstraction layer

    ▶ Data propagation layer

    ▶ DWH integration layer and Corporate Memory

  ▶ Aggregation level including

    ▶ Data marts

    ▶ Aggregation hierarchies

▶ Data retrieval level (BI applications)

The layers build modularly upon each other and thus ensure a maximum of flexibility and performance by each using the optimal technology.

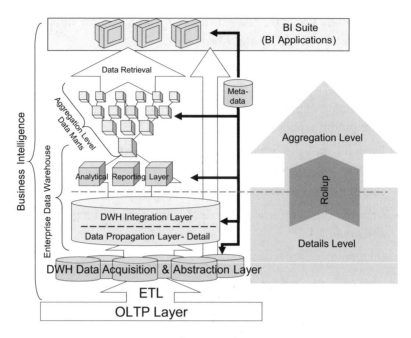

**Figure 1.10** Layer Structure in a Modern BI Landscape

EDW implemen-
tation Let us now return to Inmon's enterprise data warehouse concept. Inmon defines the following requirements for an EDW implementation:

▶ It must represent *the* single version of the truth.

▶ It allows the extraction of data from the operational systems only once in order to forward the data to different data targets at a later stage (drastic reduction of the load on operational systems: "extract once; reuse many").

▶ It serves as Corporate Memory.

▶ It supports the unknown, because it allows for redesigning the BI applications and for designing new BI applications

To fulfill these requirements, the EDW implementation should meet the following (technical) characteristics, that is, it should be:

▶ Integrated (all modules must mesh seamlessly)

▶ Comprehensive (data from all relevant operational applications)

▶ Historically complete (i.e., "historicized")

▶ Highly granular (detailed)

▶ Application-independent

▶ Under the control (and in the possession) of corporate management

When we compare these requirements with the implementation of the EDW in the new SAP NetWeaver 2004s release, all we can say is that SAP has learned from experience and that the company has developed an extremely powerful tool.

In summary, an EDW layer is indispensable to meet the growing requirements regarding scalability, data quantity, number of data sources, time-critical data, the number of BI applications, the number of end users, the complexity of problems, and so forth, both today and in future.

### 1.3.3 Real-Time Data Warehousing

In the new NetWeaver 2004s release, SAP for the first time provides an option that enables the acquisition of data in real time. But to really appreciate the advantages of this new type of data acquisition, we should look back at the history of data warehousing.

In the past (and even to a large extent today), the focus of data warehousing was on an historical view of information. Consequently, data was imported into the data warehouse at regular intervals (monthly, weekly, daily) where it was stored for a longer period of time (historicized).

Flashback

This kind of periodicity in the data-acquisition process was (and is) absolutely sufficient for most analyses and reports. Strategic reporting and time-series analyses examine data over longer periods of time and therefore do not depend on the most recent data.

Furthermore, for the few requirements in the area of tactical reporting that used to depend on time-critical data, so-called *reach-through mechanisms* were developed.[4] Those mechanisms enabled users to directly access data in the transactional systems, which entailed a significant increase in the workload of operational applications so that the mechanisms could be used for only selected tasks.

---

4 In BW 3.x, those were the *RemoteCubes* and *virtual InfoCubes*.

Real-time data
acquisition in
NetWeaver 2004s The requirement for real-time queries grew steadily with the growing maturity of data warehousing in general. The real-time data acquisition concept in NetWeaver 2004s meets this requirement exactly. The real-time data that is required for strategic decision-making processes is provided in a queue[5] by the operational applications at short intervals, for example, every minute or every hour.

For this purpose, specific InfoPackages for real-time data acquisition are created in NetWeaver BI. Those InfoPackages are scheduled using an assigned daemon[6] and are executed on a regular basis. In this way, the data is retrieved from the queue and stored in the persistent staging area (PSA). By using specific data-transfer processes for real-time data acquisition, the daemon updates the data from the PSA into DataStore objects (DSO) that have been specifically designed for this purpose. Once the data has been successfully updated in the DataStore object, it can be used for reporting purposes (see Figure 1.11).

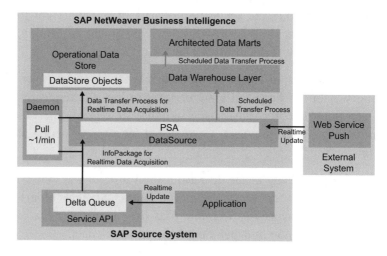

**Figure 1.11** Real-Time Data Acquisition in SAP 2004s Business Intelligence

Two types of
data sources Basically, two types of data sources can be used for real-time data acquisition:

---

5  A specific memory structure used for data transfers. The queue allows an asynchronous data transfer.

6  Batch process of the operating system. The daemon automatically performs tasks on a regular basis. In the Windows world, this is referred to as *services*.

▶ Web services that push the data in the PSA by themselves and in real time. After that, the daemon updates the data in the DSOs.

▶ SAP applications that directly write the data into the SAP Delta Queue in the source system (e.g., in a V3 update). In that case, the daemon retrieves the data from the delta queue and updates it in the DSOs.

This allows us to ensure that the additional load for the operational systems is reduced to a minimum. The analysis and reporting access to the data occurs in the data warehouse without further increasing the workload of the transactional applications.

Another advantage that we should mention is that the data will be completely available in the data warehouse for future historical examinations. Consequently, many of the usual restrictions regarding time-critical queries no longer exist.

The previous statement notwithstanding, one should still thoroughly [«] check which types of time-critical analyses are absolutely necessary and what types of data are required for them. This is especially important with regard to some transactional applications that must be customized in order to make the data available to the data warehouse, either via the delta queue or through push mechanisms (unless the application provider has already taken this into account, which is the case with SAP ERP applications).

## 1.3.4 Information Lifecycle Management and the Use of Nearline Storage

The data volume in a BI landscape grows steadily over time. Moreover, constant financial and legal changes cause companies to deal with a growing quantity of historical data that is accessed less and less. However, this historical data is indispensable when it comes to reliable historical analyses.

Having a large amount of data in a BI system generates extremely high costs and greatly affects the system's performance; in turn, this significantly increases the administrative work. In order to counteract those problems, SAP developed a data-aging strategy in SAP NetWeaver 2004s Business Intelligence. This approach provides a solution for managing historical data, based on different data storage concepts: the nearline storage concept used for historical data that still must be easily accessible for evaluation and analysis, and the archiving of historical data that is hardly ever accessed, but must be stored to comply with legal regulations.

Advantages The advantages of the data-aging strategy are as follows:

▶ Reduction of costs for data management and storage

▶ Increase of BI system performance

▶ Efficient storage of historical data for a comprehensive enterprise data warehouse

Information life- cycle management The SAP implementation of the data-aging strategy is based on an information lifecycle management (ILM) architecture.

ILM focuses on aligning the availability of data and hence the associated administrative work and costs with the commercial benefit of that data. Based on the ILM model, the data is allocated into one out of three availability classes (see Figure 1.12):

▶ **Online**
For current, important data that is regularly used

▶ **Nearline**
For less frequently used data that is still active and will probably be used at a later stage (e. g., for reliable historical analyses or time series)

▶ **Offline (Archived)**
For historical data that may be used in the future or that has to be stored due to legal regulations

As Bill Inmon states: "An ILM concept for data warehousing enables companies to effectively subdivide data according to its current operational value. Data that is actively used remains online in the data warehouse, whereas less important data is moved to a nearline storage system. Historical data and data that must be stored for legal reasons can be archived offline. If needed, this data can be restored to meet the requirements of users or to be examined in legal audits."

A fast access to online data is a decisive factor in the SAP implementation as well. The online data is located in the very powerful NetWeaver BI Repository (enterprise data warehouse), which uses storage media that has the highest possible performance values. Nearline data is first compressed and then moved to a separate, more cost-efficient repository. In this way, fast access is replaced by cost reductions. The data is still available as "quasi online" in the BI system via virtual InfoProviders and MultiProviders. It makes a lot of sense here to use less expensive storage media for this purpose. The offline data is archived in the most cost-efficient media in order to reduce the data storage costs and administration effort to a minimum. It can, however, be restored in the online repository for data modeling purposes.

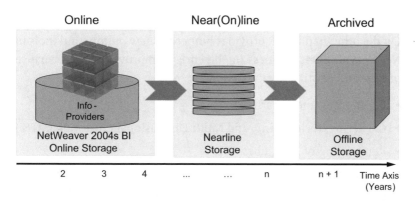

**Figure 1.12** The Three Availability Classes of the SAP ILM Architecture Along the Time Axis

## 1.3.5 Clustering (Reclustering), Partitioning (Repartitioning), and Remodeling Functions

Performance is a perpetual topic in all data warehouse installations. This holds true not only for new projects, but also—and even more acutely so—for data warehouses that have been operative for several years and were thus able to grow organically. It is exactly this growing number of users, reports, and different applications that make performance optimization mandatory.

Our experience has shown that the following additional system-external **[«]** factors also demand an optimization of the system:

▶ The growing degree of competition among companies requires extremely fast real-time analyses that must be available at each company level.

▶ A wide acceptance and use of the system can be achieved only if long runtimes for data updates and reports are avoided.

On the one hand, you can use the known optimization options that have already been in use in BW 3.x installations:

▸ Optimization of hardware, operating system, file system, and the database for business intelligence use

▸ Optimization of the BW Basis installation and BW statistics

▸ Data model and dimensions optimization

▸ Indices and aggregates

▸ OLAP cache and precalculation

New options    On the other hand, SAP provides numerous new options and tools in NetWeaver 2004s Business Intelligence to improve the performance of new and existing data warehouses:

▸ Partitioning and repartitioning

▸ Clustering, reclustering, and Multi-Dimensional Clustering (MDC)

▸ Remodeling of InfoCubes

▸ Parallelization of the rolling up, condensing, and checking of several aggregates and of the attribute change run

▸ Business Intelligence Accelerator (is described in further detail in Section 1.3.7 and Chapter 5, *Performance Optimization with Aggregates and BI Accelerator*)

So let's take a closer look at those optimization options.

Partitioning    The entire dataset of an InfoCube can be divided into several small blocks via partitioning. Those blocks are physically independent and don't overlap each other. The separation into blocks significantly increases the system's performance during reporting and when data is deleted from the InfoCube.

Although the partitioning options have been extended in SAP NetWeaver 2004s BI (in particular with regard to database support), partitioning can still be carried out only on the basis of one of the two available partitioning criteria: **Calendar month** (0CALMONTH) and **Fiscal year/period** (0FISCPER).

Repartitioning    A new feature in SAP NetWeaver 2004s BI is the option to repartition existing InfoCubes that already contain data. Repartitioning is useful if data has already been loaded into the InfoCube and if:

- The InfoCube was not partitioned at creation time
- More data was loaded into the InfoCube than was originally planned in the initial partitioning phase
- The period chosen for the partitioning is too short
- Some partitions contain only little or no data over time after a data archiving process

There are two ways to carry out a repartitioning:

- **Merging and adding partitions**
  You can merge partitions of InfoCubes at the bottom end of the partitioning schema (merge) or add them at the top (split).

- **Complete partitioning**
  In a complete partitioning, the fact tables of the InfoCube are fully converted using shadow tables that have been created via the new partitioning schema.

Repartitioning is supported by all BW databases except for DB2 UDB for UNIX, Windows, and Linux, and except for MaxDB. DB2 UDB for UNIX, Windows, and Linux supports clustering and reclustering instead.

This means that the MaxDB database neither supports partitioning and repartitioning nor clustering and reclustering up to and including SAP NetWeaver 2004s. Needless to say, this database should be used for only small data quantities.

[«]

Clustering was already supported by BW 3.x running on DB2 UDB. That kind of clustering was a so-called *index clustering*, which can be compared to partitioning. Index clustering organizes the data records of a fact table according to the sort order of an index; BW only supports the time characteristics, **Calendar month** (0CALMONTH), and **Fiscal year/period** (0FISCPER). This results in a linear partitioning based on the values of the index fields.

Multi-dimensional clustering

Conversely, Multi-Dimensional Clustering (MDC) was introduced in SAP NetWeaver 2004s. It can be set separately for each InfoCube and DataStore object. You can essentially increase the performance of database operations such as read, write, and delete accesses by using MDC. Multi-Dimensional Clustering organizes the data records of a fact table according to one or several freely selectable characteristics. The selected characteristics are referred to as *MDC dimensions*. Only data records that have identical values in the MDC dimensions are stored in a database block, which is also referred to as an *extent*. This ensures that there is always an optimal sort order so that table reorganization can be avoided even if many insertions and deletions are made.

Instead of standard indices, database-internal *block indices* are created on the characteristics. Block indices reference database blocks instead of data records, which significantly reduces their size. Therefore, they save storage space, and it takes less time to browse through them to find information. This accelerates table queries that are restricted to those characteristics.

In Multi-Dimensional Clustering, one or several dimensions can be selected for the fact tables of an InfoCube. For the active table of a DataStore object, you can select one or several InfoObjects; and for PSA tables, an MDC index is automatically created on the REQUEST field.

In SAP NetWeaver 2004s BI, MDC is only supported by the IBM DB2 Universal Database for UNIX and Windows platform. In addition to clustering new InfoProviders, you can also recluster existing InfoProviders.

**Remodeling InfoCubes**

The remodeling of InfoCubes is another optimization option. SAP NetWeaver 2004s provides tools that enable you to change the structure of InfoCubes that already contain data without losing this data. The different remodeling options available are as follows:

For characteristics:

- ▶ Addition of or replacement with:
    - ▷ Constants
    - ▷ Attribute of an InfoObject of the same dimension
    - ▷ Value of another InfoObject of the same dimension
    - ▷ Customer exit (for user-specific coding)
- ▶ Deletions

For key figures:

- ▶ Addition of:
    - ▷ Constants
    - ▷ Customer exit (for user-specific coding)

▶ Replacement with:

  ▶ Customer exit (for user-specific coding)

▶ Deletions

These tools enable you to adjust the structure of an existing InfoCube to new requirements and situations.

The repartitioning, remodeling, and reclustering tools provide invaluable support, especially in data warehouses that have been in operation for a longer time. These tools enable you to adjust the structures to new requirements and situations. This flexibility increases the lifecycle of the data warehouse and always ensures optimal system performance. There are several reasons for adjusting an InfoProvider that already contains data:

▶ A larger data quantity requires a new partitioning (or clustering) of the data.

▶ A change in the distribution of data forces requires the repartitioning (reclustering) of InfoProviders.

▶ A modified company structure requires the adjustment of the data model.

▶ New or changed requirements on the end users' side may entail both remodeling and repartitioning.

**[«]**

Parallelization of the attribute-change run, as well as of the rollup, condensing, and checking of several aggregates, is mentioned only briefly for the sake of completeness at this point. Because these parallel processes are always carried out in the background, their runtimes can be significantly reduced.

Parallelization

## 1.3.6 The New ETL Process, Including Transformation Rules and Data Transfer

A new object concept is available for the ETL process as of SAP NetWeaver 2004s. To implement the EDW layer paradigm, SAP has changed the concept of the ETL data flow and process design (Info-Package for the load into the PSA, transformation, data-transfer process for the data distribution within BI). In doing so, SAP rationalized and standardized the involved components (see Figure 1.13). This standardization and rationalization makes it much easier for companies to implement even very extensive, sometimes even complex, data warehouse architectures that map the EDW layer concept.

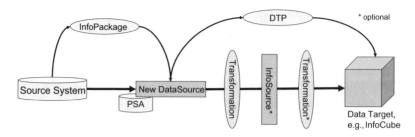

**Figure 1.13** New ETL Process Including Transformation Rules and Data Transfer Process

The most important innovations in this modified object concept are as follows:

▶ When a DataSource is activated, a PSA table is generated in the inbound layer of the BI so that data can already be loaded.

▶ The InfoPackage is only used to load the data from the source system into the PSA.

▶ This is followed by the data-transfer process (DTP) step to transfer data within the BI from one persistent object to another by using transformations and filters.

▶ The definition for which data targets the data from the DataSource is to be updated into occurs in transformations. This is also where fields of the DataSource are assigned to InfoObjects of the target objects in BI.

This separation increases the transparency of transfer processes through the various data-warehouse layers, which enables a straight-forward implementation of the EDW concept. The performance of the transfer process is further increased by an optimized parallelization of the data import process.

In line with the standardization mentioned at the beginning of this section, data-transfer processes are used for the standard data transfer as well as for real-time data acquisition and for direct data access.

### 1.3.7 The Business Intelligence Accelerator and Its Search and Classification Functions (TREX)

When observing the business analytics market, several trends are apparent:

▸ The number of BI end users is growing exponentially due to the use of intranets and extranets.

▸ The quantity of data warehouse data is growing continuously; most companies expect the data volume to double in less than three years. This problem is further compounded by the fact that the load frequency of the data warehouse is increasing steadily, and the requirements are increasingly moving more towards real-time data warehousing.

▸ The decision cycles are becoming shorter and are increasingly requiring decision alternatives. Simulations, what-if analyses, and ad-hoc queries are becoming indispensable.

▸ Good response times are a vital prerequisite for using analytical applications successfully in practice.

The SAP BI Accelerator (BIA) is SAP's answer to these challenges. Basically, it is a "black box," as it combines specialized hardware and software in one system. SAP BI Accelerator was developed in collaboration with Intel, which provides the specialized processors, as well as IBM and HP, who provide the server and storage technologies.

**SAP BI Accelerator**

> You should keep in mind, however, that SAP BI Accelerator is a *complement* to SAP NetWeaver 2004s Business Intelligence and in no way should it be considered to be a replacement. Therefore, in order to use BIA, you must have a SAP NetWeaver installation, including the necessary hardware and software components. Moreover, you should note that the current version of SAP BI Accelerator can only index InfoCubes that contain cumulative key figures.

**[«]**

But what does this SAP BI Accelerator "black box" actually hide "under the hood"? BI Accelerator is basically a highly scalable, parallelized analysis server that processes the queries of SAP NetWeaver BI users in an extremely efficient way. The uniqueness of SAP BIA is its use of the SAP-proprietary TREX search and classification technology, combined with a hardware architecture based on scalable blade servers manufactured by HP and IBM. Figure 1.14 provides a good overview of SAP BIA and its interactions with SAP NetWeaver 2004s BI.

In terms of technology, SAP BI Accelerator is based on indices that provide a transposed image of all data of an InfoCube such as fact tables, dimensions, and master data, as well as on a scalable compo-

**SAP BI Accelerator technology**

nent that processes the jobs in the main memory in parallel. The entire SAP BI Accelerator software runs on a 64-bit Linux platform, which enables it to use the full scalability of the blade-server hardware. Therefore, any extension of the hardware (e. g., the addition of blades, memory, and more or faster processors) directly increases the performance of the BI Accelerator.

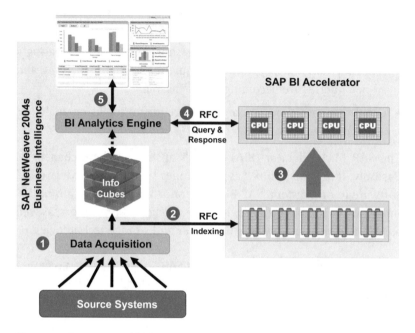

**Figure 1.14** Interaction of SAP NetWeaver 2004s BI and SAP BI Accelerator

**Functionality of SAP BI Accelerator**

Figure 1.14 also provides a rough overview of the functionality of SAP BI Accelerator:

1. The data is imported from the different source systems into an SAP NetWeaver 2004s BI InfoCube.

2. Concurrently, the data is indexed in parallel in SAP BI Accelerator, where it is also stored with the same level of granularity as the InfoCube. Those TREX indices are not stored in a database, but directly in the file system. Extremely high compression rates and a highly efficient read behavior are achieved by using transposed, column-based, decomposition indices (as opposed to the "normal" row-based and record-based indices).

3. The BI Accelerator indices are loaded in the main memory. That's where the queries are processed at runtime including their aggregations, filtering, selections, joins, and sorting. The indices are either imported automatically in the main memory during the initial call of a query, or you can have them imported upfront, for instance after each data import in the InfoCube.

4. The queries are then forwarded through the BI Analytics Engine to the BI Accelerator at query runtime.

5. The BI Accelerator provides the results transparently to the end user.

When a query is run, the BI Analytics Engine decides which of the available processing options is the best. The new SAP BI Accelerator option is one possible option in a series of alternatives here. The processing options are checked in the following sequence, from the fastest to the most resource-intensive one:

Process steps of a query

1. Does an up-to-date, precalculated result set exist?

2. Is the result set still available in the OLAP cache?

3. Does a BI Accelerator index exist for this InfoCube?
   (Tests have shown that the BI Accelerator is approximately as fast as the OLAP cache).

4. Do aggregates or materialized views exist that can be used?

5. The basic InfoProvider is used.

In summary, you can say that SAP BI Accelerator is a transparent extension to SAP NetWeaver 2004s. This extension enables the system to handle a growing number of end users and flexible queries (simulations, ad-hoc queries, what-if analyses) against a dramatically increased quantity of data.

> Our experience has shown that—depending on the combination of data model and queries—the increase in system performance can be considerable when using SAP BI Accelerator. For example, a triple-digit improvement factor is entirely possible for queries that require a lot of database read time.

[«]

### 1.3.8 Advanced Analytics Applications

Let us now return to the third step in the closed-loop process described in Section 1.1: Modeling.

Because the majority of business intelligence solutions do not consist of advanced analytics tools (and vice versa), this is where the problem begins. Incompatible tools are used that often have different databases, access different upstream systems, and are hardly able to exchange data among each other. As shown in Figure 1.15, this often results in a knowledge gap or "learning gap" that drastically interrupts and slows down the closed-loop process.

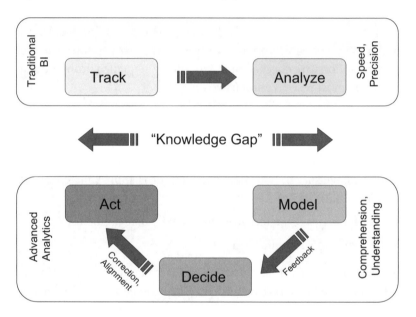

**Figure 1.15** Knowledge Gap (or "Learning Gap") in the Closed-Loop Process (Source: IDC, 2003)

**SAP Analytics Applications**

At this stage, the new *SAP Analytics Applications* come into play; these are provided with NetWeaver 2004s BI. These applications represent a kind of "business content" that consists of more than 100 applications for more than 25 different industries.

SAP Analytics Applications are model-oriented, *service-based composite applications* (see Section 1.3.10) that merge historical information and real-time information directly linked to specific business processes and transactions. SAP Analytics Applications enable users to expedite important business processes and corporate decisions based on a holistic view of the available information.

It is the combination of data from operational SAP solutions and external systems with business intelligence queries that enables the SAP Analytics Applications to provide this consistent, holistic view of all relevant business data. In this way, data silos are eliminated, and planning (analyses, modeling) and collaboration processes (acting, triggering corrective action) are seamlessly combined across different lines of business and company areas as well as organizational borders.

Consequently, the "knowledge gap" in the closed-loop business analytics process can be closed, and the process itself can be carried out faster and more smoothly from the analysis to the action, which provides a competitive advantage to the company.

### 1.3.9 BI-Integrated Planning

In the SAP world, the term *BI-integrated planning* describes the complete integration of planning and BI functions with a uniform user interface and design environment, as well as a commonly used analysis engine and data basis.

In particular, BI-integrated planning meets the following market requirements:

Spectrum

▶ Standardization of analysis and planning from the user's viewpoint. This can be achieved through:

   ▶ Uniform and consistent user interfaces

   ▶ Alignment and reusability of process and modeling logic (e. g., by using hierarchies, variables, calculated key figures, etc.)

   ▶ Common design tools (e. g., the Query Designer, Web Application Designer, etc.)

   ▶ A uniform and consistent data basis

▶ Flexible planning modeling via simple and complex multiple aggregation levels, a versioning concept, the use of hierarchies, and other capabilities

▶ Web-based modeling environment for planning applications (planning wizard and planning modeler) that is supported by the system

▶ Planning on the web and in MS Excel

▶ Barrier-free support of the planning process including

　▶ Single point of entry

　▶ Information broadcasting

　▶ Status and tracking system

Figure 1.16 contains a straightforward illustration of the standardization of analysis and planning. All planning elements of the data acquisition and data storage layers (DataStore objects, InfoProviders, aggregation levels, and so on), as well as of the data retrieval (OLAP and analytic services) and data presentation layers (query, analysis, reporting), are integrated in the business intelligence component of SAP NetWeaver 2004s.

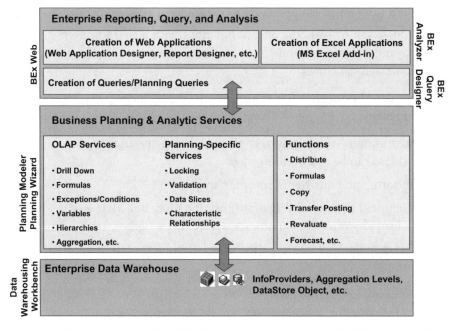

**Figure 1.16** Integration of the Planning Environment in SAP NetWeaver 2004s BI

### 1.3.10 The Composite Application Framework and Barrier-Free Applications

*"The business environment is becoming more challenging as Sarbanes-Oxley, regulation, and competition all drive organizations to evolve their business models, improve the alignment between strategy and execution, and empower their business users with actionable insights in the context of business processes."[7]*

That's where composite applications come into play. Composite applications are the way to fulfill the promise of providing a service-oriented architecture. That is, they enable the seamless combination of transaction, analysis, and collaboration processes across different lines of business, company areas, and organizational borders (see also the example of such an application shown in Figure 1.17).

**Figure 1.17** Example of a Composite Application That Combines Analytical and Operational Components

---

7  Mitch Morris, Director, Deloitte Consulting LLP.

Composite Appli-
cation Framework In order to develop composite applications quickly and easily, SAP provides a Composite Application Framework (CAF) within Net-Weaver 2004s.

SAP CAF provides a stable development and runtime environment for SAP Composite Applications, which comply with the Enterprise Services Architecture. The SAP CAF comprises development tools, methods, services and processes, an abstraction layer for objects, and libraries containing predefined user interfaces and process templates.

As shown in Figure 1.18, the most important characteristics of the SAP Composite Application Framework can be summarized by the following list:

▶ **Model-oriented architecture**
The SAP Composite Application Framework supports the model-oriented application creation so that applications can be developed with a minimum of programming work. This enables you to reduce development and implementation times and achieve an improved business-process-oriented integration for new applications.

▶ **Object access layer**
The object access layer separates the repositories of the underlying systems from the business objects and processes. This means that SAP Composite Applications can be installed in any given system landscape. The object access layer is a central interface that controls the communication with participating systems via Web services; in other words, the composite applications don't require any information as to whether services are provided by another SAP NetWeaver 2004s component or by an external service provider. The data sources for those independent "business objects" can be different heterogeneous (planning-related and operational) source systems.

▶ **Cross-company collaboration**
The Collaboration Framework enables you to establish a link between a service or object of SAP NetWeaver components and any other business object. Collaboration objects such as tasks, documents, or meetings can be accessed within the object access layer. Therefore, all applications that are based on the SAP CAF have integrated collaboration functions.

▶ **Templates for user interfaces and guided procedures**
The business objects and services of the SAP Composite Application Framework form the basis for the design of guided procedures, which, in turn, provide an application-friendly user interface for the design phase, and a process display for the runtime. Predefined workflow templates support the process definition of the guided procedures and therefore help to accelerate the application development process. Moreover, they facilitate the consistent development of barrier-free applications.[8]

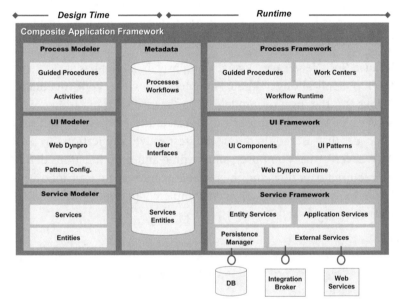

**Figure 1.18** The Model-Oriented Architecture of the SAP Composite Application Framework

The model-oriented architecture of the SAP Composite Application Framework allows for a linkage of design time components and runtime components that is based solely on metadata.

The next sections provide two examples of different development environments (Visual Composer in the frontend area and Data Warehousing Workbench in the backend area) that adhere to the aforementioned concepts.

---

8  The non-existence of barriers ensures that everyone can use technology and IT products, in particular, handicapped people. The SAP CAF was designed in such a way that it especially facilitates the development of barrier-free applications.

### SAP Visual Composer

SAP has implemented the composite applications concept in the NetWeaver context by using SAP Analytics Applications (see Section 1.3.8). The Visual Composer serves as the user interface for SAP Analytics Applications. This model-based tool allows the integration of data from different systems (both operational and planning systems), and the creation of professional frontends, including full portal integration. It provides a powerful, server-based design tool, which enables a high degree of productivity. Both the design time and runtime environments use *zero-footprint clients*, which means that the application is located on the server and doesn't need to be installed on the client.

Codefree development

Because SAP NetWeaver Visual Composer is model-based, you can develop applications without the need to write code manually. Thanks to the use of models as a basis for applications, SAP NetWeaver Visual Composer can translate the models by itself into the code that is required for the respective application. In SAP NetWeaver Visual Composer, simple drag-and-drop functions define the required data flow and thus enable you to create user interfaces on the basis of templates or even completely per your own requirements (see Figure 1.19).

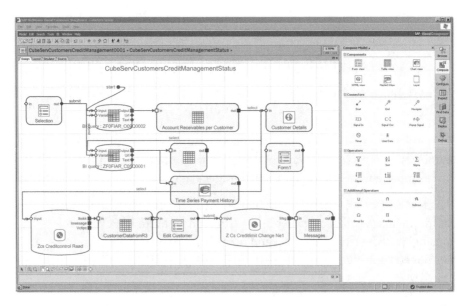

**Figure 1.19** Visual Composer Designer—the SAP Tool for Developing Frontends for Composite Applications and Analytical Applications

To ensure a simple development or enhancement of composite applications, the Visual Composer is linked to the following SAP NetWeaver components and applications:

▶ **SAP Enterprise Portal**
Easy modeling of new applications, reconfiguration of existing applications, and customization of applications

▶ **SAP NetWeaver 2004s Business Intelligence**
Access to SAP data and external data via the BI-Java interface and creation of composite applications that are closely linked with transaction data (e. g., an ERP system)

▶ **SAP Analytics**
Modeling analytical applications. To ensure the appropriate presentation of analytical information, SAP NetWeaver Visual Composer supports both Adobe Flex and HTML.

Chapter 12 provides more detailed information on SAP NetWeaver Visual Composer.

### Data Warehousing Workbench (DWB)

In SAP NetWeaver 2004s, the widely known transaction RSA1 no longer launches the Administrator Workbench, but rather the Data Warehousing Workbench (see Figure 1.20). This new name describes a newly developed and significantly extended version of the Administrator Workbench.

The high degree of modularization, as well as the new arrangement of the components and an optimized layout, enables a more efficient processing of the BI administration tasks.

In this first chapter, we tried to provide you with a comprehensive overview of the new concepts that have been implemented in SAP NetWeaver 2004s Business Intelligence. We also positioned it in the general data-warehousing world. The following chapters will now describe these innovations in greater detail.

Summary

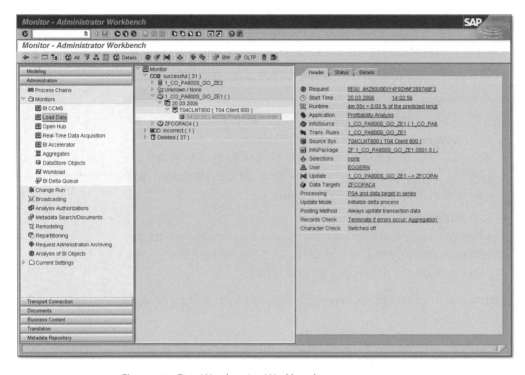

**Figure 1.20** Data Warehousing Workbench

*This chapter is intended to provide an overview of the most important new features of SAP NetWeaver 2004s and to therefore identify the major differences between this release and previous releases. This chapter does not describe any details of areas and functions that have been changed only slightly or not at all.*

# 2    New Features of SAP NetWeaver 2004s—An Overview

## 2.1    SAP NetWeaver 2004s

When SAP officially declared business intelligence to be one of the main focuses of product development and promotion in 2005, it was already apparent that the upcoming BI release would be a particularly ambitious project. The change of the product name from "SAP BW 3.5" to the originally announced "SAP BW 7.0" already indicated a quantum leap in the development that took place in the field of business intelligence.

Focus on BI

While in earlier releases, the newly added features had been relatively limited in terms of quantity and value added, in the new SAP NetWeaver 2004s Release, it is harder to get a sense of the scope of the innovations and enhancements available.

Innovations, step by step

To make it easier for you to become familiar with the new BI features of SAP NetWeaver 2004s, this chapter introduces you to the most important innovations step by step. Starting off with the introduction of individual software components, which BW administrators and users need for their daily work, the chapter then focuses on the three main components of SAP NetWeaver 2004s:

▶ **Enterprise Data Warehousing (EDW)**
The EDW area includes modeling, data retrieval, and administration. For didactical reasons, these topics are discussed in separate sections:

> ▷ Enterprise Data Warehousing: Data Modeling

> ▷ Enterprise Data Warehousing: ETL and Administration

▶ **Enterprise Reporting, Query and Analysis**
This includes the creation and formatting of queries, the integration of queries in Excel workbooks or web applications, and the printing of reports.

▶ **Business Planning and Analytical Services**
This term describes the integrated planning process using SAP NetWeaver 2004s.

Finally, the chapter provides insight into the aspects of performance and authorizations.

## 2.2 Software Components and User Interfaces

Not only does the new release contain "internal" changes to many functions, that is, changed of the program code, but the new functionality also required adjustments to and completely new developments of individual software components and user interfaces. This includes innovations in tools that you may already know from SAP BW 3.x, as well as user interfaces that have explicitly been developed for SAP NetWeaver 2004s.

### 2.2.1 Data Warehousing Workbench

RSA1 and Administrator Workbench
Every BW administrator knows the Administrator Workbench, and RSA1 is probably the most frequently executed transaction in SAP BW. This transaction still exists in the new release, but from now on it will take the administrator into the *Data Warehousing Workbench*.

[»]      The Data Warehousing Workbench is nothing more than a revised version of the Administrator Workbench.

New navigation bar
When you call the Data Warehousing Workbench, the first thing you'll notice is that the main navigation bar has changed (see Figure 2.1). Instead of the familiar tabs, **Modeling**, **Monitoring**, **Reporting Agent**, **Transport Connection**, **Documents**, **Business Content**, **Translation**, and **Metadata Repository**, you'll notice that the new release no longer contains the **Reporting Agent**, while **Monitoring** was renamed to **Administration**.

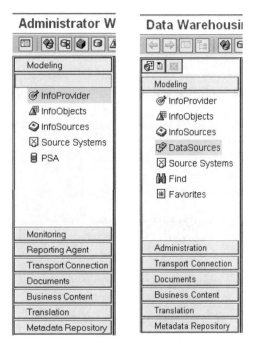

**Figure 2.1** Old and New Modeling Navigation Bars

The **Modeling** tab contains the new menu items, **DataSources**, **Find**, and **Favorites**, whereas it no longer contains the **PSA** item. The **Source Systems** item now contains only the individual source systems (the DataSources have been moved to a separate menu item). If you select the DataSource tree of a source system here, you will automatically jump to the associated menu item, **DataSources**.

Modeling tab

---

**Excursus: Object distinction according to 3.x and NetWeaver 2004s**

When using the Data Warehousing Workbench, you should note that basically there are now objects available that are based on different technologies. For that reason, there are *3.x BW objects* as well as *NetWeaver 2004s components*.

▶ The 3.x objects are prefaced with a small square box (see Figure 2.2, Step 1). These objects are the InfoSources or DataSources that were used up to and including Release 3.x.

3.x objects

▶ The NetWeaver 2004s objects are based on a new technology. In future, you should use these objects rather than the 3.x objects, because only these components will enable you to use the transformations, which are much more flexible than the transfer and update rules.

NetWeaver 2004s objects

<table>
<tr><td>Emulated<br>DataSources</td><td>*Emulated DataSources* represent an exception to the aforementioned rule. These are DataSources that have been created as 3.x DataSources in BI, which can also use the new transformation technology.</td></tr>
</table>

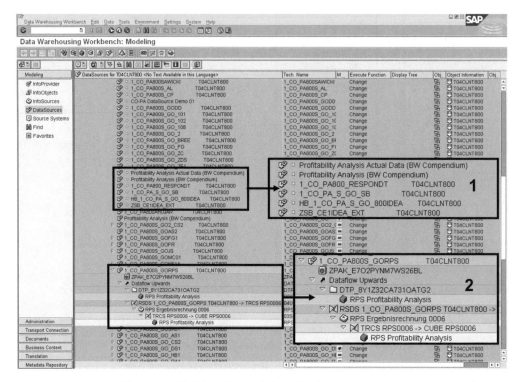

**Figure 2.2** "Modeling"Area with Tree Display

Displaying data
flow objects

As shown in Figure 2.2, Step 2, you can expand the entire data flow tree in the DataSource view as well as in other views (for example, in the InfoProvider view, which is not shown here). This enables you to display a tree of the data flow with possible navigation options to the individual objects on the left-hand side of the screen, while you can edit individual objects in the right-hand pane (see Figure 2.3).

A disadvantage here is that if you don't use a high screen resolution, you will constantly have to move the individual window panes to get an optimal view of the object you want to edit or display. On the other hand, the context menu that changes according to the object you select is a real advantage. **[+]**

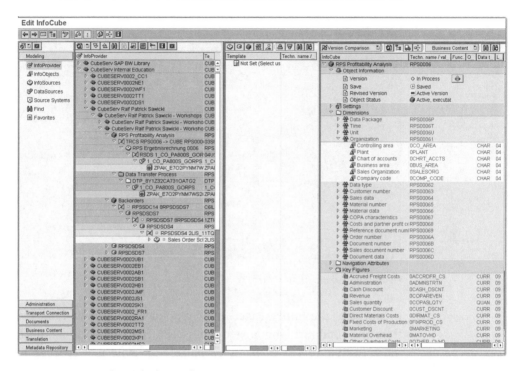

**Figure 2.3** Tree Display and Object Editing

With regard to the Administration area (see Figure 2.4), you should note that there is no longer only one monitor, but separate monitors for different areas such as extraction or Open Hub Services. Consequently, the monitor used for extraction purposes is now called *extraction monitor*.

**Administration tab**

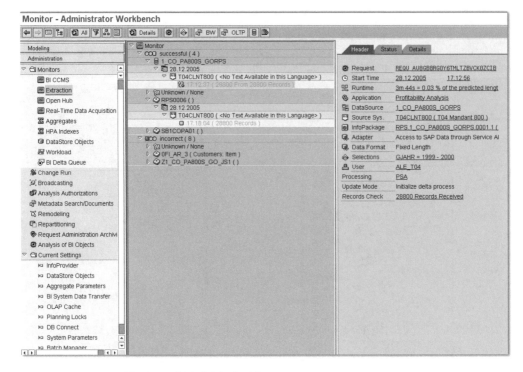

**Figure 2.4** "Administration" Area

Process chains | In addition, the InfoPackageGroups relic has finally been removed from the administration area and has been replaced with the much more flexible *process chains* (see Figure 2.5). Note that apart from this, additional, somewhat new functions have been implemented here:

- ▶ Remodeling
- ▶ Repartitioning
- ▶ Navigation to global settings of BW objects

Reporting Agent | As already mentioned, the Reporting Agent has been removed from the navigation bar of the Data Warehousing Workbench. However, you can still use Transaction Code REPORTING_AGENT to call its familiar functions in order to use them for 3.x queries and SAP BW web templates (see Figure 2.6).

[»] | The Reporting Agent is no longer developed further, because its functions have been replaced by Information Broadcasting in the new release.

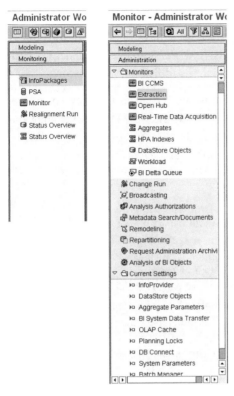

**Figure 2.5** Old and New Navigation Bars in the Administration Area

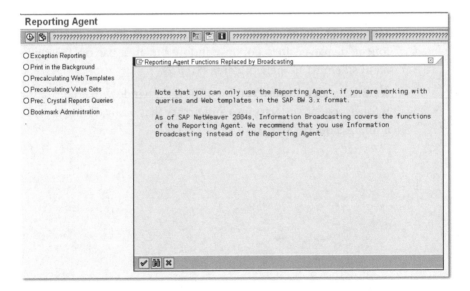

**Figure 2.6** Reporting Agent

### 2.2.2 BEx Query Designer

In NetWeaver 2004s, SAP provides a new version of the Query Designer (see Figure 2.7). This new version is a .NET-based, Unicode-enabled tool that contains some additional new features.

Compatibility

To ensure downward compatibility with queries that have been created in SAP BW 3.x, SAP delivers both the new Query Designer and the old version of the Query Designer that was used in SAP BW 3.x. The predecessor also works in SAP NetWeaver 2004s, but it cannot access the new functionality.

[!]

Note that once you have edited 3.x queries using the new version of the Query Designer, you can no longer edit using Query Designer 3.x because the queries are converted to the new technology. This also involves 3.x queries that contain reusable components such as variables, calculated or restricted key figures, or structures if at least one component has been edited using the Query Designer in SAP NetWeaver 2004s.

This means that a transition to the new version should not occur all at once, but rather step by step and for individual queries.

Changes

Compared to its predecessor, the structure of the new Query Designer has changed slightly:

▸ The areas—**Filters, Free Characteristics, Rows**, and **Columns**—are no longer displayed together. Instead you can use separate tabs to go to the individual work areas (see Figure 2.7, Step 1).

▸ The properties of selected characteristics or key figures are no longer displayed in a popup window but in a bar on the right-hand side next to the work area (Step 2).

▸ A newly added feature is the notification window that constantly informs you about warnings and errors that occur during the creation of a query (Step 3).

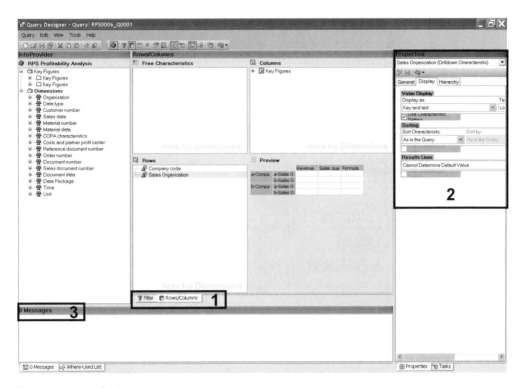

**Figure 2.7** Query Designer

The most important new functions of the Query Designer in SAP NetWeaver 2004s include the following:

New functions

- ▶ Entering and displaying Unicode texts
- ▶ Saving the filter as a global, reusable object
- ▶ Creating queries that allow the input of data for planning purposes
- ▶ Variables can have several default values
- ▶ Editing several objects at the same time (e. g., result row suppression for several characteristics in drilldown)
- ▶ Referencing the properties of structure elements (e. g., if a structure element should always display the text of the key figure assigned to it)
- ▶ Displaying warnings and messages including troubleshooting suggestions
- ▶ Navigation in the Query Designer via tabs

### 2.2.3   Report Designer

The Report Designer is a new feature that comes with SAP NetWeaver 2004s. This .NET-based Business Explorer (BEx) tool enables you to create formatted and print-optimized reports that are made available as queries or query views (see Figure 2.8).

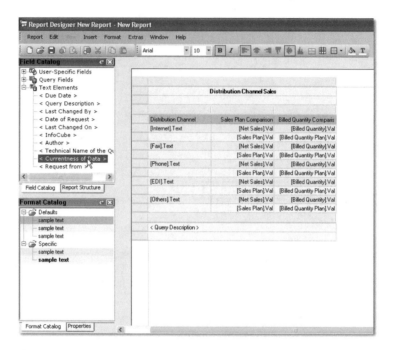

**Figure 2.8** Report Designer

You can call the Report Designer either as a standalone application or directly via the **Report** web item in the BEx Web Application Designer.

Functions   The most important functions of the Report Designer include the following:

- Standard formatting functions such as fonts, font sizes, font colors, etc.

- Integration of texts, images, and charts

- Insertion of report headers and footers, page headers and footers, line breaks, and page numbers

- Individual formatting of report rows, columns, and cells, as well as support of hierarchy formatting

### 2.2.4 Web Application Designer

SAP NetWeaver 2004s also contains a new version of the Web Application Designer (see Figure 2.9). This tool is also based on .NET and Unicode-enabled.

To ensure downward compatibility with web templates that have been created in SAP BW 3.x, SAP delivers both the new Web Application Designer (WAD) and the old version of the WAD that was used in SAP BW 3.x. The predecessor also works in SAP NetWeaver 2004s, but it cannot access the new functionality.

**Compatibility**

> Note that once you have edited 3.x templates with the new version of Web Application Designer, you can no longer edit them using WAD 3.x, because the templates are then converted into the new technology. SAP provides a migration tool for migrating web templates. Because professional web reporting usually also requires the use of specific code such as HTML, CSS, or JavaScript in the web templates and because the web templates are not always migrated correctly, it is often necessary to post-edit the templates manually.

**[!]**

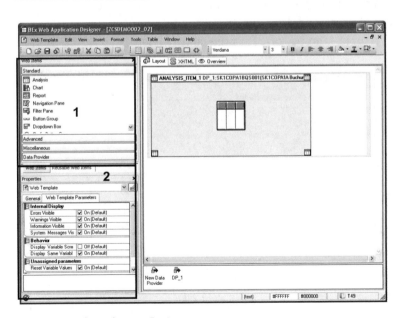

**Figure 2.9** Web Application Designer

In addition to new web items, it is particularly new wizards that have been integrated in the SAP NetWeaver 2004s Release. For example, it contains wizards for HTML tags and command tags. The user inter-

**New features**

face hasn't changed much, but what is apparent is the better grouping of web items into the categories, **Standard**, **Advanced**, and **Miscellaneous** (see Figure 2.9, Step 1) as well as the categorization of web item properties (Step 2) according to **Appearance**, **Inner Appearance**, **Behavior**, and **Data Binding**.

### 2.2.5    BEx Analyzer and Workbook Design

Despite the blatantly obvious attempt made by SAP to shift the analyses towards a more flexible web technology, SAP NetWeaver 2004s also contains an enhanced BEx Analyzer.

Standard workbook

As displayed in Figure 2.10, the layout of the new standard workbook is reminiscent of the standard web template. The workbook now also contains buttons that enable you to display the analysis results as a graphic instead of a table or to show and hide information on the current query.

Analyses by drag-and-drop

Another specific feature can be found in the user interface for analyses. You can simply exchange, add, and remove individual characteristics via drag-and-drop, while the results — both characteristics and key figures — can be sorted via the table header.

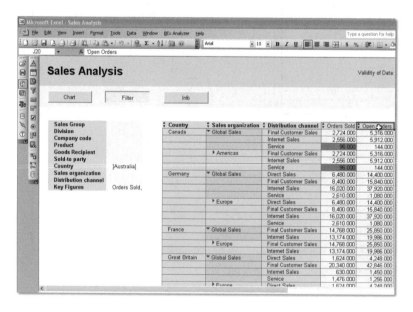

Figure 2.10  Report in BEx Analyzer

Other functions are provided in the context of workbook design. **Workbook design** Similar to Web Application Designer 3.x, you can now also create workbooks that contain elements such as dropdown boxes, radio buttons, and filters. These elements are located in a separate toolbar (see Figure 2.11, Step 1). Furthermore, improved layout and formatting options are available, as well as integrating the input of data for planning purposes in the workbooks (Step 2).

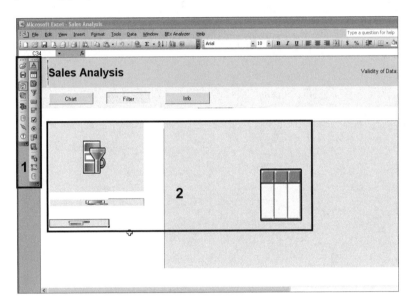

**Figure 2.11** Workbook Design Using BEx Analyzer

## 2.2.6    BEx Web Analyzer

The new standard template used for the analysis of queries on the web has also been enhanced with new functions (see Figure 2.12). Similar to the revised workbooks, you can now also insert individual characteristics and key figures via drag-and-drop into the work area of a web template, while another separate area containing dropdown boxes is provided for filtering purposes (see Figure 2.12, Step 1). Moreover, you can now carry out the sorting function at the click of a mouse (see Step 2). Another new feature is the option to print out the query result or generate a PDF file by clicking on a specific button (Step 3).

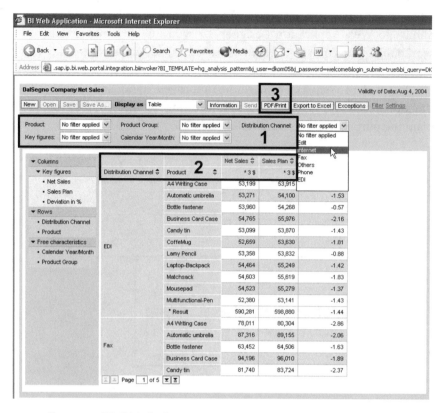

Figure 2.12  BEx Web Analyzer

### 2.2.7  Planning Modeler and Planning Wizard

BI-integrated planning

With SAP NetWeaver 2004s, SAP pushes BI-integrated planning in the area of planning applications. The planning environment is fully integrated in NetWeaver and is designed for the Enterprise Services Architecture (ESA). Contrary to planning with SEM-BPS or BW-BPS, BI-integrated planning is based on an open and flexible planning framework that was created for all SAP applications. This framework is very closely related to BW and the associated planning options along with analytical applications such as the reporting component.

Transaction BPS0

This new strategy led to the fact that a completely new planning modeling environment was required for the new basis. Although Transaction BPS0 from SEM-BPS and BW-BPS does still exist, you can only use it for the "old" planning functions. The 3.x planning concept can still be used in parallel to BI-integrated planning.

If you want to use the new possibilities of BI-integrated planning, the technical details of which are dealt with in a separate chapter, however, there's no other way than using Transaction Code RSPLAN, which takes you to the *Planning Modeler* (see Figure 2.13, Steps 1 and 2). The Planning Modeler is web-based and can be called without directly logging onto a SAP GUI; the system logon occurs via the browser. Step 1 shows the tabs that represent the individual steps in the creation of a planning application. These steps include selecting an InfoProvider, defining aggregation levels and filters, and creating planning functions and planning sequences.

**Planning Modeler via Transaction RSPLAN**

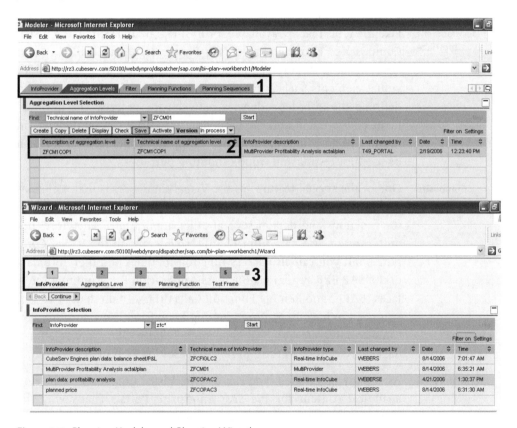

**Figure 2.13** Planning Modeler and Planning Wizard

Similar to the familiar creation of web-based planning applications and layouts using the Web Interface Builder and its integrated wizard, SAP NetWeaver 2004s also contains a tool to support the creation of planning applications on the web—the *Planning Wizard* (see Figure 2.13, Step 3). This wizard guides the user through the creation

**Planning Wizard**

of a complete planning application to the entry of test data in order to test the accuracy and functionality of the development.

### 2.2.8 Visual Composer

*Target group*

The Visual Composer is a WYSIWYG (what you see is what you get) development tool that enables you to quickly develop analytical applications (Rich Internet Applications) for the SAP Enterprise Portal without any programming knowledge. The Visual Composer is thus particularly suited for users from the business area whose IT knowledge may be rather limited.

*Development interface*

Like the tools that are available for BI-integrated planning, the Visual Composer is also web-based (see Figure 2.14). It enables you to develop complex portal applications by dragging and dropping individual elements such as tables and charts into the design area and defining the interdependencies between the objects. The development environment and the modeling procedure can be understood intuitively. In addition, the Visual Composer contains tools that can be used for testing and troubleshooting purposes.

*Composite applications*

One of the special features of the Visual Composer is that it enables you to develop *composite applications*, which are programs that use the functions and data of several other applications. Therefore, not only can you use data from BI InfoProviders with the Visual Composer, but you can also access function modules and therefore data of the SAP ERP system via Business Application Programming Interfaces (BAPIs) and Remote Function Calls (RFC). To do that, however, you need to have basic programming knowledge. Furthermore, you can also integrate non-SAP data sources (both OLAP and relational data sources) such as third-party databases via BI Java Connectors.

*Enterprise Portal*

As already mentioned, you can use the Visual Composer to develop analytical content for the SAP Enterprise Portal. That's why the Visual Composer is installed as an add-on for the SAP Enterprise Portal. The Visual Composer allows you to generate iViews for both the SAP Enterprise Portal 6.0 SP2 (Web Application Server 6.20) and SAP Enterprise Portal 6.0 on Web Application Server 6.40, which is a component of SAP NetWeaver '04. The prerequisites for the development of content on the client side currently are an up-to-date browser, an XML parser, and Adobe SVG Viewer.

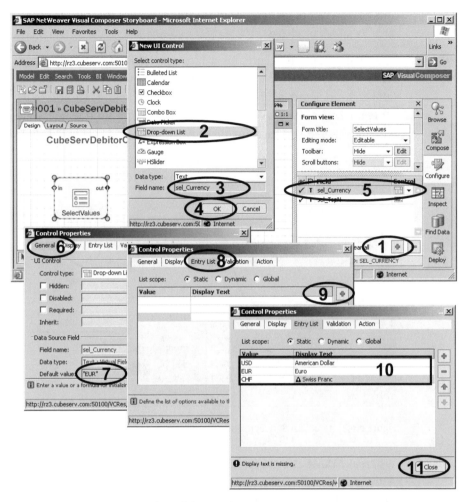

**Figure 2.14** Development Interface of the Visual Composer

Other important features of the Visual Composer are:  **Other features**

▶ Multilingual support of contents at runtime

▶ HTTPS and SSL support

▶ Input validation using regular expressions

▶ Model security: password protection for single models

▶ Java Server Pages (JSPs), HTMLB, and Flex/Flash support

Figure 2.15 provides an overview of the interaction between the  **Technical details**
individual components. The data basis can be built with both SAP

and non-SAP data. Visual Composer then models the data as objects such as tables or charts.

Flex, MXML, and
ActionScript

The Visual Composer contains a Flex server. Flex is a presentation server that is installed on a J2EE application server or servlet container. It can access a large library of Flex UI components and represents the source code as MXML and ActionScript. Both technologies were developed by Macromedia (now Adobe).

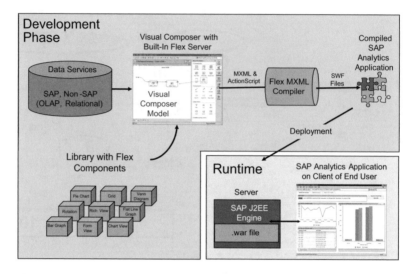

**Figure 2.15** Interaction Between Visual Composer and Flex (Source: SAP AG)

Whereas MXML is a proprietary XML format—a markup language—ActionScript represents the program-specific part. Like JavaScript, ActionScript was originally object-based, but since ActionScript 2.0, it can be thought of as an object-oriented programming language.

Shockwave and
deployment

In order to protect the source code from unwanted access, a Flex MXML compiler is switched in between, which generates a compiled and therefore only machine-readable Shockwave code (*.swf) from the readable code. The compiled applications can be deployed on the runtime engine and then be called through the portal.

**[»]**  SAP is currently planning to enhance the Visual Composer in the near future in such a way that it will also contain the functions of the Web Application Designer so that it will replace it eventually.

## 2.3 Enterprise Data Warehousing: Data Modeling

According to the new SAP philosophy, modeling is one of the two central blocks that constitute enterprise data warehousing. The other one is operation.

The data modeling field primarily involves the InfoProviders of SAP BW. These objects comprise both the InfoProviders that actually store data, such as InfoObjects, InfoCubes, and DataStore objects, and InfoProviders such as MultiProviders and InfoSets, which merely represent a logical view of the data. The following sections describe the innovations with regard to all these objects.

InfoProviders

### 2.3.1 InfoObjects

Regarding InfoObjects, many enhancements pertain to the characteristics. If you take a look at the **Business Explorer** tab, you can see that you can now specify a unit InfoObject of the **Quantity Unit** type, which must be an attribute of the InfoObject. The unit InfoObject is used to convert quantities for the master-data-bearing characteristic in the Business Explorer.

Characteristics

The configuration of the master data access is another important feature for queries (see Figure 2.16).

Master data access

Here you can select from among three different options:

► **Standard**
As usual, the values from the master data table of the characteristic are displayed at query runtime.

► **Own Implementation**
The master data can also be accessed via a custom object-oriented ABAP class that inherits information from the class, CL_RSMD_RS_BW_SPEC. For this purpose, you must implement the IF_RSMD_RS_ACCESS interface. If you want to store InfoObject-specific parameters for this master data reading class, you must also implement the IF_RSMD_RS_GENERIC interface.

► **Remote**
The **Remote** option enables direct access to data in a source system. For this purpose, however, you must mark the characteristic as an InfoProvider and configure a corresponding staging process.

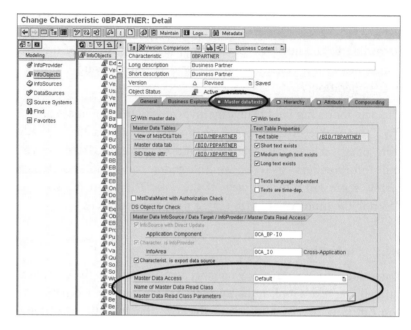

**Figure 2.16** Characteristics—"Master data/texts" Tab

**[+]** Based on our experience, we recommend using the **Standard** setting. In some specific cases, it might be necessary to use your own implementation, but for performance reasons, you should avoid using a remote implementation whenever possible.

Authorization-relevant attributes

In addition to the option to assign temporal hierarchy joins to time-dependent hierarchies of a characteristic, you can now also mark the master data attributes as authorization-relevant (see Figure 2.17). This enables you to generate authorization objects for reporting that contain this characteristic, which, in turn, allows you to run queries for only specific value ranges of the characteristic.

Key figures

Regarding the key figures, there are no visible significant changes. The distinction still exists between cumulative and non-cumulative values with their characterizing setting options. One enhancement, however, has been implemented for the exception aggregation behavior; the following two options are now also available for selection (see Figure 2.18):

► No Aggregation Along Hierarchy
► No Aggregation of Postable Nodes

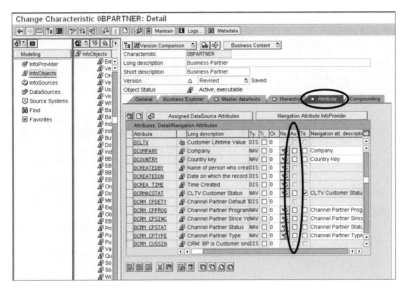

**Figure 2.17** Characteristics—"Attribute" Tab

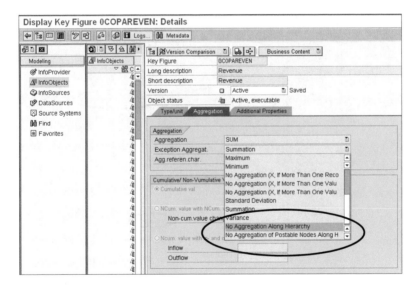

**Figure 2.18** Exception Aggregation for Key Figures

## 2.3.2 DataStore Objects

The DataStore objects (DSO) are the successors to the Operational Data Store (ODS). They are used to store data of high granularity, for example at document level, and to provide the data in aggregated form to the multidimensional data models, which are more efficient in analyses.

Chapter 3, *Data Modeling in the Data Warehousing Workbench of SAP NetWeaver 2004s BI*, provides detailed information on how to create a DataStore object.

**[»]** Technically speaking, the familiar ODS from SAP BW 3.x does still exist (see Figure 2.19), but it was simply renamed to *DataStore object* to reflect the general data-warehousing terminology.

Three DSO types    SAP NetWeaver 2004s contains three different types of DataStore objects:

▶ Standard

▶ Direct Update

▶ Write-Optimized

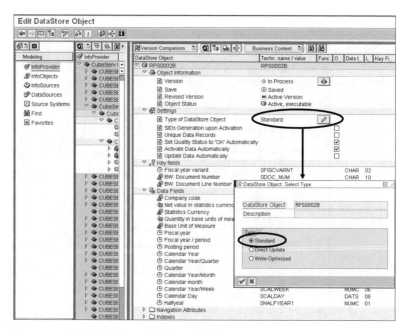

**Figure 2.19** "Standard" Type DataStore Object

Parallelized deletions    What all three types of DataStore objects have in common is that the (semantic) key can still contain 16 key fields. But, what is new is that from hereon you can delete active requests in parallel. Until now,

88

requests were deleted serially, while the new release allows you to create packages and perform a parallelized deletion process.

Contrary to previous releases, SAP NetWeaver 2004s enables you to make object-specific settings for runtime parameters of DataStore objects and to transport these settings into connected systems.

Object-specific runtime parameter settings

You can maintain the following runtime parameters:

▶ Package size for activation

▶ Package size for SID determination

▶ Maximum wait time until a process is marked as being lost

▶ Type of processing

  ▶ serial

  ▶ parallel (batch)

  ▶ parallel (dialog)

▶ Number of processes to be used

▶ Server/server group to be used

In addition to the configuration of object-specific settings, you can also define default values. Default values are used whenever no object-specific entry is available.

The **Standard** type DataStore object is the successor to the standard Operational Data Store. Both are fully compatible so that no migration is necessary. The DSO consists of the three essential tables, **Active Data, Change Log**, and **New Data**. When data is loaded, it is first stored in the **New Data** table until the activation process updates it with the corresponding logic into the **Active Data** and **Change Log** tables. Accordingly, for this DSO type, settings such as **Activate Data Automatically, Update Data Automatically**, or **SIDs Generation upon Activation** are available.

"Standard" type

The **Direct Update** type DataStore object is the familiar transactional Operational Data Store that is predominantly used with the Analysis Process Designer (APD) or for consolidation purposes. This DSO consists of an **Active Data** table; it does not contain a **Change Log**.

"Direct Update" type

The third DataStore object type, **Write-Optimized**, was specifically developed for SAP NetWeaver 2004s. The only DSO setting available

"Write-Optimized" type

here is that you can check the uniqueness of the data (see Figure 2.20).

The reason for this very small number of setting options can be found in the structure of this DataStore object type. The object type was developed with the objective of storing data as efficiently as possible in order to be able to further process the data without losing any additional time for the creation of SIDs, aggregations, and data-record-based deltas.

The Write-Optimized DSO virtually consists of only the **Active Data** table, while the Change Log and Activation Queue tables no longer exist because the data is merely updated from the source system to the table via **Insert**. An update or delta determination of the data does not occur because the obligatory activation step has also become obsolete.

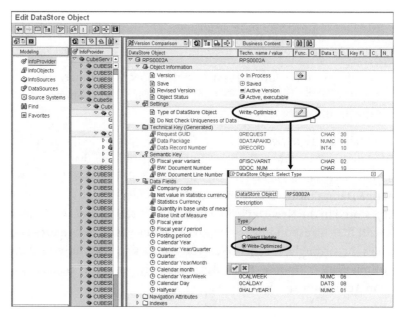

**Figure 2.20** "Write-Optimized" Type DataStore Object

You may be surprised to know that the data is available for reporting on the DSO, although no SIDs were generated during the load process. This is possible because the necessary SID values for the data are determined in the DataStore object during the query execution.

> For performance reasons, we generally don't recommend setting up a reporting process on a Write-Optimized DataStore object. On the one hand, the relational data model of the DSO table is not as well suited for an analysis as a reasonably well-structured multidimensional data model; on the other hand, the SID values must always be newly determined at query runtime. Nevertheless, you should note that the Write-Optimized DataStore object can be integrated both in MultiProviders and InfoSets.

**[+]**

As already mentioned, the data is always written to the **Active Data** table via an **Insert** command. This is possible because it is not the semantic key consisting of a maximum of 16 key fields, which is used here, but a technical key that consists of a request ID, data package, and a data record number. Therefore, each new data record has a new unique key. Note that the loaded data is not aggregated. If two data records with the same logical key are extracted from the source, both records are stored in the DataStore object. The record mode that is responsible for the aggregation is still preserved so that the data can be aggregated in a standard DSO at a later time. The **Active Data** is partitioned on the basis of the request ID.

No aggregation

The **Do Not Check Uniqueness of Data** flag tells you whether you can store several data records with the same semantic DataStore key in the **Active Data** table. The use of this flag should be carefully deliberated.

Uniqueness of data

Table 2.1 once again lists the most important differences between the three DataStore object types.

| DataStore Object Type | | Standard | Direct Update | Write-Optimized |
|---|---|---|---|---|
| **Primary use** | EDW layer | Yes | No | No |
| | ODS layer | Yes | No | Yes |
| | Delta Determination | via **After Images** at record level | No | at request level |
| | Activation | Yes | No | No |
| | Other Functions | — | For external applications and analysis processes (APD) | Staging layer for large data quantities |

**Table 2.1** Comparison of DataStore Object Types

| DataStore Object Type | | Standard | Direct Update | Write-Optimized |
|---|---|---|---|---|
| **Structure** | Active data | Yes | Yes | Yes |
| | Change Log | Yes | No | No |
| | New Data | Yes | No | No |
| **Integration in data flow** | | Via staging (DTP) | Via APIs, staging in downstream data targets possible | Via staging (DTP) |

Table 2.1 Comparison of DataStore Object Types (cont.)

Enhanced monitor for request processing    SAP NetWeaver 2004s also provides a separate, very detailed monitor that you can use for request operations carried out in DataStore objects, such as activation, rollback, and so on.

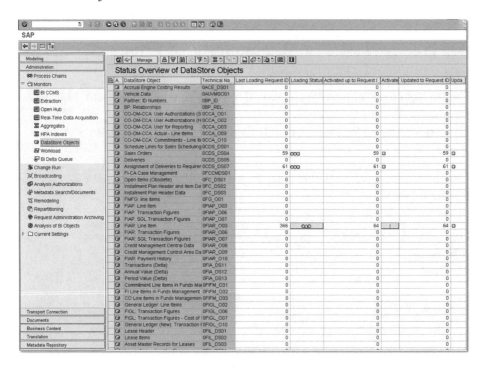

Figure 2.21 Enhanced Monitor for Request Processing in DSO

Operations that modified requests used to be displayed in the extraction monitor in previous releases. This often resulted in finding it difficult to comprehend all operations in the event of multiple executions.

### 2.3.3    InfoCubes, VirtualProviders, and MultiProviders

The InfoCubes, too, were assigned new names in SAP NetWeaver 2004s, for example, you no longer use a transactional InfoCube in planning, but a *Realtime InfoCube*.

Realtime InfoCube

InfoProviders that merely represent logical views of data and do not physically store any data are referred to as *VirtualProviders*. These include the RemoteCubes, SAP RemoteCubes, and the virtual Info-Cubes with services.

VirtualProviders

> MultiProviders and InfoSets that also have these typical properties, however, did not receive any new names.    [«]

Technically, the InfoCubes (Basic InfoCubes) and MultiProviders haven't changed that much. The most important change here is once again the way in which you can create and edit those BW objects. The look and feel of a new user interface for InfoCubes is reminiscent of the UI for DataStore objects (see Figure 2.22).

New modeling user interface

Again, you can edit the InfoCube in the right half of the Data Warehousing Workbench. The context menu enables you to create and edit dimensions. And once again, you can select the necessary characteristics and key figures from templates such as other InfoCubes, InfoSources, and so on (see Figure 2.22, Step 1), and then assign them to the individual dimensions via drag-and-drop. As before, you can also insert the InfoObjects directly into the individual dimensions by using their technical names.

Drag-and-drop

A separate folder exists for the navigation attributes. This folder contains all potential navigation attributes of the InfoCube. Some of you may be reminded of the maintenance and release of navigation attributes in Release SAP BW 3.x here. The new release also requires you to explicitly release navigation attributes.

Navigation attributes

There's something special about the key figures (Step 2). At last, it is possible to group key figures, which is something we have all been waiting for. For example, if you look at the module SAP CO-PA (profitability analysis), you'll see that it contains numerous key figures. If you want to map all key figures in the data model of the InfoCube and if the model is not account-based, you will quickly lose your overview of the individual key figures. In the new release, you can

Hierarchical structure of key figures

arrange individual elements based on their data type or business contexts, for example, in a hierarchical folder structure.

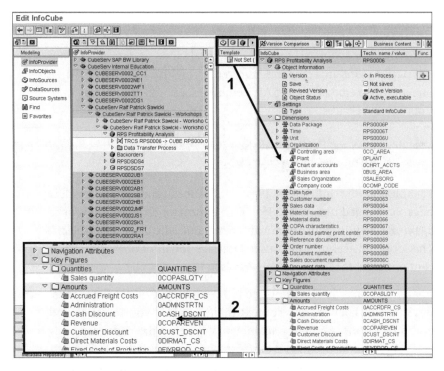

**Figure 2.22** Editing an InfoCube

Editing dimensions
Although assigning InfoObjects to dimensions via drag-and-drop is rather useful, the actual creation of dimensions is no longer as user-friendly and ergonomic as it was in previous releases. Whereas in the past you could edit the descriptions of several dimensions in one screen, you must now click through every individual dimension to make the required settings (see Figure 2.23).

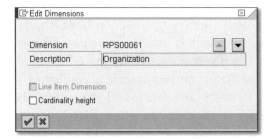

**Figure 2.23** Editing Dimensions

### 2.3.4 InfoSets

The enhancement of the previous model has substantially improved the InfoSets. In previous releases, you could create InfoSets to obtain a logical view of several InfoProviders using a join. A disadvantage of the InfoSets up to and including SAP BW 3.x was that you could integrate only relational InfoProviders such as InfoObjects (of the **Characteristic with Master Data** type) and Operational Data Stores.

It was not possible to create a join with multidimensional data structures such as a Basic InfoCube by using an InfoSet. However, SAP NetWeaver 2004s now also permits InfoCubes as potential components of an InfoSet. This makes it possible to create joins, for instance, with an InfoCube and a DataStore object or an InfoObject containing master data. Figure 2.24 shows a join that consists of an InfoCube and InfoObject 0COMP_CODE.

*Join with InfoCubes*

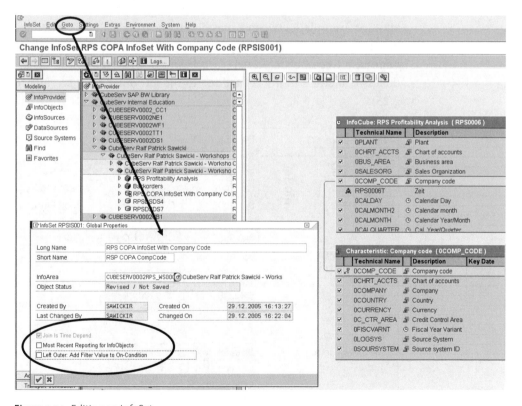

**Figure 2.24** Editing an InfoSet

Global properties You can make other technical settings that have a global effect on the InfoSet via the menu (**Goto · Global Properties**). These settings include temporal joins for time-dependent data and left outer joins.

Scenarios involving
InfoSets Thanks to the enhanced InfoSets, you can now link an InfoCube with a DataStore object using an inner join. Contrary to a similar link via a MultiProvider, only those data records are displayed whose linked keys actually exist in both InfoProviders. For MultiProviders, a union operation is used as a link; therefore, all data records from all InfoProviders are displayed. If, for example, a key combination didn't exist in all InfoProviders, the characteristics of the missing key combination were displayed by a **#** character (i. e., **not assigned**). These data records can now be avoided, provided they are correctly represented in the report.

In addition, you can still create temporary joins with time-dependent master data, as well as lists of slow moving items (i. e., a left outer join, for example, between a master-data-bearing InfoObject such as material and a DataStore object containing document data). If an item hasn't been ordered yet—if it hasn't been posted—it is nevertheless contained in the report due to the left outer join (see Figure 2.25).

| Master Data | | DataStore Object | | |
|---|---|---|---|---|
| Material No. | | Period/FYear | Material No. | Quantity |
| CS00000815 | | 001.2006 | CS00000815 | 700 Pieces |
| CS00470011 | | 001.2006 | CS22101979 | 650 Pieces |
| CS22101979 | | 002.2006 | CS00000815 | 500 Pieces |
| | | 002.2006 | CS22101979 | 400 Pieces |
| | | 003.2006 | CS22101979 | 800 Pieces |

| Inner Join | Material No. | Quantity |
|---|---|---|
| | CS00000815 | 1200 Pieces |
| | CS22101979 | 1850 Pieces |

| Left Outer Join | Material No. | Quantity |
|---|---|---|
| | CS00000815 | 1200 Pieces |
| | CS00470011 | 0 Pieces |
| | CS22101979 | 1850 Pieces |

**Figure 2.25** Inner Join and Left Outer Join

For performance reasons, you cannot (yet) use an InfoCube as a right operand of a left outer join.    **[«]**

### 2.3.5    Modeling Aspects: Remodeling and Partitioning

The InfoProviders of SAP BI are modeled and filled with data on the basis of specific requirements so that the end users can analyze the data. However, what needs to be done if the data model is modified at a later stage whereas data has already been loaded into the Info-Providers? Small changes such as the inclusion of an additional characteristic into a MultiProvider, which already exists in the underlying InfoCube or DataStore object, or the release of navigation attributes can be done easily even after the data has been loaded.

*Remodeling problem*

"Bigger" actions such as the deletion of a characteristic, or the replacement of one key figure InfoObject by another key figure, always used to involve a reload of the InfoProvider in order to change the data model in previous releases up to and including SAP BW 3.5.

*Procedure up to and including Release 3.5*

You could rely on two useful solution approaches to do just that (see Figure 2.26).

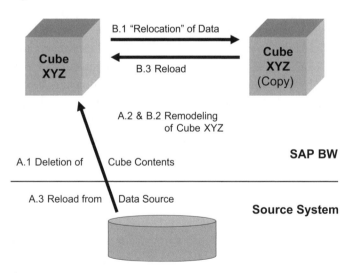

**Figure 2.26** Classic Remodeling Procedure

In our example, we want to exchange a key figure InfoObject of an InfoCube.

▶ **Approach A: Reload from the source system**
In this procedure, the InfoCube is completely deleted. After that, the existing key figure InfoObject can be replaced by a new one. Because the mapping of the update rules has also changed in this process, the update rules must be adjusted and activated. In the final step, the data is reloaded from the data source into the Info-Cube.

▶ **Approach B: Relocating the data into a copy of the InfoCube**
This second procedure is a bit more complex than the first, however, it enables you to preserve a "frozen history" of the status of the data at the time it was originally loaded. First, you must create a copy of the InfoCube that you want to modify. Next, you must reload the data into the new InfoCube via the export DataSource of the InfoCube that you just copied. Then, the data of the "old" InfoCube is also deleted as it was in the first procedure, the key figure is replaced, and the data is reloaded via the export Data-Source of the copied InfoCube, including an accurate adjusted mapping of the update rules.

Both approaches required a lot of work and proved rather time-consuming due to the reload processes, which is why they were often performed over the weekend.

NetWeaver 2004s: Remodeling Toolbox

For this reason, a simplification of the remodeling process has been long awaited. SAP NetWeaver 2004s provides a tool that meets this requirement exactly: the *Remodeling Toolbox* (see Figure 2.27) This application, which is integrated in the Data Warehousing Workbench and can be called via the **Workbench** menu or the **Administration** tab enables you to retroactively implement changes to characteristics and key figures of InfoCubes. Chapter 6, *Redesign Functions: Repartitioning and Remodeling*, contains a detailed description of how to use the Remodeling Toolbox.

Remodeling rules

The new remodeling options allow you to add, delete, and replace characteristics and key figures (see Figure 2.28, circled part). These operations are then summarized into a *remodeling rule*.

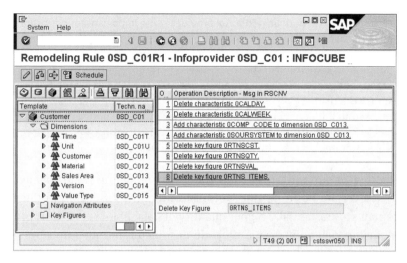

**Figure 2.27** Remodeling Toolbox

The attributes of a *characteristic* to be added can only be enriched via constants, a customer exit, or by using the attributes of another characteristic or using another characteristic that is located directly in the dimension specified for the new characteristic. Key figures, on the other hand, can be loaded only via a constant or customer exit prior to the next data load to the InfoCube.

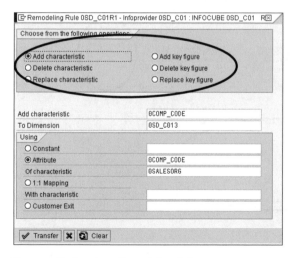

**Figure 2.28** Creating a Remodeling Rule

[**»**]    Although the Remodeling Toolbox provides some important functions for a retroactive remodeling of InfoCubes, there is still one option missing, which we regard as equally important: the retroactive adjustment and addition of dimensions. This option is important regarding the performance of the data model and can be a critical factor if 13 line item dimensions are already being used. In that case, the Remodeling Toolbox cannot be used to add a new characteristic. Moreover, the Remodeling Toolbox can currently be used for only InfoCubes. An extension for DataStore objects or InfoObjects still needs to be developed.

Partitioning filled InfoCubes    Another important aspect concerning data modeling is *partitioning*. If, at a certain point in time, you realize that the modeled InfoCube contains a substantially higher quantity of data than expected, from a modeling viewpoint, you can divide this filled InfoCube into several partitions at database level. Figure 2.29 shows such a partitioning based on the time characteristic **0CALMONTH**. A great advantage of a good partitioning is that it optimizes the read access to data in the queries.

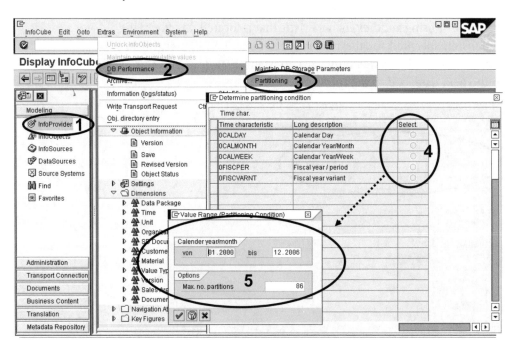

**Figure 2.29** Partitioning InfoCubes

This subject is also described in greater detail in Chapter 6, *Redesign Functions: Repartitioning and Remodeling*.

## 2.4 Enterprise Data Warehousing: ETL and Administration

As described in Chapter 1, *Business Intelligence Concepts—Innovations*, with SAP NetWeaver 2004s, SAP follows the philosophy of a classic enterprise data warehouse with several layers. To transparently present and clearly structure the architecture and data flow as much as possible, making changes in the areas of data retrieval (extraction, transformation, loading) and administration was inevitable. We address these aspects in the following sections.

### 2.4.1 Data Flow Concept in SAP NetWeaver 2004s

Figure 2.30 illustrates the traditional data flow with 3.x components (old concept): Here, data is delivered to SAP BW via an extractor of the DataSource. Optionally, the data can then be temporarily stored in the inbound memory of BW—the persistent staging area (PSA). The PSA was created in the system when the transfer rules were activated. From the PSA, the data is transferred through the InfoSource to the data target. Transfer and update rules, which enable the processing of the data, are located before and after the InfoSource. The entire data flow from the data source to the data target is controlled by an InfoPackage.

*Data flow with 3.x components*

SAP NetWeaver 2004s employs a new data flow concept. Here, a PSA is generated during the creation of a DataSource. The InfoPackage is only used to load the data from the source system into the PSA. In another step, the *data transfer process* (DTP), the data can be retrieved from the PSA and updated into the data target. The DTP can be compared to an InfoPackage (see also Section 2.4.4). One of the reasons why the process was divided into several steps was to obtain a clean and transparent separation of the individual levels of the staging process and to improve the performance of parallel data load processes.

*Data flow in SAP NetWeaver 2004s*

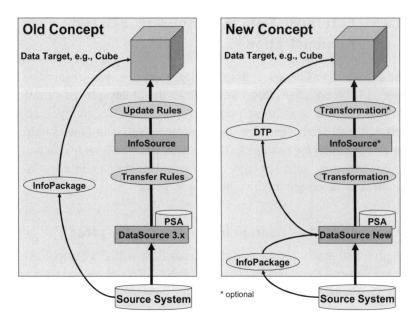

Figure 2.30 Old and New Data Flow Concepts

Transformations

You can still edit the data after it has been loaded from the Data-Source (and thus the PSA) and before it is updated into the data target. Contrary to the old concept of using transfer and update rules, you can now use *transformations*.

One-level and two-level data flows

These transformations, in turn, can be located before and after the InfoSource. In fact, they can be there, but they don't have to be, the reason being that in the new concept, the InfoSource is no longer mandatory because you can also load data directly from the Data-Source into the data target. Depending on the respective scenario, we refer to a *one-level* or *two-level data flow*. You can find additional information on transformations in Section 2.4.3.

### 2.4.2 Source Systems and DataSources

As before, DataSources are assigned to individual source systems. Prior to SAP NetWeaver 2004s, the source systems connected to SAP BW were arranged in a single-level list (Transaction Code RSA13). With thirty, forty, or even more connected source systems, a specific search was very difficult and inconvenient.

As of SAP NetWeaver 2004s, the source systems are grouped according to the source system type and are addressed via the relevant source system type folder (see Figure 2.31).

Grouping by source system type

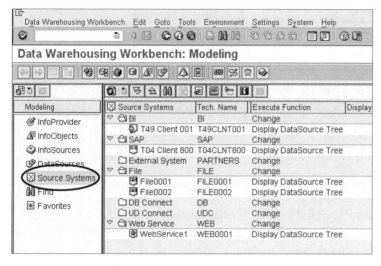

**Figure 2.31** Grouping by Source System Type

The following source system groups are differentiated from each other:

▶ BI (e. g., the Myself system)

▶ SAP (e. g., SAP R/3 Enterprise)

▶ External system (e. g., Ascential Datastage)

▶ File

▶ DB Connect

▶ UD Connect

▶ Web Service

This useful grouping helps you to get a better overview of already connected SAP systems or databases (via DB Connect).

You can display the DataSource tree either by double-clicking on the respective source system in the source system view, or by selecting the source system directly in the DataSource view (see Figure 2.32, Step 1). If you use the second option, then only those source systems are displayed for which a DataSource tree actually exists, regardless of whether DataSources have already been created.

Selecting the Data-Source tree

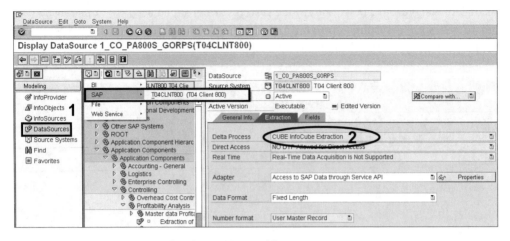

**Figure 2.32** DataSource View and Properties

**Uniform look & feel**
The display of the DataSource has also been revised and standardized as much as possible for all DataSource types. Instead of the three tabs for a CO-PA transaction data DataSource shown in Figure 2.32, some DataSources have additional tabs. For example, a file DataSource has one additional tab for previewing the data to be extracted (see Figure 2.33, Step 1).

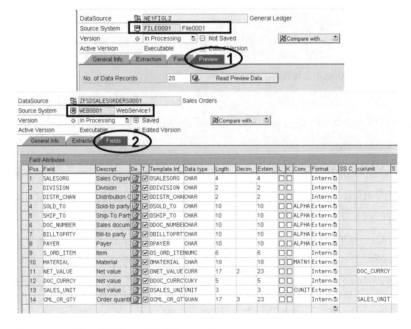

**Figure 2.33** Tabs of Different DataSource Types

Another useful new feature is that the DataSource maintenance displays information on the extractor, in particular, on the delta process being used (see Figure 2.32, Step 2). To get information on the delta process used in previous releases, you had to display the contents of tables such as RSOLTPSOURCE or ROOSOURCE.

Useful additional information

Moreover, the display of the InfoObjects used in the DataSource including their fields, data types, and conversion routines has also become much clearer. You can obtain this new display in the **Fields** tab in Figure 2.33, Step 2.

The DataSources are divided into 3.x (R3TR ISFS) and SAP NetWeaver 2004s Data Sources (R3TR RSDS). The new RSDS virtually always provides direct access to the data so that you don't need to (additionally) store the data in SAP BW; for example, this would make a remote access to master data possible.

ISFS vs. RSDS

Furthermore, you can also directly create DataSources (Web services) in the Web services area. Up to and including SAP BW 3.5, you first had to create an InfoSource with transfer rules for a file DataSource to do that before you could generate the function module for the extraction via SOAP connection or as a Web service.

Web services

It is possible to migrate 3.x DataSources to the new DataSources.

Migration

> Please note, however, that objects depending on 3.x DataSources, such as mappings or transfer rules, are deleted unless they are exported as optional backup and stored for a potential restore.

[«]

### 2.4.3 Transformation

In the data staging process, transformations are predominantly used to cleanse and harmonize the data, but they can also be used to enrich and modify the delivered data. Thus they always represent a link between a data input and a (newly generated) data output. In SAP NetWeaver 2004s, for example, you can use transformations for the following BW objects:

Usage scenarios

► Sources in the data flow such as DataSources, InfoSources, InfoObjects, DataStore objects, InfoCubes, and now also InfoSets

► Target objects or intermediate objects in the data flow such as InfoSources, InfoObjects, DataStore objects, and InfoCubes

New type of transfer and update rules

In this way, transformations represent a new type of transfer and update rules. Note that you can still use update rules. Update rules use the same symbol as transformations, but they are preceded by a small square box (see Figure 2.34, Step 1). You can create update rules by selecting **Additional Functions** from the associated context menu (see Figure 2.34, Step 2).

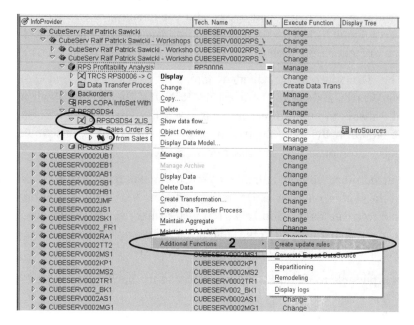

**Figure 2.34** Traditional Update Rules

### Excursus: Transfer and update rules

Transfer and update rules are based on a "procedural" programming concept, which becomes obvious, for instance, by the form call in the start routines or in the ABAP routines during the derivation of the target InfoObjects (see Figure 2.35). In addition, these rules use different source structures: Transfer rules can access fields of the transfer structure, while update rules process fields of the communication structure. Both types of rules provide the additional option to store a start routine.

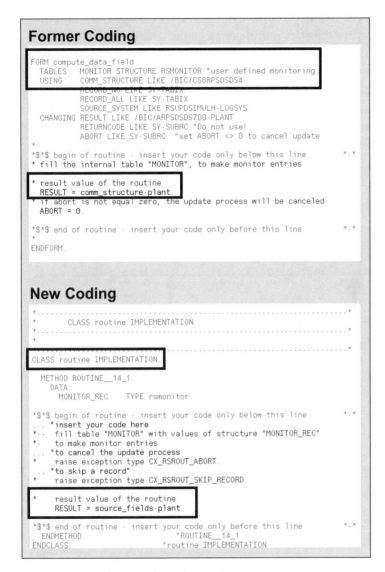

**Figure 2.35** Procedural vs. Object-Oriented Start Routines

Transformations, on the other hand, are programmed as object-oriented (see Figure 2.35). Not least due to the encapsulation of the objects, which is made possible by the use of classes, you can now use the transformations at those stages, which required the use of transfer and update rules up to and including SAP BW 3.x, because the access to individual fields was carried out via the uniform SOURCE_FIELDS type.

**Object-oriented transformations**

**Start and end** In addition to a start routine, you can now also store an end routine.
**routines** You can use the start routine to stage the data prior to the transformation. Typical examples of this include the deletion of data that is not required for the update, or the one-time buffering of tables in internal tables for downstream processing rules. The end routine, on the other hand, enables an additional processing step after the data transformation. Possible scenarios here are validations, or the deletion of data that is no longer relevant to the update process due to values that have been determined during the data transformation. Figure 2.36 shows the new process that occurs during the transformation.

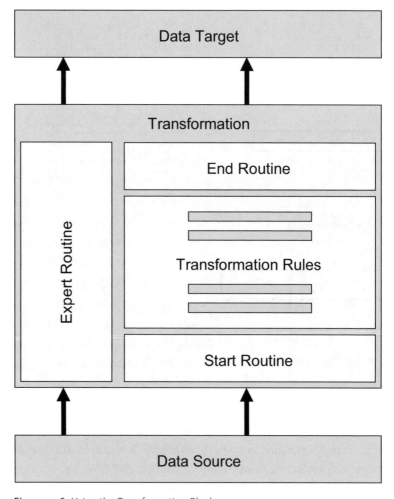

**Figure 2.36** Using the Transformation Blocks

As an alternative to the start and end routines (see Figure 2.37, Step 1) and the individual transformation rules, you can also use the *expert routine* (Step 2).

**Expert routine**

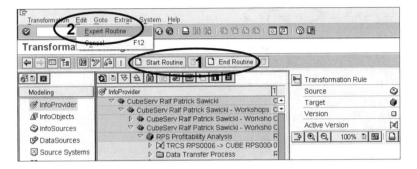

**Figure 2.37** Start, End, and Expert Routines

This routine can be used to obtain a more efficient coding in specific scenarios than it would be possible to obtain by simply using the standard framework of the transformation. Furthermore, an expert routine greatly facilitates the transition of a key-figure-based data model into an account-based data model, which corresponds to the return table principle in the update rules in SAP BW 3.x. As shown in Figure 2.37, you can activate the expert routine via the menu.

Similar to SAP BW 3.x, SAP NetWeaver 2004s also provides transformations as **Direct Assignment**, **Initial Value**, **Formula with Formula Editor**, **ABAP Routine**, or **Constant**. In addition to these transformation types, you can also use the *currency and unit conversion*. The unit calculation is a new feature that can be compared to the currency translation in the steps to be prepared. You must first define a conversion type via Transaction RSUOM (see Figure 2.38, Steps 1 through 5). Only then can you use the conversion type in the transformation rules (see Figure 2.38, Step 6).

**Transformation types**

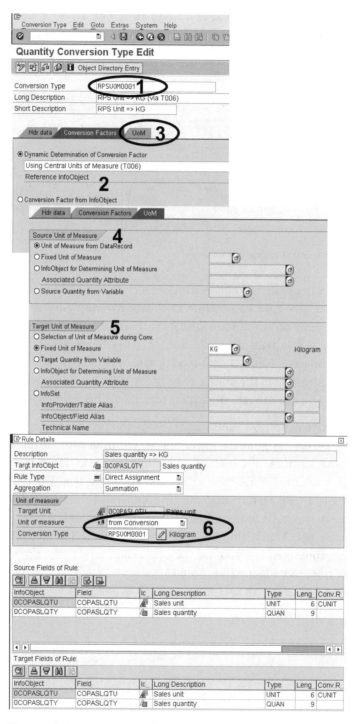

**Figure 2.38** Converting Units of Measure

A new user interface allows you to edit the transformations. The **New user interface**
individual assignments can be implemented via drag-and-drop. For
large structures, it is helpful to use the provided navigation window
(see Figure 2.39). Similar to zooming in and out of a geographical
map, you can jump to the relevant place in the transformation area
when using the navigation window.

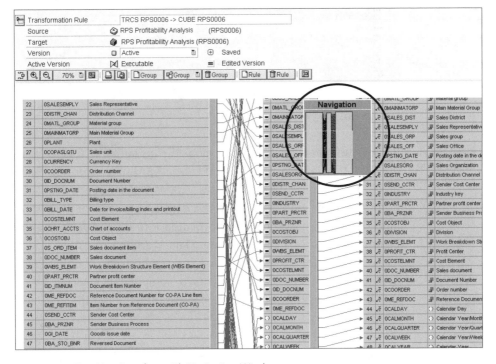

**Figure 2.39** New User Interface with Navigation Window

## 2.4.4 Controlling the Data Flow with InfoPackages and DTP

As already described, the concept of controlling the data flow has **Data transfer**
changed in such a way that from now on InfoPackages will only be **process**
used to update the data in the PSA. On the other hand, the data transfer process (DTP) is used for further processing among the InfoProviders of SAP BW (see Figure 2.40).

Within the data transfer process, you can access an *error stack*. For **Error handling**
example, if errors occur during the loading of data from the PSA into
a DataStore object, the error-free data records can be updated into
the DSO; however, those data records that contain errors are stored

in an additional table, the error stack, where they can be corrected and then further updated. This type of error handling is not available for InfoPackages.

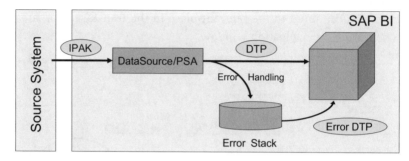

**Figure 2.40** Data Flow with Error Stack

Control components in the data flow

Because InfoPackages are only responsible for updating the data into the PSA, that is, into the inbound layer of SAP BW, you can create them as soon as an SAP NetWeaver 2004s DataSource is available. Contrary to this, you cannot define a data flow process in the system until the data target and a transformation into it have been created. Figure 2.41 shows a section of the Data Warehousing Workbench. Even in the InfoProvider view you can see both the complete data flow into the data target and the control components associated with the flow such as the data transfer process (Step 1) and the InfoPackage (Step 2).

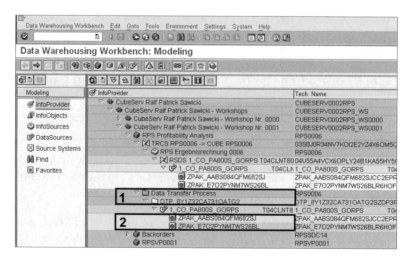

**Figure 2.41** DTP and InfoPackage in the Data Flow

Regarding the InfoPackage maintenance you should note that similar to the DataSource maintenance, SAP NetWeaver 2004s now also contains an **Extraction** tab (see Figure 2.42, Step 1). Previous SAP BW releases did not have this tab. The tab contains information on the data format and the adapter being used. The **Processing** tab (Step 2) no longer allows the settings that were still possible in SAP BW 3.5 and earlier. The only option available here is the **PSA** processing type (Step 3).

*InfoPackage*

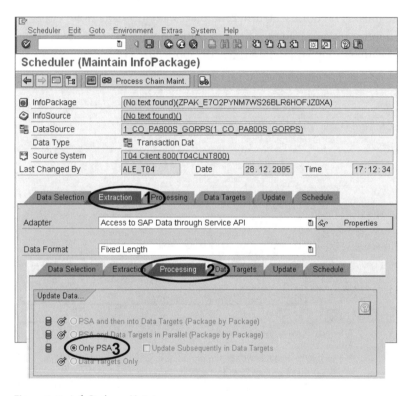

**Figure 2.42** InfoPackage Maintenance

Similar to the InfoPackage in SAP BW 3.x, the data transfer process in SAP NetWeaver 2004s enables you to load data using the extraction modes, **Full** and **Delta**. In this context, it is not necessary to load all data available because you can store filtering criteria via multiple selections, OLAP variables, and routines.

*Data transfer process*

These filtering criteria are very useful if you want to benefit from one of the new properties of the data transfer process which, unfortunately, were not available in the "old" InfoPackages. From now on,

*Separating the delta mechanism*

the DTP controls the data flow, which allows you to separate the delta mechanism for different targets. This enables you to also implement different data selections via different DTPs for one or more data targets. Therefore, you can establish a transparent "data distribution" among different layers.

Debugging The debugging option provided for the data transfer process is another new feature (**Execute** tab). A serial processing in a dialog (see Figure 2.43, Step 1) enables a simulation of the update. You can set various breakpoints at different places in the data flow (Step 2). Therefore, you no longer have to contend with the tedious creation of endless loops in update rules for debugging tasks.

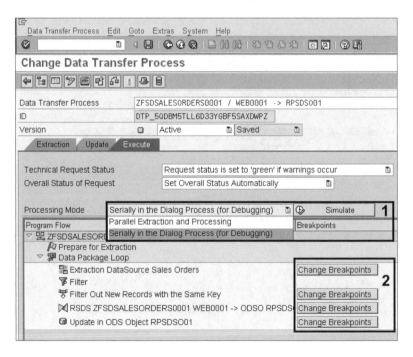

**Figure 2.43** Debugging the Data Transfer Process

Error stack We already discussed using an error stack (i. e., a request-based database table) to handle erroneous data records during an update into DataStore objects in the data transfer process. The exact technical structure of the error stack is defined via the DTP (see Figure 2.44, Step 1). The **Semantic Groups** button enables you to define a combined key containing a maximum of 16 fields. This number is based on the maximum number of key fields allowed for the DSO. Note that the error stack does not necessarily have to contain the same number of key fields as the DataStore object associated with it.

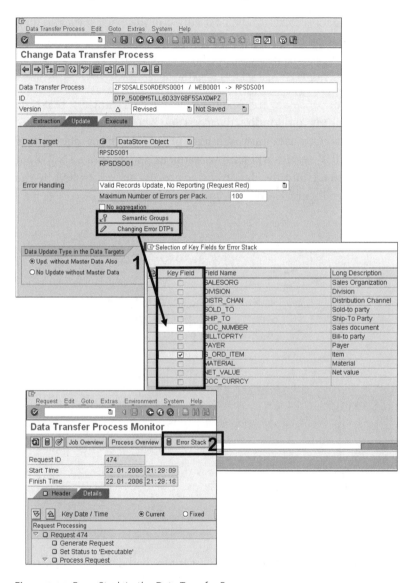

**Figure 2.44** Error Stack in the Data Transfer Process

As before, you can define the behavior for each DTP separately in case of an error:

▶ Abort at a specific number of erroneous data records that cause an incorrect (red) request

▶ Update valid records without reporting

▶ Process valid records and reporting

Erroneous data records can be post-edited in the error stack and then be updated. You can access the error stack, for instance, through the data transfer process monitor (see Figure 2.44, Step 2). Here you can also see that the DTP instance is a request.

Data transfer processes are used for standard data transfers, real-time data acquisition, and for directly accessing data. Real-time data acquisition describes a daemon-based load process from the delta queue of the SAP BW Service API with subsequent update into a DSO. Both the InfoPackage and the data transfer process are controlled by the daemon (see Figure 2.45).

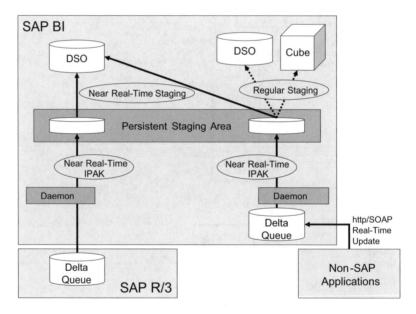

**Figure 2.45** Real-Time Data Acquisition

This concept is used whenever you want to load data at shorter time intervals (every hour or every minute) into SAP BW than are used in the regular load process (daily or weekly). This, however, contradicts the classic principle of a data warehouse: The real-time data acquisition scenario (which is actually a *near-real-time scenario*) supports operational reporting during one day.

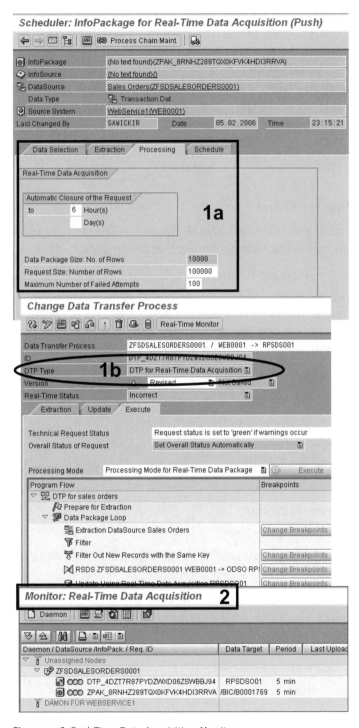

**Figure 2.46** Real-Time Data Acquisition Monitor

**Daemon-based control**
You can transfer data both from SAP source systems and through Web services via push mode. The daemon is responsible for the actual control of the data transfer into the PSA and the subsequent update into the DataStore object. A prerequisite for the usability of InfoPackages and DTPs is that those control objects are marked as real-time-enabled (see Figure 2.46, Steps 1a and 1b). Transaction Code RSCRT provides access to the monitor for real-time data acquisition (Step 2) where you can make the settings for the daemon, Info-Package, and DTP.

### 2.4.5 Process Chains

With regard to process chains, SAP NetWeaver 2004s contains some new enhancements and improvements that are long awaited for.

**New process types**
In SAP NetWeaver 2004s, the InfoPackageGroups are eventually replaced by the more flexible process chains. Placing the focus on process chains meant that additional important process types had to be introduced in the new release. In contrast to SAP BW 3.5, the new process types listed below are now available (see Figure 2.47).

- ▶ General Services
  - ▷ Interrupt Process
  - ▷ Decision Between Multiple Alternatives
- ▶ Load Process and Post-Processing
  - ▷ Update DataStore Object Data (Further Update)—this replaces the update of ODS data
  - ▷ Data Transfer Process
- ▶ Data Target Administration
  - ▷ Activate DataStore Object Data—this replaces the activation of ODS data
  - ▷ Archive Data from an InfoProvider
- ▶ Other BW Processes
  - ▷ Deletion of Requests from the Change Log
  - ▷ Execute Planning Sequence
  - ▷ Switch Realtime InfoCube to Plan Mode
  - ▷ Switch Realtime InfoCube to Load Mode

▶ Other

    ▷ Last Customer Contact Update (Retraction)

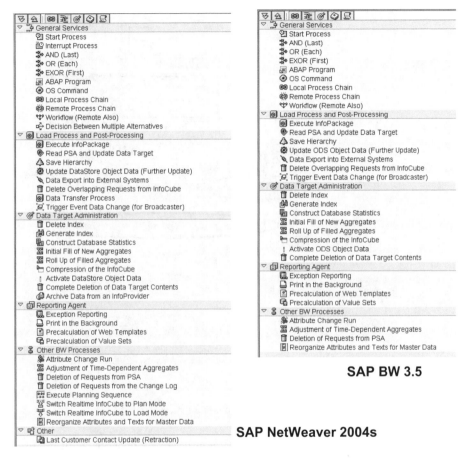

**Figure 2.47** Comparison of Old and New Process Types

Perhaps the most important new process type is the **Decision Between Multiple Alternatives** (see Figure 2.48, Step 3). This process type enables you to control the flow of a process chain based on multiple-value decisions. For example, you can use the formula editor to formulate conditions based on which the flow of the process chain is controlled (Steps 1 and 2). This means that the process does not necessarily end completely successfully or with an error. Instead, in case of a successful completion a decision is made as to how the further flow of the process chain is to be carried out, for example, based on a specific date (Step 5).

Multiple-value decisions

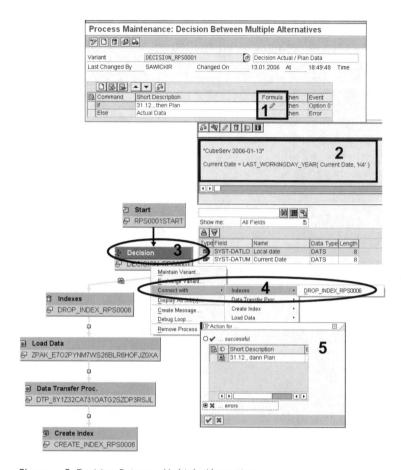

**Figure 2.48** Decision Between Multiple Alternatives

**Connecting processes**

The additional context menu functions in the process chain mainte-nance constitute another new feature (see Figure 2.48, Step 4). These functions eliminate the necessity of connecting the individual pro-cess variants via drag-and-drop. Instead, you can select the individual variants grouped by their type via the context menu. In this context, a check is carried out for possible links to ensure that no redundant targets are provided for selection.

**Display mode**

Regarding process chains, SAP NetWeaver 2004s distinguishes explicitly between the *display* and *change modes*. Up to and including SAP BW 3.5, only one user at a time could display a process chain and change it, if necessary. Other users weren't even able to display the same process chain at the same time. This problem was elimi-nated in the new release.

The copying of process chains is another new feature (see Figure 2.49, Step 1). If you want to copy an existing process chain, including its references to the process variants, you must perform the following steps:

**Copying chains**

▶ Select the process chain to be copied.

▶ Copy the process chain (e. g., via the menu, as shown in Step 1).

▶ Assign a technical name and description to the new chain.

▶ Exchange the start process variant (this step is mandatory because a start process variant can be assigned to only one process chain in the system).

▶ Save the new chain and, if necessary, activate and schedule it.

You can now also use the process chains in a client-dependent application (see Figure 2.49, Step 2).

**Other functions**

> We're rather skeptical about the usefulness of this option, however, because an SAP BW system can run on only one client.

**[«]**

You can also define an explicit user to execute the process chain. As in the Data Warehousing Workbench, a tree display is available to provide accessibility (Step 3) so that you don't need to use the network graphic.

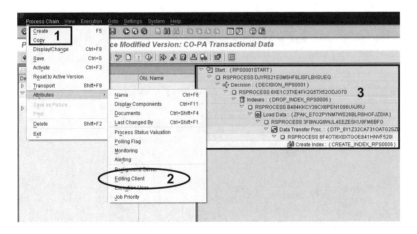

**Figure 2.49** New Features of the Process Chains

## 2.5    Enterprise Reporting, Query, and Analysis

Old and new func-
tions and compo-
nents
The Business Explorer Suite contains individual tools such as the Query Designer and the Web Application Designer, which have again been provided in a 3.x version in order to ensure downward compatibility with previously created 3.x objects. But, if you save the old objects using the new components—sometimes it will suffice to simply open the elements in the new frontend—a conversion is carried out depending on the respective object type. You may, however, encounter a situation whereby you cannot carry out a conversion because the new release no longer supports specific elements such as the **Role Menu** web item in the Web Application Designer. Nonetheless, new functionality is only provided with the new components.

Components of the
Business Explorer
Suite
Figure 2.50 shows the individual components of the *Business Explorer (BEx) Suite*. Presumably the most important innovation in the field of enterprise reporting is the *Report Designer* that is used to format reports and is provided for the first time in SAP NetWeaver 2004s. Familiar tools such as the Query Designer, Web Application Designer, and BEx Analyzer are still provided by SAP, though with a new user interface and changed functionality.

[»]    Note that the new functions of the Business Explorer Suite require the use of an SAP Enterprise Portal.

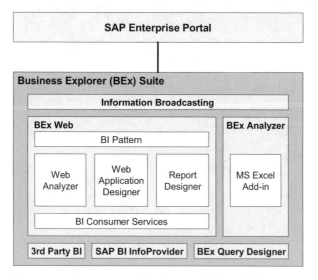

**Figure 2.50**  Components of the Business Explorer Suite

### 2.5.1 Query Design

Compared to the familiar Query Designer 3.x, the user interface of the Query Designer provided with SAP NetWeaver 2004s has changed significantly, as is indicated by the separation into individual work areas. In earlier versions, four areas were displayed simultaneously: **Filter**, **Free Characteristics**, **Rows**, and **Columns**. Now, you must use tabs and the toolbar to navigate between the filter area and the section containing the row and column definitions (see Figure 2.51, Step 1).

*Work areas*

The filter area consists of the **Characteristic Restrictions** (Step 2) that cannot be changed later on when the query is executed, and the **Default Values** area (Step 3) in which you can restrict characteristics that can be navigated, for instance, from the query row area.

*Filter area*

What is new about the characteristics in filters is that you can now store them in the new release like structures and calculated or restricted key figures, which means you can reuse them in other queries.

*Global filters*

If you use variables as well, you no longer have to restrict the variable names to eight characters. This often leads to incomprehensible abbreviations and to a multitude of variables, because it is easier to create a new variable than to examine the properties of each existing variable. The only workaround for this dilemma was to examine Table RSZGLOBV. Fortunately, the restriction of the short technical name was eliminated in SAP NetWeaver 2004s.

*Variable names*

In the new release, the **Properties** of individual elements or of the query no longer need to be displayed in a popup window, because the system displays them in a separate area for each selected element (see Figure 2.51, Step 4).

*Properties*

The area below the query definition is also new. As you can see in Figure 2.52, the system outputs error messages or warnings, sometimes replete with suggested corrections. It is very helpful in this context that the check is constantly refreshed so that errors are reported in real time, which prevents you from conducting error analyses once the query is completed. You should note that we didn't observe any significant prolongation of the runtime that might have been caused by these checks.

*Displaying messages*

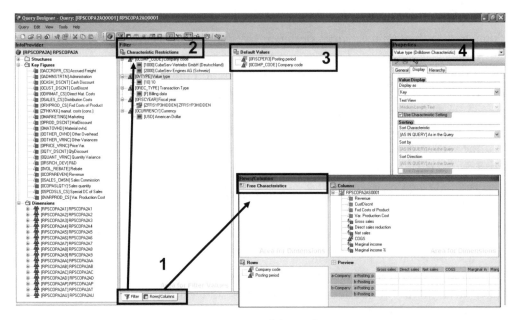

**Figure 2.51** New Arrangement of the Work Areas

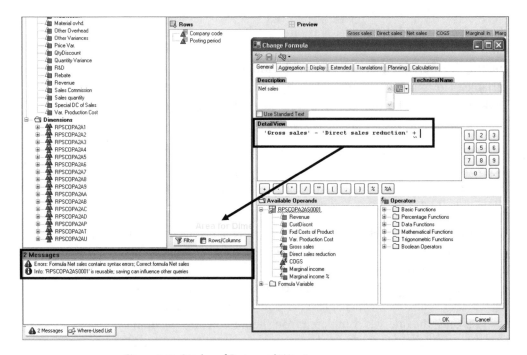

**Figure 2.52** Display of Errors and Warnings

Another useful feature is the option to mark multiple elements and process them simultaneously. Figure 2.53, Step 1, shows the multiple selections of several key figures and the properties area that applies to all the selected key figures. Thanks to this feature, you can now carry out formatting tasks much faster (e. g., the number of decimal places or scaling for key figures, the display of text/key or the handling of result rows for characteristics).

During the design of queries, you can also mark individual key figures as plannable so that the query works as a data-entry layout during its execution on the web or in a workbook. This feature is also new (Step 2).

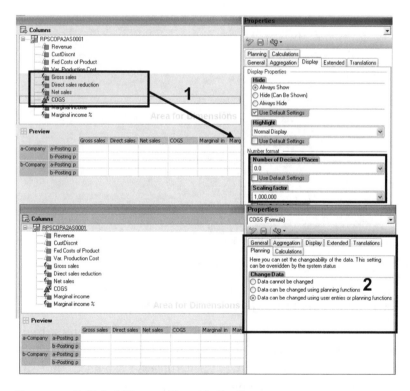

**Figure 2.53** Multiple Editing and Plannable Key Figures

Once you have defined the query, you can run it on the web and thus through the portal or integrate it in a workbook (see Figure 2.54). As we already mentioned, using SAP Enterprise Portal along with SAP NetWeaver 2004s is necessary if you want to use the new functions of the Query Designer.

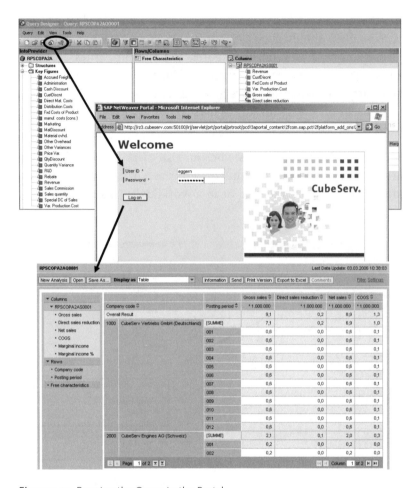

**Figure 2.54** Running the Query in the Portal

### 2.5.2 MS Excel Integration and Workbook Design

Although n the context of reporting SAP clearly promotes a trend towards web reporting, the MS Excel-based analysis using the Business Explorer Analyzer was nevertheless extended in SAP NetWeaver 2004s and equipped with new functions.

Intuitive navigation

You can run analyses in the new workbook template, but it is not mandatory. Unlike previous navigation options, SAP now also provides an intuitive user interaction via drag-and-drop (see Figure 2.55, Steps 1 and 2). Here, you can add and remove new characteristics via drag-and-drop, and you can exchange individual columns. Furthermore, all Information Broadcasting features are still available.

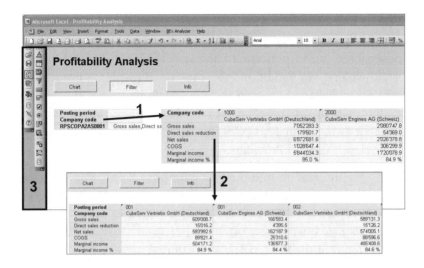

**Figure 2.55** BEx Analyzer

In addition to the navigation options, the new BEx Analyzer also supports the development of applications in Excel. The application elements (see Figure 2.55, Step 3) can be compared to those in the Web Application Designer: filters, dropdown boxes, radio buttons, and so on.

*Application building and workbook design*

Moreover, the tool is better integrated in Excel. In previous releases, it often happened that the popup window for the variable entry disappeared in the background if several applications were open and you frequently changed between the applications. In the future, you can circumvent this annoying behavior via the integration in Excel.

For an attractive design of the workbooks, you can use all formatting functions available in Excel, and you can access all cells of the result set using Excel formulas.

> Note, however, that you can no longer use the macros provided up to SAP BW 3.x in the new applications without modifying them.    **[«]**

Application building is further supported by transferring functionality from the area of BI-integrated planning. Not only can you create efficient analysis workbooks, but also Excel-based workbooks containing areas for the entry of planning data at planning aggregation levels and the use of planning functions.

*Planning integration*

### 2.5.3    BEx Web Analyzer

Multiple
DataProviders

The BEx Web Analyzer is integrated into the SAP NetWeaver Portal and enables you to perform ad-hoc analyses based on multiple BI DataProviders. In addition to the DataProviders from SAP NetWeaver 2004s, these also include DataProviders of third-party vendors, which can be connected to the business warehouse via ODBO or XML for Analysis (XML/A). Therefore, you can use queries, query views, and InfoProviders.

Saving the query

Due to the integration into the SAP Enterprise Portal, you can save the current navigation status of a query either in the BEx Portfolio or in the Favorites in the Knowledge Management area of the portal. If you create new query views using the BEx Web Analyzer, this metadata is stored in the BI Metadata Repository.

Navigation

Figure 2.56 shows an ad-hoc report in the BEx Web Analyzer. Arrows in the column headers enable you to sort the columns in ascending or descending order. You can obtain a different navigation status by dragging and dropping elements from the pool into the display area or vice versa. You can also exchange columns via drag-and-drop.

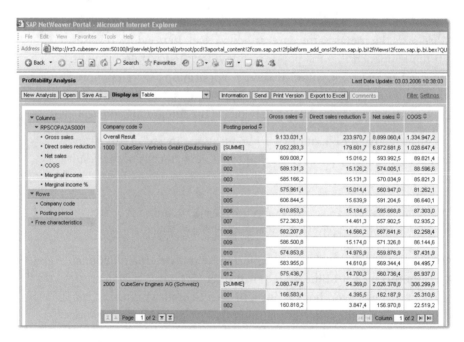

**Figure 2.56** Ad-Hoc Query in the BEx Web Analyzer

To display the report, you can either use the classic table display, a chart, or a combination of the table and the chart.

Table and chart

You can also use other features such as Information Broadcasting or result printing.

## 2.5.4 Formatted Reports

The Report Designer enables you to format reports in an attractive way so that they can be used for enterprise reporting purposes and be displayed on the web. The Report Designer is also part of the Business Explorer Suite and is provided for the first time in SAP NetWeaver 2004s.

Enterprise reporting

The data for all formatted reports is either provided through queries or query views. You can insert one or more data sources into the report page (see Figure 2.57, Step 1). In addition, the field catalog (Step 2) enables you to include other DataProvider-specific information such as text elements or all fields of the DataProvider in the report. To optimize the report display, you can change the settings of the page layout (see Step 3) such as the orientation (portrait or landscape) or the page margins.

DataProviders and page layout

In addition to the data contents, you can, of course, also use other page elements such as a page header or footer to further lay out the reports in a professional manner (see Figure 2.58, Step 1). For example, you could add a query description from the text elements via drag-and-drop (Step 2). You can also format all cells of the report using familiar styles such as font type, font size, font color, text orientation, or background colors (Step 3). You can perform the formatting tasks using the menu, the toolbar, or the respective context menu.

Page elements and formattings

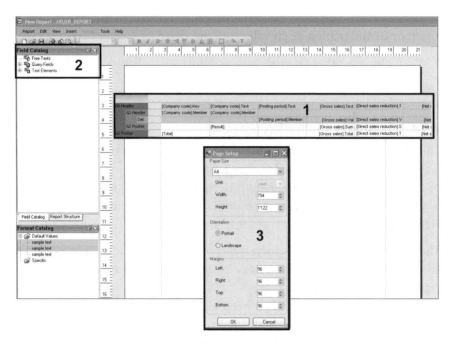

**Figure 2.57** Page Formatting in the Report Designer

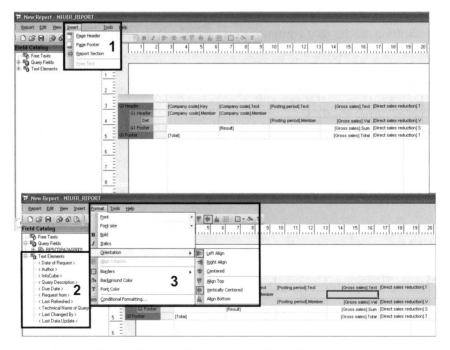

**Figure 2.58** Page Elements, Field Catalog, and Formattings

You can format elements both cell by cell and across entire rows or columns. The latter is referred to as a *row-pattern concept*. This concept also allows you to insert new columns and rows whose height and width you can define individually (see Figure 2.59).

Row-pattern concept

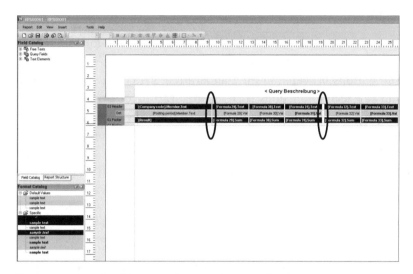

**Figure 2.59** Completed Report with Inserted Rows and Columns

Depending on the DataProvider that is used, you can distinguish between *static* and *dynamic sections*. Queries that contain two structures—one in the rows and the other in the columns—are referred to as *static*, because the structure of the report is defined and fixed. Queries that have only one (key figure) structure and at least one characteristic in the drilldown are referred to as *dynamic*, because their length or width can vary depending on the number of characteristic values.

Static and dynamic sections

Therefore, static reports provide only very restricted navigation options; usually that's only the filtering of attributes. Because the layout is fixed due to the two structures, each cell can be uniquely identified and positioned anywhere in the report.

Static reports

In dynamic reports, you cannot uniquely identify the cells, which is why here you can change only the position of cells within the same group in a section of the report. Fields that belong to higher levels of the report can be downgraded to lower levels. The navigation options available in this type of report are the filtering and expand-

Dynamic reports

ing of hierarchies, for example, to which you can also apply the respective formatting.

Cell manipulation

During the design phase of a report, you can also manipulate the contents of cells; for example, you can add texts or units without any problem.

Running a report in the portal

Once the report has been completely formatted, you can either integrate it into a web application or run it in the portal (see Figure 2.60). The buttons provided in the standard template of the report enable you to execute functions such as broadcasting or printing. Because the page settings of the report don't override any client-side browser settings, you should ensure that you use the function provided by SAP instead of the print function of the browser. Thanks to the Adobe Document Service integrated in Web Application Server, you can also convert the report into PDF format.

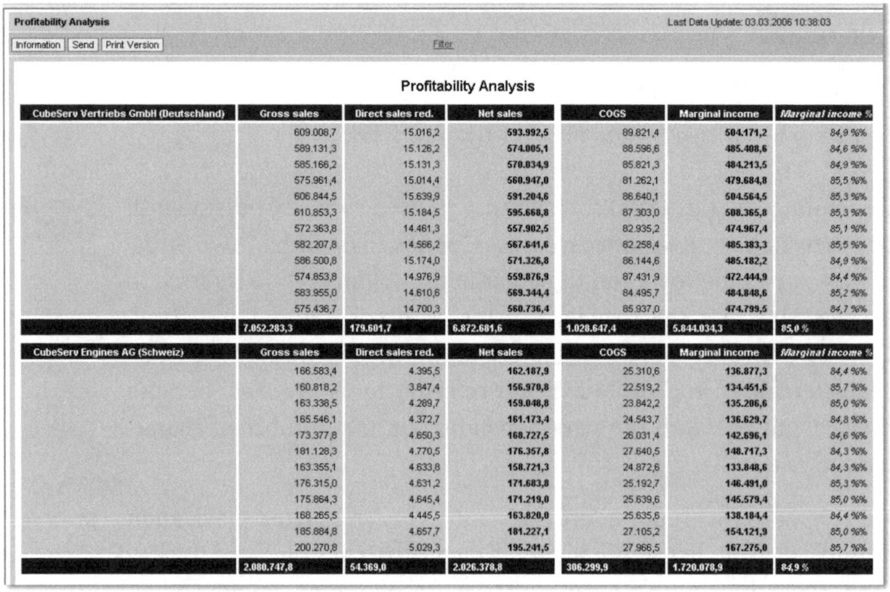

**Profitability Analysis**  Last Data Update: 03.03.2006 10:38:03

Information | Send | Print Version  Filter

### Profitability Analysis

| CubeServ Vertriebs GmbH (Deutschland) | Gross sales | Direct sales red. | Net sales | COGS | Marginal income | Marginal income % |
|---|---|---|---|---|---|---|
| | 609.008,7 | 15.016,2 | 593.992,5 | 89.821,4 | 504.171,2 | 84,9 %% |
| | 589.131,3 | 15.126,2 | 574.005,1 | 88.596,6 | 485.408,6 | 84,6 %% |
| | 585.168,2 | 15.131,3 | 570.034,9 | 85.821,3 | 484.213,5 | 84,9 %% |
| | 575.961,4 | 15.014,4 | 560.947,0 | 81.262,1 | 479.684,8 | 85,5 %% |
| | 606.844,5 | 15.639,9 | 591.204,6 | 86.640,1 | 504.564,5 | 85,3 %% |
| | 610.853,3 | 15.184,5 | 595.668,8 | 87.303,0 | 508.365,8 | 85,3 %% |
| | 572.363,8 | 14.461,3 | 557.902,5 | 82.935,2 | 474.967,4 | 85,1 %% |
| | 582.207,8 | 14.566,2 | 567.641,6 | 82.258,4 | 485.383,3 | 85,5 %% |
| | 586.500,8 | 15.174,0 | 571.326,8 | 86.144,6 | 485.182,2 | 84,9 %% |
| | 574.853,8 | 14.976,9 | 559.876,9 | 87.431,9 | 472.444,9 | 84,4 %% |
| | 583.955,0 | 14.610,6 | 569.344,4 | 84.495,7 | 484.848,6 | 85,2 %% |
| | 575.436,7 | 14.700,3 | 560.736,4 | 85.937,0 | 474.799,5 | 84,7 %% |
| | **7.052.283,3** | **179.601,7** | **6.872.681,6** | **1.028.647,4** | **5.844.034,3** | **85,0 %** |
| **CubeServ Engines AG (Schweiz)** | **Gross sales** | **Direct sales red.** | **Net sales** | **COGS** | **Marginal income** | **Marginal income %** |
| | 166.583,4 | 4.395,5 | 162.187,9 | 25.310,6 | 136.877,3 | 84,4 %% |
| | 160.818,2 | 3.847,4 | 156.970,8 | 22.519,2 | 134.451,6 | 85,7 %% |
| | 163.338,5 | 4.289,7 | 159.048,8 | 23.842,2 | 135.206,6 | 85,0 %% |
| | 165.546,1 | 4.372,7 | 161.173,4 | 24.543,7 | 136.629,7 | 84,8 %% |
| | 173.377,8 | 4.650,3 | 168.727,5 | 26.031,4 | 142.696,1 | 84,6 %% |
| | 181.128,3 | 4.770,5 | 176.357,8 | 27.640,5 | 148.717,3 | 84,3 %% |
| | 163.355,1 | 4.633,8 | 158.721,3 | 24.872,6 | 133.848,6 | 84,3 %% |
| | 176.315,0 | 4.631,2 | 171.683,8 | 25.192,7 | 146.491,0 | 85,3 %% |
| | 175.864,3 | 4.645,4 | 171.219,0 | 25.639,6 | 145.579,4 | 85,0 %% |
| | 168.265,5 | 4.445,5 | 163.820,0 | 25.635,6 | 138.184,4 | 84,4 %% |
| | 185.884,8 | 4.657,7 | 181.227,1 | 27.105,2 | 154.121,9 | 85,0 %% |
| | 200.270,8 | 5.029,3 | 195.241,5 | 27.966,5 | 167.275,0 | 85,7 %% |
| | **2.080.747,8** | **64.369,0** | **2.026.378,8** | **306.299,9** | **1.720.078,9** | **84,9 %** |

**Figure 2.60** Formatted Report in the Browser

### 2.5.5 Web Applications and Web Printing

The basic tool to use for the creation of web applications is the BEx Web Application Designer. The BEx tool in SAP NetWeaver 2004s contains new layout and navigation elements, as well as an improved layout and code editing engine. Figure 2.61 shows the new user interface.

The web items are divided into the following categories (see Figure 2.61, Step 1):

▸ **Standard**
The most frequently used web items

▸ **Advanced**
Less often used web items

▸ **Miscellaneous**
Special items

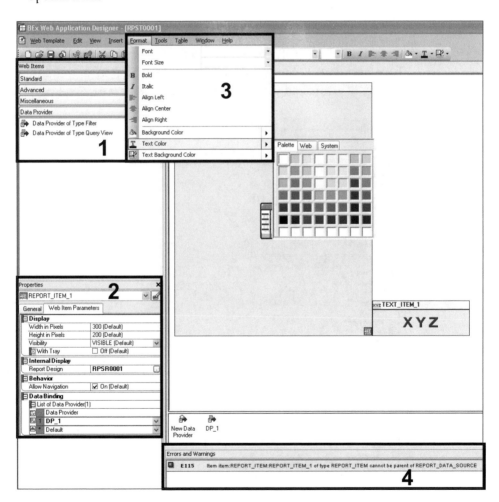

**Figure 2.61** User Interface of the Web Application Designer

The properties of the web items are grouped according to the following criteria (see Figure 2.61, Step 2):

▸ **Display**
All properties needed to render the items, such as width, height, and visibility

▸ **Internal Display**
All item-specific properties that refer to rendering the item, such as alternative styles of table rows in the analysis (table) item

▸ **Behavior**
Item-specific behavior

▸ **Data Binding**
Assignment of a DataProvider

Moreover, the WYSIWYG settings for font, positioning, and color have been greatly improved (see Figure 2.61, Step 3) as well as the display of errors and warnings in a separate work area (Step 4).

**Figure 2.62** Web Items Sorted by Categories

With regard to web items, SAP implemented quite a few new features. Some web items have been completely removed, others were changed, and some new ones have been added (see Figure 2.62). The following section provides a brief overview of the changes. You can find more detailed information on individual web items in Chapter 7, *BEx Query Designer*.

SAP NetWeaver 2004s contains the following new web items:

New web items

► **Container Layout**
This item enables a layout design for inserted web items similar to (invisible) HTML tables.

► **Filter Pane**
This item allows you to display several filter dropdowns of a DataProvider. The filtering restriction can be carried out automatically, as predefined, or at runtime via drag-and-drop.

► **Menu Bar**
This item enables you to generate a menu—similar to desktop applications—into which you can integrate commands for the template.

► **Properties Pane**
This item enables you to display the properties of a specific web item at runtime and modify these properties, if necessary.

► **Tab Pages**
This item represents a grouping option for individual DataProviders.

► **Button Group**
This item allows you to group multiple buttons, which, in turn, contain defined commands.

► **Link**
This item enables you to display and execute a command. The display type can be compared to an HTML hyperlink.

► **Group**
This item enables you to group one or several web items.

► **Input Field**
This item can be used to enter planning data.

▶ **System Messages**
This item displays errors, warnings, information, and other system messages.

▶ **Listbox**
This item enables you to make multiple selections of a characteristic from one or several DataProviders.

▶ **Report**
This item allows you to integrate the reports formatted with the new BEx Report Designer into the web template.

▶ **Context Menu**
This item is now available as a separate web item and no longer depends on the properties of the web template itself. Unlike the context menu in SAP BW 3.x, with this context menu, you no longer need to switch between the standard menu and the advanced menu.

Obsolete
web items
The following web items are no longer provided with SAP NetWeaver 2004s:

▶ **Role Menu**
This item is replaced by the role-based display of BI content in the SAP Enterprise Portal.

▶ **Alert Monitor**
This item is replaced by the Universal Worklist (UWL) of the portal. Due to the integration of Information Broadcasting and the Alert Framework, you can now distribute and display any type of alert via the same infrastructure and user interface.

▶ **Broadcaster**
This item is now available as an iView in SAP NetWeaver Portal and can be included in web pages, roles, or favorites.

▶ **Ad-hoc Query Designer**
The BEx Web Analyzer replaces the Ad-hoc Query Designer in SAP NetWeaver 2004s.

▶ **ABC Analysis**

▶ **Simulation Prediction**

Modified
web items
The following web items, which are already familiar from SAP BW 3.x, have been significantly modified in the new release:

▶ **Analysis (formerly Table)**

The new version makes navigating easier due to the drag-and-drop functionality. You can now change between different navigation statuses. Moreover, the integration of planning in the queries enables you to enter planning data through the Analysis item. During the course of writing this book, the table interface (web API) for the Analysis item was not available. We continue to hope, however, that SAP will change its strategy here and integrate this powerful tool again.

▶ **Dropdown Box**

The familiar functionality of the Dropdown Box has been combined with that of the **Query View Selection** web item. So you can now select individual characteristic values to filter data and define your own items for the Dropdown Box. The ONLY_VALUES parameter is no longer supported.

▶ **Navigation Pane**

The new navigation block now also provides drag-and-drop functionality; however, unfortunately, the table interface was removed here as well.

▶ **Radio Button Group**

The HORIZONTAL_ALIGNMENT and HORIZONTAL_NUMBER parameters have been combined and replaced by the new COLUMN parameter. Thus you only need to specify one value for the display.

▶ **Checkbox Group**

This item was modified in the same way as the Radio Button Group item.

▶ **Chart**

The **Chart** web item provides three new chart types (see Figure 2.63):

▷ **Gantt Chart** for the graphical display of project schedules

▷ **Milestone Trend Analysis** (MTA) to determine the project completion date

▷ **Heatmap** to determine the efficiency of marketing campaigns

▶ **Hierarchical Filter**

The hierarchy is no longer rendered dynamically at runtime, but it is provided as a static tree structure that can be expanded and collapsed.

▶ **Map**

You can execute individual key figures for each level so that a query that contains several key figures can be used for several levels. You can display or hide the legend for each level individually.

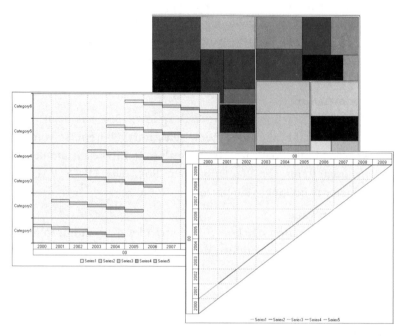

**Figure 2.63** New Chart Types

▶ **Text**

This item is an enhancement of the **Label** web item: You can now display language-dependent texts via table control, which means the texts no longer need to be integrated as language-dependent text elements of an ABAP report into the web template.

▶ **Information Field**

This item summarizes the various pieces of information provided by filter and text elements of previous releases.

▶ **Single Document/Document List**

These new items enable you to call Knowledge Management applications. Furthermore, you can directly integrate a single document into the web application (without using frames or iFrames). In the document lists, you can display and hide meta-information on the documents; however, you can no longer use the two document BAdIs, RSOD_ITEM_DOC, and RSOD_ITEM_DOC_LIST.

The code generation wizards represent another substantial improve- **Code generation**
ment in the new release. In addition to simple HTML codings such as **wizards**
tables and styles, a command wizard is available (see Figure 2.64)
that enables you to easily generate commands (command URLs) such
as the closing of a browser window, calling the BEx Broadcaster, or
various navigation options on the DataProvider. Therefore, the Java-
Scripts in the web templates will only play a minor role in the future.

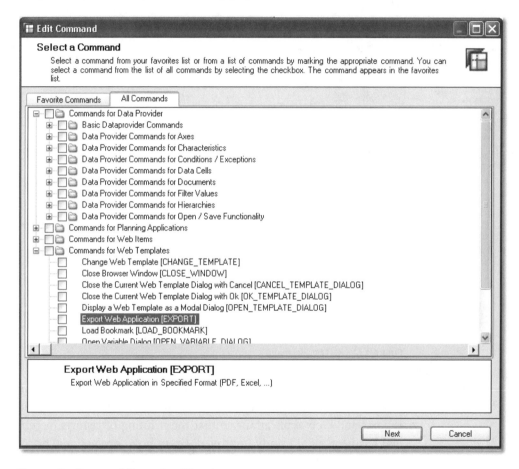

**Figure 2.64** Command Generation Wizard

Another new feature is that the source code is now XML-based **XHTML source**
(instead of HTML):XHTML (see Figure 2.65). **code**

[»] For manual code manipulations, this means that you must have some specific knowledge of this format because the coding must be set up in a correspondingly clean manner, that is, it must be well formed and valid. In HTML, on the other hand, an unclean coding was not a big problem, because the browsers have a certain error tolerance to carry out corrections by themselves.

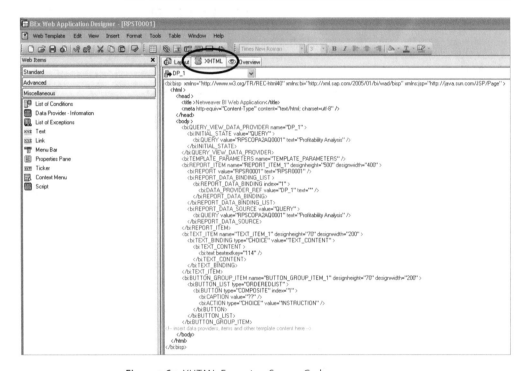

**Figure 2.65** XHTML Format as Source Code

**PDF generation and web printing** Thanks to the integration of the Adobe Document Service into SAP NetWeaver Web AS, you can now generate PDF documents from the reports and web applications so that the printing of reports in general has been significantly improved. Up to now, professional printing solutions for web applications with all web items including charts have only been possible by using third-party tools. The new web printing feature now also provides options such as page orientation, margins, and header and footer texts (see Figure 2.66). You can either define these print settings globally or override them individually.

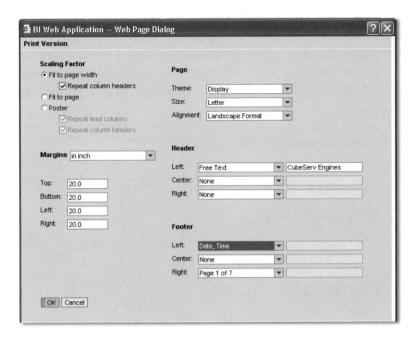

**Figure 2.66** "Print Version" Dialog of a Web Application

## 2.5.6    Information Broadcasting

Information Broadcasting, that is, the distribution of information, enables you to provide reports containing business intelligence data to a wide range of users and to tailor these reports to the respective information requirements. This functionality was provided for the first time in SAP BW 3.5. In SAP NetWeaver 2004s, it was extended and further integrated into the portal.

From hereon, you can use BEx queries, views, workbooks, web applications, and formatted enterprise reports as a basis for the provision of information. As before, the reports can be distributed to the data as (zipped) HTML, (zipped) MHTML, workbook, and online link. New features are the PDF format and print formats such as Post-Script.

Technical details

The information can still be distributed via email or posted into the portal. Thanks to the *Multi-Channel Broadcasting* feature, you can create several distribution channels with the same setting in SAP NetWeaver 2004s. This avoids separate creations for email and portal.

SAP Alert Framework

The broadcast can be triggered either ad-hoc, scheduled, or via *exceptions*. Due to the integration of Information Broadcasting with the SAP Alert Framework, you can therefore define alerts based on exceptions (see Figure 2.67). These alerts can be checked in the background by the broadcaster, which, if necessary, can then trigger an alert through the SAP Alert Framework.

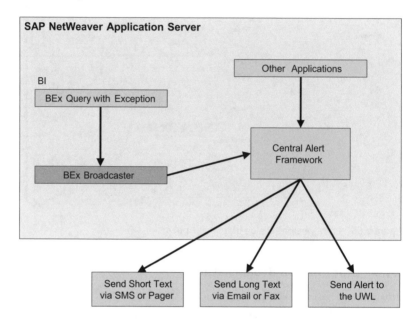

**Figure 2.67** Exception Broadcasting

## 2.6 Business Planning and Analytical Services

With SAP NetWeaver 2004s, SAP strongly pushes the concept of BI-integrated planning. In contrast to SEM-BPS and BW-BPS, the planning uses the objects from SAP BW more intensely than before, particularly the components of the Business Explorer Suite. The following sections describe the concept of BI-integrated planning and the most important innovations.

### 2.6.1 BI-Integrated Planning

The version of BI-integrated planning that comes with SAP NetWeaver 2004s is fully integrated in SAP NetWeaver and aligned with the strategy of the Enterprise Services Architecture (ESA).

Up to and including SAP BW 3.5, objects for planning with BPS and those for data warehousing were developed in parallel and didn't have much in common. Interfaces between these two fields existed only in the data model, the real-time InfoCube (then referred to as "transactional basic InfoCube"), and reports on selected InfoCubes or MultiProviders, provided these reports existed. Variables, data-entry layouts, or hierarchies are just a few examples of elements that were either developed exclusively in the BPS or parallel to data warehousing in the BPS. Regarding the hierarchies, you even had to accept some functional losses on the BPS side.

Redundant functions

When SAP decided to unveil the redundant interfaces between planning and data warehousing and to combine them, the concept of *BI-integrated planning* was born.

Figure 2.68 shows the new architecture of BI-integrated planning. The metadata from SAP BW forms the basis. In addition to the real-time InfoCubes and the InfoObjects that contain master data, it is particularly the MultiProvider that plays a major role in planning. You can use the MultiProvider only as a substitute for the multi-planning area and therefore to establish a link between actual data and planning data.

Objects of BI-integrated planning

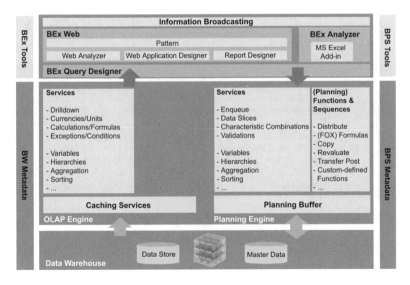

**Figure 2.68** Architecture of BI-Integrated Planning (Source: SAP AG)

Innovations   The planning models including the planning functions are created on the basis of the data model. You should note that you can now also use variables and hierarchies from SAP BW for planning purposes, which enables you to avoid redundant metadata, especially with regard to the variables. To enter the planning data, you no longer need to create any data-entry layouts. Instead, you need queries with key figures that are ready for input. You can enter the data, for instance, on the web or in Excel workbooks. This closes the circle of BI-integrated planning in the analysis area. The familiar reporting components of the Business Explorer Suite are used, which means that objects such as formulas are automatically available as well.

For the planning models, new terminology has been introduced along with BI-integrated planning. Figure 2.69 contains a comparison of old and new objects.

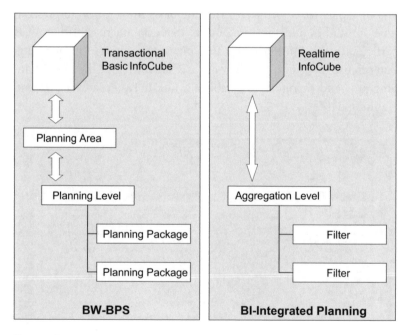

**Figure 2.69** BW-BPS vs. BI-Integrated Planning

If you are planning to migrate to SAP NetWeaver 2004s, you will have to deal with the following question: Which planning objects that have been created using BW-BPS or SEM-BPS do you want to keep using in the new release? SAP's answer is: All of them! Both planning versions—the old one and BI-integrated planning—can be operated in parallel. However, if you want to use the new functions and options, a migration is inevitable. In this context, you must first manually rebuild the objects that work as front-ends, such as data-entry layouts, web interfaces, and so on.

**[«]**

### 2.6.2 Planning Modeler

The central development tool for BI-integrated planning is the web-based Planning Modeler (see Figure 2.70, Steps 1 and 2) that can be called via Transaction Code RSPLAN and replaces the familiar Transaction BPS0 or BW-BPS and SEM-BPS. This tool handles the entire modeling and customizing processes in BI-integrated planning. Alternatively, you can also call the Planning Wizard (Step 3), which is very useful when developing a planning application.

Transaction RSPLAN

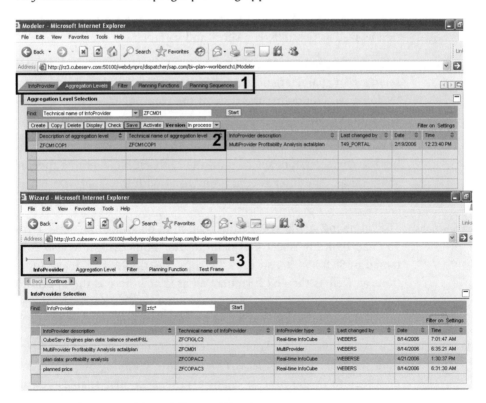

**Figure 2.70** Planning Modeler and Planning Wizard

**Development procedure**

If you want to develop a planning application, you must carry out the following basic steps:

- Create the BW data model, i. e., at least one real-time InfoCube.
- Create a planning model.
- Create planning functions.
- Create a query for the data entry.
- Create a workbook (with query integration) and/or a web application.
- Execute the planning application.

Let's take a closer look at these steps. Chapter 11, *BI-Integrated Planning*, contains detailed instructions for the creation of planning applications with SAP NetWeaver 2004s.

**Planning model**

Once you have created a real-time InfoCube as a data model basis for BI-integrated planning, you can create a planning model. For this planning model, you must first select the real-time InfoCube. In this step, you must also create the relationships between the characteristics, as well as possible data slices and variables.

**Aggregation levels**

Next, you have to create the aggregation levels, which represent a selection of characteristics and key figures for the planning process. In doing so, you define the flow of the planning process (e. g., top-down or bottom-up).

The last step in the creation of a planning model consists of restricting the characteristics selected on the aggregation level to a specific value range. The filter is commonly used with the Query Designer. To obtain a flexible application, we recommend using variables here.

**Planning functions**

The following step involves the creation of planning functions. Here you can basically select the planning functions that were also contained in SAP BW 3.x such as the copy, distribute, and delete functions as well as the Fox formula. What is new here is the option to develop customized functions by deriving an OO class. These customized functions are then based on standard functions.

**Integration in process chains**

You can automate the planning functions by merging them into planning sequences. The process type **Execute Planning Sequence** is a new feature in the process chain maintenance that enables you to schedule automatisms as batch jobs, a function that has been long awaited. Another process type is **Switch from Realtime InfoCube**. In previous releases this function had to be carried out either manually via the Data Warehousing Workbench or by calling the relevant function module.

Once you have completed working on the planning model basics, you can turn to the user interfaces for the entry of planning data. For this purpose, you must first create a query at a defined aggregation level. Such queries can retransfer values into an InfoProvider if the relevant key figures have been defined correctly. Data can be changed via (user input or) planning functions.

Planning-compatible queries

Finally you must integrate the newly created query into a workbook or a web application. After that BI-integrated planning can begin.

Workbook and/or web application

## 2.7 Performance Optimization

Performance has and will always be integral to all data warehouse projects. Today fast and real-time report analyses are absolutely mandatory, especially because of the increasing number of users, reports from different applications, and the growing competition among companies. Under these circumstances and in order to promote a wide system acceptance, you must ensure that long runtimes for data updates and long report runtimes caused by performance optimization measures can be avoided.

Even a strong hardware infrastructure is not enough if you don't undertake basic performance measures regularly, or if you don't use them at all. Up until SAP BW 3.5, you could ensure a good system performance by using the following measures:

Traditional performance optimzation measures

► Good data model
► Use of aggregates
► Updating database statistics
► Deletion and recreation of indices when loading data
► Indices on master data attributes
► OLAP cache
► Pre-calculation of the Reporting Agent or Information Broadcasting

SAP NetWeaver
2004s

These methods and options are also available in SAP NetWeaver 2004s. In addition to those, you can use the repartitioning and remodeling functions for data modeling, as well as write-optimized DataStore objects and increased parallelization in the context of data staging, in order to attain improvements in the reporting behavior. This includes the use of BI accelerators and delta caching, which are both described in the following sections.

### 2.7.1 BI Accelerator

Indexing struc-
tured and unstruc-
tured data

For quite some time now, many search engines have been browsing several hundreds of millions of unstructured data on the World Wide Web very fast and have thereby returned rather acceptable results. In doing so, these search engines use the technique of indexing documents. So why shouldn't it be possible for SAP to apply this technique to structured BI data as well, especially since SAP's TREX search engine has already established itself, predominantly with regard to unstructured data.

BI Accelerator
vs. TREX

The answer to this new SAP strategy is the *BI Accelerator*. SAP provides the BI Accelerator that is based on the TREX technology along with a separate server. However, you cannot use the BI Accelerator as a standard Knowledge Management functionality, while a TREX installation, in turn, cannot be used as a BI Accelerator.

Hardware
and setup

The preconfigured BI Accelerator is located in a black box, which contains blade servers with 64-bit Intel Xean CPUs and the Linux operating system. It is currently available with hardware from Hewlett-Packard or IBM; other vendors will probably be added soon. Because you don't need to configure the BI Accelerator, you can connect it to an SAP NetWeaver 2004s BI system within a couple of minutes and immediately start operating it.

Indexing

Figure 2.71 illustrates the architecture and functionality of the BI Accelerator. By indexing InfoCube data—currently only this type of InfoProvider with cumulative values is supported—the data is transferred from the data warehouse to the BI Accelerator Server, where it is processed and stored as BI Accelerator indices. A BI Accelerator index contains replicated data and indices (one index per table, i. e., vertically), which represent the star schema. Internally, these indices are stored as packed numbers, which is even more efficient regarding performance than storing the star schema in BW. The update of BI Accelerator indices (for instance, a rollup or change run) when data in the BW has changed is much faster than the familiar BW processes.

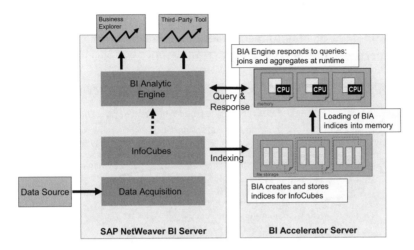

**Figure 2.71** BI Accelerator Architecture (Source: SAP AG)

The indices are loaded into the main memory of the BI Accelerator Server. This occurs either through a specific process or during the first execution of a query. The queries are entirely processed in the main memory where the data is aggregated. Then, the data is joined and transferred to the BI Analytic Engine.

Queries

The BI Analytic Engine determines whether the BI Accelerator Server must be accessed. In a query evaluation, the following sequence is adhered to so that the best and most efficient option is always used:

BI Analytic Engine

► Precalculation and Information Broadcasting
► OLAP cache
► BI Accelerator
► Aggregates
► InfoProviders

If the BI Accelerator continues to be successful, it is very likely that it will be extended so that it can handle other InfoProviders and non-cumulative key figures as well. Because the BI Accelerator is provided as a separate server that is not integrated in BI, it is conceivable

A look ahead

that the BI Accelerator will eventually also be used for "regular" large SAP ERP tables.

### 2.7.2 Delta Caching

Query Monitor *Delta caching* is another new feature in SAP NetWeaver 2004s. You can set delta caching for each query individually through the query properties in the Query Monitor (Transaction RSRT, see Figure 2.72).

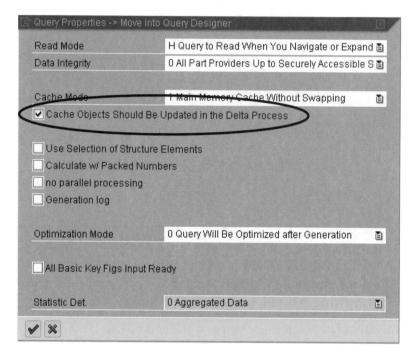

**Figure 2.72** Delta Caching in the Query Monitor

Procedure If you use this function, the query reads the data from the OLAP cache. Additional requests, that is, delta information, are read from the InfoCube, and the OLAP cache is updated with this data. However, if the InfoCube is compressed, no delta can be determined so that the entire cache content must be updated.

## 2.8 User Management and Analysis Authorizations

With regard to the authorization concept, there are also substantial differences between SAP NetWeaver 2004s and its predecessors. In SAP NetWeaver 2004s, reporting authorizations are referred to as *analysis authorizations*. In order to differentiate between the authorizations of the standard authorization concept in SAP NetWeaver and the analysis authorizations in BI, the term *standard authorization* is used. The maintenance of these analysis authorizations occurs through the new central Transaction RSECADMIN (see Figure 2.73).

Analysis authorizations

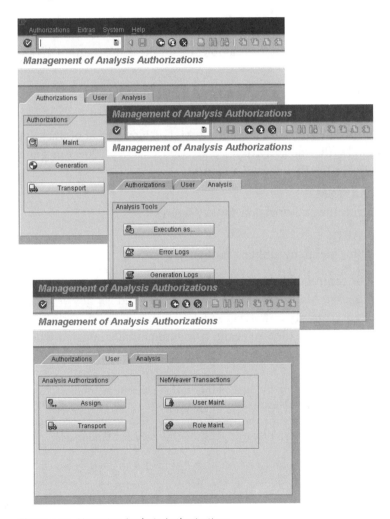

**Figure 2.73** Managing Analysis Authorizations

Essential new
features You can now mark individual navigation attributes as authorization-relevant. To do that, you must set the authorization check flag for the navigation attributes of the InfoObject. In this context, the referencing characteristic does not necessarily have to be authorization-relevant.

Regarding the hierarchy authorizations, you can now also use the variables in the authorization concept, which enables you to flexibly and dynamically determine hierarchy nodes.

With regard to the new analysis authorizations, some new InfoObjects have been implemented that control the authorization concept. These InfoObjects include:

► **0TCAACTVT**
Used for the activity, for example, 03 for the display authorization

► **0TCAIPROV**
Grants authorization to access individual InfoProviders

► **0TCAVALID**
Controls the authorization duration for a given period of time; for example, the interval from 01.xx.2006 to 01.yy.2006 can grant access for the first days of a month

► **0TCAKYFNM**
Controls the authorization for key figures

► **0TCTAUTH**
Used for hierarchy authorizations

0BI_ALL  A specific control of the authorizations occurs via 0BI_ALL. Similar to SAP_ALL, 0BI_ALL is generated automatically and cannot be modified. 0BI_ALL grants authorization for all values of the characteristics marked as authorization-relevant. It is automatically updated whenever a new InfoObject is defined as authorization-relevant.

**[»]**  SAP recommends using the new authorization concept as soon as possible, because the old concept is no longer supported. You can find detailed migration instructions for the ABAP migration tool RSEC_MIGRATION that comes with SAP NetWeaver 2004s in SAP Service Marketplace.

## 2.9    Conclusion

With SAP NetWeaver 2004s Business Intelligence, SAP has managed very well to strengthen its position against other data warehousing products.

Compared to previous releases, many of the modified functions and possibilities as well as the new features represent a significant improvement and, if used correctly and professionally, they will add to an increase in the quality of information management, while at the same time reduce the total cost of ownership (TCO).

For this reason, we recommend a migration to SAP NetWeaver 2004s Business Intelligence as soon as possible so that you can benefit from the advantages described here as a BI user, BI administrator, and as a company as a whole. **[+]**

*With SAP NetWeaver 2004s BI, a number of important*
*extensions and changes have been introduced in the area of*
*data modeling. This chapter describes the most significant of*
*these changes.*

# 3 Data Modeling in the Data Warehousing Workbench of SAP NetWeaver 2004s BI

## 3.1 Introduction

In its new version of SAP BW, SAP has made changes to both the user interface and the functionality in terms of data modeling and the associated parts of the Data Warehousing Workbench. In this chapter, we will use a sample scenario to show you the most important changes. Our objectives are as follows:

► To introduce you to new elements of the changed user interface (InfoObject and InfoCube configuration) from a number of different aspects

► To explain the new master data access function

► To present data store objects (formerly ODS, Operational Data Store) and their new properties

► To demonstrate the procedure for creating InfoCubes in the new interface

► To give you an insight into the procedure for creating MultiProviders in the new user interface

## 3.2 Sample Scenario

Our sample enterprise, CubeServ Engines (see the Introduction to this book), requires a sales order reporting function, complete with orders, order items, and various key figures for amounts and quanti-

Requirement for sales order reporting function

ties (such as net value of sales order items, and cumulative order quantity in sales units (SUs)).

Layers
The data model will contain the following: a *data warehouse integration layer* consisting of DataStore objects for the sales order header and sales order items, which are mandatory basis data; and an *analytical reporting layer* consisting of InfoCubes with the same granularity along with a MultiProvider to combine them. Business content objects will be used as the basis for data modeling.

Corrections to business content
Any gaps in the data model (in terms of InfoObjects) will be filled, and any required links will also be made. To do this, we will create an extra InfoObject called "harmonized version." We will also provide any additional data that may be required, such as time characteristics, and correct any weaknesses that may exist in the modeling of the business content objects (e. g., InfoCube dimensions).

## 3.3    Creating an InfoObject

First, create the "harmonized version" InfoObject in the *Modeling* transaction (Transaction RSA1) of the **Administrator Workbench.**

Prerequisites
The necessary InfoArea structure and the associated InfoObjectCatalogs must already exist.

### Creation Procedure

[▪]
▸ To do this, in the **InfoObjects** view, right-click on the selected **InfoObjectCatalog** folder to open the context-sensitive menu, and select the **Create InfoObject** function (see Figure 3.1, Steps 1 to 3).

▸ The **Create Characteristic** popup opens. Enter the technical name of your InfoObject (**ZFVERSION** in our case) and a long text for the description in the **Char.** field (Step 4).

▸ Confirm your entries by clicking on the **Continue** button (Step 5).

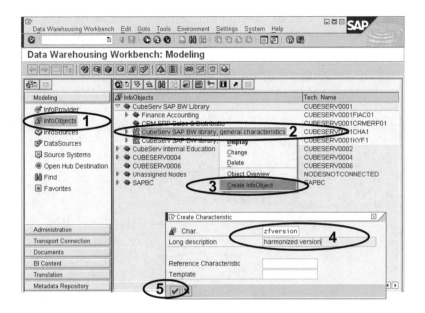

**Figure 3.1** Create InfoObject

**New User Interface**

Next, the dialog for configuring the properties of our InfoObject opens. SAP has provided a new user interface (UI) for this purpose.

▶ The navigation structure displayed in the left-hand frame (for switching on and off the tabs Modeling, Administration, etc.) and the InfoArea/InfoObjectCatalog/ InfoObject tree displayed in the middle frame remain visible (see Figure 3.2).

Overview

▶ The dialog for configuring the InfoObject is displayed in an extra frame on the right-hand side of the screen.

▶ Also, the InfoObject maintenance functions are available as pull-down menus (see Figure 3.2, Step 1).

Proceed as follows to create a new UI:

▶ Specify the properties of your sample InfoObject in the right-hand frame. Enter the short description for the InfoObject, and in the *General* tab, enter the data type CHAR and the length 10. You don't need a conversion routine here (see Figure 3.2, Steps 2 to 5).

[▪]

Hide Tree ▸ If you don't want the tree (in this case, the InfoArea/InfoObject-Catalog / InfoObject tree) to be visible, click on the **Show/Hide Tree** button (Step 6).

▸ The dialog is then displayed as shown in Figure 3.3.

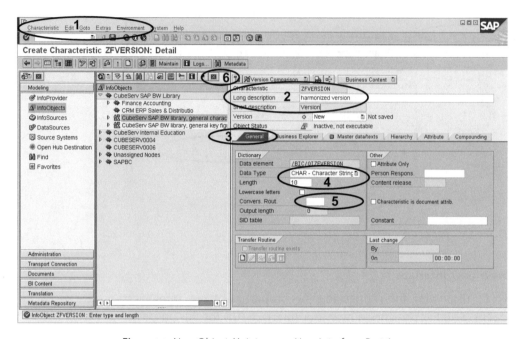

**Figure 3.2** New Object Maintenance User Interface, Part 1

Show tree ▸ If you want to re-show a hidden tree, click on the **Show/Hide Tree** button again (see Figure 3.3, Step 1).

Master Data/Text Properties ▸ You don't need to assign any master data attributes to your InfoObject. Therefore, open the **Master Data/Texts** tab and deactivate the **With master data** property (Steps 2 and 3).

▸ Because you want your texts to be language-specific long texts, you retain the default setting, **Texts language dependent**. You also select the **Long text exists** option (Steps 4 and 5).

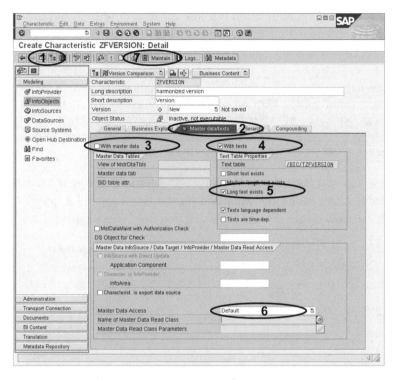

**Figure 3.3** New Object Maintenance User Interface, Part 2

We now come to the new property for setting InfoObject-specific master data access. SAP provides the following information on this property in the context-sensitive Help:

*New: Master Data Access*

*You have three options for accessing master data at query runtime:*

**1. Default**
*The values from the master data table for the characteristics are displayed.*

**2. Own Implementation**
*You can implement access to master data yourself by determining an ABAP class. This ABAP class has to inherit from class CL_RSMD_RS_ BW_SPEC.*

**3. Remote**
*If the characteristic is flagged as an InfoProvider and as an InfoSource with direct update, you can access data in a source system remotely. If this option is set, the master data InfoSource must be connected to the required DataSource.*

The general recommendation is to use the default setting, and this is what we will do here, because the instances of the current InfoObject do not come from any source system (see Figure 3.3, Step 6).

**[+]** Even if the master data instances for characteristics did come from source systems (such as SAP R/3), we would still need to be very careful about using alternative methods of master data access, as using remote access is suitable only for special cases. You should avoid using remote master data in performance-critical scenarios in particular.

Maintain
Master Data

Now, you will open the master data access function for your harmonized version, using the **Maintain** button (see Figure 3.3, Step 7). You can now create the instances that you need (see Figure 3.4).

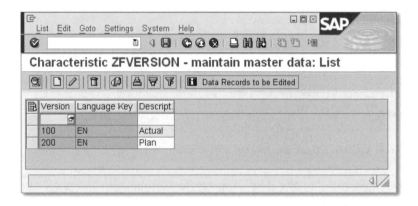

**Figure 3.4** Instances of the "Harmonized Version" InfoObject in the Sample Scenario

## 3.4 "Sales Order Header" Data Model

### 3.4.1 "Sales Order Header" DataStore Object

For your sample scenario, you will now create a cleaned-up DataStore object that is a copy of the business content object **Orders** (0SD_O03), based on the business content components for the sales order header data.

### Activate business content object

Activate the business content DataStore object on the tab of the same name in the **Data Warehousing Workbench** (using Transaction RSA1).

▸ In the **BI content** tab, select the **Object Types** selection type (see Figure 3.5, Steps 1 and 2), then select the **In Data Flow Before** grouping type from the dropdown menu (Steps 3 and 4).

**[▪]**

▸ To select the business content objects that you want to activate, select the **DataStore Object** folder in the **All Objects According to Type** frame and double-click on the **Select Objects** entry to activate your selection (Step 5).

Select business content objects

▸ In the **Input help for Metadata** popup, select the **Object Name** column and click on the **Set Filter** button (Steps 6 and 7).

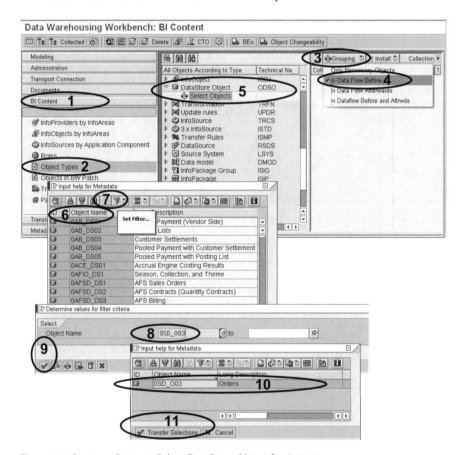

**Figure 3.5** Business Content: Select DataStore Object for Activation

- ▶ Next, the **Determine values for filter criteria** popup is displayed.
- ▶ In the **Object Name** selection field, enter the required business content object (in this case, **0SD_O03**) and click on the **Execute** button (Steps 8 and 9).
- ▶ The selected object is then displayed in the **Input help for Metadata** popup. Select the object you want by clicking on the row containing it, and then click on the **Transfer Selections** button (Steps 10 and 11). This transfers the object into the list of collected objects (see Figure 3.6, Step 1).

Activate business content objects
- ▶ To activate the collected business content objects, click on the **Install** button and select the **Install** entry from the dropdown list (see Figure 3.6, Step 2).
- ▶ If the business content objects that you want to activate have been changed, the differences are displayed for comparison purposes in the **Merge** dialog.
- ▶ In this case, you want to use all the business content settings, so you click on the **Transfer all without dialog** button (Step 3).

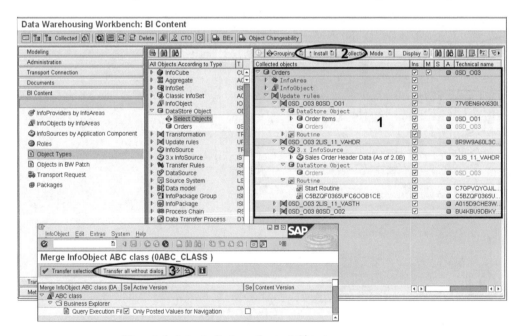

**Figure 3.6** Activate Business Content Objects

Activation results
- ▶ After the activation request has been processed, the log is displayed in the frames in the lower part of the screen. In this exam-

ple, the activation was carried out successfully (see circled section in Figure 3.7).

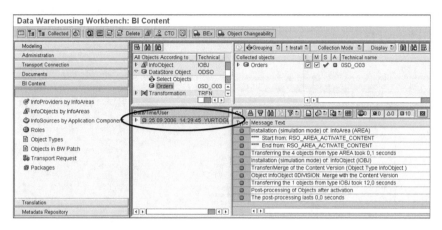

**Figure 3.7** Activation Results

▶ Open the **InfoProvider** view in the **Modeling** tab in the **Data Warehousing Workbench** to display the activated business content objects.

New display in new release

▶ Select an activated object (in this case, DataStore object **0SD_O03**) by clicking on it, and then click on the **Expand Subtree** button (see Figure 3.8, Steps 1 and 2) to display the entire activated data flow for the selected object as a subtree (see Step 3).

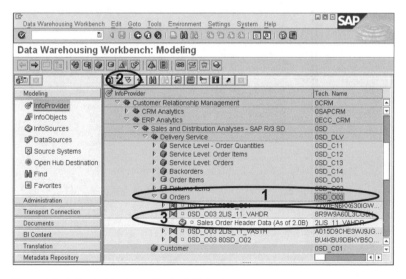

**Figure 3.8** Activated Business Content Objects

Activated Data-
Store object

▶ To analyze the DataStore object, first, right-click on the object to open its context-sensitive menu, and select the **Display** function.

▶ After the various folders for settings, key fields, and data fields are opened, the configuration of the DataStore object is displayed (see Figure 3.9).

**Figure 3.9** Activated DataStore Object 0SD_O03

### Recommended Changes to Business Content DataStore Object 0SD_O03

As with all business content objects, you need to critically analyze the activated DataStore object. If you compare the DataStore object fields with the update rules of the InfoSource **Sales order header 2LIS_11_VAHDR**, you'll see that most of the DataStore object fields are not updated (see Figure 3.10).

Non-updated fields

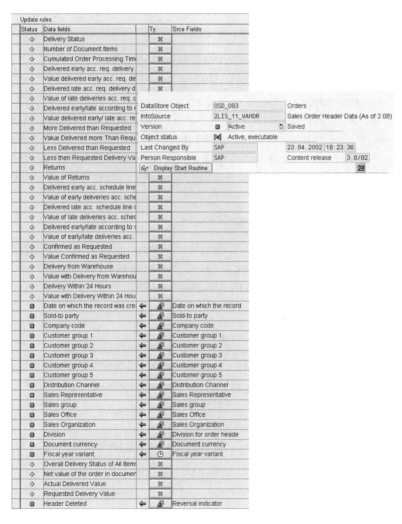

**Figure 3.10** Fields of DataStore Object 0SD_O03 That Are Updated by InfoSource 2LIS_11_VAHDR

**[+]** Because the DataStore object in this scenario will serve as the data prop-agation layer in the Data Warehouse Integration Layer, we recommend that you use only the fields that were updated by the associated Data-Source. Therefore, most of the fields in the business content DataStore object are superfluous for your purposes.

**[+]** To update the DataStore object in the next-highest data warehouse layer, we recommend (unlike with SAP business content) that you create a version InfoObject in the DataStore object.

### Creating a Customer-Specific DataStore Object as a Copy of Business Content Object 0SD_O03

For your sample scenario, then, you will create a customer-specific DataStore object that is a copy of the business content object, which contains only the recommended InfoObjects of the SAP business content DataStore object—that is, those that are updated from the sales order header—and to which the InfoObject **Version** (ZFVER-SION) is added to make it complete.

Prerequisite The required InfoArea structure exists.

**[■]**  ▸ To create a dedicated DataStore object, select the required InfoArea in the **Modeling** view of the **Data Warehousing Work-bench** (Transaction RSA1), and right-click on it to open the con-text-sensitive menu (see Figure 3.11, Steps 1 and 2).

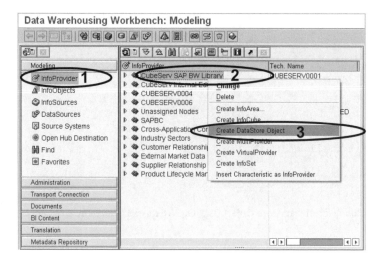

Figure 3.11 Creating a DataStore Object, Part 1

▶ Select the **Create DataStore Object** function (Step 3).

▶ The **Edit DataStore Object** popup opens. Here, you need to enter the technical name (in this case, **ZFSDO03**), the description (in this case, **"Sales Order Header"**), and the name of the object that you want to use as a template (in this case, **0SD_O03**) (see Figure 3.12, Steps 1 to 3).

▶ Confirm your entries by clicking on the **Create** button (Step 4).

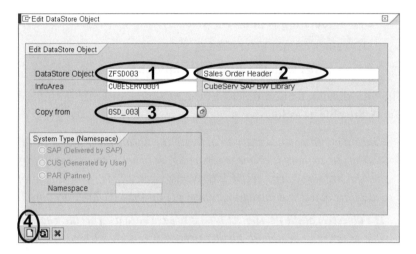

**Figure 3.12** Creating a DataStore Object, Part 2

▶ Next, the **Edit DataStore Object** screen opens (see Figure 3.13).

The new SAP BW version for DataStore objects provides a new DataStore object type ("Write-Optimized;" see Figure 3.13, Step 1) (also see the SAP BW online documentation).[1]

▶ **Standard DataStore objects** have the following properties:

  ▷ Data population is done via the data transfer process.

  ▷ SID values can be created.

  ▷ Data records with the same key are aggregated during the activation process.

  ▷ Data remains available for reporting purposes after activation.

---

1 *http://help.sap.com/saphelp_nw2004s/helpdata/en/F9/*
  *45503C242B4A67E10000000A114084/frameset.htm*

▶ **Write-Optimized DataStore objects** have the following properties:

- ▶ Data population is done via the data transfer process.
- ▶ SID values cannot be created.
- ▶ Data records with the same key cannot be aggregated.
- ▶ Data is immediately available for reporting purposes after loading.

▶ **Direct Update DataStore objects** have the following properties:

- ▶ Data population is done via APIs.
- ▶ SID values cannot be created.
- ▶ Data records with the same key cannot be aggregated.

The SAP documentation describes the new type of write-optimized DataStore objects as follows:

*"Until now, it was necessary to activate the data loaded into a DataStore object to make it visible to reporting, or to be able to update it further for InfoProviders. As of SAP NetWeaver 2004s, a new type of DataStore object was introduced: the write-optimized DataStore object.*

*The objective of the new object type is to save data as efficiently as possible in order to be able to further process it quickly without the need for additional effort to generate SIDs, aggregation, and data-record based delta.*

*Data that is loaded into write-optimized DataStore objects is available immediately for further processing. The activation step that has been necessary until now is no longer required. Note that the loaded data is not aggregated. If two data records with the same logical key are extracted from the source, both records are saved in the DataStore object. The record mode responsible for aggregation remains, however, so that the aggregation of data can take place at a later time in standard DataStore objects.*

*Furthermore, during loading, for reasons of efficiency, no SID values can be determined for the loaded characteristics. The data is still available for reporting. However, in comparison to standard DataStore objects, you can expect to lose performance because the necessary SID values have to be determined during evaluation".[2]*

---

[2] *http://help.sap.com/saphelp_nw2004s/helpdata/en/cb/ 351042f664e12ce10000000a1550b0/frameset.htm*

**Selecting Type "Write-Optimized DataStore Object"**
Because the DataStore object we want to create acts as a component of the data propagation layer in the data warehouse integration layer, the standard reporting function is not available in this case. Therefore, we use the new type: **write-optimized DataStore object**.

▶ To do this, click on the corresponding button next to **Type of** [.] **DataStore Object** (see Figure 3.13, Step 1). Select the property **Write-Optimized** from the **DataStore Object: Select Type** popup and confirm your entry by clicking on **Continue** (Steps 2 and 3).

▶ This automatically changes the available settings to match the DataStore object type. We do **not activate** the **Do Not Check Uniqueness of Data** setting here, because the technical key that is automatically created in the update process guarantees that the data can be uniquely identified (Step 4) (see the SAP online documentation above):

  ▶ Request GUID (0REQUEST)

  ▶ Data package (0DATAPAKID)

  ▶ Data record number (0RECORD)

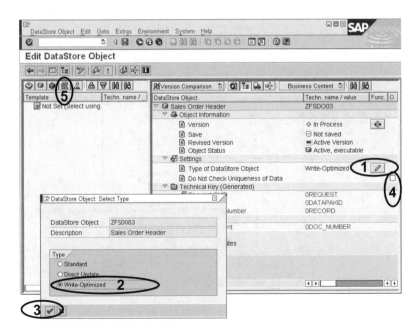

**Figure 3.13** Creating a DataStore Object, Part 3: DataStore Object Type

**Selecting an InfoObjectCatalog as a Template**

You also need to assign the **Version** (ZFVERSION) to the DataStore object that you are creating. Because this InfoObject is available in an InfoObjectCatalog, you can select this InfoObjectCatalog as a template for the InfoObject.

[.•]
- ▸ To do this, click on the **InfoObjectCatalog** button (see Figure 3.13, Step 5).

- ▸ Select the required catalog (see Figure 3.14, Step 1) from the **Select InfoObjectCatalog** popup that opens, and copy it by clicking on **Continue** (Step 2).

Adding more
InfoObjects
- ▸ The catalog is now displayed in the template frame on the left-hand side of the screen. Click on the directory structure to open it and drill down until the InfoObject you require is displayed (Step 3).

- ▸ Select the InfoObject, then drag-and-drop it to the **Delivery Status** InfoObject in the DataStore object (ODLV_STS, see Step 4).

- ▸ This inserts the newly-added InfoObject **Version** (ZFVERSION) above the **Delivery Status** InfoObject ODLV_STS (Step 5).

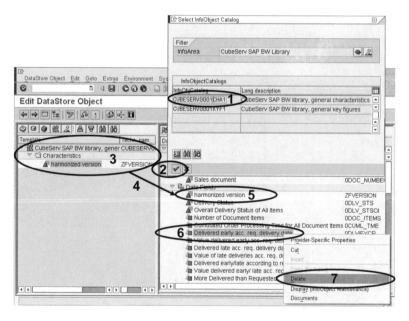

**Figure 3.14** Creating a DataStore Object, Part 4: Adding and Removing an InfoObject

**Removing InfoObjects**

As described in relation to Figure 3.10 (see above), you need to remove any fields in the DataStore object that were not updated by the InfoSource.

▸ Select any InfoObjects of this kind in the DataStore that you are creating, and right-click on them to open the context-sensitive menu (see the sample InfoObject, **Delivered early acc. req. delivery date** (0DLVIEYCR)).  **[✦]**

▸ Select **Delete** from this menu (see Figure 3.14, Steps 6 and 7). You then need to execute the delete function for the following unused InfoObjects (see the remaining data fields in Figure 3.15, Step 1):

  ▸ Delivery Status (0DLV_STS)

  ▸ Number of Document Items (0DOC_ITEMS)

  ▸ Cumulated Order Processing Time for All Document Items (0CUML_TME)

  ▸ Delivered early acc. req. delivery date (0DLVIEYCR)

  ▸ Value delivered early acc. req. delivery date (0DLVVEYCR)

  ▸ Delivered late acc. req. delivery date (0DLVILECR)

  ▸ Value of late deliveries acc. req. delivery date (0DLVVLECR)

  ▸ Delivered early/late according to delivery date (0DLVIELCR)

  ▸ Value delivered early/late acc. req. delivery date (0DLVVELCR)

  ▸ More Delivered than Requested (0DLVIOVER)

  ▸ Value Delivered more Than Requested (0DLVVOVER)

  ▸ Less Delivered than Requested (0DLVIUNDR)

  ▸ Less then Requested Delivery Value (0DLVVUNDR)

  ▸ Returns (0DITM_RET)

  ▸ Value of Returns (0VAL_RET)

  ▸ Delivered early acc. schedule line (0DLVIEYSC)

  ▸ Value of early deliveries acc. schedule line (0DLVVEYSC)

  ▸ Delivered late acc. schedule line (0DLVILESC)

  ▸ Value of late deliveries acc. schedule line (0DLVVLESC)

▸ Delivered early/late according to schedule line (0DLVIELSC)

▸ Value of early/late deliveries acc. to schedule line (0DLVVELSC)

▸ Confirmed as Requested (0ICOASREQ)

▸ Value Confirmed as Requested (0VCOASREQ)

▸ Delivery from Warehouse (0ISHP_STCK)

▸ Value with Delivery from Warehouse (0VSHP_STCK)

▸ Delivery Within 24 Hours (0DLV_24)

▸ Value with Delivery Within 24 Hours (0VAL_24)

▸ Date on which the record was created (0DLV_STSOI)

▸ Net value of the order in document currency (0NET_VAL_HD)

▸ Actual Delivered Value (0DLV_VAL)

▸ Requested Delivery Value (0REQU_VAL)

▶ Lastly, activate the DataStore object (see Figure 3.15, Step 2).

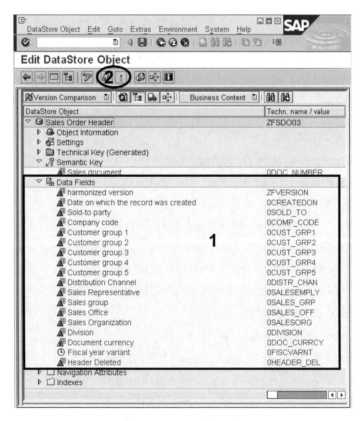

**Figure 3.15** DataStore Object ZFSDO03 After Changes

### 3.4.2 "Sales Order Header" InfoCube

We will now update our DataStore object in the **Service Level Orders** (0SD_C13) InfoCube in SAP Business Content.

**Analyzing the Business Content InfoCube**

An analysis of the business content InfoCube illustrates the necessity of creating a corrected copy of the InfoCube for the following reasons:

▶ The data model of the SAP Business Content InfoCube **Service Level Orders** (0SD_C13) does not use the maximum number of dimensions (six instead of 16). The dimension tables are therefore larger than is ideal.

*Problems with dimension modeling*

▶ In the individual dimensions, characteristics with multiple (and possibly a growing number of) instances are mixed with characteristics with only a small number of instances; for example, dimension 1 contains the status (InfoObjects **0STS_DLV_C, 0DLV_STSOI, 0DLV_STS**) as well as **Date on which the record was added** (0CREATEDON).

▶ The various characteristics of dimension 1 are not updated by all ETL processes, which have the result that, for example, the ETL process based on the sales order header updates only the InfoObject **Date on which the record was added** (0CREATEDON) with characteristic attributes. The initial statuses remain. This procedure is not optimal from the point of view of avoiding empty cells.

▶ No line item dimensions are modeled for characteristics with a large number of attributes.

▶ The **Date on which the record was added** characteristic (0CREATEDON) is the basis for updates to the time dimension, and is located there in the **Calendar Day** InfoObject with full granularity. Storing this InfoObject in another dimension (and thus duplicating it) does not enhance the analysis options and therefore would unnecessarily reduce the quality of the dimension.

▶ The time dimension attribute of the SAP business content InfoCube **Service Level Orders** (0SD_C13) is not optimal.

*Problems with time dimension*

  ▷ It does not have any calendar-based or fiscal time characteristics, which are prerequisites for useful previous year's comparisons (for example, InfoObjects **0FISCPER3, 0FISCYEAR, 0CALMONTH2**, and **0CALYEAR**).

▶ Other time characteristics are also missing, some of which are required for quarterly, half-year, and weekday comparisons (0CALQUART1, 0CALQUARTER, 0HALFYEAR1, and 0WEEKDAY1).

Because the **Calendar Day** InfoObject (0CALDAY) already exists in the InfoCube, using the full attribute with the key figures in question does not increase the size of the dimension. Consequently, all time characteristics are copied into the corrected InfoCube.

Empty cells due to non-updated key figures ▶ The key figures are only partially updated by the various ETL processes. This results in a high number of empty cells.

▶ For example, with the ETL process that is based on the sales order header, only the **Number of Orders** (0ORDERS) key figure is updated. The result is that 29 out of 30 key figures are initial; in other words, more than 96% of the key figures in the fact table are empty.

Missing navigation attributes ▶ No navigation attributes are used in the business content InfoCube. For that reason, you cannot perform analyses of sold-to parties or of the latest customer groups (as distinct from those that are valid at the time of the update in accordance with dimension 2).

Therefore, an InfoCube is created that contains only the characteristics and the key figure that are actually updated.

**Designing your own "Sales order header" InfoCube**

We will now eliminate the problems described above in a copy of the business content InfoCube. We will also make other corrections and extensions in the re-modeling process:

▶ Discard all the characteristics of dimension 1, as the status is not updated by the ETL process on the basis of the sales order header, and the **Date on which the record was added** InfoObject (0CREATEDON) is already located in the time dimension with full granularity (see the analysis above).

▶ Save the **Sold-To Party** InfoObject (0SOLD_TO) in the newly-emptied dimension 1.

▶ Re-transfer the **Version** InfoObject (ZFVERSION) to the InfoCube.

▶ Re-transfer the **Header Deleted** InfoObject (0HEADER_DEL) to the InfoCube.

► Because, in any case, the combination of **Calendar Day** (0CALDAY) and sold-to party (0SOLD_TO) often gives rise to a high level of granularity approaching document-level granularity—as our model company, CubeServ Engines, has only a medium-level quantity structure—the **Sales Document** InfoObject (0DOC_NUMBER) is also copied again to the InfoCube.

► The dimensions with individual characteristics are defined as line item dimensions.

**Figure 3.16** Data Model of the Business Content InfoCube 0SD_C13

### Activating the Business Content InfoCube

For your sample scenario, you will now create a clean InfoCube that is a copy of the business content InfoCube **Service Level Orders** (0SD_C13), based on the business content components for the sales order header data (see Figure 3.16).

[⬝⬝]
▸ Activate the business content InfoCube in the tab of the same name in the **Data Warehousing Workbench** (using Transaction RSA1). Open the **BI Content** tab and click on the **Object Types** selection type to select it (see Figure 3.17, Steps 1 and 2).

▸ Next, select the **Grouping** type **In Dataflow Before** from the dropdown menu (Steps 3 and 4).

▸ To select the business content objects you want to activate, select the InfoCube folder in the **All Objects According to Type** frame and double-click on the **Select Objects** entry to activate your selection (Step 5).

▸ In the **Input help for Metadata** popup, select the **Object Name** column and click on the **Set Filter** button (Steps 6 and 7).

▸ Next, the **Determine values for filter criteria** popup is displayed. In the **Object Name** selection field, enter the required business content object (in this case, **0SD_C13**) and click on the **Execute** button (Steps 8 and 9).

▸ The selected object is then displayed in the **Input help for Metadata** popup. Select the object you want by clicking on the row containing it, and then click on the **Transfer Selections** button (Steps 10 and 11).

▸ This transfers the object into the list of collected objects (see Figure 3.18, Step 1).

▸ To activate the collected business content objects, click on the **Install** button and select the **Install** entry from the dropdown list (Steps 2 and 3).

▸ If the business content objects that you want to activate have been changed, the differences are displayed for comparison purposes in the **Merge** dialog. In this case, you want to use all the business content settings, so you click on the **Transfer all without dialog** button (Step 4).

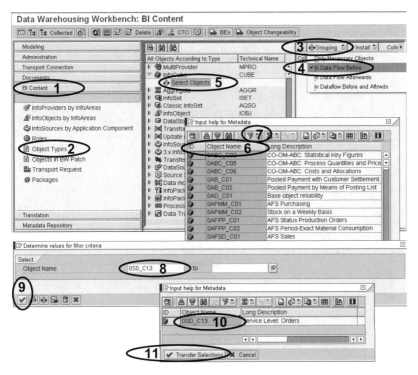

**Figure 3.17** Business Content: Selecting InfoCube for Activation

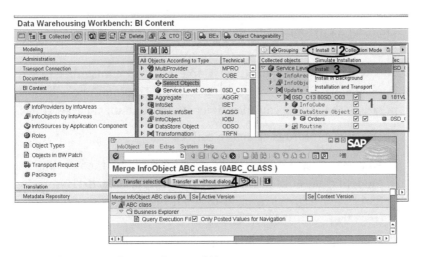

**Figure 3.18** Activating Business Content Objects

▶ After you successfully activate them, the business content objects are displayed in the **InfoProvider** view of the **Modeling** tab in the **Data Warehousing Workbench**.

**After activation**

▶ Select an activated InfoCube (in this case, **0SD_C13**) by clicking on it, and then click on the **Expand Subtree** button (see Figure 3.19, Steps 1 and 2) to display the whole activated data flow for the selected object as a subtree (see Step 3).

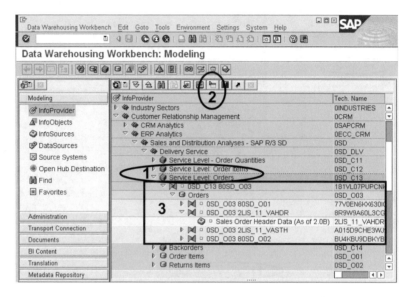

**Figure 3.19** Business Content InfoCube In Dataflow Before

### Creating a Customer-Specific InfoCube as a Copy of Business Content

You will now create for your sample scenario a customer-specific InfoCube that is a copy of business content. This InfoCube will incorporate the modeling considerations discussed in the analysis above.

Prerequisite    The required InfoArea structure exists.

[▪]  ▶ To create a separate InfoCube, select the required InfoArea in the **Modeling** view of the **Administrator Workbench** (Transaction RSA1), and right-click on it to open the context-sensitive menu (see Figure 3.20, Steps 1 and 2).

▶ Select the **Create InfoCube** function (Step 3).

▶ The **Edit InfoCube** popup opens. Here, you must enter the technical name (in this case, **ZFSDC13**), the description (in this case, **"Sales Order Header"**), and the name of the object that you want to use as a template (in this case, **0SD_C13**) (see Figure 3.21, Steps 1 to 3).

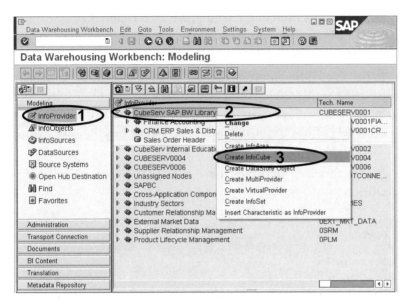

**Figure 3.20** Creating an InfoCube, Part 1

▶ Confirm your entries by clicking on the **Create** button (Step 4).

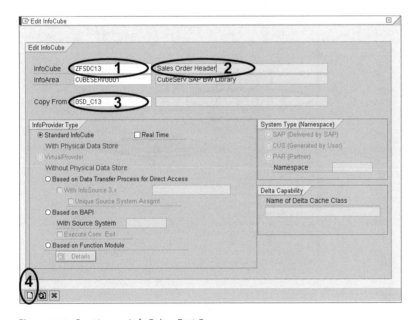

**Figure 3.21** Creating an InfoCube, Part 2

New user interface   ▶ Next, the **Edit InfoCube** screen opens (see Figure 3.22). SAP has completely re-designed the dialog for editing InfoCubes in the new version of SAP BW.

Deleting Info-
Objects from the
InfoCube   ▶ In the post-editing process, the first thing that needs to be done is to remove superfluous characteristics. To do this, select the InfoObject that you want to delete, right-click on it to open the context-sensitive menu, and select the **Delete** function (see Figure 3.22, Steps 1 and 2).

  ▶ Repeat this step until you have removed all superfluous Info-Objects.

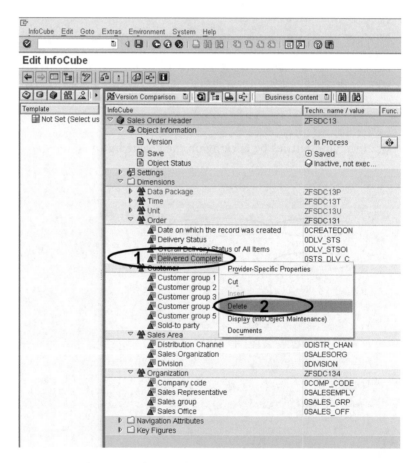

**Figure 3.22** Deleting Superfluous InfoObjects from the InfoCube

### Adding Dimensions

According to your design considerations, you now have to add new dimensions in order to use the maximum number of 16 dimensions.

▸ To do this, select the **Dimensions** folder, activate its context-sensitive menu by right-clicking on it, and select the **Create New Dimensions** function (see Figure 3.23, Steps 1 and 2). **[▪]**

▸ In the **Create Dimensions** popup, keep clicking on the **Create Additional Dimensions** button until you reach the maximum of 16 (Step 3).

▸ Then confirm your entry (Step 4).

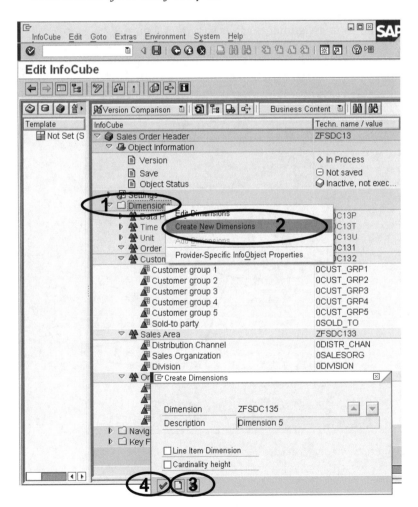

**Figure 3.23** Creating New Dimensions

### Moving Characteristics to Other Dimensions

To minimize the size of the dimensions tables, in accordance with your design considerations, you now need to move the characteristics to the new dimensions.

**[»]**
- ▶ To do this, select a characteristic (in your example, the InfoObject **Distribution Channel**) and drag-and-drop it to one of the (empty) dimensions (in your example, **Dimension 5**) (see Figure 3.24, Steps 1 to 3).

- ▶ The characteristic has now been removed from the original dimension and re-assigned to the new one.

- ▶ Once you have moved all the characteristics, the characteristic-to-dimension assignments are as shown in Figure 3.25, Step 1.

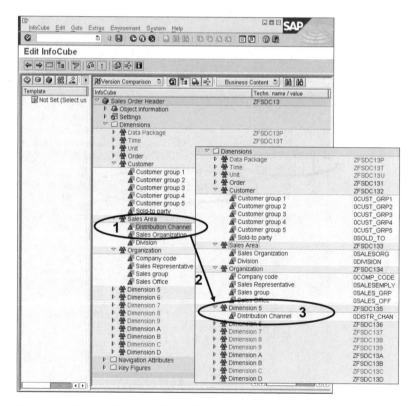

**Figure 3.24** Moving Characteristics to Other Dimensions

**DataStore Object Template**

In the next step, you must complete the InfoCube by adding the remaining characteristics.

▶ To do this, click on the **DataStore Object** button, and select the DataStore object **ZFSDO03** that you created earlier in the **Select DataStore Object** popup (see Figure 3.25, Steps 2 and 3).

**[▪]**

▶ Then click on **Continue** (Step 4).

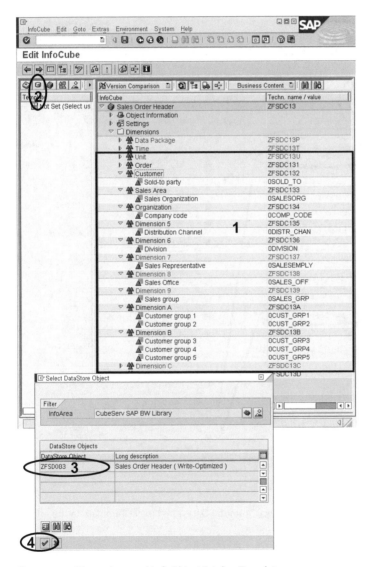

**Figure 3.25** Dimensions and InfoObjectCatalog Template

▶ Once the DataStore object has been transferred as a template, open the folder of the object so that the InfoObjects in the **Semantic Key** and **Data Fields** folders are displayed (see Figure 3.26).

▶ Finally, transfer the InfoObjects **Sales document** (0DOC_ NUMBER), **harmonized version** (ZFVERSION), and **Header Deleted** (0HEADER_DEL) to dimensions 1, C, and D (see Figure 3.26, Steps 1 to 3). To do this, mark each of them and drag-and-drop them to the relevant dimension.

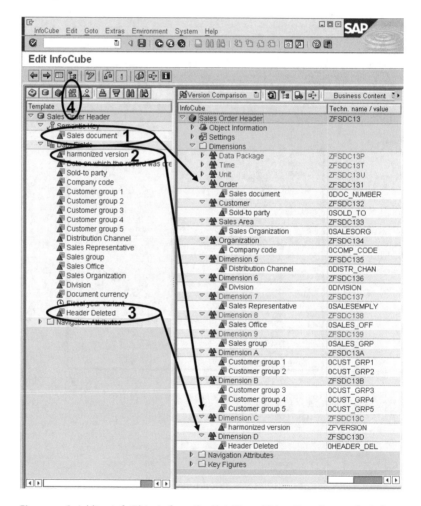

**Figure 3.26** Adding InfoObjects from the DataStore Object Template to the Info-Cube

### Adding Time Characteristics

In the next step, you will add the missing time characteristics to reflect your design considerations.

► To do this, click on the **InfoObjectCatalog** button (see Figure 3.26, Step 4).

[▪]

► In the **Select InfoObject Catalog** popup, click on the **All InfoObject Catalogs** button (see Figure 3.27, Step 1).

► Then click on **Search**. In the **Determine Search Criterion** popup, select the **Object Name** search option and enter the generic search term *TIM* (Steps 2 and 3).

► Click on **Continue** to start the search (Step 4).

► The entry **0TIMNOTASSIGNED** ("**Not assigned time characteristics**") is then highlighted in the list. Select this entry and transfer it as a template by clicking on **Continue** (Steps 5 and 6).

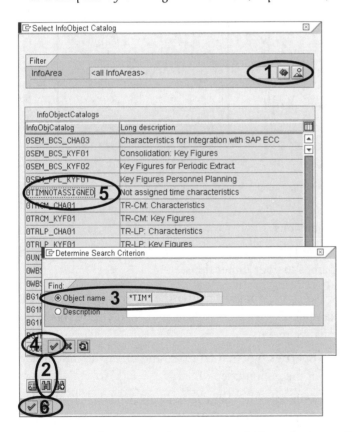

**Figure 3.27** Transferring "Time Characteristics" InfoObjectsCatalog as a Template

▶ To transfer all the time characteristics when the template is open, select the first time characteristic, then keep the **Shift** key pressed and select the last characteristic in the list. This selects all the entries in the list (see Figure 3.28, Step 1).

▶ Next, drag-and-drop the objects to the **Time** dimension. The missing time characteristics have now been added to the InfoCube (Steps 2 and 3).

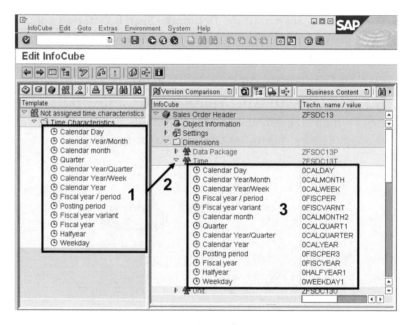

**Figure 3.28** Transferring Multiple Time Characteristics

**Renaming Dimensions**

As a last measure in your dimension modeling, you need to assign meaningful names to your dimensions.

**[▪]**

▶ To do this, select one dimension after the other (see **Dimension D** in your example, Figure 3.29, Step 1), and right-click to open the context-sensitive menu.

▶ Select the **Properties** function (Step 2), and enter the description you require in the popup (Step 3).

▶ Dimensions with only one characteristic are also assigned the **Line Item Dimension** property (Step 4).

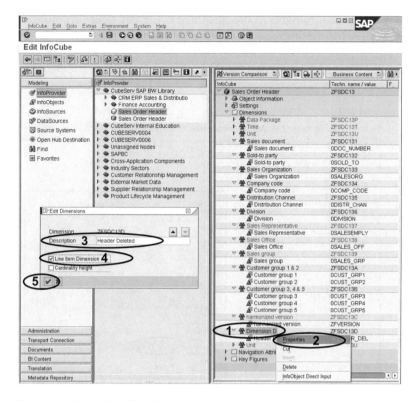

**Figure 3.29** Properties of the Dimension

### Deleting Key Figures

You must delete any key figures that are not relevant to the InfoCube to reflect your design considerations.

▶ To do this, open the **Key Figures** folder in the **Edit InfoCube** screen. **[»]**

▶ Select the first non-relevant key figure (in our example, InfoObject **Returns**; see Figure 3.30, Step 1), keep the **Shift** key pressed, and select the last key figure you want to delete from the list (in our example, InfoObject **Value with Delivery from Warehouse**).

▶ Right-click on the selected range to open the context-sensitive menu, and select the **Delete** function (Step 2).

▶ Repeat this step for the key figures from Net value of the order in document currency (0NET_VAL_HD) to **Perfect Order Fulfillment (Value)** (0DLVVPOF).

▶ Now all that remains in the InfoCube is the key figure **Number of Orders** (0ORDERS) (see Figure 3.31, Step 1).

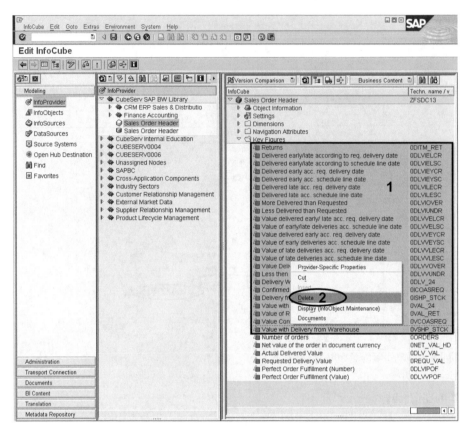

**Figure 3.30** Deleting Key Figures

### Activating Navigation Attributes

You will now release the navigation attributes required for the Info-Cube, in accordance with the considerations of your data model.

[■] ▶ To do this, open the **Navigation Attributes** folder (see Figure 3.31, Step 2).

▶ In this folder, activate the required navigation attributes (in your example, **Country of Sold-to Party (0SOLD_TO__0COUNTRY)** and **Region (state, county) (0SOLD_TO__0REGION)**) by clicking on the checkbox for the InfoCube in question (Steps 3 and 4).

▶ Finally, activate the InfoCube (Step 5).

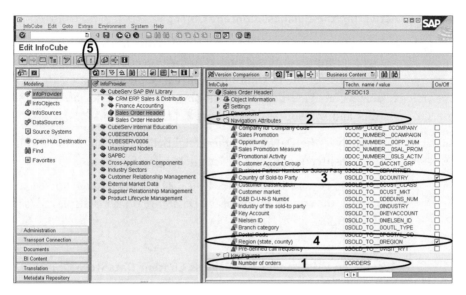

**Figure 3.31** Releasing Navigation Attributes and Activating the InfoCube

## 3.5 "Sales Order Items" Data Model

### 3.5.1 "Sales Order Items" DataStore Object

SAP business content provides DataStore object **0SD_O01** for sales order item data. It is on the basis of this object that you will now create a clean DataStore object that is a copy of the business content object **Order Items** for your sample scenario.

Using a business content DataStore object as a starting point

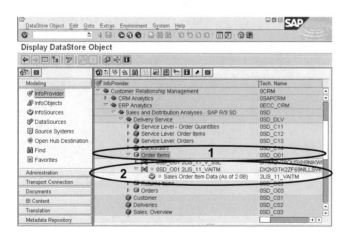

**Figure 3.32** Activated DataStore Object "Order Items" (0SD_O01) with Update Rules and InfoSources

**Activating the Business Content Object**

[▪] ▶ First, we need to activate the business content DataStore objects. The procedure for this is similar to the procedure described in Section 3.4.1 for the **In Dataflow Before** grouping method. After you do this, activate the DataStore object with its associated update rules and InfoSources (see Figure 3.32, Steps 1 and 2).

Activated Data-Store object

▶ To analyze the DataStore object, right-click on it to open its context-sensitive menu, and select the **Display** function.

▶ After the various folders for settings, key fields, and data fields are opened, the configuration of the DataStore object is displayed (see Figure 3.33).

**Recommended Changes to Business Content DataStore Object 0SD_C01**

Non-updated fields

As with all business content objects, you need to critically analyze the activated DataStore object. If you compare the DataStore object fields with the update rules of the InfoSource **Order Item Data** (from 2.0B) (**2LIS_11_VAHDR**), you'll see that most of the DataStore object fields are not updated (see Figure 3.34).

[+] Because the DataStore object in this scenario will serve as the **data propagation layer** in the data warehouse integration layer, we recommend that you use only those fields that were updated by the associated Data-Source. Therefore, the non-updated fields of the business content DataStore object are superfluous for our purposes.

[+] To update the DataStore object in the next-highest data warehouse layer, we recommend (unlike with SAP Business Content) that you create a version InfoObject in the DataStore object.

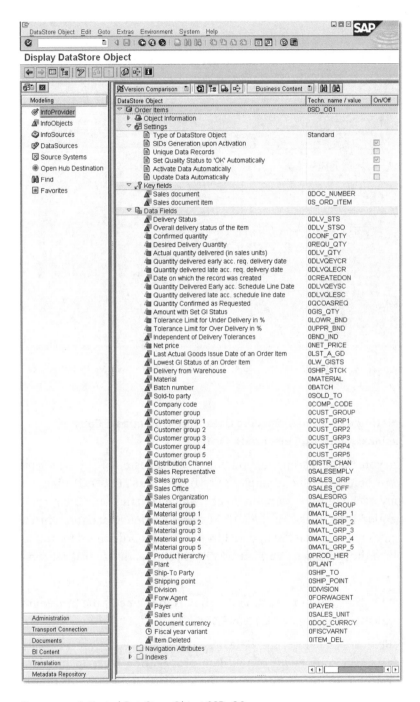

**Figure 3.33** Activated DataStore Object 0SD_O0

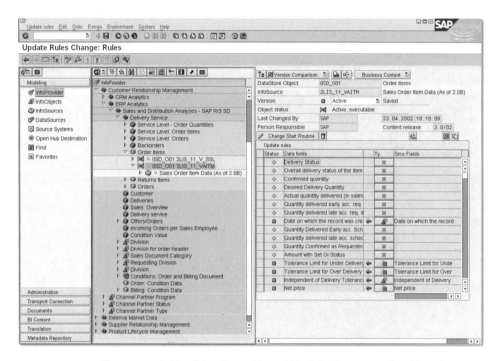

**Figure 3.34** Fields of DataStore Object 0SD_O01 That Are Updated by InfoSource 2LIS_11_VAITM

### Creating a Customer-Specific DataStore Object as a Copy of Business Content Object 0SD_O01

For your sample scenario, you will create a customer-specific Data-Store object (in this example, sales order item **ZFSDO01**) that is a copy of the business content object, which contains only the recommended InfoObjects of the SAP Business Content DataStore object, i. e., only those that are updated from the sales order headers and to which the InfoObject **Version** (ZFVERSION) is added to make it complete.

[•] ▸ The procedure for creating the copy is the same as the procedure illustrated in Figures 3.11 to 3.15.

▸ Because, as before, the DataStore object that you want to create acts as a component of the **data propagation layer** in the **data warehouse integration layer**, the standard reporting function is not available here. Therefore, you will use the new **write-optimized DataStore object** for DataStore object **ZFSDO01** as you did before.

▶ As described in relation to Figure 3.34 above, you must remove any fields in the DataStore object that were not updated by the InfoSource. Delete the following InfoObjects in accordance with the procedure described for DataStore object **ZFSDO03**:

Deleting non-relevant InfoObjects

- ▶ Delivery Status (0DLV_STS)
- ▶ Overall delivery status of the item (0DLV_STSO)
- ▶ Confirmed quantity (0CONF_QTY)
- ▶ Desired Delivery Quantity (0REQU_QTY)
- ▶ Actual quantity delivered (in sales units) (0DLV_QTY)
- ▶ Quantity delivered early acc. req. delivery date (0DLVQEYCR)
- ▶ Quantity delivered late acc. req. delivery date (0DLVQLECR)
- ▶ Quantity Delivered Early acc. Schedule Line Date (0DLVQEYSC)
- ▶ Quantity delivered late acc. schedule line date (0DLVQLESC)
- ▶ Quantity Confirmed as Requested (0QCOASREQ)
- ▶ Amount with Set GI Status (0GIS_QTY)
- ▶ Last Actual Goods Issue Date of an Order Item (0LST_A_GD)
- ▶ Lowest GI Status of an Order Item (0LW_GISTS)

▶ Unlike with business content, in the DataStore object, key figures that are provided by the business content InfoSource **2LIS_11_VAITM** should be updated. This applies to the following InfoObjects:

Key figures to add

- ▶ Subtotal 1 (0SUBTOTAL_1)
- ▶ Subtotal 2 (0SUBTOTAL_2)
- ▶ Subtotal 3 (0SUBTOTAL_3)
- ▶ Subtotal 4 (0SUBTOTAL_4)
- ▶ Subtotal 5 (0SUBTOTAL_5)
- ▶ Subtotal 6 (0SUBTOTAL_6)
- ▶ Target quantity in sales units (0TARGET_QTY)
- ▶ Target value with outline agreement in document currency (0TARG_VALUE)
- ▶ Tax Amount in SD Document Currency (0TAX_VALUE)
- ▶ Tolerance Limit for Over Delivery in % (0UPPR_BND)
- ▶ Volume of Order Item (0VOLUME_AP)
- ▶ Cumulative confirmed quantity in base units (0CML_CD_QTY)
- ▶ Cumulative confirmed quantity in sales units (0CML_CF_QTY)

- ▸ Cumulative order quantity in sales units (0CML_OR_QTY)
- ▸ Cost in document currency (0COST)
- ▸ Denominator (divisor) for conversion of sales qty into SKU (0DENOMINTR)
- ▸ Factor for converting sales units to base units (target qty) (0DENOMINTRZ)
- ▸ Credit data exchange rate for requested delivery date (0EXCHG_CRD)
- ▸ Exchange rate for pricing and statistics (0EXCHG_RATE)
- ▸ Exchange rate for statistics (0EXCHG_STAT)
- ▸ Gross Weight of Sales Item (0GROSS_WGT)
- ▸ Tolerance Limit for Under Delivery in % (0LOWR_BND)
- ▸ Cumulative required delivery qty (all dlv-relev.sched.lines) (0REQDEL_QTY)
- ▸ Sales Order Item (0ORD_ITEMS)
- ▸ Numerator for Converting Sales from Target Qty to Qty Stored (0NUMERATORZ)
- ▸ Numerator (Factor) for Conversion of Sales Quantity into SKU (0NUMERATOR)
- ▸ Net weight of item (0NET_WT_AP)
- ▸ Net value of the order item in document currency (0NET_VALUE)

**Direct Entry of InfoObjects**

One option for entering the additional key figures into DataStore object **ZFSDO01** is to input them directly.

[▪] ▸ To do this, right-click on the **Data Fields** folder to open its context-sensitive menu, and select the **InfoObject Direct Input** function (see Figure 3.35, Steps 1 and 2).

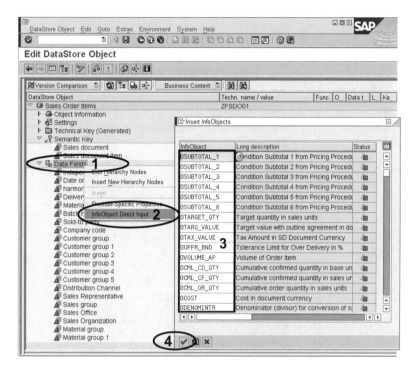

**Figure 3.35** Directly Entering InfoObjects into DataStore Object ZFSDO01

▶ Enter the key figures in the input fields of the **Insert InfoObjects** popup (Step 3), and click on the **Continue** button to transfer them (Step 4).

▶ Finally, activate the DataStore object. The object you have just edited is now available for use (see Figure 3.36).

Activating the DataStore object

▶ In the **Edit InfoCube** popup, enter the technical name you want to assign to the InfoCube and a description (in this case, **ZFSDC12, Sales Order Items**) and click on the **Create** button (Steps 4 to 6).

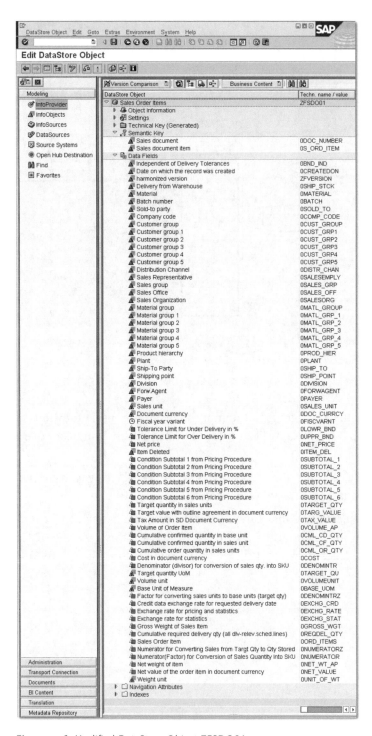

**Figure 3.36** Modified DataStore Object ZFSDO01

## 3.5.2 "Sales Order Items" InfoCube

You will now update our DataStore object in the **Service Level Order Items** (0SD_C12) InfoCube in SAP Business Content.

### Analyzing Business Content InfoCube 0SD_C12

An analysis of the business content InfoCube and the updated Data-Source **2LIS_11_VAITM** illustrates the necessity of changing the business content InfoCube or creating a new InfoCube, because this is the only way of making the information in the DataSource available for reporting purposes via the InfoCube.

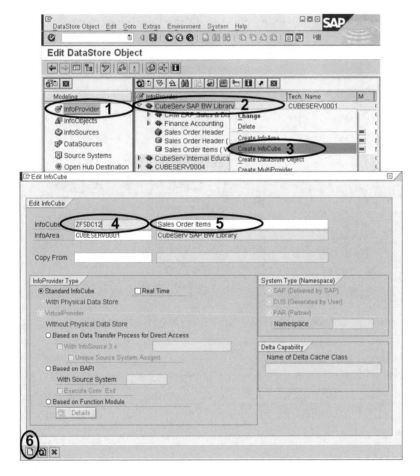

**Figure 3.37** Creating InfoCube ZFSDC12

[▪] ► To do this, open the **InfoProvider** view in the **Modeling** function of the **Administrator Workbench**. Then, right-click on the relevant InfoArea to open the context-sensitive menu (see Figure 3.37, Steps 1 and 2).

► Next, select the **Create InfoCube** function (Step 3).

Creating the maximum number of dimensions

► In the **Edit InfoCube** dialog, right-click on the **Dimensions** folder to open the context-sensitive menu, and select the **Create New Dimensions** function (see Figure 3.38, Steps 1 and 2).

► In the **Create Dimensions** popup, keep clicking on the **Create Additional Dimensions** button until you reach the maximum number (Step 3).

► Confirm your entries by clicking on the **Continue** button (Step 4).

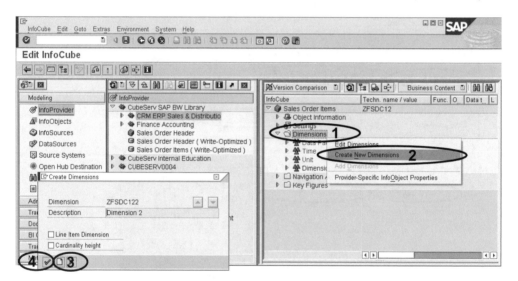

**Figure 3.38** Creating the Maximum Number of Dimensions in InfoCube ZFSDC12

### Assigning InfoObjects

We will use the InfoObjects of our previously created DataStore object for the InfoCube. Because our example has only a moderate quantity structure, the DataStore is copied to the InfoCube with its full granularity.

[▪] ► Therefore, select the DataStore object you previously created as a template for the InfoCube. To do this, click on the **DataStore Object** button, select the template object you require (in this case, **ZFSDO01**), and click on **Continue** (see Figure 3.39, Steps 1 to 3).

▶ Now, the InfoObjects of the DataStore object are available in the template frame (Step 4).

▶ You can now drag-and-drop the InfoObjects to the InfoCube (Step 5), similarly to the procedure described above (see the information on Figure 3.26).

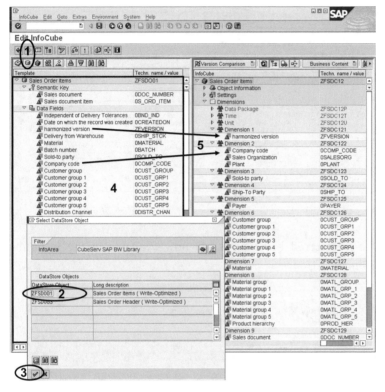

**Figure 3.39** Selecting Template Object ZFSDO01 and Transferring Characteristics to InfoCube ZFSDC12

▶ To transfer key figures, select all the key figures you require in the template object (either by selecting the first and last object that you want to transfer, or by selecting them individually while keeping the **Ctrl** key pressed), and drag-and-drop them to the **Key Figures** folder (see Figure 3.41, Steps 1 and 2).

Transferring key figures

▶ You can now define the properties of the dimensions, similarly to the procedure described above (see the text relating to Figure 3.29). The automatically generated dimension names are replaced by meaningful ones, and dimensions with only one characteristic are declared as line item dimensions (e. g., see Figure 3.40, Steps 1 to 5).

Defining the dimensions

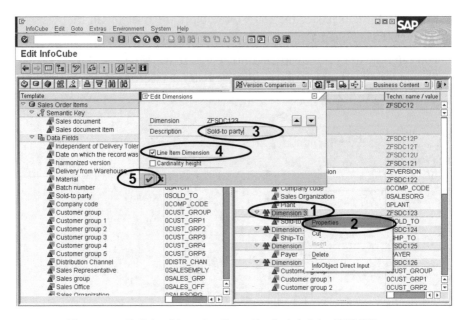

**Figure 3.40** Defining Dimension Properties for InfoCube ZFSDC12

▸ The transferred key figures are now available in the InfoCube (Step 3).

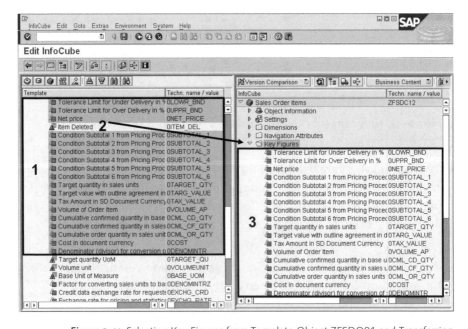

**Figure 3.41** Selecting Key Figures from Template Object ZFSDO01 and Transferring InfoObjects to InfoCube ZFSDC12

## Using Key Figure "Number of Document Items"

In addition to the key figures for the template object, the key figure **Number of Document Items** (0DOC_ITEMS) should also be used (similarly to the business content InfoCube **Service Level Order Items** (0SD_C12)). This is done in the same way as the transfer of InfoObjects from the template DataStore object.

▸ Select InfoCube **0SD_C12** as a template object (see Figure 3.42, Step 1). [✦]

▸ Then select the key figure to be transferred and transfer it via drag-and-drop to a key figure that you want to edit in the Info-Cube (Steps 2 to 4).

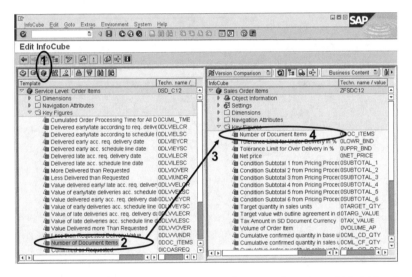

**Figure 3.42** Selecting Key Figure 0DOC_ITEMS from Template Object 0SD_C12 and Transferring InfoObjects to InfoCube ZFSDC12

▸ Likewise, similar to the procedure described above (see Figures 3.27 and 3.28), transfer all time characteristics to the InfoCube (see Figure 3.43, Steps 1 to 3). **Transferring all time characteristics**

▸ Now, to map the aggregation requirements using the basic characteristics, activate the required navigation attributes by clicking on the **On/Off** flag (see Figure 3.44, Step 1). **Activating navigation attributes**

▸ Finally, activate the InfoCube by clicking on the button of the same name (Step 2). **Activating the InfoCube**

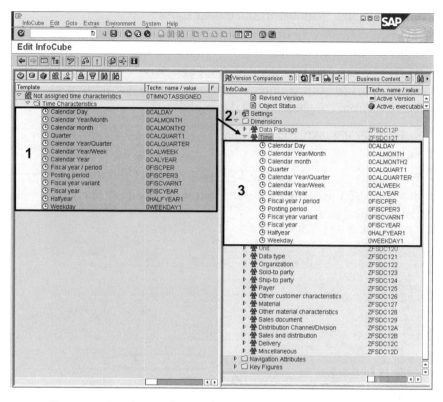

**Figure 3.43** Transferring All Time Characteristics to InfoCube ZFSDC12

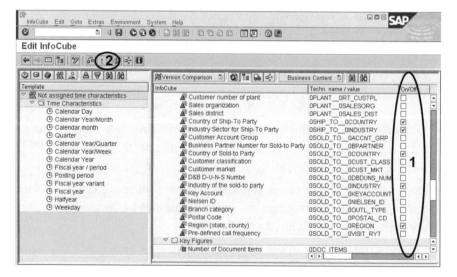

**Figure 3.44** Activating Navigation Attributes for InfoCube ZFSDO01 and Activating the InfoCube

## 3.6 "Sales Order Header and Item" MultiProvider

As a general rule, analyses of the sample scenario should use Multi-Providers to access data in InfoCubes. To enable this, you will now create a MultiProvider called **Sales Order Header and Item** (ZFSDM10) that contains InfoCube **Sales Order Header** (ZFSDC13) and InfoCube **Sales Order Items** (ZFSDC12). This "linking" MultiProvider will contain all the characteristics and key figures of the basic underlying InfoCube.

MultiProviders for sales order reporting

### Creating the "Sales Order Header and Item" MultiProvider

▶ To create a MultiProvider, open the **InfoProvider** tab in the **Modeling** view of the **Data Warehousing Workbench** in SAP BW (Transaction RSA1) (see Figure 3.45, Step 1).

[▪]

▶ Place your cursor on the InfoArea under which you want to create your MultiProvider (Step 2) (in our case, InfoArea **CubeServ SAP BW Library** (CUBESERV0001)), and right-click on it to open its context-sensitive menu.

▶ Then select the **Create MultiProvider** function (Step 3).

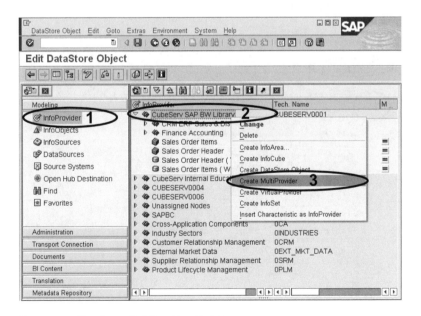

**Figure 3.45** Creating a MultiProvider, Part 1

Specifying the name and description of the Multi-Provider

▶ Next, the **Edit MultiProvider** popup opens. Enter the technical name (in this case, **ZFSDM10**) and description of the MultiProvider (in this case, **Sales Order Header & Items**) and click on **Create** (see Figure 3.46, Steps 1 and 2).

MultiProvider: selecting relevant InfoProviders

▶ Then the **MultiProvider: Relevant InfoProviders** popup opens. In the **InfoCubes** tab page (Step 3) of this popup, click on the relevant checkboxes to select the two InfoCubes **ZFSDC12** and **ZFSDC13** (Step 4).

▶ Lastly, click on **Continue** (Step 5).

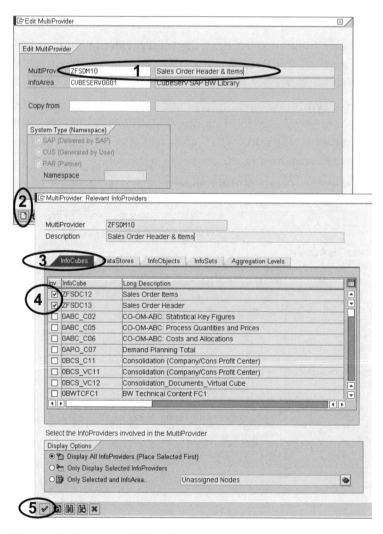

**Figure 3.46** Creating a MultiProvider, Part 2

▶ Similar to the procedure described above (see Figures 3.27 and 3.28), in the **Edit MultiProvider** dialog, transfer all time characteristics of InfoCube **ZFSDC12** to the MultiProvider (see Figure 3.47, Steps 1 to 3).

Transferring time characteristics of InfoCube ZFSDC12

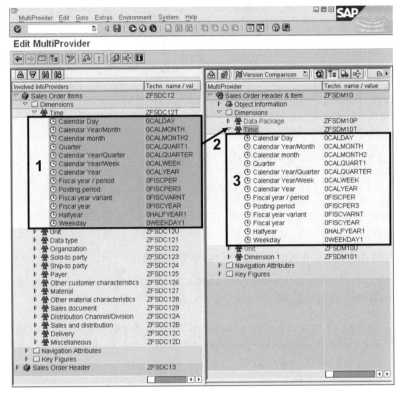

**Figure 3.47** Transferring All Time Characteristics of InfoCube ZFSDC12 to the MultiProvider

▶ Now, delete the empty template **Dimension 1** in the MultiProvider. To do this, right-click on it to open the context-sensitive menu (see Figure 3.48, Step 1) and select **Delete** (Step 2).

Deleting empty dimension 1

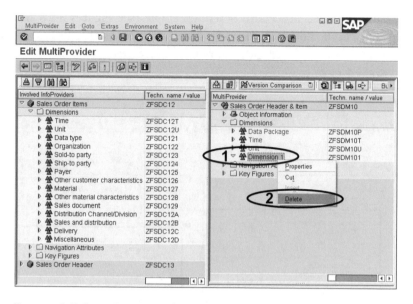

**Figure 3.48** Deleting Empty Template Dimension 1

### Transferring Dimensions and Characteristics

Next, you need to transfer the dimension and characteristics of the InfoCube **ZFSDC12** to the MultiProvider.

[■]
- ▶ To do this, select a dimension of the InfoCube **ZFSDC12**, and drag-and-drop it to the **Dimensions** folder in the MultiProvider (see Figure 3.49, Steps 1 to 3).
- ▶ This automatically adds the dimension transferred in each case (if possible, as is the case here) to the MultiProvider as the next dimension in that MultiProvider. Likewise, all characteristics of the transferred dimension are automatically added to the new dimension of the MultiProvider (if possible, and again, this is the case here).
- ▶ Proceed in the same way for all dimensions of the **Sales Order Item** InfoCube.
- ▶ Thus, with the exception of the **Header Deleted** characteristic (0HEADER_DEL), all characteristics of the **Sales Order Header** InfoCube are now contained in the MultiProvider. Using the same procedure, also transfer the 0HEADER_DEL characteristic of the **ZFSDC13** InfoCube to the **Miscellaneous** dimension of the Multi-Provider.

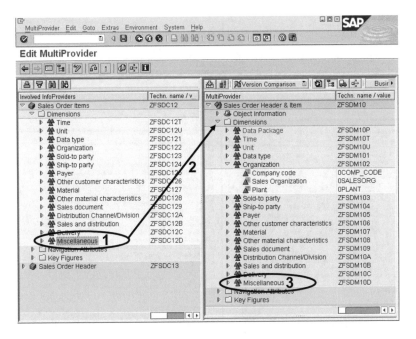

**Figure 3.49** Transferring Dimensions and Characteristics

### Transferring Key Figures

▶ In the **Edit MultiProvider** dialog, transfer the key figures of the **[»]**
ZFSDC12 InfoCube to the MultiProvider, similar to the procedure
described above (see Figures 3.27 and 3.28); in other words, drag-
and-drop the block of selected key figures in the InfoCube to the
folder of the same name in the MultiProvider (see Figure 3.50,
Steps 1 to 3).

▶ Then, following the same procedure, transfer the **0ORDERS** key
figure to the **ZFSDC13** InfoCube in the MultiProvider.

▶ To select the InfoCube(s) to which a key figure belongs, right-click    Selecting key
on the key figure in question to open the context-sensitive menu    figures
(see Figure 3.51, Step 1), and select the **Select (Assign)** function
(Step 2).

▶ You can now select the origin of the key figures. You do this in the    Creating a pro-
**Selection of Key Figures Involved** popup. Because all the key fig-    posal for all key
ures in our example originate from the same source InfoCube, you    figure assignments
can simply click on the **All** button (Step 3).

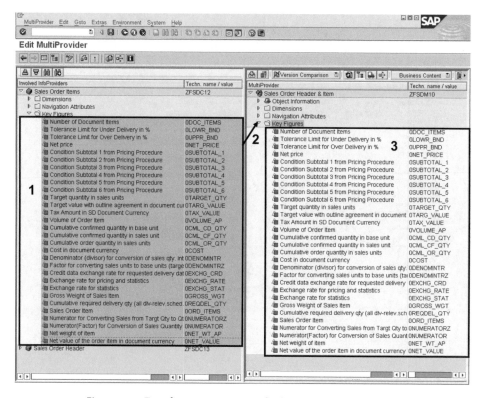

**Figure 3.50** Transferring Key Figures of InfoCube ZFSDC12 to the MultiProvider

▶ Next, the assignment proposal is generated, and an **Information** popup opens containing the message "**A proposal for ALL InfoObjects has been created.**"

▶ Confirm this popup by clicking on the **Continue** button (Step 4). This unique selection has now been created for every key figure in the MultiProvider.

▶ Close the **Selection of Key Figures Involved** popup by clicking on **Continue** again (Step 5).

Defining navigation attributes of the MultiProvider

▶ To define the navigation attributes you require, open the **Edit MultiProvider** dialog, then open the **Navigation Attributes** folder (see Figure 3.52, Step 1).

▶ Select the navigation attributes you want (Step 2).

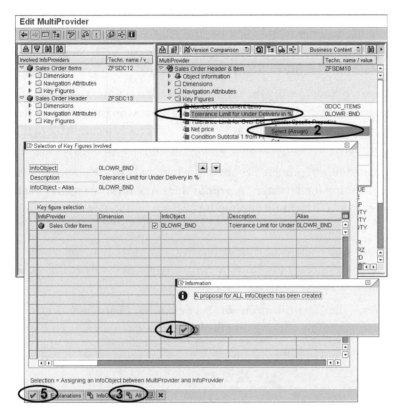

**Figure 3.51** Assigning Key Figures

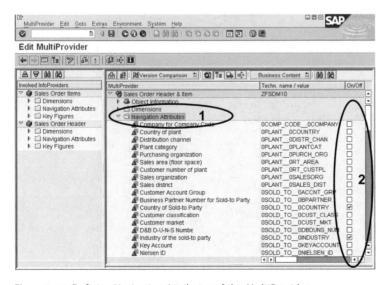

**Figure 3.52** Defining Navigation Attributes of the MultiProvider

Identifying
characteristics

▶ To identify a characteristic, or the InfoCube(s) to which a characteristic belongs, right-click on the characteristic in question to
open the context-sensitive menu (see Figure 3.53, Step 1), and
select the **Identify (Assign)** function (Step 2).

Creating a
proposal for all
characteristic
assignments

▶ You can now identify the origin of the characteristic. You do this in
the **Identification of Participating Characteristics/Nav. Attr.**
popup. Because you want to use all the characteristics available in the
InfoCubes in your example, simply click on the **All** button (Step 3).

▶ Next, the assignment proposal is generated, and a popup opens
containing the message "**A proposal for ALL InfoObjects has been
created.**" Confirm this popup by clicking on the **Continue** button
(Step 4).

▶ Now, every characteristic in the MultiProvider that you want to
assign to one or both InfoCubes is assigned to the basic InfoCube
that contains the characteristic in question.

▶ Close the **Identification of Participating Characteristics/Nav.
Attr.** popup by clicking on **Continue** again (Step 5).

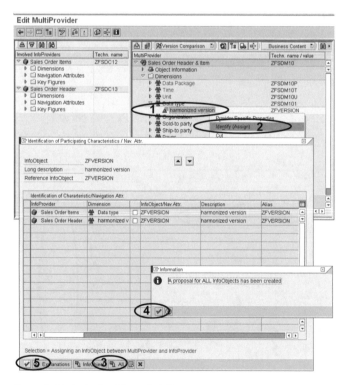

**Figure 3.53** Assigning Characteristics

### Assigning Characteristics Manually

You must now check the assignments. Any characteristics and navigation attributes for which a unique proposal cannot be created and/or for which the proposed assignment is not ideal must be manually assigned.

▶ To do this, right-click on a characteristic or navigation attribute to open the context-sensitive menu and select the **Identify (Assign)** function (see Figure 3.54, Step 1).

[◢]

▶ Complete or correct the assignments in the **Identification of Participating Characteristics/Nav. Attr.** popup, and confirm your entries (Step 2). In this case, you assign all the existing characteristics and navigation attributes from both assigned InfoCubes to the InfoProvider on a 1–1 basis.

▶ Confirm your settings (Step 3).

▶ Finally, activate the MultiProvider **ZFSDM10** by clicking on the button of the same name (see Figure 3.54, Step 4).

Activating the MultiProvider

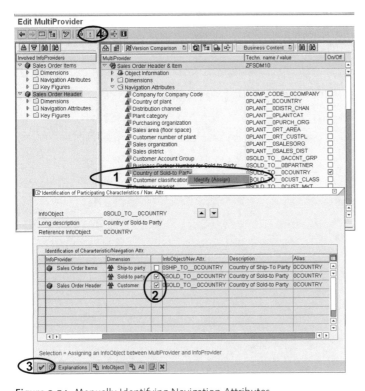

**Figure 3.54** Manually Identifying Navigation Attributes

Your newly created MultiProvider is now displayed hierarchically in the Data Warehousing Workbench with its assigned InfoCubes (see Figure 3.55, circled text).

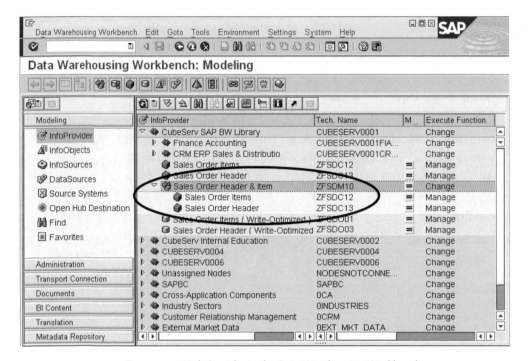

**Figure 3.55** MultiProvider in the Data Warehousing Workbench

*Data retrieval, which consists of data extraction, transformation, and loading (ETL), represents the first layer of the data warehouse architecture. With NetWeaver 2004s, SAP provides extended and revised data retrieval functions, and places particular emphasis on unifying the components. This chapter uses a sample scenario to illustrate how to use the 3.x ETL components of SAP NetWeaver 2004s, and to describe the fundamental functions of native NetWeaver 2004s ETL components.*

# 4    Data Retrieval

## 4.1    Sample Scenario

In this chapter, you will load master data and transaction data into SAP BW. This data will enable you to generate a profitability analysis for your model company, CubeServ Engines. The ETL processes in question are based partly on the 3.x data retrieval components and partly on the new NetWeaver 2004s components.

3.x data retrieval and NetWeaver 2004s components Master data

Using the InfoObject **Division** (0DIVISION) as an example, we will explain the configuration of ETL processes on the basis of 3.x data retrieval with NetWeaver 2004s components. During the course of the scenario, you will configure and execute the data retrieval process for the master data of this InfoObject.

Using a profitability analysis as an example, we will explain the configuration of flexible updates for transaction data on the basis of 3.x data retrieval with NetWeaver 2004s components.

Transaction data

## 4.2    DataSources

From SAP NetWeaver 2004s, SAP differentiates between the earlier 3.x DataSources and the new DataSources available from NetWeaver 2004s onwards. Therefore, DataSources are marked accordingly in the new version of SAP BW.

### Calling the DataSource Tree

There is a new way of calling the DataSource tree in SAP NetWeaver 2004s.

[▪] ▸ In the **Source Systems** view of the Data Warehousing Workbench (Transaction RSA1), click on the folder that contains the various system types and open it (see Figure 4.1, Steps 1 to 3).

▸ Right-click on the relevant source system to open its context-sensitive menu, and select the **Display DataSource Tree** function (Step 4).

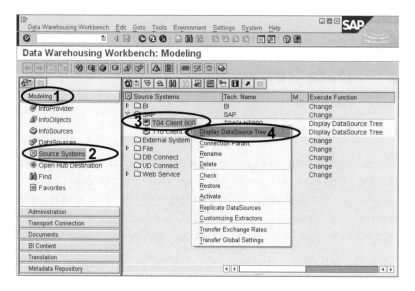

**Figure 4.1** Calling the DataSource Tree

▸ The active view now changes from **Source Systems** to **DataSources**, and the DataSources tree is displayed (see Figure 4.2, Steps 1 and 2).

3.x DataSources ▸ 3.x DataSources are now identified in SAP BW by a square-shaped icon in front of the DataSource description (Step 3).

NetWeaver 2004s—BI Data-Sources ▸ The new SAP NetWeaver 2004s DataSources are displayed in SAP BW as normal; that is, there is no icon in front of their descriptions (see Figure 4.3, Steps 1 to 3) (compare this with 3.x DataSources; see Figure 4.3, Step 4).

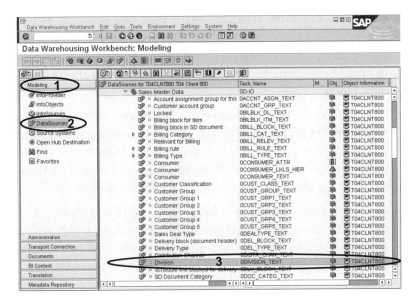

**Figure 4.2** Display of 3.x DataSources in SAP NetWeaver 2004s

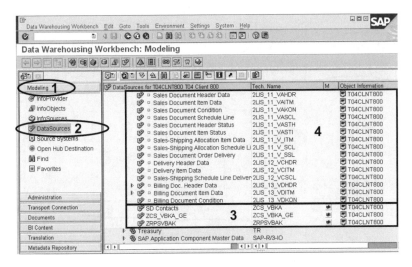

**Figure 4.3** SAP NetWeaver 2004s DataSources and 3.x DataSources

## Replicating DataSources and Selecting the DataSource Type

▶ If you want to transfer to SAP BW DataSources that do not yet **[»]**
exist, open the DataSource tree in the **DataSources** view of the
Data Warehousing Workbench (see Figure 4.4, Steps 1 and 2).

▶ Then, drill down the DataSource tree until you reach the source system application component for which you want to transfer the DataSources (in this example, it is **Sales Master Data**), right-click to open the context-sensitive menu, and select the **Replicate Metadata** function (Step 3).

▶ If the system finds a DataSource that has not yet been replicated, the **Unknown DataSource** popup opens. This popup asks you to decide whether you want to transfer this unknown DataSource to SAP BW as an SAP NetWeaver 2004s **DataSource** or as a **3.x DataSource** (Step 4). Make and confirm your selection (Step 5).

▶ Another popup then opens, asking you whether you want to activate the DataSource as a **Background** or as a **Dialog** (Step 6). In this example, after it is activated, the new DataSource will be available in a dialog as an SAP NetWeaver 2004s DataSource in SAP BW.

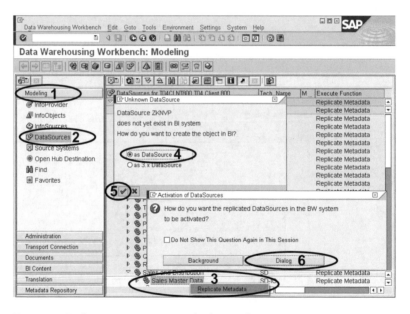

**Figure 4.4** Replicating DataSources and Selecting the DataSource Type

Migration  Section 4.4 explains how to migrate a DataSource from a 3.x DataSource to an SAP NetWeaver 2004s DataSource.

## 4.3 Emulating the 3.x Data Retrieval Process in SAP NetWeaver 2004s

### 4.3.1 Direct Update

If you want to keep using the data retrieval process from an earlier SAP BW version or to set up a new data retrieval process with 3.x emulation, the starting point has to be a 3.x DataSource (in this example, InfoObject **Division**, DataSource 0DIVISION_TEXT; see Figure 4.5, Steps 1 to 3).

**Starting point: 3.x DataSource**

▶ In the **InfoSource** view of the Data Warehousing Workbench, right-click on an InfoObject to open its context-sensitive menu and select the **Create Transfer Rules** function from the submenu (see Figure 4.5, Step 4 to 7).

**[»]**

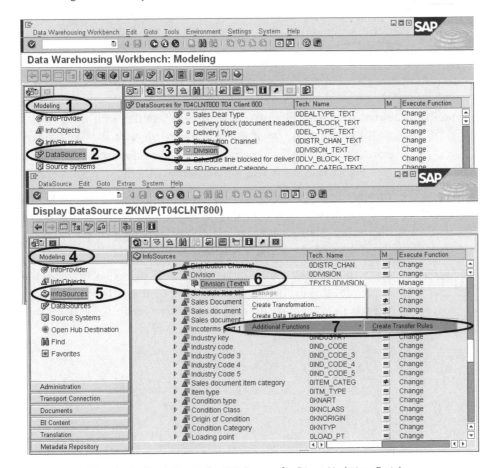

**Figure 4.5** Setting Up 3.x Emulation in the ETL Process for Direct Updating, Part 1

▶ As in earlier SAP BW versions, the **Master Data—InfoSource: Assign Source System** popup now opens. Select the source system and confirm your selection (see Figure 4.6, Steps 1 and 2).

▶ Then select the DataSource from the **Available DataSources** popup. Confirm this selection and click on **Yes** in the **Save Changes?** dialog (Steps 3 to 5).

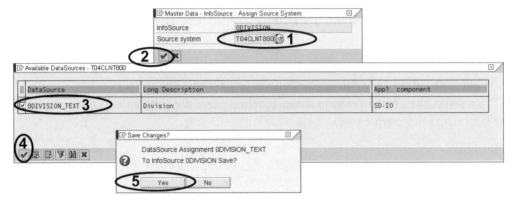

**Figure 4.6** Setting Up 3.x Emulation in the ETL Process for Direct Updating, Part 2

Transfer rules in 3.x emulation

▶ Next, similar to the procedure we are familiar with from earlier SAP BW versions, open the InfoSource view of the Data Warehousing Workbench, maintain the transfer rules for 3.x emulation (see Figure 4.7, Steps 1 to 4), and activate them (Step 5).

New hierarchy display

▶ Another new feature in the Data Warehousing Workbench is that ETL components are now displayed in a hierarchy structure (see Figure 4.7, Step 3). This example illustrates the process from the DataSource to the transfer rules to the InfoObject.

InfoPackage in 3.x emulation

▶ Once you have activated the transfer rules, right-click on the Data-Source (again, in the **InfoSource** view of the Data Warehousing Workbench) to open its context-sensitive menu (see Figure 4.8, Steps 1 to 3).

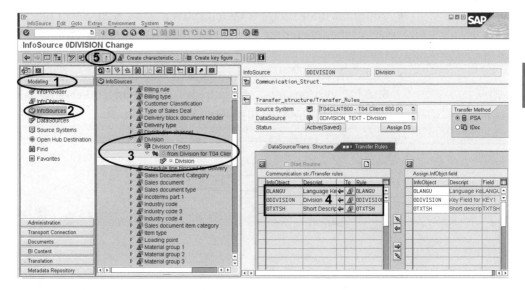

**Figure 4.7** Transfer Rules in 3.x Emulation

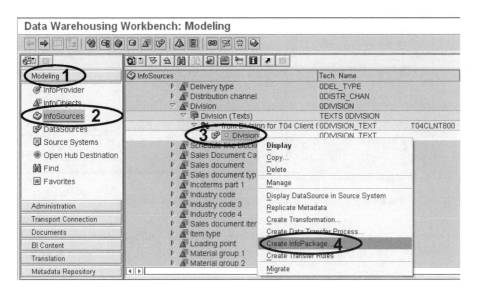

**Figure 4.8** Configuring the InfoPackage for 3.x Emulation, Part 1

▶ Select the **Create InfoPackage** function. In the **Create InfoPackage** popup that opens, enter a name for your new InfoPackage, click on the relevant row to select the DataSource, and then click on **Save** (see Figure 4.9, Steps 1 to 3).

▶ Your new InfoPackage is then displayed in the component hierarchy of the **InfoSource** view in the Data Warehousing Workbench (Step 4).

▶ Maintain the InfoPackage in the same way that you do in earlier SAP BW versions, and, if required, start it from the **Schedule** tab in the InfoPackage maintenance (Steps 5 to 7).

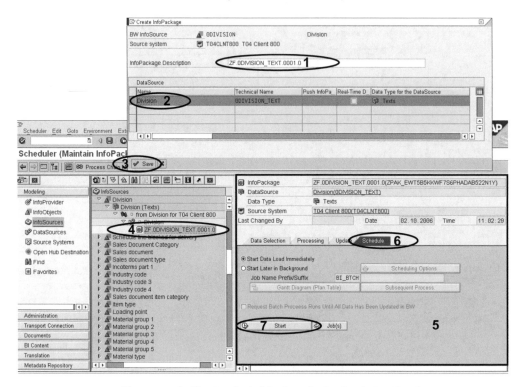

**Figure 4.9** Configuring the InfoPackage for 3.x Emulation, Part 2

Monitoring direct updating

▶ Click on the **Open BI Object Monitor** button (see Figure 4.10, Steps 1 to 4) to display the updated requests in the new **Monitor** frame.

▶ Click on an update request (Step 5) to display the details of the request in the frame on the right (Step 6).

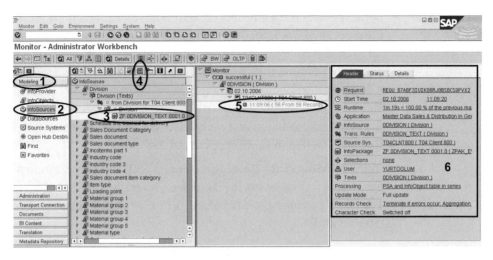

Figure 4.10 Monitoring Direct Updating

## 4.3.2 Flexible Updating

If you want to keep using the existing data retrieval process from an earlier SAP BW version or set up a new data retrieval process with 3.x emulation, the starting point must be a 3.x DataSource.

Starting point: 3.x DataSource

▶ In this example, you will use the transaction data DataSource **Profitability Analysis SAP BW-Library 1** (1_CO_PA800S_GO_ZE1) (see DataSource tree in the SAP BW Data Warehousing Workbench, Figure 4.11, Steps 1 to 3).

[•]

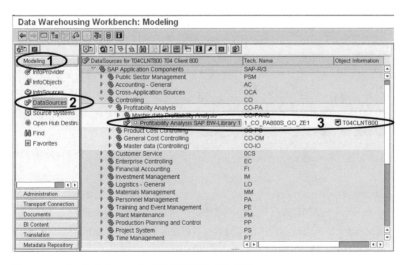

Figure 4.11 3.x DataSource 1_CO_PA800S_GO_ZE1

Creating the
InfoSource

▶ Because this is not a business content DataSource, you must create the associated 3.x InfoSource yourself. The easiest way to do this for 3.x DataSources is to use the DataSource as a template, employing almost the same procedure as was used for SAP BW 3.5. To do this, right-click on the required DataSource in the Data-Source tree of the SAP BW Data Warehousing Workbench to open the context-sensitive menu, and select the **Create Transfer Rules** function (see Figure 4.12, Steps 1 and 2).

▶ In the **InfoSource for DataSource** popup, confirm the assignment proposal by clicking on the **Transfer (Enter)** button and answer **Yes** when prompted to save changes in the **Save changes?** popup (Steps 3 and 4).

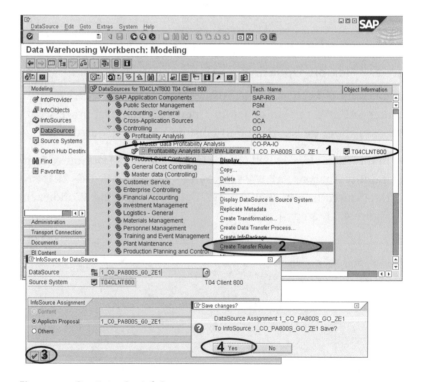

**Figure 4.12** Creating a 3.x InfoSource

Creating transfer
rules

▶ If InfoObjects were assigned to all fields of the DataSource, and if you want SAP BW to propose transfer rules, click on the button of the same name in the **Change InfoSource...** dialog (see Figure 4.13, Step 1).

▶ If an information popup with a warning message opens, simply confirm this by clicking on **OK** (Step 2).

▶ Lastly, activate the transfer rules by clicking on the button of the same name (Step 3).

Activating the 3.x InfoSource

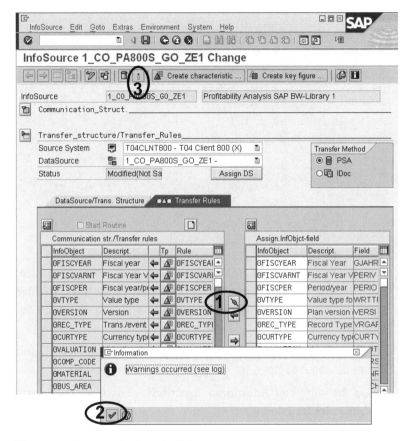

**Figure 4.13** Proposing 3.x Transfer Rules

▶ Once the InfoSource has been activated, the data flow components are displayed hierarchically in the InfoSource view of the Data Warehousing Workbench (see Figure 4.14, Steps 1 to 3).

New data flow display

▶ Now, all components types that are linked by a data flow can be edited in any of the views (**InfoProvider, InfoObjects, Info-Sources,** and **DataSources**).

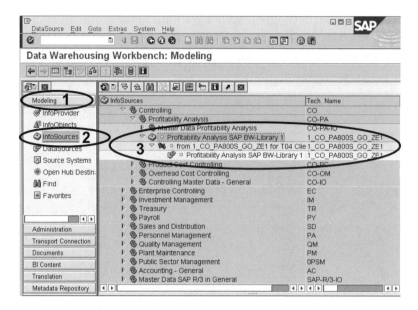

**Figure 4.14** New Display of Component/Data Flow Hierarchy in the Data Ware-housing Workbench

Creating 3.x
update rules

▶ 3.x update rules can be created for a previously configured Info-Provider (in this case, InfoCube **ZFCOPAC4**) in the **InfoProvider** view of the Data Warehousing Workbench (see Figure 4.15, Step 1).

▶ To do this, click on the InfoProvider in question to select it, and right-click on it to open the context-sensitive menu (Step 2).

▶ Open the submenu **Additional Functions**, and select the **Create update rules** function (Step 3).

▶ In the **Update Rules Create: Start** popup, select the InfoSource that you want to assign (see Figure 4.16, Step 1), and confirm your selection by clicking on the **Continue** button (Step 2).

▶ If update rules cannot be created for all key figures, an information popup containing the message **Key Figures was set to 'no update'** is displayed. Again, confirm this popup by clicking on **Continue** (Step 3).

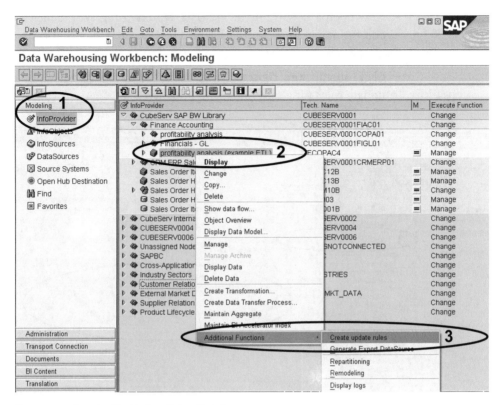

**Figure 4.15** Creating 3.x Update Rules, Part 1

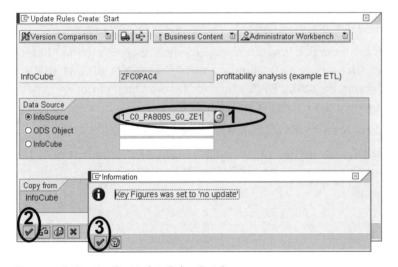

**Figure 4.16** Creating 3.x Update Rules, Part 2

<table>
<tr><td>Editing and<br>activating 3.x<br>update rules</td><td>▶ Now open a new frame in the Data Warehousing Workbench to edit the update rules for the selected InfoProvider and its assigned InfoSource (see Figure 4.17, Steps 1 and 2).</td></tr>
</table>

▶ Click on the **Key Figure** button to start the process of editing update rules for a selected key figure (Step 3).

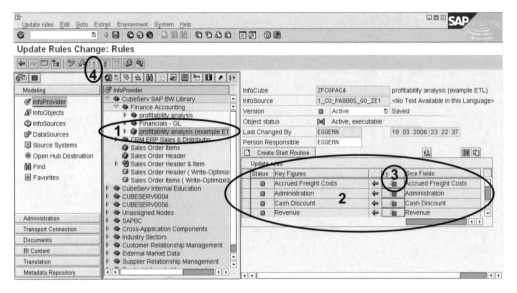

**Figure 4.17** Editing and Activating 3.x Update Rules, Part 1

▶ Make the required settings in the **Key Fig. Calculation**, **Chars.**, and **Time Ref.** tabs (see Figure 4.18, Steps 1 and 2 (examples)).

▶ In this example, you can change the field mapping in the **Characteristics** tab by assigning the source field **0CRM_BILDAT (Billing Date)** to the **0BILL_DATE** (Date for Invoice) target InfoObject contained in the InfoProvider (Step 3).

▶ Then, transfer the settings using the **Transfer** button (Step 4).

▶ Lastly, activate the update rules by clicking on the button of the same name (see Figure 4.17, Step 4).

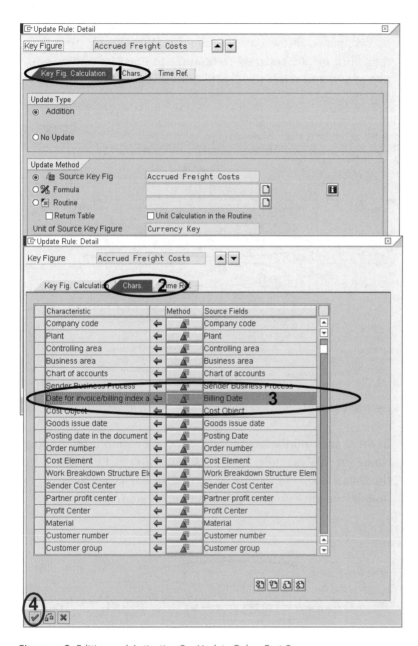

**Figure 4.18** Editing and Activating 3.x Update Rules, Part 2

▸ The update rules are then displayed in the data flow tree in the Data Warehousing Workbench (see Figure 4.19).

Creating a
3.x InfoPackage

▶ InfoPackages can now be created from within the data flow tree that is opened in the Data Warehousing Workbench. To do this, right-click on the assigned DataSource to open its context-sensitive menu, and select the **Create InfoPackage...** function (Steps 2 and 3).

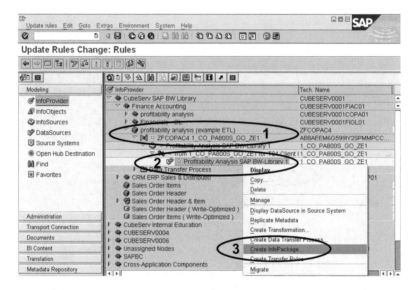

**Figure 4.19** Creating Update Rules in Data Flow Tree and 3.x InfoPackage

▶ In the **Create InfoPackage** popup, enter the required **InfoPackage Name** (in this example, **ZF.1_CO_PA800S_GO_ZE1.0001.0**), select the DataSource you require (if more than one DataSource is proposed), and click on **Save** (see Figure 4.20, Steps 1 to 3).

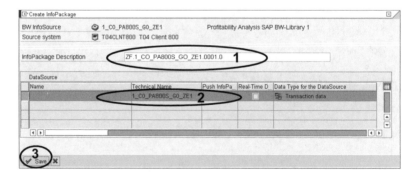

**Figure 4.20** Configuring and Starting the 3.x InfoPackage, Part 1

▶ You can configure the InfoPackage in the next dialog, **Scheduler (Maintain InfoPackage)** (see Figure 4.21, Step 1). In your example, select the **Initialize Delta Process** option in the **Update** tab (Steps 2 and 3).

Configuring the 3.x InfoPackage

▶ Go to the **Schedule** tab (Steps 4 and 5) and click on the **Start** button to execute the data request (Step 6).

Starting the 3.x InfoPackage

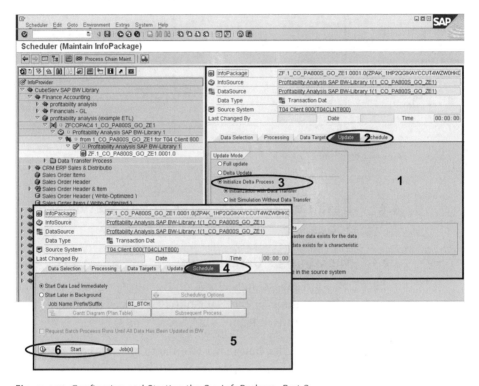

**Figure 4.21** Configuring and Starting the 3.x InfoPackage, Part 2

▶ Once an InfoPackage has been created, it is displayed in the data flow tree of the Administrator Workbench (see Figure 4.22, Step 1).

Monitoring the data request

▶ To display a list of monitor entries, select the InfoPackage by clicking on it and click the **Open BI Object Monitor** button (Steps 2 and 3).

▶ Then, to display detailed information on the data request, select a monitor entry and click on the **Details** button (Steps 4 and 5). The detailed information is displayed in a new frame. As you can see, in this example, 43,200 data records were transferred in four minutes and 55 seconds, and updated to InfoProvider **ZFCOPAC4**.

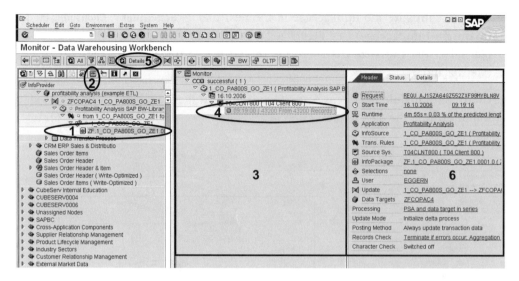

**Figure 4.22** Monitor for 3.x InfoPackage

## 4.4 Data Retrieval Processes in SAP NetWeaver 2004s

### 4.4.1 Migrating 3.x DataSources

If a 3.x DataSource exists in SAP BW on NetWeaver 2004s, it can be migrated. This is done in the DataSources view of the Data Warehousing Workbench (see Figure 4.23, Steps 1 to 3).

[■] ▶ To do this, right-click on the DataSource to open its context-sensitive menu, and select the **Migrate** function (Steps 3 and 4).

▶ This opens the **Migration of a 3.x DataSource** popup. This popup contains two migration variants: **W/O Export** and **With Export**.

Option to restore the 3.x DataSource
▶ If you want to be able to restore the 3.x DataSource, click on the **With Export** option (see Figure 4.24). This exports the 3.x objects as part of the migration process. These objects then serve as a basis if you want to restore the 3.x DataSource at a later stage.

▶ In the migration process, the 3.x DataSource is deleted and transferred to the SAP NetWeaver 2004s DataSource. The mapping object and the transfer structure are deleted. If data requests already exist, the InfoPackages and the PSA with the loaded requests are transferred to the DataSource.

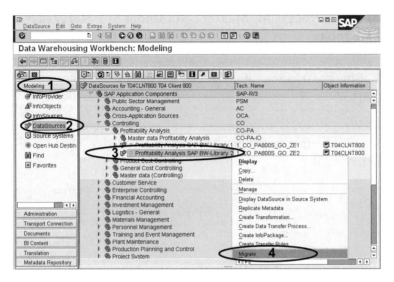

**Figure 4.23** Migrating a 3.x DataSource, Part 1

▶ In this example, use the **W/O Export** option. To do this, click on the button of the same name, as before (see Figure 4.24, Step 1). The migration process then runs automatically.

▶ Once the migration is completed, the DataSource is displayed in the Data Warehousing Workbench as an SAP NetWeaver 2004s DataSource (Step 2).

NetWeaver 2004s DataSource

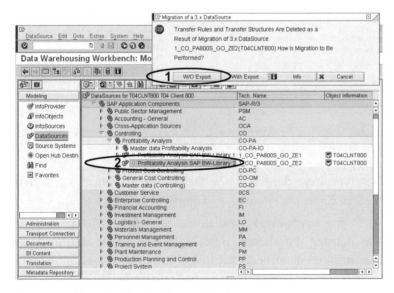

**Figure 4.24** Migrating a 3.x DataSource, Part 2

### 4.4.2 ETL Process for Master Data Under SAP NetWeaver 2004s

We will now demonstrate how to set up data retrieval for master data, using the **Division** InfoObject (0DIVISION).

[•] ▸ To set up the ETL process for a 3.x DataSource using SAP NetWeaver 2004s components, you need to migrate the Data-Source (see the description in Section 4.4.1) (see Figure 4.25, Steps 1 to 5).

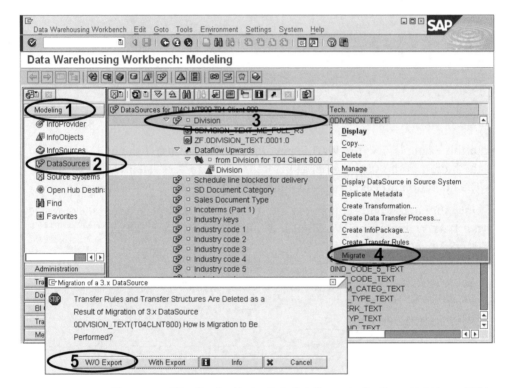

**Figure 4.25** Migrating 3.x Master Data DataSource to Configure NetWeaver 2004s ETL Components

▸ Once you have done this, the DataSource is available as a Net-Weaver 2004s DataSource (see Figure 4.26, Steps 1 to 3).

Creating a transformation
▸ Go to the **InfoSources** view in the modeling area of the Data Warehousing Workbench. Here, right-click on the icon for texts and attributes underneath the InfoObject to open the context-sensitive menu, and select the **Create Transformation** function (see Figure 4.27, Steps 1 to 4).

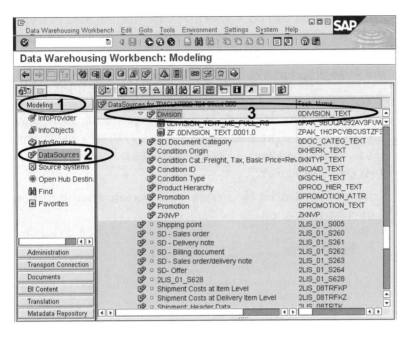

**Figure 4.26** Creating a Single-Level (Direct) Transformation, Part 1

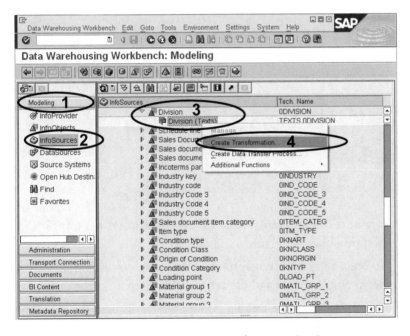

**Figure 4.27** Creating a Single-Level (Direct) Transformation, Part 2

▶ The **Assign InfoArea** popup opens. Specify the InfoArea to which you want to assign the InfoObject (in this example, **0SD**), and confirm your entry by clicking on the **Assign InfoArea** button (see Figure 4.28, Steps 1 and 2).

Source and target of the transformation

▶ This action opens the **Create Transformation** popup. The target of the transformation is already known. To complete the data, enter the source of the transformation (in this example, object type DataSource, **DataSource 0DIVISION_TEXT**, **Source System T04CLNT800)** (Step 3).

▶ Confirm these entries by clicking on the **Create Transformation** button (Step 4).

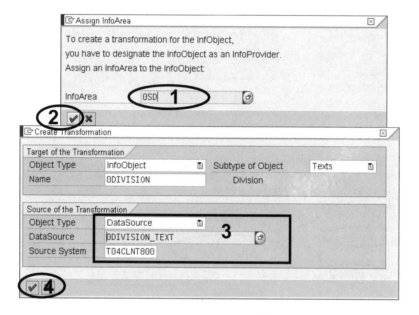

**Figure 4.28** Creating a Single-Level (Direct) Transformation, Part 3

Configuring and activating the transformation

▶ The next dialog, **Transformation Create**, displays the transformation proposal (see Figure 4.29, Step 1).

▶ To open and edit a transformation rule, double-click on the arrow between the source and the target fields (Step 2).

▶ This opens the **Rule Details** popup, which displays the rule type (**Direct Assignment**), and the source fields (**KEYI**) and target fields (InfoObject **0DIVISION**) of the rule (see Figure 4.30, Steps 1 to 3).

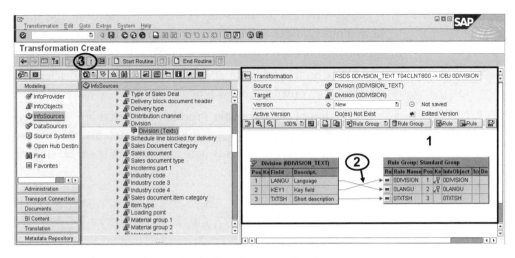

Figure 4.29  Configuring and Activating the Transformation, Part 1

▶ Close the Maintenance function by clicking on the **Transfer Values** button (Step 4).

▶ Lastly, activate the transformation by clicking on the button of the same name (see Figure 4.29, Step 3).

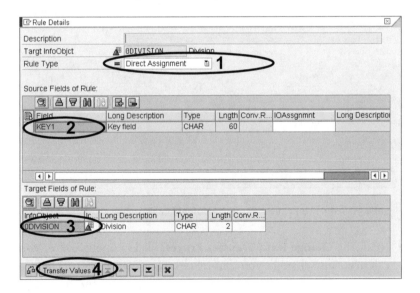

Figure 4.30  Configuring and Activating the Transformation, Part 2

Creating a data
transfer process

▶ If you now refresh the **InfoSources** view, the transformation and a new, empty folder called **Data Transfer Process** are displayed under the InfoObject (see Figure 4.31, Step 1).

▶ Right-click on this folder to open the context menu and select the **Create Data Transfer Process** function (Step 2).

▶ The **Creation of Data Transfer Process** popup that opens displays the source-target assignments of the data transfer process. You can also change these assignments here and confirm them by clicking on **Continue** (Step 3).

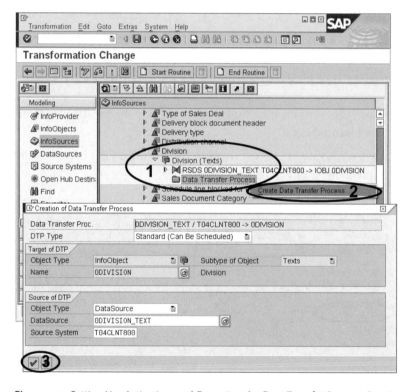

**Figure 4.31** Setting Up, Activating, and Executing the Data Transfer Process, Part 1

Set up, activate,
and execute data
transfer process

▶ Next, the **Change Data Transfer Process** dialog opens. Here, you can make any changes you require (see Figure 4.32, Step 1) before activating the data transfer process by clicking on the button of the same name (Step 2).

▶ After opening the **Execute** tab, start the data transfer process by clicking on the **Execute** button (Steps 3 and 4).

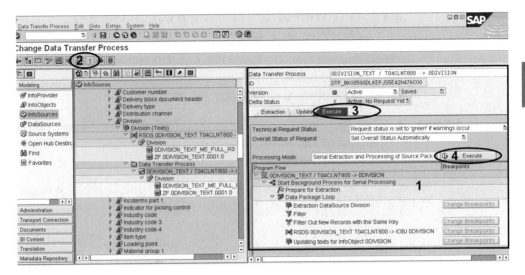

**Figure 4.32** Setting Up, Activating, and Executing the Data Transfer Process, Part 2

▶ After the data retrieval process starts, the **Request Status** popup opens. This popup asks you whether you want to display the request monitor. Click on **Yes** (see Figure 4.33, Step 1) to open the data transfer process monitor.

Data transfer process monitor

▶ In this example, the monitor shows that 58 data records with texts for the InfoObject **0DIVISION** have been successfully updated (Step 2).

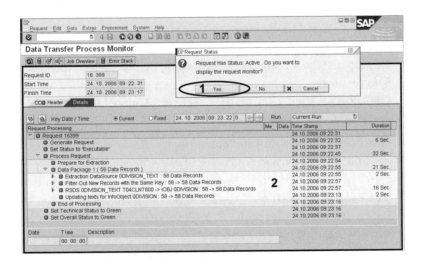

**Figure 4.33** Monitoring the Data Retrieval Process

### 4.4.3 ETL Process for Transaction Data Under SAP NetWeaver 2004s

We will now demonstrate how to set up data retrieval for transaction data and non-business-content-based ETL components, using the CO-PA DataSource **1_CO_PA800S_GO_ZE2**.

[▪] ▸ Open the context-sensitive menu for the SAP NetWeaver 2004s DataSource and select the **Create Transformation** function (see Figure 4.34, Steps 1 to 4).

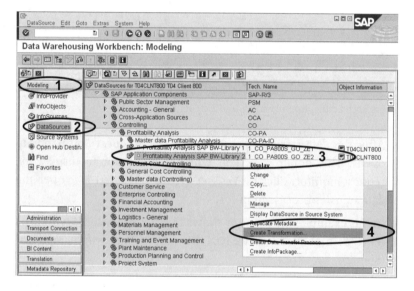

**Figure 4.34** Creating a Transformation for Transaction Data (Variant 1), Part 1

▸ This opens the **Create Transformation** popup. Select the Info-Source object type and enter the required InfoSource name (**ZFCOPAC4**). Then, click on the **Create InfoSource** button (see Figure 4.35, Steps 1 and 2).

*Creating an Info-Source using a template (variant 1)*

▸ This opens the **Create InfoSource** popup. Enter a description of the InfoSource you want to create, specify the application component to which you want to assign the InfoSource (**ZCUBESERV0001COPA01**), and set the template object type to DataSource (**DataSource 1_CO_PA800S_GO_ZE2** and source system **T04CLNT800**, Steps 3 and 4).

▸ Confirm these entries by clicking on the **Create Transformation** button (Step 5).

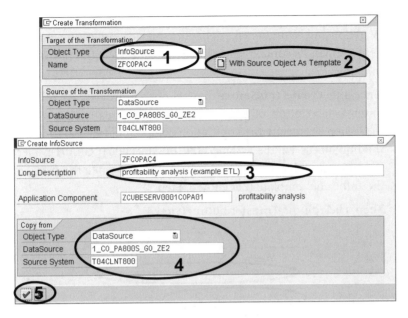

**Figure 4.35** Creating a Transformation for Transaction Data (Variant 1), Part 2

▶ The **InfoSource Maintain: Overview** dialog opens. This dialog allows you to assign an InfoObject to every source field (see Figure 4.36, highlighted fields). However, considering the large number of fields to be assigned, this process would be very time-consuming and subject to error.

| Key | InfoObject | Short Description | In... | Int... | T... | Check object | InfoObject of Unit | Type | Lngth | De... | Field | Conv... | Pos. |
|-----|-----------|-------------------|-------|--------|------|--------------|--------------------|------|-------|-------|-------|---------|------|
| ☐ | | | ⊗ | ☐ | | | | NUMC | 4 | | GJAHR | | 1 |
| ☐ | | | ⊗ | ☐ | | | | CHAR | 2 | | PERIV | | 2 |
| ☐ | | | ⊗ | ☐ | | | | NUMC | 7 | | PERIO | | 3 |
| ☐ | | | ⊗ | ☐ | | | | NUMC | 3 | | WRTTP | | 4 |
| ☐ | | | ⊗ | ☐ | | | | CHAR | 3 | | VERSI | | 5 |
| ☐ | | | ⊗ | ☐ | | | | CHAR | 1 | | VRGAR | | 6 |
| ☐ | | | ⊗ | ☐ | | | | CHAR | 2 | | CURTYPE | | 7 |
| ☐ | | | ⊗ | ☐ | | | | NUMC | 1 | | VALUTYP | | 8 |
| ☐ | | | ⊗ | ☐ | | | | CHAR | 4 | | BUKRS | | 9 |
| ☐ | | | ⊗ | ☐ | | | | CHAR | 18 | | ARTNR | | 10 |
| ☐ | | | ⊗ | ☐ | | | | CHAR | 4 | | BRSCH | | 11 |
| ☐ | | | ⊗ | ☐ | | | | CHAR | 4 | | GSBER | | 12 |
| ☐ | | | ⊗ | ☐ | | | | CHAR | 4 | | KOKRS | | 13 |
| ☐ | | | ⊗ | ☐ | | | | CHAR | 10 | | KNDNR | | 14 |

InfoSource Maintain: Overview

InfoSource    ZFCOPAC4         profitability analysis (example ETL)

**Figure 4.36** Creating a Transformation for Transaction Data (Variant 1), Part 3

▶ A far better alternative is to go to the **InfoSources** view of the Data Warehousing Workbench, right-click on an application component to open its context-sensitive menu, and select the **InfoSource** function.

▶ Once the **Create InfoSource** popup opens, proceed as follows. Enter a description of the InfoSource to be created (see Figure 4.37, Step 1); specify the application component (Step 2) to which the InfoSource will be assigned (**ZCUBESERV0001COPA01**); select the **InfoCube** object type template; and lastly, enter the name of the InfoCube template (**ZFCOPAC4**, Step 3).

▶ Then, click on the **Transfer** button (Step 4).

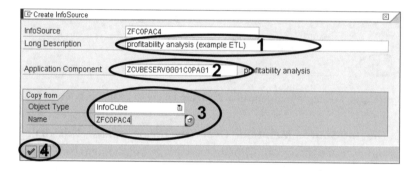

**Figure 4.37** Creating a Transformation for Transaction Data (Variant 2), Part 1

[»]   Make sure that you select the InfoCube using the SAP input help function.

▶ Next, the **InfoSource Maintain: Overview** dialog opens. This dialog contains the relevant InfoObjects, which are now automatically available by template type. Finally, save and activate the Info-Source (see Figure 4.38, Steps 1 to 3).

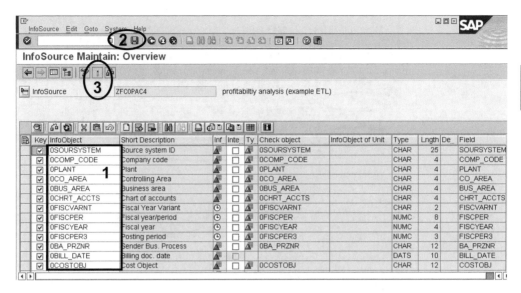

**Figure 4.38** Creating a Transformation for Transaction Data (Variant 2), Part 2

▶ The newly created InfoSource is now displayed in the application component hierarchy in the **InfoSources** view of the Data Warehousing Workbench. Open the context-sensitive menu of the new InfoSource (see Figure 4.39, Steps 1 through 3), and select the **Create Transformation** function (Step 4).

▶ The **Create Transformation** popup opens. In this popup, enter the required source (in our example, **DataSource 1_CO_PA800S_GO_ZE2** in **Source System T04CLNT800**), and click on the **Transfer** button (Steps 5 and 6).

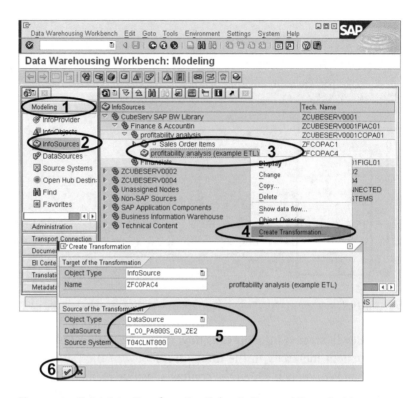

**Figure 4.39** Maintaining Transformation Rules via Drag-and-Drop, Part 1

Maintaining trans-
formation rules

▶ This opens the **Transformation Create** dialog with the transformation rules proposed by the system. In this example, only rules for
the source field **Company Code (0COMPCODE)** and the target
InfoObject of the same name, **0COMPCODE**, are proposed (see
Figure 4.40, Step 1). You now need to complete these rules.

Creating transfor-
mation rules using
drag-and-drop

▶ You can create a simple field-to-InfoObject transformation rule
using drag-and-drop. To do this, drag the mouse from the source
field to the target InfoObject. This creates a dotted line between
the source field and the target InfoObject (see **Company Code**
example, Step 2), which turns into an arrow when you release the
mouse (Step 3).

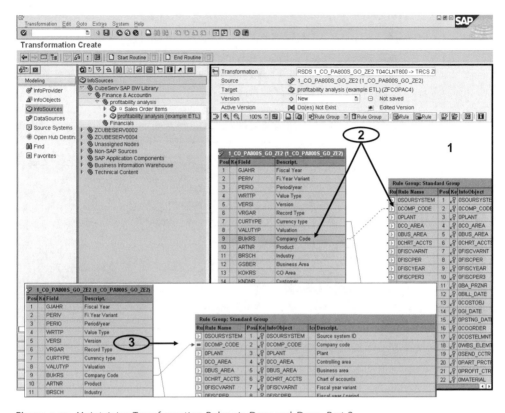

**Figure 4.40** Maintaining Transformation Rules via Drag-and-Drop, Part 2

▶ It is often impractical to maintain normal DataSources using drag-and-drop, as this involves dragging the arrows across multiple screens. A preferable alternative is to open the context-sensitive menu for the target InfoObject in question and choose the **Rule Details** function (see Figure 4.41, Step 1).

Creating transformation rules by field assignment in popup

▶ This opens the **Rule Details** popup. Here, you can select the rule type **Direct Assignment** for field-to-InfoObject assignments (Step 2).

▶ Press the + button (Step 3) to view the list of available source fields. Click on the required field to select it and then click on the **Transfer button**. A simpler alternative is to double-click on the source field to transfer it directly (see Figure 4.42, Step 1).

▶ The source field in question is now transferred and displayed in the **Rule Details** popup (Step 2).

▶ Confirm these entries by clicking on the **Transfer Values** button (Step 3).

243

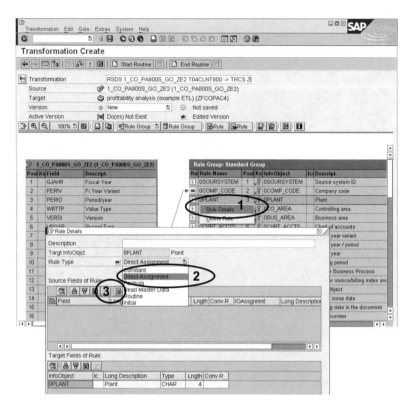

**Figure 4.41** Maintaining Transformation Rules in Rule Details Popup, Part 1

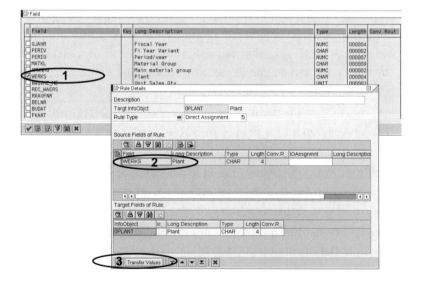

**Figure 4.42** Maintaining Transformation Rules in Rule Details Popup, Part 2

▸ To assign InfoObjects to constants, open the **Rule Details** popup for this InfoObject (see Figure 4.41, Step 1) and select the **Constant** rule type (see Figure 4.43, Step 1).

Assigning constants

▸ A new input field, **Constant Value**, opens. Here, you can enter the value you want, either manually or using the input help function (Steps 3 and 4).

▸ Confirm this setting by clicking on the **Transfer Values** button (Step 5).

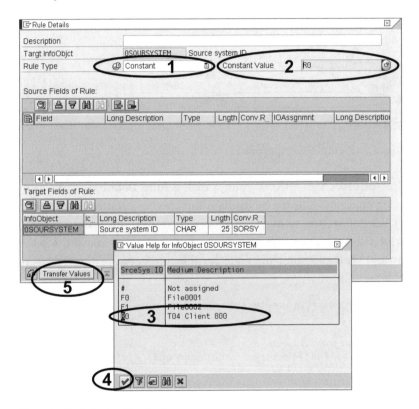

**Figure 4.43** Assigning Constants

▸ If you intend to use routines for transformations, again open the **Rule Details** popup for the InfoObject in question and select the **Routine** rule type (see Figure 4.44, Step 1).

Routines

▸ Select the source field(s) as shown in Figure 4.44 (Steps 2 to 4).

▸ Then click on the newly displayed **Change Rule** button (Step 5).

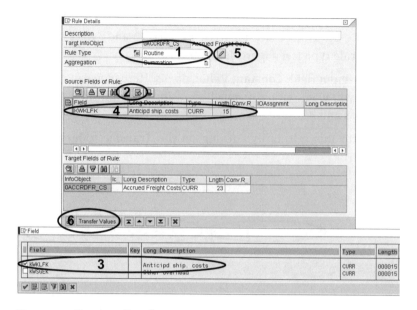

**Figure 4.44** Creating a Transformation Routine, Part 1

This displays the ABAP/4 coding dialog **Rule Details** for programming routines. This dialog displays the specified source fields in the TYPES declaration under type _ty_s_SC_1 (see the listing below), which serves as the reference for the SOURCE_FIELDS (again, see the listing). You can enter the code for the rule between the following comment lines:

`*$*$ begin of routine—insert your code only below this line`

and

`*$*$ end of routine—insert your code only before this line`

In this example, you want to store revenue reductions and costs in the InfoCube and mark them with a minus sign. To do this, you negate the KWKLFK source field and transfer it to the RESULT target field:

**RESULT =−SOURCE_FIELDS-KWKLFK.**

As you can see in the sample code, the structure of the ABAP/4 routine has been changed considerably in the new release (parts of the generated code have been replaced by "..." in order to save space):

```
PROGRAM trans_routine.
*-------------------------------------------------------------------*
*        CLASS routine DEFINITION
*-------------------------------------------------------------------*
*
*-------------------------------------------------------------------*
CLASS routine DEFINITION.
  PUBLIC SECTION.

    TYPES:
      BEGIN OF _ty_s_SC_1,
*        Field: KWKLFK Anticipd ship. costs.
        KWKLFK            TYPE P LENGTH 8 DECIMALS 2,
      END   OF _ty_s_SC_1.
    TYPES:
      BEGIN OF _ty_s_TG_1,
*        InfoObject: 0ACCRDFR_CS Accrued Freight Costs.
        ACCRDFR_CS        TYPE /BIO/OIACCRDFR_CS,
      END   OF _ty_s_TG_1.
  PRIVATE SECTION.

    TYPE-POOLS: rsd, rstr.

*$*$ begin of global—
insert your declaration only below this line  *-*
... "insert your code here
*$*$ end of global—
insert your declaration only before this line   *-*

    METHODS
      compute_0ACCRDFR_CS
        IMPORTING
          request                type rsrequest
          datapackid             type rsdatapid
          SOURCE_FIELDS           type _ty_s_SC_1
        EXPORTING
          RESULT                 type _ty_s_TG_1-ACCRDFR_CS
          monitor                type rstr_ty_t_monitor
        RAISING
          cx_rsrout_abort
          cx_rsrout_skip_record
          cx_rsrout_skip_val.
    METHODS
      invert_0ACCRDFR_CS
        IMPORTING
          i_r_selset_outbound        TYPE REF TO cl_rsmds_set
```

```
            i_th_fields_outbound          TYPE HASHED TABLE
            i_r_selset_outbound_complete TYPE REF TO cl_rsmds_set
            i_r_universe_inbound          TYPE REF TO cl_rsmds_
                                          universe
        CHANGING
          c_r_selset_inbound              TYPE REF TO cl_rsmds_set
          c_th_fields_inbound             TYPE HASHED TABLE
          c_exact                         TYPE rs_bool.
ENDCLASS.                      "routine DEFINITION


*-------------------------------------------------------------------*
*        CLASS routine IMPLEMENTATION
*-------------------------------------------------------------------*
*
*-------------------------------------------------------------------*
CLASS routine IMPLEMENTATION.

  METHOD compute_0ACCRDFR_CS.

*    IMPORTING
*      SOURCE_FIELDS-KWKLFK TYPE P LENGTH 000008 DECIMALS 000002

    DATA:
      MONITOR_REC     TYPE rsmonitor.

*$*$ begin of routine—
insert your code only below this line       *-*
... "insert your code here
*-- fill table "MONITOR" with values of structure "MONITOR_
REC"
*- to make monitor entries
... "to cancel the update process
*    raise exception type CX_RSROUT_ABORT.
... "to skip a record
*    raise exception type CX_RSROUT_SKIP_RECORD.
... "to clear target fields
*    raise exception type CX_RSROUT_SKIP_VAL.

*     EXPORTING
*       RESULT type _ty_s_TG_1-ACCRDFR_CS
      RESULT =-SOURCE_FIELDS-KWKLFK.

*$*$ end of routine—
insert your code only before this line       *-*
  ENDMETHOD.                    "compute_0ACCRDFR_CS
```

```
*------------------------------------------------------------*
*        Method invert_0ACCRDFR_CS
*------------------------------------------------------------*
*
*        This subroutine needs to be implemented only for direct
*        access (for better performance) and for the Report/
*        Report Interface (drill through).
*        The inverse routine should transform a projection and
*        a selection for the target to a projection and a
*        selection for the source, respectively.
*        If the implementation remains empty all fields are
*        filled and all values are selected.
*
*------------------------------------------------------------*
*
*------------------------------------------------------------*
  METHOD invert_0ACCRDFR_CS.

*$*$ begin of inverse routine—
insert your code only below this line*-*
... "insert your code here
*$*$ end of inverse routine—
insert your code only before this line *-*

  ENDMETHOD.                        "invert_0ACCRDFR_CS
ENDCLASS.                           "routine IMPLEMENTATION
```

▶ After you have finished coding (see Figure 4.45, Step 1), exit the **Saving the routine**
ABAP/4 programming dialog by clicking on the **Save** button (Step 2).

▶ Then, the application returns to the **Rule Details** popup, where you click on **Transfer Values** to complete the rule editing process (see Figure 4.44, Step 6).

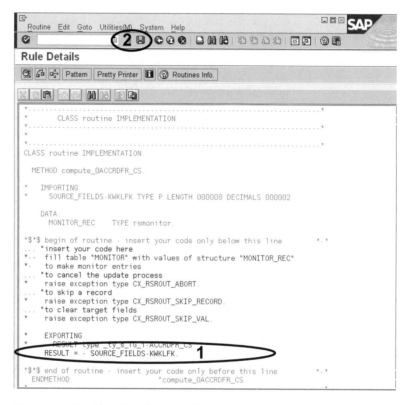

**Figure 4.45** Creating a Transformation Routine, Part 2

▸ For each edited key figure, the source field/target field assignment is illustrated by the kind of arrow shown in Figure 4.46 (highlighted arrow) and the icon indicating an ABAP/4 routine, similar to the convention for field mapping.

**Figure 4.46** Displaying the Transformation Routine in Transformation Rules

Completing the
transformation
rules
▸ Complete the transformation rules in such a way that you use field/field mappings and negate revenue reductions and costs, where possible. The transformation rules are then displayed as shown in Figure 4.47, Step 1.

▸ Finally, activate the transformation rules (Step 2).

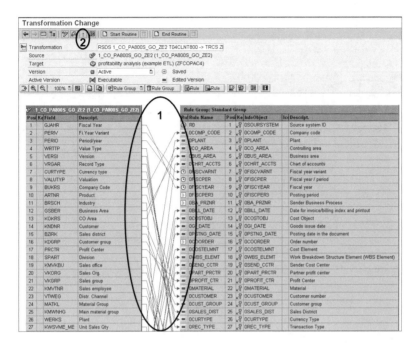

**Figure 4.47** Transformation Rules Display

▶ Once they have been activated, the transformation rules are displayed accordingly in the data retrieval tree in the **InfoSources** view of the Data Warehousing Workbench in SAP BW (see Figure 4.48, Steps 1 to 3).

Display of SAP NetWeaver 2004s transformation

▶ To transfer data from a source system to SAP BW, right-click on the **DataSource** item in the data retrieval tree to activate the context-sensitive menu, and select the **Create InfoPackage** function (Step 4). This opens the **Create InfoPackage** popup.

Create InfoPackage

▶ Enter the InfoPackage name and click on the **Save** button (see Figure 4.49, Steps 1 and 2).

▶ The data request is triggered when you open the **Schedule** tab in the InfoPackage that is then displayed, and click on the **Start** button (Steps 3 and 4).

Starting the data request

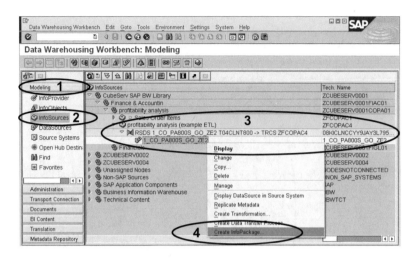

Figure 4.48 Transformation Rules in the Data Retrieval Tree

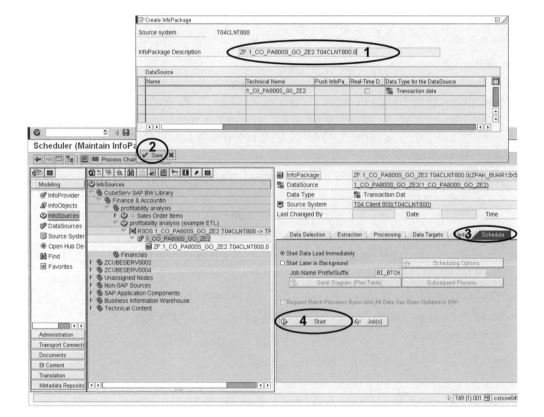

Figure 4.49 Creating the InfoPackage and Requesting Data

▸ To start the data retrieval monitoring process, select the InfoPackage, and click on the **Open BI Object Monitor** button (see Figure 4.50, Steps 1 and 2).

Monitoring the data retrieval process

▸ A new frame opens that contains a log of the progress and results of data retrieval processes (Step 3).

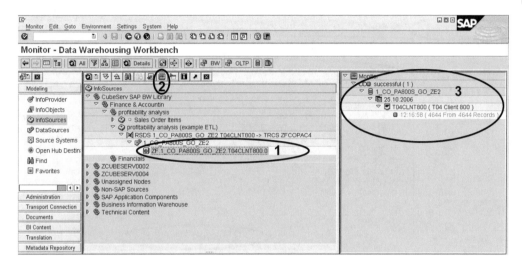

**Figure 4.50** Monitoring Data Retrieval from the Source System

▸ Transformation rules are also used to transfer data from an SAP NetWeaver 2004s InfoSource to a data target (in this example, InfoCube **ZFCOPAC4**). To do this, go to the **InfoProvider** view in the Data Warehousing Workbench of SAP BW, open the context-sensitive menu, and select the **Create Transformation** function (see Figure 4.51, Steps 1 to 5).

InfoSource transformation rules • Data target

▸ Based on the function you selected, the object type **InfoCube** and the object **ZFCOPAC4** are already defined as the **Target of the Transformation** (Step 4).

Creating a transformation

▸ Now select the transformation source (in this example, object type **InfoSource** and the object **ZFCOPAC4**), and confirm your selection by clicking on the **Create Transformation** button (Steps 5 and 6).

If the same InfoObjects are used in the source (InfoSource) and the target (InfoCube), SAP BW creates a proposal for the transformation rules. In some cases, this can be transferred directly.

Proposed transformation rules

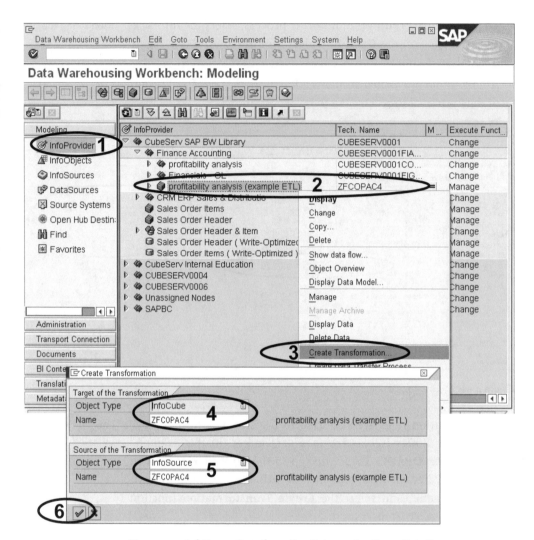

**Figure 4.51** InfoSource Transformation Rules → Creating a Data Source

Deleting transfor-
mation rules

If you want to create another rule, you can do this by deleting and
recreating a rule.

[▪] ▸ To do this, select the rules that you want to delete, right-click to
open the context-sensitive menu, and select the **Delete** function
(see Figure 4.52, Step 1).

▸ This removes the transformation rule (Step 2).

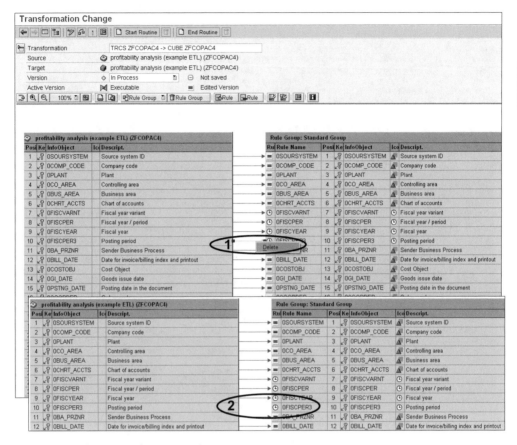

**Figure 4.52** Deleting Transformation Rules

You also follow a procedure similar to that explained above for creating a DataSource → InfoSource transformation when mapping different fields.

Mapping different fields

▶ Drag an arrow from the source InfoObject, **Fiscal Year/Period** (0FISCPER), to the target InfoObject, **Posting Period** (0FISCPER3) (see Figure 4.53, Step 1).

[▪]

▶ To edit the rule, select the target InfoObject, open its context-sensitive menu, and select the **Rule Details** function (Step 2). This opens the **Rule Details** popup.

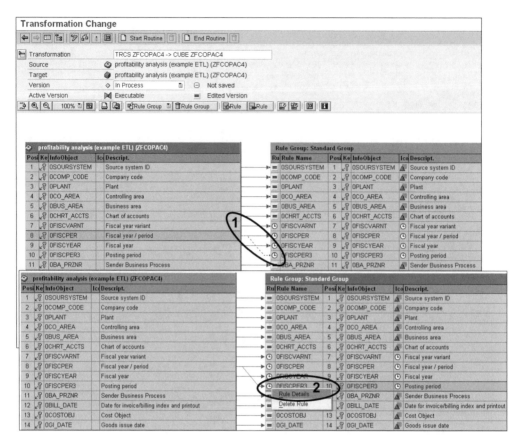

**Figure 4.53** Deleting Proposed Transformation Rules and Creating New Rules, Part 1

▶ In this case, SAP BW automatically recognizes the involvement of time characteristics, and sets up the **Time Characteristic** rule type with the appropriate time conversion formula (see Figure 4.54, Step 1).

▶ Exit the **Rule Details** popup by clicking on the **Transfer Values** button (Step 2).

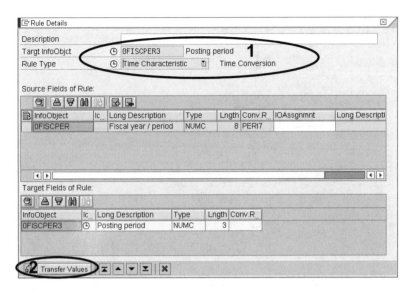

**Figure 4.54** Deleting Proposed Transformation Rules and Creating New Rules, Part 2

There is also the following alternative method of changing the transformation rules.

Changing the rule details popup

▶ To replace the source field **Harmonized Version** (ZFVERSION) with the source InfoObject **Value Type for Report** (0VYTPE), open the context-sensitive menu of the InfoObject whose transformation rules you want to change (in this case, the **Harmonized Version** InfoObject), and select the **Rule Details…** function (see Figure 4.55, Step 1).

[⋅]

▶ Then, to assign an alternative InfoObject, click on the **Add Source Fields** button in the **Rule Details** popup (Step 2). This opens the **InfoObject** popup.

▶ Double-click on the required source InfoObject, **Value Type for Reporting** (0VYTPE) (see Figure 4.56, Step 1).

▶ The newly added source InfoObject is now displayed in the **Rule Details** popup. Select the source InfoObject that you do not require, **Harmonized Version** (ZFVERSION), by clicking on it; then click on the **Remove Source Field** button (see Figure 4.55, Steps 3 and 4).

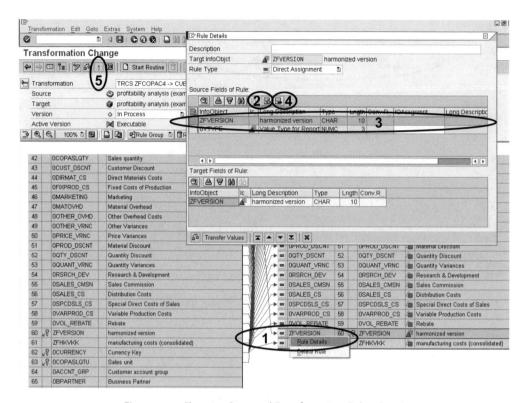

**Figure 4.55** Changing Proposed Transformation Rules, Part 1

▶ The unwanted source InfoObject is then removed (see Figure 4.56, Step 2).

▶ Confirm these entries by clicking on the **Transfer Values** button (Step 3).

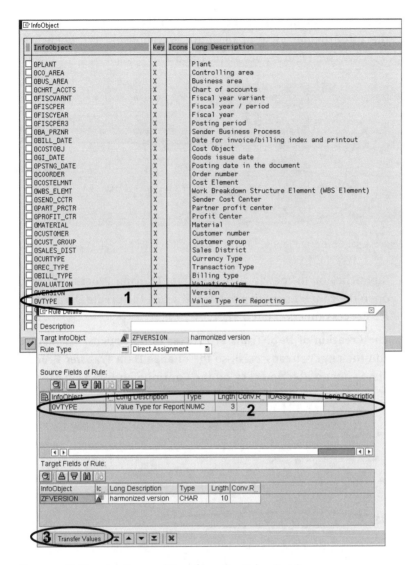

**Figure 4.56** Changing Proposed Transformation Rules, Part 2

▸ The newly configured transformation rules are then assigned to the application in the **Change Transformation** dialog (see Figure 4.57, highlighted text).

▸ Finally, activate the transformation by clicking on the button of the same name (see Figure 4.55, Step 5).

Activating the transformation

259

▶ The transformation is then displayed in the data retrieval tree in the **InfoProvider** view of the Data Warehousing Workbench in SAP BW (see Figure 4.58, Steps 1 and 2).

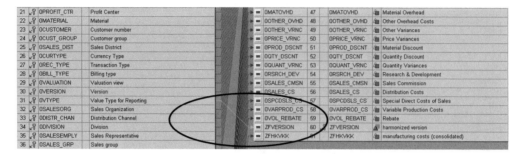

**Figure 4.57** Changing Proposed Transformation Rules, Part 3

Create data transfer process

▶ Right-click on the newly displayed **Data Transfer Process** folder to open the context-sensitive menu and select the **Create Data Transfer Process** function (Step 3).

▶ The **Creation of Data Transfer Process** popup opens. The source and the target already exist, so the **Change Data Transfer Process** dialog opens after you click on the **Continue** button (Step 4).

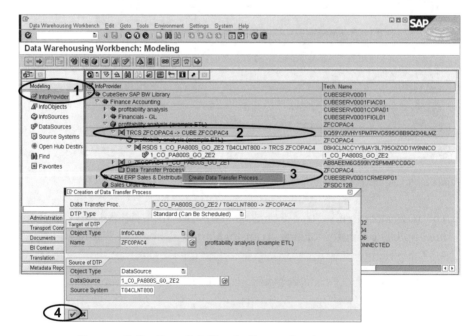

**Figure 4.58** Creating a Data Transfer Process, Part 1

▶ You do not want to transfer all data for the current data transfer process, so you will therefore set up a filter to select the data that you want. To do this, click on the **Filter** button in the **Change Data Transfer Process** dialog (see Figure 4.59, Step 1).

Defining filters in the data transfer process

▶ This opens the **Filter** popup. Now, select the data in company code 1000 by entering the values in the selection field and clicking on **Continue** (Steps 2 and 3).

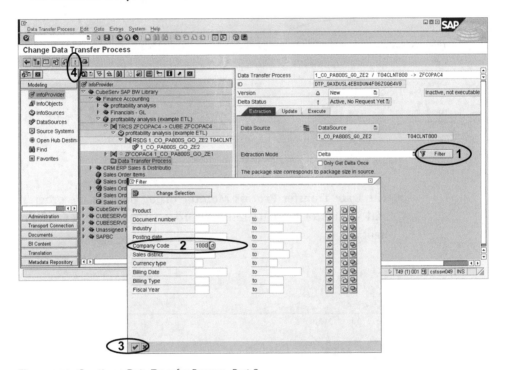

**Figure 4.59** Creating a Data Transfer Process, Part 2

▶ Activate the data transfer process by clicking on the button of the same name (see Figure 4.59, Step 4).

Activating the data transfer process

▶ Next, the data transfer process is displayed in the data retrieval hierarchy in the **InfoProvider** view of the Data Warehousing Workbench (see Figure 4.60, Step 1).

▶ To execute the data retrieval process, open the **Execute** tab (Step 2) in the **Change Data Transfer Process** (or **Display Data Transfer Process**) dialog, and click on the **Execute** button (Step 3).

Executing the data retrieval

▶ The **Request Status** popup opens. Click on **Yes** here to open the Request Monitor (Step 4).

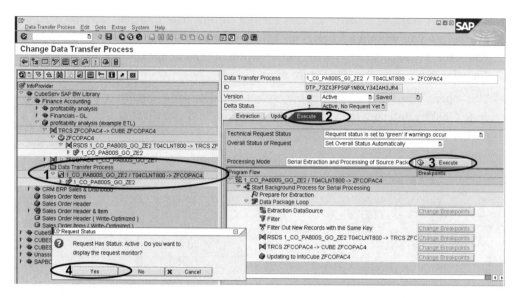

**Figure 4.60** Executing the Transaction Data Retrieval, Part 1

▶ The **Data Transfer Process Monitor** dialog displays the progress and success of the data retrieval process (see Figure 4.61, highlight).

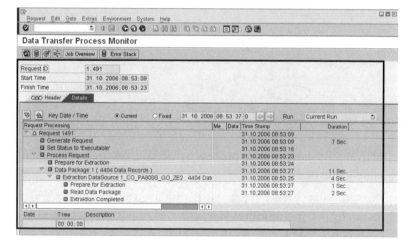

**Figure 4.61** Executing the Transaction Data Retrieval, Part 2

*Good response times for analytical applications are essential for a data warehouse, provided that the data you use is relevant and correct. In addition to the tried and tested functions, the new BI Accelerator technology in SAP Business Information Warehouse provides you with new performance optimization options that enable you to handle very large quantities of data. This chapter describes the new technology and highlights the differences with the functions that have been available in previous releases.*

# 5 Performance Optimization with Aggregates and BI Accelerator

## 5.1 Introduction

Good response times are an essential prerequisite for the success of analytical applications. People often don't react until the response times of analytical applications prompt criticism from users, or until the operation of a data warehouse in general is challenged. In this context, they frequently resort to what is referred to as "performance optimization measures."

*Good response times as an essential prerequisite*

The term *performance optimization*, however, is already confusing because it suggests that applications must be developed first, and only then can measures be taken to obtain adequate response times. We, the authors of this book, have encountered this kind of approach in many reviews. Often the users of analytical tools were frustrated, sometimes even angry. Of course, this approach usually works if you implement performance-optimizing measures to raise the overall performance to a required level; however, this "retroactive" way of handling poor performance often results in unnecessarily high implementation and operation costs. Furthermore, this approach seldom helps you to attain the minimum of response times that can actually be achieved.

*Problem of the performance optimization approach*

Performance management from design to operation

The basic concept should therefore not only consist of a (retroactive) performance optimization, but a systematic performance management as well. Systematic performance management begins with the design of the data models and ends with the operation of the applications. It comprises both database- and application-related aspects. For example, the selection of an appropriate InfoProvider, the modeling of an InfoCube, or an intelligent data compression management are necessary for a good performance of analytical applications and must be determined well before aggregates or the new technology (SAP NetWeaver 2004s BI Accelerator) are implemented.

Old or new technology?

As is typical with new tools, the new BI Accelerator technology can be mistakenly regarded as a new panacea and therefore used to solve every existing problem, at least until this unrealistic view of the new technology fails in the public eye. The questions to be answered are therefore as follows (provided that good performance management is in place): In which areas should the new technology be used? Are there any constraints for this technology? Are there still any areas of use where the previously available aggregate technology has its advantages and should therefore be the preferred choice?

If these questions—and certainly some others too—are answered systematically and seriously, the new BI Accelerator technology will offer you a new performance dimension at acceptable costs.

## 5.2 Reporting without Performance Optimization Measures

### 5.2.1 Sample Query for Performance Optimization

Based on profitability analysis data, the following performance optimization measures need to be taken for a specific query:

Time series

▶ The response time of a query, **CubeServ Time Series Revenue per Posting Period** (ZCSCOPAQ0001), that's used to display the posting periods of a selected fiscal year must be optimized. Moreover, the response time must be optimized with regard to the filtering and drilling down by characteristic values for the InfoObjects **Sold-to Country** and **Invoice Number**.

Filter

▶ During the execution of query **ZCSCOPAQ0001** the following values are selected (see Figure 5.1):

▶ F (invoice data) for characteristic **Transaction Type** (ZCSVR-GAR)

▶ V9 (October-September with 4 special periods) for characteristic **Fiscal Year Variant** (0FISCVARNT), and

▶ 001 (Actual) for characteristic **Version** (ZCSVERS)

▶ The selection for the Calendar Year characteristic (0CALYEAR) occurs through the 0P_CALYE variable.

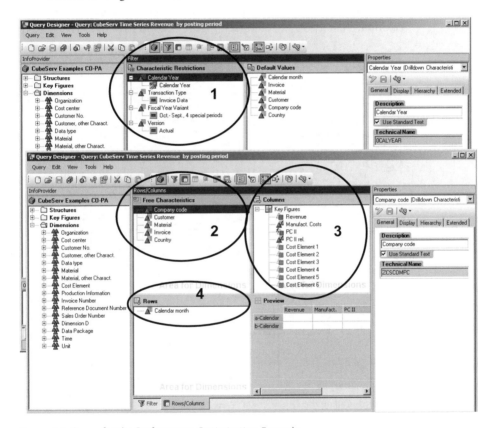

**Figure 5.1** Query for the Performance Optimization Example

▶ The rows contain the **Calendar Months** (**0CALMONTH2** characteristic) that become available after you have made the selections above, while the columns represent the key figures, **Revenue**, **Cost Elements of Goods Manufactured**, and the formulas of manufacturing costs (**Manufact. Costs**), profit contribution II (**PC II**), and relative profit contribution (**PC II rel.**), i.e., PC II in relation to revenue.

Rows and columns

265

▸ The free characteristics available are the following InfoObjects: **Company code** (ZCSCOMPC), **Customer** (ZCSCUST), **Material** (ZCSMAT), **Invoice** (ZCSZRENR), and **Sold-to Country** (ZCSLAN-DAG). These characteristics can be used for filtering and/or drill-down purposes.

### Sample Scenario, Step 1: Calling the Report

In Step 1 of the sample scenario, you must call the sample query with calendar year 2004 selected (see Figure 5.2, Steps 1 to 3).

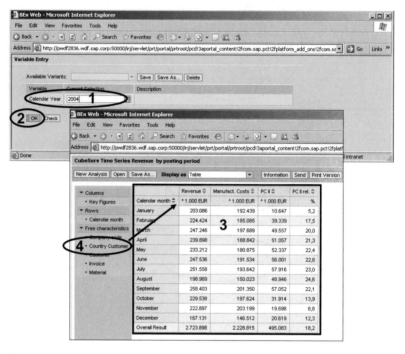

**Figure 5.2** Calling the Query, Initial View

## Sample Scenario, Step 2: Drilldown "Sold-to Country"

In Step 2 of the sample scenario, you add the country of the sold-to party to the existing calendar month drilldown by using a free characteristic (see Figure 5.2, Step 4, and Figure 5.3, Step 1).

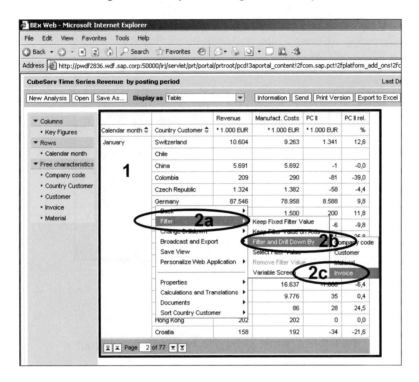

**Figure 5.3** Drilldown by Calendar Month and Country

## Sample Scenario, Step 3: Filter by Country, Drilldown by Calendar Month

In Step 4 of the sample scenario, you filter the country of the sold-to party, Germany, and display the existing invoice numbers for this selection (see Figure 5.3, Step 2, and Figure 5.4, highlight).

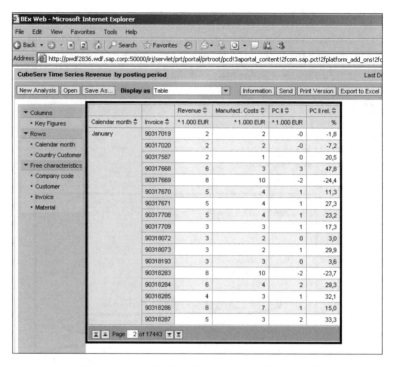

**Figure 5.4** Drilldown by Calendar Month and Invoice Number with Selection of Sold-to Country Germany

### 5.2.2 Response Time Behavior without Performance Optimization

When you call the sample query and use the navigations described above without implementing any performance optimization measures, the following response time behavior occurs:[1]

Data basis
- The InfoCube being used contains 108 Requests (101 compressed and 7 uncompressed ones) with a total of 17,303,206 records (2,637,082 compressed records and 14,666,124 uncompressed records).

- Selection for Steps 1 and 2 (see above): For **Calendar Year 2004**, fiscal year variant **V9**, version **Actual** (characteristic value 1), the fact table contains 860,925 data records, while the E table with the

---

1 Because the hardware configuration used for the SAP BW system being used here does not provide a high performance, we decided to use a very small quantity structure for our example. Powerful systems can process a quantity of data of 1000 times higher within the same amount of time.

compressed requests contains 218,891 data records, which add up to a total of 1,079,816 data records.

▸ Selection for Step 3: For the combination of the described selections, complemented by the **Sold-to Country Germany** selection (characteristic value DE), the fact table contains 455,022 data records, while the E table contains 115,749 data records, which adds up to a total of 570,771 data records.

**Behavior in Sample Scenario Step 1: Call and Initial View**

Without the implementation of performance optimization measures, a total of 860,925 data records are read from the fact table and 218,891 data records are read from the E table for the call of calendar year 2004 described above. The total response time is 84.7s, 80.8s of which (= 12.05 + 68.78, see Figure 5.5) are required for accessing the database.

**Behavior in Sample Scenario Step 2: Additional Drilldown by Sold-to Country**

Without the implementation of performance optimization measures,

860,925 data records are read once again from the fact table, and 218,891 data records are read from the E table for the call of calendar year 2004 with the additional drilldown by the sold-to country described above.

The total response time is 68.8s, 64.01s of which are required for accessing the database.

**Behavior in Sample Scenario Step 3: Additional Drilldown by Invoice Number with Selection of Sold-to Country Germany**

Without the implementation of performance optimization measures, a total of 455,022 data records is read from the fact table, and 115,749 data records from the E table for the call of calendar year 2004 by invoice number with the additional selection of the sold-to country Germany described above. The total response time is 228.7s, 64.9s of which (= 10.02 + 54.87, see Figure 5.5) are required for accessing the database. 52.3s are required for the **OLAP: Read texts** event, 86.0s are required for the **OLAP: Data transfer** event (see Figure 5.5, Steps 1 and 2).

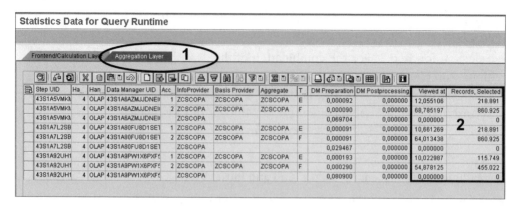

**Figure 5.5** Statistics Data at Query Runtime in the Query Monitor

Time required for
database access

In Steps 1 and 2, you can see that the database access requires a substantial portion of the total response time. The very high values for reading the texts and for the data transfer in Step 3 result in a very small portion of time for the database access, which leads to an extremely poor overall response time.

## 5.3    Performance Optimization Using Aggregates

### 5.3.1    The Concept of Aggregates

Redundant
MiniCubes based
on basic InfoCubes

The "old" technology of aggregates[2] is based on the fact that the number of data records to be read is minimized in order to reduce the query runtimes. For this purpose, (predominantly small) redundant cubes that are based on basic InfoCubes are created (exclusively) for InfoCubes. If required, SAP BW manages the synchronization of the aggregate updates with the underlying basic InfoCubes.

Aggregating by
omitting charac-
teristics

The minimization of the number of data records is basically carried out via aggregation. By omitting characteristics, SAP BW performs an aggregation across the remaining columns of an InfoCube (characteristics and navigation attributes used as well as key figures). This can reduce the remaining number of data records drastically (see Figure 5.6). Access paths are analyzed for selected queries and aggregates, as

---

2  See SAP documentation: *http://help.sap.com/saphelp_nw2004s/helpdata/en/7d/
eb683cc5e8ca68e10000000a114084/frameset.htm.*

small as possible, are defined for single queries or, if possible, groups of queries.

Another way to minimize the number of data records to be read by a query is via the *fixed value selection*. This method uses filters to define an additional aggregate that contains a significantly smaller number of data records than the InfoCube, which would normally be processed.

Fixed value selection

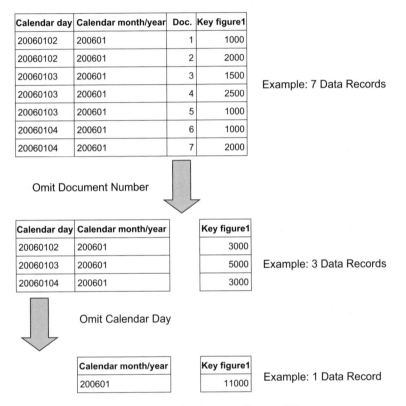

| Calendar day | Calendar month/year | Doc. | Key figure1 |
|---|---|---|---|
| 20060102 | 200601 | 1 | 1000 |
| 20060102 | 200601 | 2 | 2000 |
| 20060103 | 200601 | 3 | 1500 |
| 20060103 | 200601 | 4 | 2500 |
| 20060103 | 200601 | 5 | 1000 |
| 20060104 | 200601 | 6 | 1000 |
| 20060104 | 200601 | 7 | 2000 |

Example: 7 Data Records

Omit Document Number

| Calendar day | Calendar month/year | Key figure1 |
|---|---|---|
| 20060102 | 200601 | 3000 |
| 20060103 | 200601 | 5000 |
| 20060104 | 200601 | 3000 |

Example: 3 Data Records

Omit Calendar Day

| Calendar month/year | Key figure1 |
|---|---|
| 200601 | 11000 |

Example: 1 Data Record

**Figure 5.6** Aggregates: Aggregating by Omitting Characteristics

If you want to use hierarchies to display a characteristic in queries, you can do so by defining aggregates using the respective hierarchy level. For this, you must select a dedicated hierarchy and specify the maximum level of detail (hierarchy level) at which the aggregate to be defined can be used. This way you can aggregate (and "omit") lower levels of detail and precalculate the hierarchy nodes at the lowest level that you want to use. This also reduces the number of data records to be read significantly.

Hierarchy level

Basic InfoCubes as the basis
You can create aggregates only via basic InfoCubes. If a MultiProvider contains several InfoCubes, SAP BW uses the aggregates that are available for those InfoCubes, provided that is possible.

If you define several aggregates that form an aggregate hierarchy, SAP BW always tries to read the optimal aggregate that can satisfy the query. "Optimal" here means that the aggregate should contain as few data records as possible. If necessary, one or several aggregates are read subsequently when navigating to a low level.

Note that you cannot apply this method to DataStore objects.

Several or even many aggregates?
The creation of efficient aggregates requires a certain degree of technological know-how and experience regarding user behavior in relation to the use of analytical applications. Creating aggregates involves implementation costs, while the operation of aggregates utilizes system resources. You should consider these aspects when using the aggregate technology. But, in addition to the real-life aspects, there are numerous (and often) irrational reservations that result in the partial or even complete avoidance of aggregates, which, in turn, leads to intolerable query response times.

Rational considerations
If you want to use this technology, it is helpful to determine the requirements, expectations, costs, and benefits, and take these aspects into account in the design phase of projects.

### 5.3.2    Defining Aggregates

#### Calling the Aggregate Maintenance

You can define aggregates in the **InfoProvider** view of the Data Warehousing Workbench of SAP BW (see Figure 5.7, Step 1).

[▪]
- ▶ To do this, right-click on the relevant InfoCube to open its context-sensitive menu, and select the **Maintain Aggregate** function (see Figure 5.7, Steps 2 and 3).

- ▶ If no aggregates have yet been configured for the selected InfoCube, the **Proposals for Aggregates** popup window is displayed. Then click on the **Create by Yourself** button (Step 4).

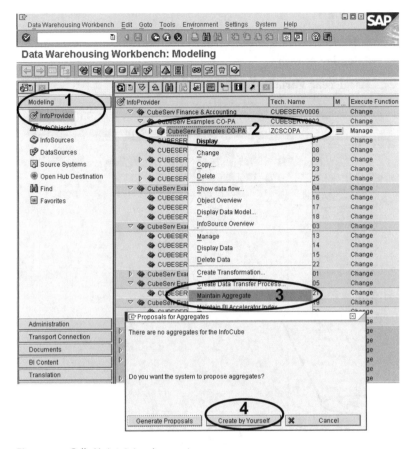

**Figure 5.7** Call: Maintaining Aggregates

### Configuring an Aggregate for the Initial Query View

▶ This opens the **Maintenance for Aggregate** dialog. Open the object   **[»]**
hierarchy in the left-hand frame in such a way that you can drag-
and-drop the **Calendar Year** (0CALYEAR) InfoObject into the
empty frame on the right (see Figure 5.8, Step 1).

▶ This action opens the **Enter Description for Aggregate** popup in
which you must enter a **short** and a **long description**. Then confirm your entries by clicking on the **Next** button (Steps 2 and 3).

▶ The InfoObject is then displayed in the aggregate configuration
work area. To comply with the query definition, you must also
transfer the following InfoObjects into the aggregate work area
(see Figure 5.9, Step 1):

- ▶ **Version**

- ▶ **Transaction Type**

- ▶ **Calendar Month**

- ▶ **Fiscal Year Variant**

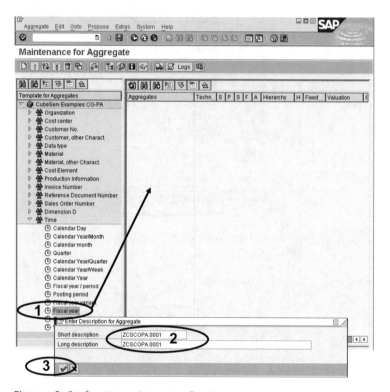

**Figure 5.8** Configuring an Aggregate, Part 1

Fixed value
selection

- ▶ To minimize the size of the aggregate to be configured, you must use fixed value selections. To do this, right-click on the **Calendar Year** InfoObject to open its context-sensitive menu, and select the **Fixed Value** function (see Figure 5.9, Steps 2 and 3).

- ▶ This opens the **Input Help** popup window for the selected InfoObject. Click on the required value (in the example: **Calendar Year 2004**) and then click on the **Transfer** button (Steps 4 and 5).

- ▶ Complete the fixed value selections by selecting the following fixed values:

  - ▷ **Fiscal Year Variant V9**

  - ▷ **Transaction Type F**

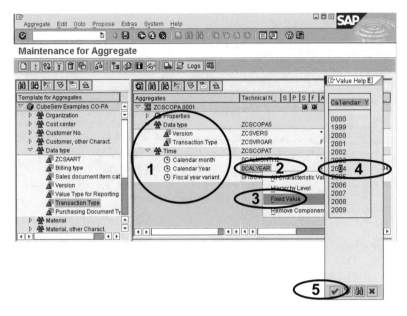

**Figure 5.9** Configuring an Aggregate, Part 2

### Activating Aggregates and Populating Aggregates

▶ Once you have completed the fixed value selections, highlight the top node with the aggregate name and click on the **Activate** button (see Figure 5.10, Steps 1 and 2). This opens the **Subsequently Aggregate the Aggregates of an InfoCube** popup. Click on the **Start** button to generate the aggregate (Step 3).

[✓]

▶ When the aggregate has been generated successfully, the **Execution time of the aggregation** popup opens. Click on the **Immediate** button (see Figure 5.11, Step 1).

Populating the aggregate

▶ Then close the **Subsequently Aggregate the Aggregates of an InfoCube** popup by clicking on the respective button (see Figure 5.10, Step 4).

▶ Once the data has been aggregated, the system displays the green status and the number of records in the aggregate (here: 50) as well as the approximate aggregation factor (in the example: 21596, see Figure 5.11, Step 2).

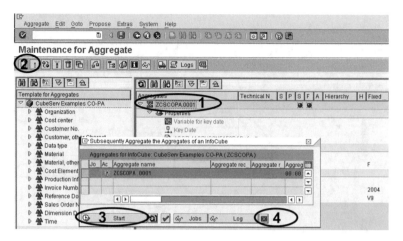

**Figure 5.10** Activating the Aggregate

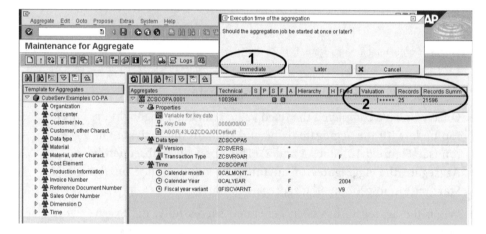

**Figure 5.11** Populating the Aggregate

### Defining Additional Aggregates

▶ To minimize the query runtime when drilling down by the sold-to country, you must define an other aggregate, **ZCSCOPA.0002**, that contains the additional characteristic **Sold-to Country** (see Figure 5.12, Step 1)

▶ Finally, to minimize the query runtime for an additional drill-down by the invoice number when selecting Sold-to Country Germany, you must define an additional aggregate, **ZCSCOPA.0003**, that contains the other characteristic, **Invoice Number**, and the fixed value selection, **Sold-to Country Germany** (Step 2).

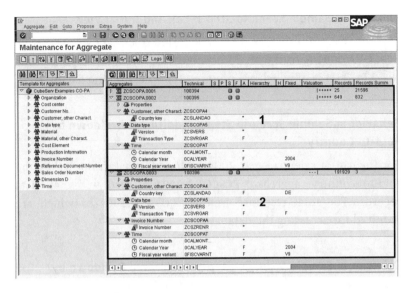

**Figure 5.12** Additional Aggregates

### Aggregate Sizes

These three aggregates minimize the number of database accesses for the described navigations. The aggregates now contain only a fraction of the data records of the InfoCube (0.0001% to 1.1%, see Table 5.1).

| Aggregate | Records | % InfoCube |
|---|---|---|
| ZCSCOPA.0001 | 25 | 0.043021% |
| ZCSCOPA.0002 | 649 | 0.106012% |
| ZCSCOPA.0003 | 191,929 | 9.476936% |

**Table 5.1** Aggregates, Number of Records, and Relation to the InfoCube

For this reason, when using aggregates, the number of accesses to the data records to be read is minimized compared to an access via the InfoCube.

*Minimizing records to be read*

### 5.3.3 Functionality of Aggregates

When calling the query and the navigations described, the following response time behavior occurs due to the provision of aggregates (see access specifications in Section 5.2.2):

**Behavior in Sample Scenario Step 1: Call and Initial View**

For the call of calendar year 2004 described above, aggregate **ZCSCOPA.0001** is read with 25 data records. The total response time is 1.93s, 0.043s of which are required for accessing the database.

**Behavior in Sample Scenario Step 2: Additional Drilldown by Sold-to Country**

For the call of calendar year 2004 with additional drilldown by the sold-to country, aggregate **ZCSCOPA.0002** is read with 649 data records. The total response time is 2.03s, 0.106s of which are required for accessing the database.

**Behavior in Sample Scenario Step 3: Additional Drilldown by Invoice Number with Selection of Sold-to Country Germany**

For the call of calendar year 2004 with additional drilldown by the invoice number and selection of the sold-to country Germany, aggregate **ZCSCOPA.0003** is read with 191,929 data records. The total response time is 174.7s, 9.47s of which are required for accessing the database (see Figure 5.13, Steps 1 and 2).

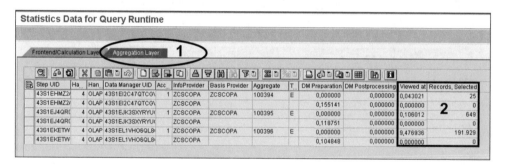

**Figure 5.13** Reducing the Number of Data Records to be Read and the Response Time by Using Aggregates

Portion of data-
base access

The accesses described above show that the database access times can be significantly reduced if you use aggregates. Consequently, the query runtime is reduced as well, corresponding to the portion of total response time required for the database access. In Steps 1 and 2, in which the database access time represents an essential part of the total response time, the reduction of query runtime is therefore considerable. Due to the high values for reading the texts and the data transfer in Step 3, the use of the aggregate does not lead to any significant reduction of the query runtime.

The degree of effectiveness of the aggregate is based on the small number of data records to be read (see Table 5.2). In Steps 1 and 2, these are clearly less than 1% of the data records that are to be read from the F and E tables when accessing the InfoCube. For Step 3, there is a reduction of almost 67%, even though this doesn't have any positive effect on the response time (see above).

**Effectiveness**

| | InfoCube | Read by InfoCube | % | Read by aggregate | % |
|---|---|---|---|---|---|
| Step 1 | 17,303,206 | 1,079,816 | 6.2 | 25 | 0.002 |
| Step 2 | 17,303,206 | 1,079,816 | 6.2 | 649 | 0.06 |
| Step 3 | 17,303,206 | 570,771 | 3.3 | 191,929 | 33.63 |

Table 5.2 Degree of Effectiveness of Aggregates Concerning Data Records to Be Read

**Assessment**

The example shows that the number of data records to be read can be significantly reduced by using aggregates. Provided you have implemented the right configurations, you can also reduce the query runtime significantly. Consequently, using aggregates is generally useful and highly recommended.

> Note, however, that aggregate synchronizations place a considerable load on the system and that the configuration of aggregates involves quite some work. For the small example described above, at least one or maybe even two aggregates would make sense.

**[«]**

This extra work represents a major disadvantage of the aggregate technology.

## 5.4 Performance Optimization Using BI Accelerator

### 5.4.1 The Concept of the BI Accelerator

The BI Accelerator integrated in SAP NetWeaver 2004s is a new technology provided for SAP BW, which, for the first time, is a departure from the traditional concept of materialized relational structures. The SAP documentation describes it as follows:

> *"BI Accelerator enables quick access to any data in the InfoCube with low administration effort and is especially useful for sophisticated scenarios with unpredictable query types, high volumes of data, and a high frequency of queries."[3]*

Indexing BI Accelerator is based on the principle of *indexing* (see Figure 5.14). This is described in the documentation as follows:

> *"A BI Accelerator index is a redundant data store of a BI InfoCube on the BI Accelerator server ... A BI Accelerator index contains all the data of a BI InfoCube in a compressed but not aggregated form. The BI Accelerator index stores the data at the same level of granularity as the InfoCube. It consists of several, possibly split indexes that correspond to the tables of the enhanced star schema and a "logical" index which, depending on the definition of the star schema, contains the metadata of the BI Accelerator index."[4]*

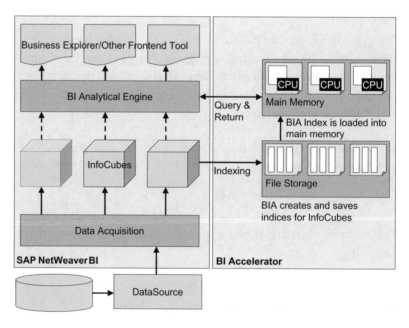

**Figure 5.14** The Operating Principle of BI Accelerator

---

3 See SAP documentation: *http://help.sap.com/saphelp_nw2004s/helpdata/en/06/49c0417951d117e10000000a155106/content.htm.*
4 Ibid.

Therefore, the BI Accelerator is based on optimizing the access via indexing and buffering techniques in the BI Accelerator server.

Optimal access instead of aggregation

*"The BI Accelerator server is a TREX system as an installation of a BI Accelerator engine. The data of the BI InfoCube is kept and processed entirely in the main memory of the BI accelerator server."*[5]

### 5.4.2 BI Accelerator: Technical Background

The backbone of the BI Accelerator is the blade technology (see Figure 5.15). This technology provides an extremely compact design, low upgrade costs, and you can easily integrate individual *server blades* into the *chassis* by inserting them into dedicated *server slots*. The chassis connects all servers with the central administration module.

Blade technology

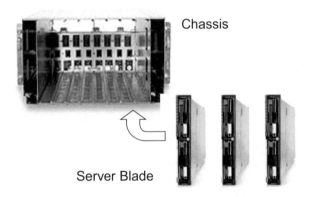

**Figure 5.15** The BI Accelerator Is Based on the Blade Technology

A server blade can host up to 4 CPUs and provide up to 64GB of memory. A chassis, in turn, can host 8 x 4 CPUs/64GB slots. This allows for configurations of up to 32 CPUs and 512 GB of main memory.

The operating system used is the 64-bit version of SUSE Linux Enterprise Server 9. This operating system is the basis for the SAP component, TREX, which is known as a search engine. This enables you to index the contents of the BI query in the cache of the blade infrastructure and to handle individual queries directly in the main memory.

Operating system

---

5 Ibid.

Due to the large number of CPUs and because all data is stored in the main memory, TREX can handle numerous processes simultaneously, which results in a much higher throughput rate than can be expected from the BI system.

As mentioned, BI Accelerator uses SAP's TREX technology. You should note, however, that this technology is not to be mistaken with the TREX that is used as a search engine for unstructured data. These are two different types of installations.

### BI Accelerator Configuration

"Out in a box"  SAP provides BI Accelerator as "out in a box" and with a "ZERO administration" architecture.

RFC connections  The connection between BI Server and BI Accelerator is established via an RFC connection; however, this connection must provide very fast access to BI Accelerator. It is therefore mandatory that you provide BI Accelerator with the fastest networking technology (1GBit or higher) in the same subnet as the BI system.

**[»]**  You can connect BI Accelerator within a few minutes to the BI system and use the new functionality immediately.

Technical process  If an InfoCube is prepared for use in BI Accelerator, the data is indexed, partitioned, and highly compressed in BI Accelerator. Data that is prepared in this way is then saved in the BI Accelerator disk subsystem and stored actively in the main memory (cache).

### A Separate Disk Subsystem for BI Accelerator

Why does BI Accelerator need a separate disk subsystem? Suppose you want to index a large quantity of data. With each restart of the system, the entire data quantity would have to be read and transferred to BI Accelerator. Not only would this take a lot of time, it would also require many system resources.

Data storage in the disk subsystem  Because the data is stored in BI Accelerator, the system can access the entire indexed dataset stored in the main memory within minutes in the event of a restart of BI Accelerator.

To make this possible, a very fast disk subsystem must be available to BI Accelerator (see Figure 5.16).

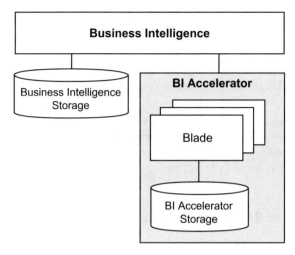

**Figure 5.16** Data Storage

**BI Accelerator Sizing**

Regarding the use of BI Accelerator, SAP has entered close collaborations with several hardware vendors. Based on a blade-storage technology, these vendors provide an out-of-a-box solution for BI Accelerator. This solution is only available as a total solution consisting of hardware and software.

*SAP and hardware vendors*

If you want to implement the BI Accelerator solution as an SAP customer, you can choose from the following configurations:

- ▶ Small T-shirt size
    - ▷ 10 parallel user sessions
    - ▷ 250 million rows total
    - ▷ 500 bytes/row → 500 GB file system
- ▶ Medium T-shirt size
    - ▷ 50 parallel user sessions
    - ▷ 500 million rows total
    - ▷ 500 bytes/row → 1 TB file system
- ▶ Large T-shirt size
    - ▷ 100 parallel user sessions
    - ▷ 1000 million rows total
    - ▷ 500 bytes/row → 2 TB file system

*Small T-shirt size*

*Medium T-shirt size*

*Large T-shirt size*

Depending on the configuration required, the hardware partner delivers BI Accelerator on the respective platform that is defined for the categories listed above.

[»] At the time this book was written, SAP did not intend to provide BI Accelerator as a DVD source download.

The reason for this decision is that SAP and its hardware partners have designed an optimally configured version for each hardware platform, and only an optimally configured hardware and software infrastructure can meet the high requirements of BI Accelerator.

### 5.4.3 Definition of BI Accelerator Indices

#### Calling the BI Accelerator Index

You can set up the BI Accelerator application in the **InfoProvider** view of the Data Warehousing Workbench of SAP BW (see Figure 5.17, Step 1).

[■] ▸ To do this, right-click on the relevant InfoCube to open its context-sensitive menu, and select the **Maintain BI Accelerator Index** function (Steps 2 and 3).

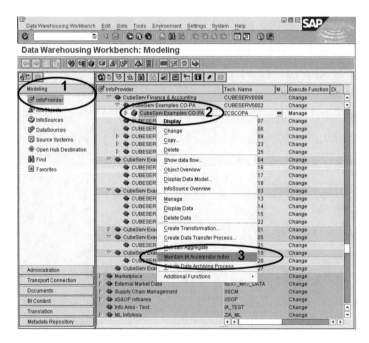

**Figure 5.17** Calling the BI Accelerator Index Maintenance

▶ If the BI Accelerator index has not yet been created for the selected InfoCube, the popup **Step 1: Create a BIA Index** opens displaying the message, **Do you want to create the BIA index for InfoCube 'ZCSCOPA'?** (see Figure 5.18, Step 1).

Activating the BI Accelerator index

▶ Click on **Continue** to activate the BI Accelerator index (Step 2).

▶ Once you have successfully created the BI Accelerator index, the popup **Step 2: Fill a BIA Index** opens displaying the message, **Do you want to fill the BIA index for InfoCube 'ZCSCOPA'?** (Step 3).

Filling the BI Accelerator index

▶ Click on the **Continue** button (Step 4).

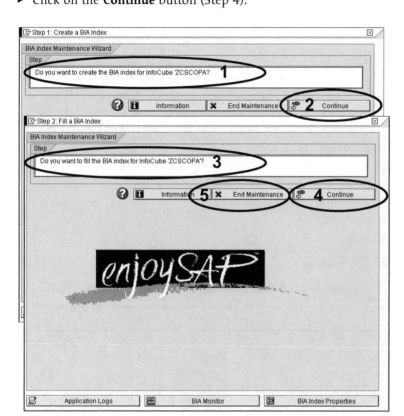

**Figure 5.18** Call: Creating and Filling the BIA Index

▶ After that, the **Start Time** popup opens that allows you to parameterize the job that fills the BIA index. You must parameterize the job accordingly. In this example, it starts immediately. Therefore, you should click on the **Immediate** button and then click on the **Save** button (see Figure 5.19, Steps 1 and 2).

Scheduling the BIA index filling job

Job monitoring ▶ The procedure described in the previous sections schedules a job into standard SAP job scheduling. If necessary, you can trace the BIA filling job using the SAP job monitoring function via the following menu path: **System · Services · Jobs · Job Overview**.

▶ The **Job Overview** dialog displays the status and progress of the selected job (Step 3).

Indexing ▶ Depending on the quantity structure and complexity, the creation of indices occurs either in one or in several parallel processes. In this complex data model containing more than 17.3 million data records in the InfoCube, the process is carried out within 61 minutes and consists of several parallel indexing processes (Step 4).

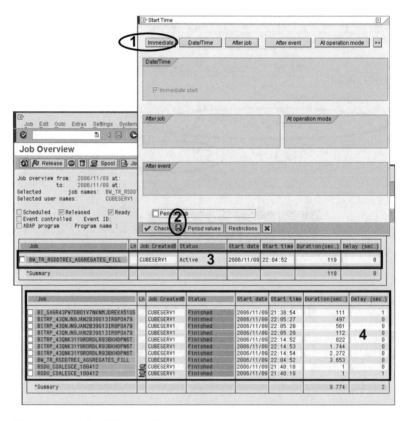

**Figure 5.19** Job for Filling the BIA Index

Completing the ▶ Click on the **End Maintenance** button in the **Fill a BIA Index** maintenance popup to return to the Data Warehousing Workbench (see Figure 5.18, Step 5).

### Deleting an Existing BIA Index

When you call the BI Accelerator maintenance again (see Figure 5.20), the popup **Step 1: Delete a BIA Index** opens.

► Click on the **Continue** button (see Figure 5.20, Step 1) and answer the security prompt in the popup **Deletion of BIA Indexes** by clicking on the **Yes** button (Step 2). [▪]

► Then you can exit the dialog by clicking on the **End Maintenance** button (Step 3).

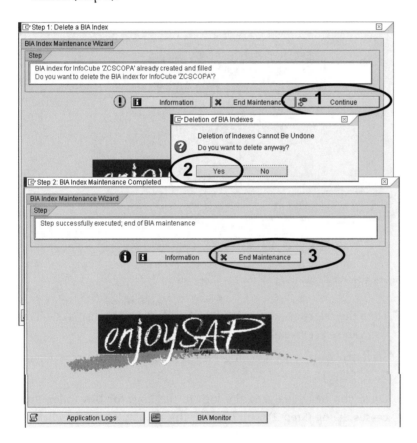

**Figure 5.20** Deleting a BIA Index

► The popup **Step 1: Delete a BIA Index** also allows you to call the application logs for display. This is imperative in the event of a termination, erroneous processing, or when a runtime analysis is required. To display the logs, click on the **Application Logs** button (see Figure 5.21, Step 1).

Application logs

▶ In the **Log Selection** popup, select the required log by clicking on it (in this example, that is the log for the initial filling job) and confirm the selection by clicking on the **Next** button (Steps 2 and 3).

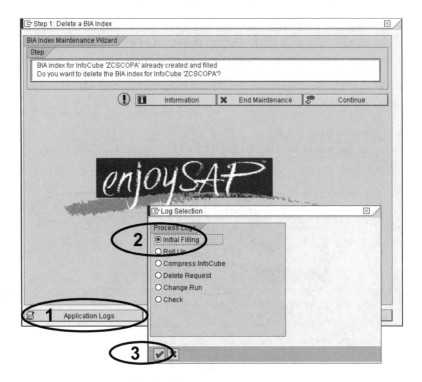

**Figure 5.21** Application Log for the BIA Index, Part 1

▶ Then the selection screen **Analyse Application Log** displays where you can select specific logs, if necessary.

▶ Start the display by clicking on the **Execute** button (see Figure 5.22, Step 1).

▶ Once you have analyzed the logs in the **Logs for BIA Index Processes** dialog (Step 2), you can exit this display screen by clicking twice on the **Back** button (Step 3).

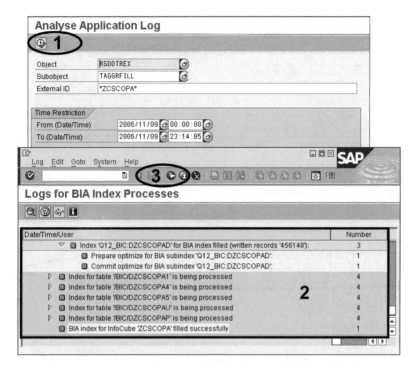

**Figure 5.22** Application Log for the BIA Index, Part 2

### BIA Monitor

You can also call the BIA Monitor in the popup **Step 1: Delete a BIA Index**. [•]

▶ To do this, click on the **BIA Monitor** button (see Figure 5.23, Step 1).

▶ This displays the quick overview of the BIA Monitor (Step 2). Here you can click on the **More Extensive Monitor** button (Step 3) to open the **BI Accelerator Monitor** dialog.

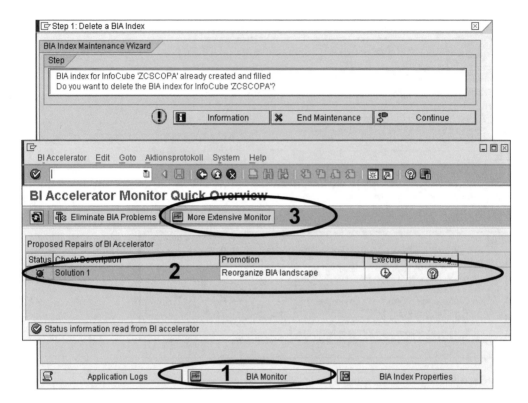

**Figure 5.23** BIA Monitor, Part 1

▶ There you can analyze and resolve the problem that was displayed in the quick overview. Select the **Current Results** tab (see Figure 5.24, Step 1) and analyze a current problem either by calling the long description[6] (Step 2) or by clicking on the **Execute** button (Step 3).

▶ You can exit the BIA Monitor by clicking on the **Back** button twice (Step 4).

---

6 SAP documentation: "This action reorganizes the indices on the blades in order to obtain an equal distribution of the indices and to improve system utilization. During the reorganization you can still perform search actions, whereas the BI Accelerator Server is locked for other actions. You can start this action from the BI system."

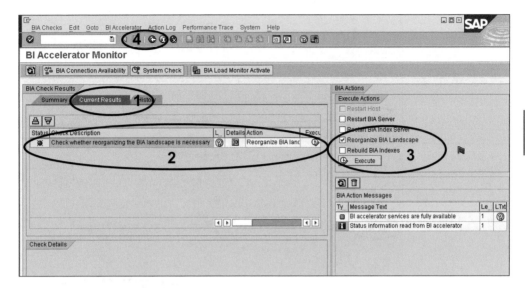

**Figure 5.24** BIA Monitor, Part 2

**Maintaining BIA Index Properties**

You can also maintain the BIA index properties in the popup **Step 1: Delete a BIA Index**.

▸ To do this, click on the **BIA Index Properties** button (see Figure 5.25, Step 1).   **[»]**

▸ In the **Maintain BIA Index Properties** popup, you can then select the respective option to either deactivate an existing BIA index (without deleting it) or to reactivate a deactivated BIA index (Step 2).

▸ You can also store the entire dataset in the main memory by selecting the corresponding option (Step 3).

▸ Finally, you can save the changed settings by clicking on the **Confirm Values** button (Step 4).

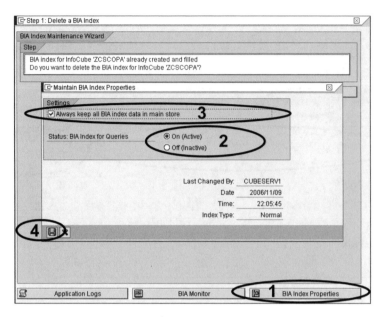

**Figure 5.25** Maintaining BIA Index Properties

### 5.4.4 The Functionality of BI Accelerator Indices

When calling the query and the navigations described, the following response time behavior occurs due to the provision of aggregates (see access specifications in Section 5.2.2):

**Behavior in Sample Scenario Step 1: Call and Initial View**

For the call of calendar year 2004 described earlier in this chapter, 1,079,816 data records are read via the BIA index (**ZCSCOPA$X**). The total response time is 0.72s, 0.41s of which are required for accessing the database.

**Behavior in Sample Scenario Step 2: Additional Drilldown by Sold-to Country**

For the call of calendar year 2004 with the additional drilldown by the sold-to country, 1,079,816 data records are read via the BIA index (**ZCSCOPA$X**). The total response time is 1.01s, 0.44s of which are required for accessing the database.

### Behavior in Sample Scenario Step 3: Additional Drilldown by Invoice Number with Selection of Sold-to Country Germany

For the call of calendar year 2004 with the additional drilldown by the invoice number and selection of sold-to country Germany, 570,771 data records are read via the BIA index (**ZCSCOPA$X**). The total response time is 174s, 8.70s of which are required for accessing the database (see Figure 5.26, Steps 1 and 2).

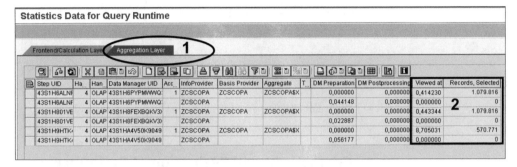

**Figure 5.26** Reducing the Response Time Using BI Accelerator

The accesses described above show that the database access times can be significantly reduced if you use BI Accelerator. Consequently, the query runtime is reduced as well, corresponding to the portion of total response time required for the database access. In Steps 1 and 2, in which the database access time represents an essential part of the total response time, the reduction of query runtime is therefore considerable. Due to the high values for reading the texts and the data transfer in Step 3, the use of the aggregate does not lead to any significant reduction of the query runtime.

**Time required for database access**

The degree of effectiveness of using BI Accelerator depends on the access optimization for the BIA index. In Steps 1 and 2, the BIA index reduces the database access time by 98% and 88% respectively, compared to the situation without aggregates and BI Accelerator. In Step 3, the database access time does not represent a significant portion of time. This BI Accelerator does not cause any significant improvement for this access.

**Effectiveness**

**Assessment**

The example shows that you can significantly reduce the database access time by using BI Accelerator (see Table 5.3). Provided you have implemented the right configurations, you can also reduce the query runtime considerably. Consequently, using BI Accelerator is generally useful and highly recommended.

| Process step | Read by InfoCube | DB time for InfoCube access | DB time with BI Accelerator | Change of access time in % |
|---|---|---|---|---|
| Step 1 | 1,079,816 | 80.8 | 0.41 | −99.5% |
| Step 2 | 1,079,816 | 64.01 | 0.44 | −99.3% |
| Step 3 | 570,771 | 64.9 | 8.70 | −86.6% |

**Table 5.3** Degree of Effectiveness of the BIA Index Regarding Access Times

## 5.5 Comparison and Evaluation of Performance Optimization Tools

**[+]** Both technologies (aggregates and BI Accelerator) provide considerable improvements with regard to the database access times. For this reason, we recommend using these technologies.

*Advantages and disadvantages of the aggregate technology*

The advantages of using aggregates are that you can create optimal aggregates for dedicated accesses, which results in extremely minimized response times. The disadvantages of using aggregates are that the work and therefore the costs involved in creating and maintaining aggregates can be very high and that extremely long runtimes can occur when filling aggregates (see Table 5.4).

*Advantages and disadvantages of BI Accelerator*

The advantages of the BI Accelerator are that a minimum amount of work is required in implementing this tool and in creating the BIA index. Moreover, only little know-how is required and the technology can be used with all types of accesses (and not only to dedicated ones, as in the case of aggregates). The disadvantages of the BI Accelerator are that this tool requires that you make hardware investments and that it doesn't optimally support certain accesses (see Table 5.4).

| Process step | DB time with aggregates | DB time with BI Accelerator | Access time BIA vs. Aggregates in % |
|---|---|---|---|
| Step 1 | 0.043 | 0.41 | +863% |
| Step 2 | 0.106 | 0.44 | +318% |
| Step 3 | 9.47 | 8.70 | –8% |

**Table 5.4** Comparison Between Aggregates and BI Accelerator

**Usage Recommendation**

To achieve optimal system performance, you should use both BI Accelerator and aggregates. Important InfoCubes are supported by BI Accelerator, while others may not be supported. For queries that are not sufficiently supported by BI Accelerator, you should use dedicated aggregates.

Use the following access flow:

1. Access to BIA index, if available and not deactivated

2. Access to aggregates if appropriate aggregates are available and no previous BI Accelerator access occurred

3. Access to InfoCubes if neither the BIA index nor aggregates can be used

For this reason, you must deactivate the use of BI Accelerator for those **[+]** queries that are to use aggregates.

▶ In the current version, you can deactivate BI Accelerator by main- **[⬝]** taining the **Reports Directory (RSRREPDIR)** table (see Figure 5.27, Step 1).

▶ To enable the deactivation, you must fill the field **No HPA Index (NOHPA)** with an **X** character (Step 2). This means that BI Accelerator is no longer used for the query in question and that if aggregates exist, the aggregates will be accessed.

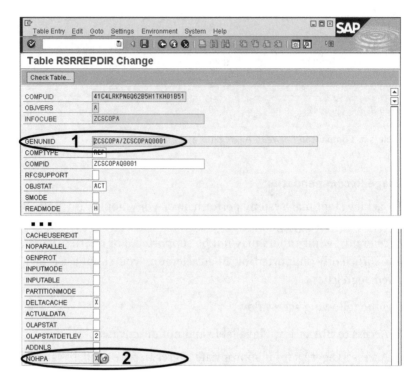

**Figure 5.27** Deactivating the BIA Index Access for Individual Queries

*In many SAP BW installations, the need to redesign the data model arises after several years of operation. SAP meets this requirement by providing the first redesign components: repartitioning and remodeling.*

# 6 Redesign Functions: Repartitioning and Remodeling

## 6.1 Redesign Requirements in SAP BW Applications

Many SAP BW applications were designed and implemented several years ago so that today there is a need to redesign them. Some of today's redesign options are new, sometimes the growing quantity of data and its specific values requires changes, and sometimes an inappropriate data model has been implemented for a particular reason, all prompting the need to redesign requirements.

Redesign requirements

In SAP NetWeaver 2004s, SAP provides the repartitioning and remodeling functions for InfoCubes in SAP BW as the first redesign components.

First redesign components

## 6.2 Repartitioning InfoProviders

### 6.2.1 An Overview of the Functionality

The partitioning process splits datasets into separate, redundant-free units and is used for optimizing the performance for both reporting and the modification of datasets. Partitioning can be done using the time characteristics 0CALMONTH (calendar year/month) and fiscal year/period (0FISCPER) as a basis.

Partitioning

For example, if partitioning is based on 0CALMONTH (calendar year/month) and partitions are needed for the calendar months of the years 2000 through 2006, a total of 12 partitions is generated for each of these seven years, as well as two additional partitions for the calendar months smaller than 01.2000 and 12.2006.

Mandatory: consistent time characteristics A critical factor for increasing the performance is that the time dimension is constant, that is, that all characteristics of the time dimension of the InfoCube in question are contained in the logical time hierarchy. For example, this would not be the case if an entry with calendar day 00.00.0000 (initial) existed for calendar month 02.2006 (see Figure 6.1).

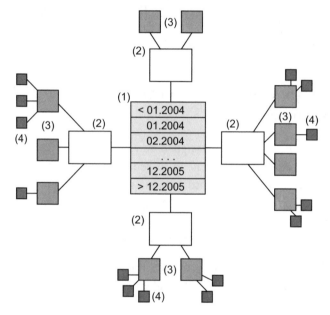

**Figure 6.1** Partitioning the Fact Table of an InfoCube
(1 = Fact Table, 2 = Dimension Tables, 3 = SID Tables, 4 = Master Data)

The release information for SAP NetWeaver 2004s contains the following description in the section on enterprise data warehousing (EDW):

SAP documentation on repartitioning

*"With partitioning, the runtime for reading and modifying access to InfoCubes and DataStore objects can be decreased. Using repartitioning, non-partitioned InfoCubes and DataStore objects can be partitioned, or the partitioning schema for already partitioned InfoCubes and DataStore objects can be adapted".[1]*

---

1 See SAP documentation: *http://help.sap.com/saphelp_nw04s/helpdata/en/62/ f71342eb11de2ce10000000a1550b0/content.htm.*

Repartitioning of InfoCubes is supported for the following databases:

- ▶ UDB for UNIX/WINDOWS
- ▶ DB2 for z/OSDB2/OS390
- ▶ DB2/AS400
- ▶ ORACLE
- ▶ MSSQL

The repartitioning of DataStore objects is currently supported only on DB2 for UNIX/WINDOWS.[2]

## 6.2.2 Sample Scenario for Repartitioning

Contrary to partitioning, which can only be carried out if no data is contained in the InfoCube, repartitioning can be performed if data has already been loaded (see **Administrator Workbench · InfoProvider · Manage Data Targets**, Figure 6.2, highlight).

Data in InfoCube ·
Repartitioning

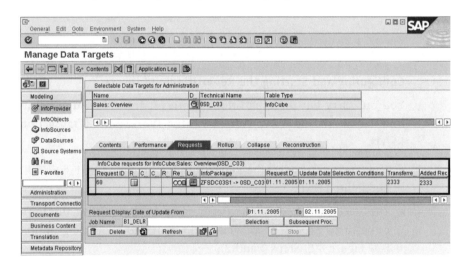

**Figure 6.2** Repartitioning and Preserving Existing Data

In the following example, the business content InfoCube **0SD_C03** **(Sales and Distribution: Overview)** contains data from a large period of time. As this InfoCube has never been partitioned before, you now want to repartition it in order to optimize performance (see **Administrator Workbench · Display InfoCube**, Figure 6.3, Steps 1 to 4).

---

2  Ibid.

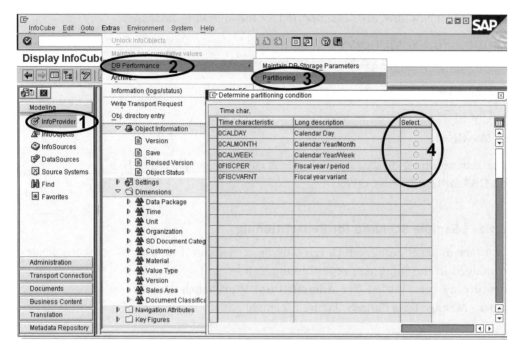

**Figure 6.3** Non-Partitioned InfoCube

### Configuring and Starting the Repartitioning Process

You can carry out the repartitioning process from the **Administra-tion** tab in the **SAP BW Administrator Workbench** (Transaction RSA1).

**[▪]**
- There you must select the **Repartitioning** function (see Figure 6.4, highlighted text).

- The selection screen for repartitioning displays. Select the Info-Cube to be processed as well as the required processing option (see Figure 6.5, Steps 1 and 2).

The following processing options are available:

- Adding Partitions
- Merging Partitions
- Complete Repartitioning

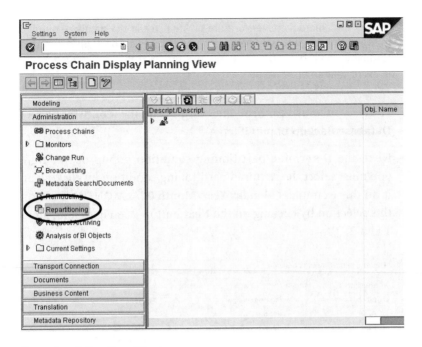

**Figure 6.4** Calling Repartitioning

▶ Because the InfoCube selected for the sample scenario has not been partitioned yet, you use the **Complete Repartitioning** option.

▶ Then click on the **Initialize** button of the repartitioning request (Step 3).

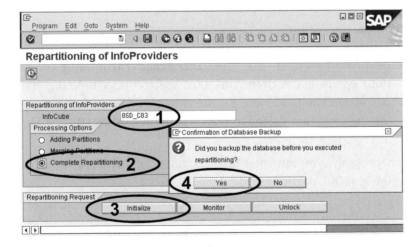

**Figure 6.5** Selection Screen for Repartitioning

[!] Because fundamental conversions are taking place in the database during the repartitioning process, SAP recommends that you back up the database before the process starts; otherwise, you run the risk of losing data in the event that an error occurs.

▶ Lastly, you must confirm the warning in the **Confirmation of Database Backup** popup (Step 4).

Determining the partitioning condition

▶ Next, the **Determine partitioning condition** popup opens. Here you must select the required partitioning condition by clicking on it (in this example, **Calendar Year/Month 0CALMONTH**). Confirm this selection by clicking on the **Next** button (see Figure 6.6, Steps 1 and 2).

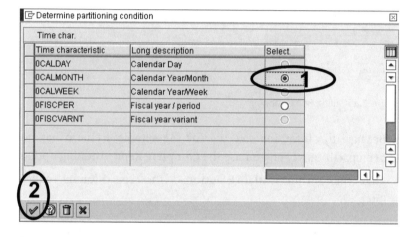

**Figure 6.6** Determining the Partitioning Condition

Determining the value range

▶ Once you have done that, the **Value Range (Partitioning Condition)** popup opens. Here you must specify the value range for which you want to create partitions based on the selected partitioning condition **Calendar Year/Month (0CALMONTH)** (see Figure 6.7, Step 1).

▶ Optionally, you can enter the maximum number of partitions in the **Max. no. partitions** field (Step 2).

[!] If the value you enter here is smaller than the result of the formula ("Number from value range + 2"), SAP will determine the partitions that will not correspond to the entry of the value range.

▶ The settings are transferred using the **Next** button (Step 3).

▶ In the **Aggs** popup, you must then specify whether you want the aggregates to be rebuilt after the repartitioning process. Confirm this by clicking on the **Yes** button (Step 4).

▶ Finally, an information popup displays, indicating that a repartitioning request (with background program execution) has been created for the selected InfoCube. Confirm this popup as well (Step 5).

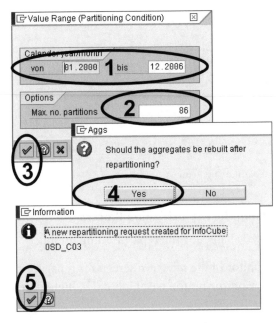

**Figure 6.7** Determining the Value Range for Partitioning

### Scheduling the Repartitioning Request

The request that has been created based on the above definitions must now be scheduled. Scheduling the repartitioning request is carried out in compliance with the requirements that exist in traditional SAP job scheduling.

▶ In the sample scenario, you must choose the **Immediate** option in the **Start Time** popup. Then, save the setting (see Figure 6.8, Steps 1 and 2).

▶ Next, confirm the information popup regarding the start of the repartitioning request (Step 3).

[**⚷**]

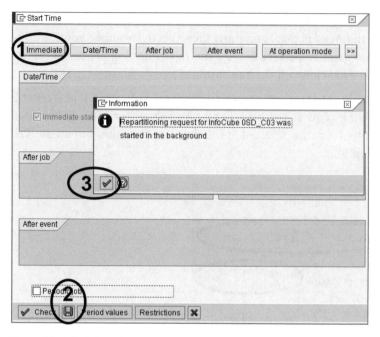

**Figure 6.8** Scheduling the Repartitioning Request

### Monitoring and Controlling the Repartitioning Process

A monitoring function is available for the repartitioning option.

[■] ▶ You can launch the monitor in the selection screen for repartitioning by clicking on the **Monitor** button (see Figure 6.9, highlighted
text).

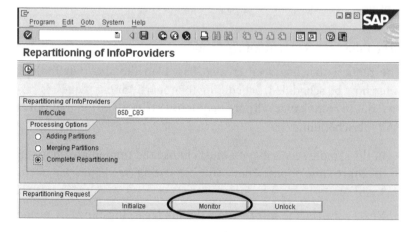

**Figure 6.9** Calling the Repartitioning Monitor

- ▶ The monitor logs the steps carried out during repartitioning along with the respective results (see Figure 6.10, highlighted text).

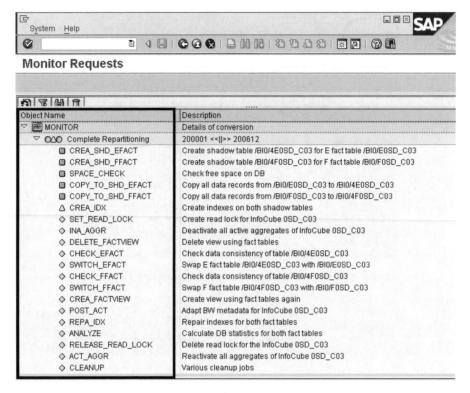

| Object Name | Description |
|---|---|
| ▽ 🖳 MONITOR | Details of conversion |
| ▽ ⊘⊘ Complete Repartitioning | 200001 <<‖>> 200612 |
| ☐ CREA_SHD_EFACT | Create shadow table /BI0/4E0SD_C03 for E fact table /BI0/E0SD_C03 |
| ☐ CREA_SHD_FFACT | Create shadow table /BI0/4F0SD_C03 for F fact table /BI0/F0SD_C03 |
| ☐ SPACE_CHECK | Check free space on DB |
| ☐ COPY_TO_SHD_EFACT | Copy all data records from /BI0/E0SD_C03 to /BI0/4E0SD_C03 |
| ☐ COPY_TO_SHD_FFACT | Copy all data records from /BI0/F0SD_C03 to /BI0/4F0SD_C03 |
| △ CREA_IDX | Create indexes on both shadow tables |
| ◇ SET_READ_LOCK | Create read lock for InfoCube 0SD_C03 |
| ◇ INA_AGGR | Deactivate all active aggregates of InfoCube 0SD_C03 |
| ◇ DELETE_FACTVIEW | Delete view using fact tables |
| ◇ CHECK_EFACT | Check data consistency of table /BI0/4E0SD_C03 |
| ◇ SWITCH_EFACT | Swap E fact table /BI0/4E0SD_C03 with /BI0/E0SD_C03 |
| ◇ CHECK_FFACT | Check data consistency of table /BI0/4F0SD_C03 |
| ◇ SWITCH_FFACT | Swap F fact table /BI0/4F0SD_C03 with /BI0/F0SD_C03 |
| ◇ CREA_FACTVIEW | Create view using fact tables again |
| ◇ POST_ACT | Adapt BW metadata for InfoCube 0SD_C03 |
| ◇ REPA_IDX | Repair indexes for both fact tables |
| ◇ ANALYZE | Calculate DB statistics for both fact tables |
| ◇ RELEASE_READ_LOCK | Delete read lock for the InfoCube 0SD_C03 |
| ◇ ACT_AGGR | Reactivate all aggregates of InfoCube 0SD_C03 |
| ◇ CLEANUP | Various cleanup jobs |

**Figure 6.10**  Display of the Repartitioning Monitor

- ▶ You can trace the job by calling Transaction **Job Overview** (SM37). [Job log] Once you have selected the relevant job and clicked on the **Execute** button, the job overview displays (see Figures 6.11 and 6.12, highlighted text, Job RSDU_IC_COMP_REPART/0SD_C03).

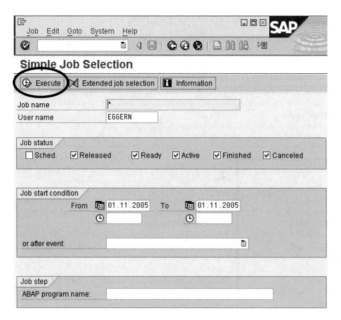

Figure 6.11 Calling the Job Overview for the Repartitioning Request

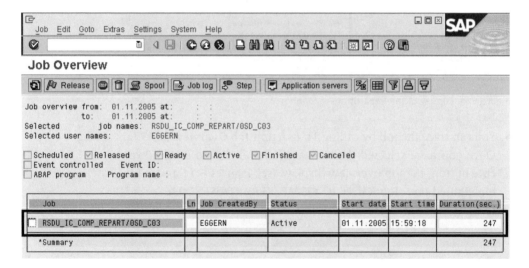

Figure 6.12 Job Overview for the Repartitioning Request

New partitioning
setting

▶ When you call the InfoCube definition, as shown in Figure 6.3, the new partitioning setting is displayed in the **Determine partitioning condition** popup once the repartitioning run is completed (see Figure 6.13, highlighted text).

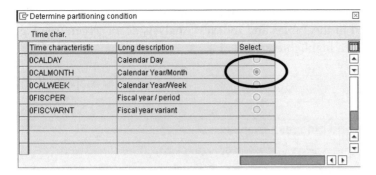

**Figure 6.13** Display of the New Partitioning Setting

▶ You can trace the changes to the database using Transaction **DB02** (Tables and Indexes Monitor). In the **Database Performance: Tables and Indexes** selection screen, click on the **Detailed analysis** button in the **Tables and indexes** section (see Figure 6.14, highlighted text).

**Changes to the database**

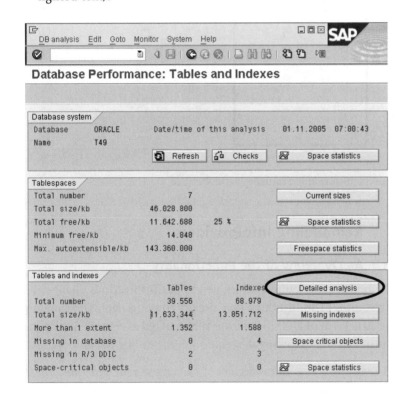

**Figure 6.14** Calling the Tables and Indexes Monitor (DB02)

▶ The partitions created for the fact table of the InfoCube are displayed in the **Tables and Indexes: Analysis** detail screen (see Figure 6.15, highlighted text).

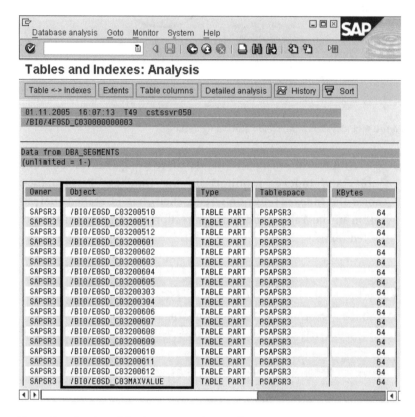

**Figure 6.15** Display of the Partitions in the Database

## 6.3 Remodeling InfoProviders

### 6.3.1 An Overview of the Functionality

The remodeling function
The remodeling function enables you to perform various changes to the structures of an InfoCube that already contains data. The changes to the structures of an InfoCube are summarized as remodeling rules. SAP provides the following description in the online documentation:

*"A remodeling rule is a collection of changes to your InfoCube. These changes are executed at the same time.*

*For InfoCubes, you have the following remodeling options:*

*For characteristics:*

▶ *Inserting or replacing characteristics with:*

▷ *Constants*

▷ *Attribute of an InfoObject within the same dimension*

▷ *Value of another InfoObject within the same dimension*

▷ *Customer exit (for user-specific code)*

▶ *Delete*

*For key figures:*

▶ *Inserting:*

▷ *Constants*

▷ *Customer exit (for user-specific code)*

▶ *Replacing key figures with:*

▷ *Customer exit (for user-specific code)*

▶ *Delete"*[3]

It is highly recommended that you consider the information provided by SAP with regard to using the remodeling function:

Prerequisites for remodeling

*"As a precaution, make a backup of your data before you start remodeling.*

*In addition, ensure that:*

▶ *You have stopped any process chains that run periodically and affect the corresponding InfoProvider. Do not restart these process chains until remodeling is finished.*

▶ *There is enough tablespace available on the database.*

▶ *After remodeling, check which BI objects that are connected to the InfoProvider (transformation rules, MultiProviders, queries and so on) have been deactivated. You have to reactivate these objects manually".* [4]

---

3  See SAP documentation: *http://help.sap.com/saphelp_nw04s/helpdata/en/58/ 85e5414f070640e10000000a1550b0/content.htm.*

4  Ibid.

### 6.3.2 Sample Scenario for Remodeling

In most SAP BW installations, you will always find the same reasons that warrant a remodeling:

▸ The chosen data model is inappropriate.

▸ The time dimension is inadequate and inconsistent, as is the case in numerous business content InfoCubes.

▸ Important characteristics are missing.

▸ Unused characteristics or key figures inflate the data model and (in the case of key figures) the quantity structure to a great extent.

For our sample scenario, we'll use the business content InfoCube 0SD_C01 (customer). The following redesign requirements exist for this InfoCube in our sample company:

▸ An InfoStructure of the Sales Information System has always been used as a data source and we'll continue to do so. For this reason, the data has always been delivered with only one time characteristic—here: **0CALMONTH (Calendar Year/Month)**—since this InfoCube was provided the first time.

▸ However, this means that the update of the other time characteristics of this InfoCube via the business content update rules occurs as initial (see Figures 6.16 and 6.17). Therefore, on the one hand, the time dimension is inconsistent (for example, see the previous remarks on partitioning). On the other hand, the existence of generally initial time characteristics in InfoCubes is not useful and rather confusing.

| Transfer Structure | | | | | | Communication Structure | | | | |
|---|---|---|---|---|---|---|---|---|---|---|
| Description | InfoObject | Type | Length | Field Name | | Description | InfoObject | Type | Length | Item |
| Calendar Day | 0CALDAY | DATS | 0008 | SPTAG | ➡ | Calendar Day | 0CALDAY | DATS | 0008 | 0002 |
| Calendar Year/Month | 0CALMONTH | NUMC | 0006 | SPMON | ➡ | Calendar Year/Month | 0CALMONTH | NUMC | 0006 | 0003 |
| Calendar Year/Week | 0CALWEEK | NUMC | 0006 | SPWOC | ➡ | Calendar Year/Week | 0CALWEEK | NUMC | 0006 | 0004 |
| Fiscal year/period | 0FISCPER | NUMC | 0007 | SPBUP | ➡ | Fiscal year/period | 0FISCPER | NUMC | 0007 | 0010 |
| Fiscal Year Variant | 0FISCVARNT | CHAR | 0002 | PERIV | ➡ | Fiscal Year Variant | 0FISCVARNT | CHAR | 0002 | 0011 |

**Figure 6.16** Business Content Transfer Rules for DataSource 2LIS_01_S001 into the InfoSource of the Same Name

| Communication Structure | | | | | InfoCube | | | |
|---|---|---|---|---|---|---|---|---|
| Description | InfoObject | Type | Length | | Description | InfoObject | Type | Length |
| **Time Characteristics** | | | | | | | | |
| | | 🗓 | K4 | ➡ | Fiscal year variant | OFISCVARNT | CHAR | 0002 |
| Calendar Day | 0CALDAY | DATS | 0008 | ➡ | Calendar Day | 0CALDAY | DATS | 0008 |
| Calendar Year/Month | 0CALMONTH | NUMC | 0006 | ➡ | Calendar Year/Month | 0CALMONTH | NUMC | 0006 |
| Calendar Year/Week | 0CALWEEK | NUMC | 0006 | ➡ | Calendar Year/Week | 0CALWEEK | NUMC | 0006 |
| Fiscal year / period | 0FISCPER | NUMC | 0007 | ➡ | Fiscal year / period | 0FISCPER | NUMC | 0007 |

**Figure 6.17** Business Content Update Rules for InfoSource 2LIS_01_S001 in Info-Cube 0SD_C01

▶ The characteristics that identify the sales area exist. However, the **0COMP_CODE (company code)** characteristic, which is usually very important, is not contained in the InfoCube. This makes the creation of useful MultiProviders and report-report interfaces to data from financial reporting and controlling very difficult if not impossible.

▶ In order to identify the data of the different source systems to be updated in the future, you want to include the **0SOURCESYSTEM (Source System ID)** characteristic in the InfoCube and initialize it using the source system ID of the source system that has been used up to now.

▶ The key figures regarding returns are not used for reporting purposes in the sample company and are therefore not needed in the InfoCube.

The starting point for the scenario is InfoCube **0SD_C01 (Customer)**, which is already filled with data (see Figure 6.18).

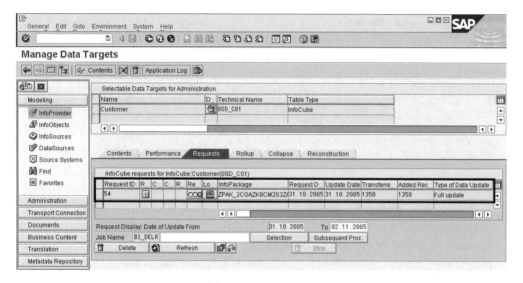

Figure 6.18 Remodeling and Preserving Existing Data

**Remodeling Rule for Implementing the Required Redesign**

[✦] ▸ To implement the redesign requirements, you must delete the inconsistent time characteristics **0CALDAY (Calendar Day)** and **0CALWEEK (Calendar Week)** from the **Time** dimension (see Figure 6.19, Step 1). These characteristics are provided in the source system only at the calendar year/month level and can therefore not be filled so that it makes sense.

▸ The **Sales Area** dimension (Step 2) must be complemented with the **0COMP_CODE (Company Code)** and **0SOURCESYSTEM (Source System ID)** characteristics. The **Company Code** characteristic must be initialized using the **0COMP_CODE** attribute of the **0SALESORG** characteristic (**Sales Organization**). The **Source System ID** is to be initialized using a constant.

▸ Finally, you must delete the key figures **0RTNSCST**, **0RTNSQTY**, **0RTNSVAL**, and **0RTNS_ITEMS** from the InfoCube as they are not relevant for reporting in our sample company.

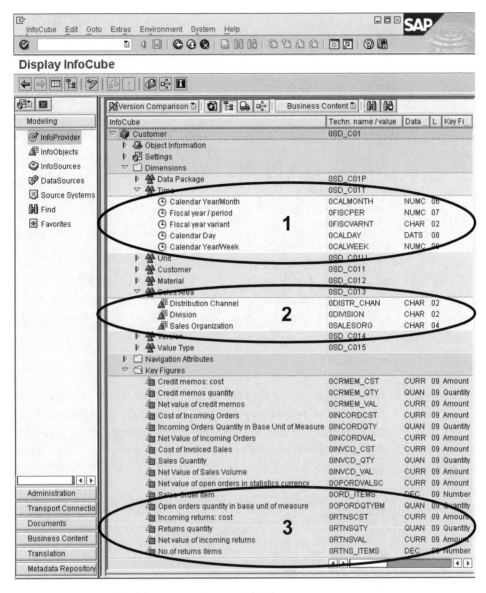

**Figure 6.19** Data Model of the Business Content InfoCube

## Configuring and Starting the Remodeling Process

You can carry out the remodeling process from the **Administration** tab in the **SAP BW Administrator Workbench** (Transaction RSA1).

► Select the **Remodeling** function (see Figure 6.20, Step 1).          [■]

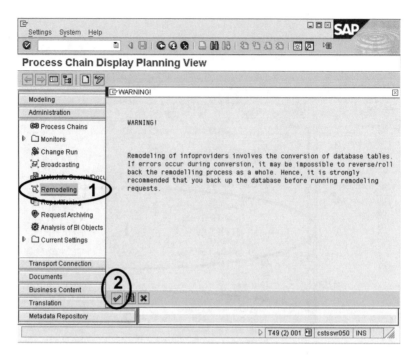

**Figure 6.20** Calling the Remodeling Function

▶ In the initial screen for remodeling, you must enter the technical name for the **remodeling rule** to be created (in the example that's **0SD_C01R1**) and the **InfoProvider** to be changed (here InfoCube **0SD_C01**). Click on the **Create** button (see Figure 6.21, Steps 1 and 2).

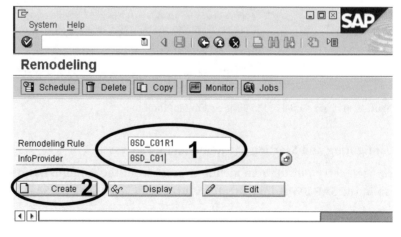

**Figure 6.21** Initial Remodeling Screen

▶ The **Remodeling** popup opens in which you can enter a description of the remodeling rule. You can complete your entries by clicking on the **Transfer** button (see Figure 6.22, Steps 1 and 2).

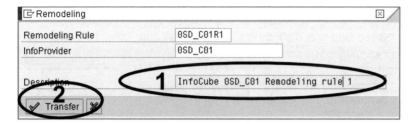

**Figure 6.22** Description for the Remodeling Rule

▶ The **Remodeling Rule ... REMODELING** dialog allows you to configure the remodeling. To do that, click on the **Add Operation to List** button (see Figure 6.23, Step 1).

Maintaining the remodeling rule

▶ Then a popup opens in which you can specify an operation. To delete the time characteristic **0CALDAY**, select the **Delete characteristic** operation (Step 2).

"Delete characteristic" operation

▶ Enter the technical name of the InfoObject to be deleted in the input field (Step 3) and confirm your entries by clicking on the **Transfer** button (Step 4).

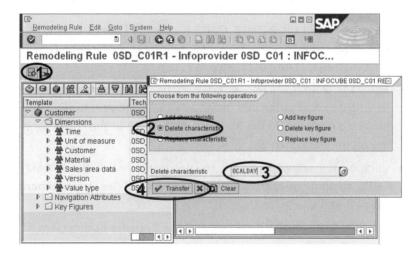

**Figure 6.23** Creating a Remodeling Rule

▶ The configured operation is then displayed in the remodeling rule (see Figure 6.24, highlighted text).

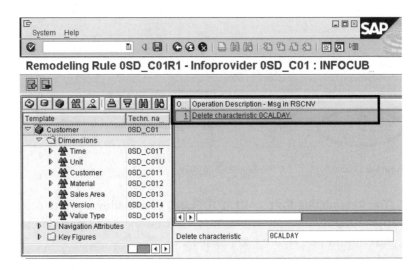

**Figure 6.24** Operation in the Remodeling Rule

Adding other operations ▶ Keep clicking on the **Add Operation to List** button to add other operations (see also Figure 6.23, Step 1).

### Adding the "Company Code" Characteristic with Attribute Derivation

▶ In order to add the **0COMP_CODE** (**Company Code**) characteristic to the data model, you must first select the **Add characteristic** operation (see Figure 6.25, Step 1).

▶ Enter the technical name, **0COMP_CODE**, of the characteristic to be added as well as the dimension to which you want to assign the new characteristic (in the example, **0SD_C013**) in the corresponding input fields (Step 2).

▶ Click on the relevant options to specify the use of the **0COMP_CODE** attribute of characteristic **0SALESORG (Sales Organization)** (Steps 3 and 4).

▶ Confirm these entries by clicking on the **Transfer** button (Step 5).

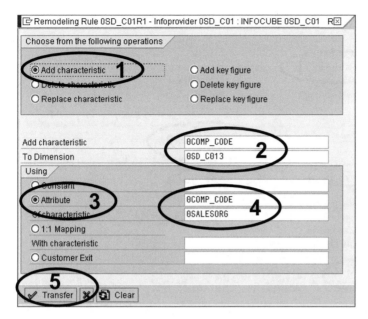

**Figure 6.25** Adding a Characteristic with Attribute Derivation

### Adding the Source System ID Characteristic with a Constant

▶ In order to add the **0SOURSYSTEM (Source System ID)** characteristic to the data model you must again select the **Add characteristic** operation (see Figure 6.26, Step 1).

▶ Enter the technical name, **0SOURSYSTEM**, of the characteristic to
be added as well as the dimension to which you want to assign the
new characteristic (in the example, **0SD_C013**) in the corresponding input fields (Step 2).

▶ Select **Using** of the **Constant** and specify the key value (in the
example, **F1**) (Steps 3 and 4).

▶ Confirm these entries by clicking on the **Transfer** button (Step 5).

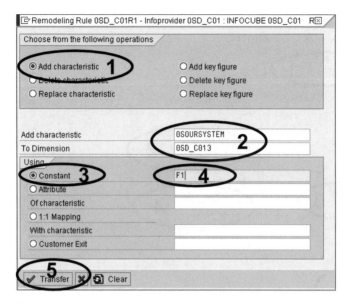

**Figure 6.26** Adding a Characteristic with Constant

### Deleting Key Figures

▶ To delete key figures from the InfoCube, you must proceed in a similar way as when removing characteristics. Select the **Delete key figure** operation (see Figure 6.27, Step 1).

▶ Enter the technical names, **0RTNSCST** (and so on), of the key figures to be deleted in the input field (Step 2), and confirm your entries by clicking on the **Transfer** button (Step 3).

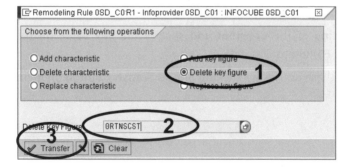

**Figure 6.27** Removing Key Figures

### Saving and Scheduling the Remodeling Rule

▶ Lastly, you must **save** your remodeling rule (see Figure 6.28, Step 1).

▶ Once you have saved the remodeling rule, the **Schedule** button displays. Click on this button to execute the remodeling process (Step 2).

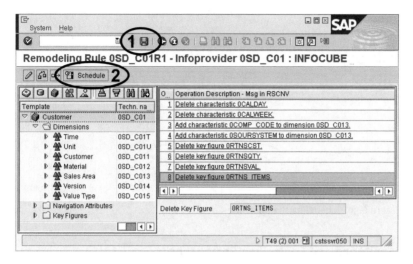

**Figure 6.28** Operations in the Remodeling Rule

▶ Confirm that you will back up the database before running remodeling request in the **Warning** popup by clicking on the **Next** button (see Figure 6.29, highlighted text).

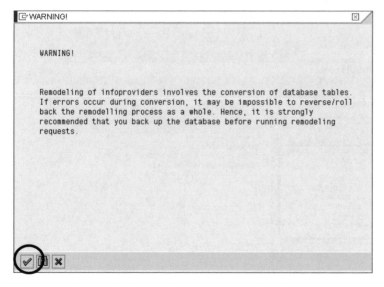

**Figure 6.29** Warning: Follow the Recommendations by SAP

Carrying out a
conversion

▶ Next, the selection screen for scheduling the remodeling process is displayed (**Schedule conversion for ...**). Select the start option, which in the example is **Start immediately** (see Figure 6.30, Step 1).

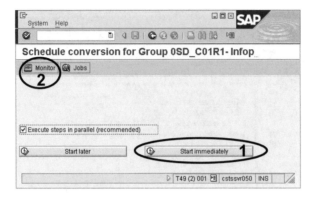

**Figure 6.30** Scheduling the InfoCube Conversion

### Monitoring and Controlling Remodeling

A monitor is available for the remodeling function.

**[»]**

▶ To call the monitor, click on the **Monitor** button in the scheduling selection screen (see Figure 6.30, Step 2).

▶ Then the remodeling monitor displays (see Figure 6.31, high-lighted text).

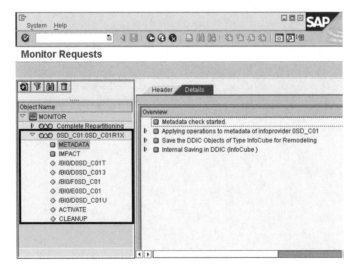

**Figure 6.31** The Remodeling Monitor

▶ The display of the data model in the Administrator Workbench
shows the structural results of the remodeling process (see Figure
6.32, highlighted text in 1, 2, and 3), including the added characteristics and the deleted key figures and characteristics.

Result

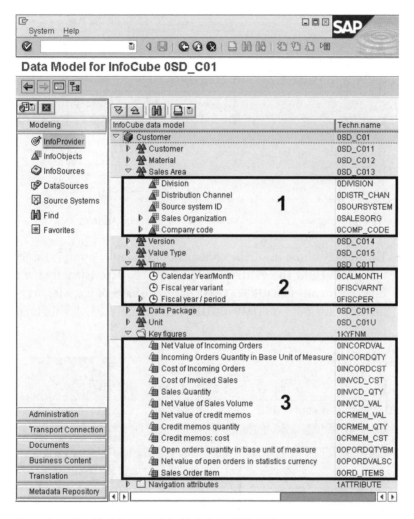

**Figure 6.32** Modified Data Model of InfoCube 0SD_C01

▶ The display of preserved and added data in the InfoCube shows
the changes to the contents caused by the remodeling process. The
company code was derived from the sales organization attribute
of the same name (see Figure 6.33).

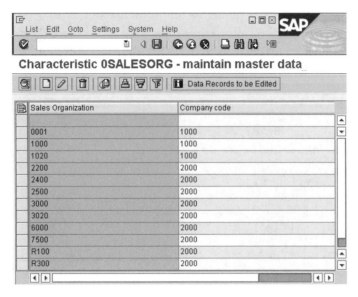

**Figure 6.33** Company Code Based on the Sales Organization Attribute

Result: content changes

▶ The display of the InfoCube contents (for example, using Transaction LISTCUBE) shows the newly added characteristics that are filled constantly (**0SOURSYSTEM**), or on the basis of the sales organization attribute (**0COMP_CODE**) (see Figure 6.34, highlighted text).

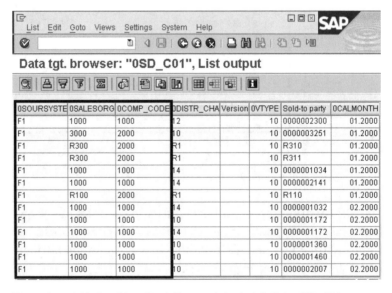

**Figure 6.34** Added and Initialized Characteristics in InfoCube 0SD_C01

## 6.4 The First Redesign Functions: An Interim Result

The availability of the first redesign functions in SAP NetWeaver 2004s Business Intelligence is timely and very useful to meet the constantly growing redesign requirements in existing applications.

Useful redesign functionality

The repartitioning function already meets existing requirements.

Repartitioning

The existing remodeling functions are also helpful as they exist today. For further optimization, it would be very useful to complement the currently available operations with the following two additional functions: The creation of new dimensions including the assignment (and filling) of characteristics, and the reassignment of characteristics between different dimensions.

Remodeling

*SAP NetWeaver 2004s contains many new and revised reporting and analysis functions in the Business Explorer (BEx) Suite. BEx Query Designer serves as a basis for these reporting and analysis tools. This chapter describes the most important changes as well as selected new functions.*

# 7 BEx Query Designer

## 7.1 Reporting and Analysis—An Overview

The modeling and display of reporting functions is carried out via the Business Explorer Suite, which is a collection of programs and plug-ins for analyzing existing data (see Figure 7.1).

Business Explorer Suite

The Business Explorer Suite consists of the following tools: BEx Query Designer, BEx Web Application Designer, BEx Broadcaster, and BEx Analyzer.

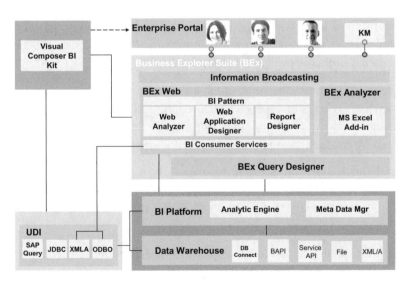

**Figure 7.1** Business Explorer Suite (Source: SAP AG)

Business Explorer query

The basis for all reporting processes is a query. A query is a process that extracts data from defined InfoProviders in a specific view. You can generate queries and roughly define their structure using the BEx Query Designer. When you create a query, you define the key figures and characteristics to be displayed, and the filters and characteristics based on which future navigations should be possible.

Depending on the purpose of the report and the task to be performed by the respective user group, the display of the queries created in this way can occur in several ways.

Business Explorer Analyzer

For example, a user group that wants to use the reports to perform calculations, even after the reporting process has ended, will most likely use the functions provided by the BEx Analyzer, an MS Excel plug-in that displays the provided data in a spreadsheet. BEx Analyzer is fully compatible with Excel as of MS Office 98, whereas its functionality is limited if it is used with earlier versions of MS Office.

Business Explorer Web Application

Another user group is interested in a representative presentation of the information and would probably prefer the functions of a web-based presentation that can be created using the BEx Web Application Designer or the formatted output of the Report Designer, which can then be displayed in the SAP Enterprise Portal. The output for web-based reporting occurs via pre-generated HTML pages, which are referred to as web templates. All you need to display the web report is an up-to-date browser. Internet Explorer Version 5.5 or higher is probably the best solution here.

Business Explorer Web Application Designer

Web applications can be created using the BEx Web Application Designer. This software is contained in SAP GUI and must be installed on the frontend. Web applications created using the BEx Web Application Designer can be called via a specific URL.

Business Explorer Broadcaster

And finally, we should mention that a third user group wants to include their reports in a daily delivery process. Those users can use the BEx Broadcaster that enables you to dispatch precalculated information, for instance, via email.

All these tools enable you to filter or drill down data according to specific characteristics in order to obtain a view that represents the facts in question precisely. This chapter focuses on the description of BEx Query Designer, while the following chapters (i.e., Chapter 8, 9, and 10) introduce the other tools of the Business Explorer Suite.

## 7.2    BEx Query Designer in Detail

BEx Query Designer serves as a basis for the reporting and analysis tools. It is used to define queries that are provided to the user via the frontend.

The creation of individual queries is based on a specific InfoProvider. The queries can only contain key figures and characteristics that are also available in the underlying InfoProvider. In addition, you can define your own key figures or restricted key figures that are based on the basic key figures. You can then use the customized key figures to restrict or change the basic key figures.

The screen of the Query Designer can roughly be divided into four areas (see Figure 7.3):

*Work areas of the Query Designer*

▶ The InfoProvider view that contains available key figures and characteristics for the respective InfoProvider

▶ The query modeling area

▶ The properties area where you can set the relevant properties

▶ A message window at the bottom of the screen

The following key figures and characteristics are available: basic key figures and characteristics contained in the InfoProvider, as well as key figures that have been calculated and restricted at a later stage and globally defined structures and key figures.

*Characteristics and key figures*

The work area provided for modeling the queries comprises the restriction to filters, the definition of rows and columns that determine the general layout of the queries, and actions for individual cells—the so-called *exception cells* or cell definitions. You can use tabs to switch between these three views.

*Query modeling*

Depending on the selected object, the properties are filled and are changeable. The message window displays warnings and errors. Contrary to previous versions, an error message does not disrupt the workflow; it is only displayed in the message window and indicated by a color highlighting of the object.

*Properties*

You can change the appearance of the standard screen via the menu item, **View**. There you can hide either the **Messages** or the **Properties** area.

*Hiding areas*

New features    In addition, BEx Query Designer provides some supporting features that are supposed to facilitate the user's work. These features include the error-handling function with the aforementioned correction help, a task management function for inexperienced users, the use of placeholders for a definition at a later stage, automatic creation of technical names for reusable objects, mass processing of objects of the same type, and the option to store properties as reusable.

> **[»]**    The Query Designer is a frontend program that is installed with the Business Explorer Suite. You must log onto the connected SAP BW system if you want to use it.

### 7.2.1 Sample Scenario

We now want to introduce you to some important query functions and query properties as well as the new user interface of BEx Query Designer. To do that, we'll use a sample scenario for our model company, CubeServ Engines.

Functions of the example    During the course of the example, we'll describe the configuration of static and variable filters, dynamic lists of characteristic values, fixed structures with any kind of subtotals for characteristic values, as well as calculations using key figures and the configuration of the display in several steps.

Structure of the example    In the final step in designing the query, we want to create a display of a simple contribution margin scheme in the columns of the query, while the rows should display months (periods), quarterly subtotals, and the annual total. We want to select the company code, CubeServ Engines AG (Jona), statically. We also want to ensure that the fiscal year to be analyzed has already been included at the time the query is executed.

### 7.2.2 Getting Started with BEx Query Designer

Because BEx Query Designer can be operated intuitively, experienced users will quickly familiarize themselves with it. But, since the latest version has been comprehensively redesigned, we should also take a brief look at its basic principles.

## Starting the Query Designer

▶ You can launch BEx Query Designer via the following menu item: **[▪]**
**Business Explorer** • **Query Designer** (see Figure 7.2, Step 1).

▶ Log in to your system (Step 2).

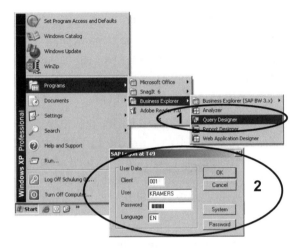

**Figure 7.2** Calling the BEx Query Designer

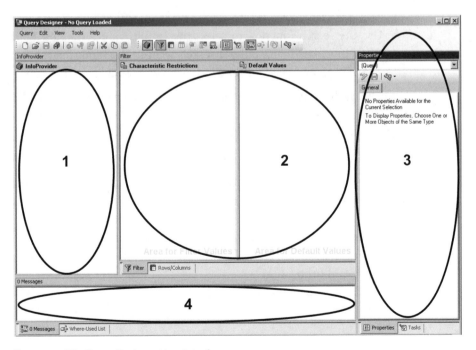

**Figure 7.3** BEx Query Designer User Interface

▶ Figure 7.3 displays the areas described above: key figures and characteristics (highlight 1), query modeling (highlight 2), properties (highlight 3), and the message window (highlight 4). These areas are empty because we haven't opened any query yet.

### Creating a Query and Selecting an InfoProvider

In the next step, you'll create the query. As already mentioned, queries are assigned to InfoProviders and are stored in the system in relation to those InfoProviders. For this reason, you must select the underlying InfoProvider if you want to create a query.

InfoProvider as data basis

There are several ways to select the InfoProvider for the query. The system initially provides a selection based on the history, that is, those InfoProviders that were opened last are provided in a list. Alternatively, you can navigate through the available InfoAreas or perform a search run. Lastly, you can also enter the technical name of the InfoProvider directly.

[▪]

▶ To create a new query, click on the **New Query** button in the header bar of BEx Query Designer (see Figure 7.4, Step 1).

▶ This opens the **New Query: Select InfoProvider** popup.

▶ Use the search function to select the InfoProvider: Click on **Find** (the binoculars icon), enter a search term in the input field (here: ZCSCOPA), and click on the **Find** button (Steps 2 to 4).

▶ The system now lists the InfoProviders that correspond to the search term (Step 5).

▶ Click on the relevant InfoProvider to select it and confirm this selection by clicking on **Open** (Step 6).

Once you have initialized a query in this way, the area for key figures and characteristics lists the key figures that are available, as well as the characteristics including attributes, navigation attributes, and variables, sorted by the modeled dimensions. You can transfer these key figures and characteristics into the modeling area of the query via drag-and-drop.

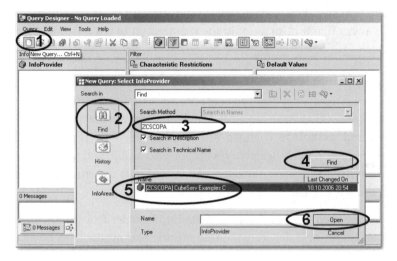

**Figure 7.4** Creating a New Query

### Components of the Modeling Area

The modeling area is divided into three subareas that are separated by tabs.

▶ **Filters**

The Characteristic Restrictions area contains the filters that restrict the query, whereas the Default Values area contains suggested values for an initial drilldown. Characteristics that are used to filter the query are not available for a drilldown.

▶ **Rows/Columns**

Here you can define which characteristics and key figures you want to include in the initial drilldown of the query. For example, you can determine the level of granularity for the analysis. When you execute the query, all those characteristics are displayed that result from the filtering operations you set.

Moreover, you can define the free characteristics here that enable flexible navigation. The arrangement within rows and columns can be defined using structures. To check the schematic design of the created query, a rudimentary preview block is available.

▶ **Cells**

This tab contains the cell definitions or exception cells within a query. This tab only displays if you use two structures and if you have stored formulas via the Cells button.

In the next step, you must now use filters to restrict the new query in such a way that it displays only the required set of data.

### 7.2.3    Filters in a Query

Filtering
characteristics

As mentioned above, filtering characteristics are fixed restrictions set in the query. They have already been defined before the query is executed and cannot be changed afterwards, which is why they are referred to as non-navigatable restrictions. Basically, you can use any characteristic as a filter; however, you should only use characteristics that are not needed for navigation purposes.

Filters are used to limit the data of the InfoProvider to a specific part of the dataset in order to make this specific part available to certain groups of users.

The restriction can be implemented via a popup that displays the possible values of the characteristic. Furthermore, you can specify variables in this popup to ensure dynamic filter selection.

Selection list

To restrict the selection, you can display the selection list in different ways.

▶ **History**
The settings selected last are displayed.

▶ **Favorites**
The restrictions that have been selected most frequently by the user are displayed.

▶ **Single values**
The complete list is displayed. Because such lists can be very long, you can perform a search run here.

▶ **Value ranges**
Here you can define value ranges. You can define an interval or a threshold value from which or up to which the value range applies. The characteristic value is then selected based on this value range.

▶ **Variables**
A selection of possible variables is displayed.

You can transfer the selected restriction via drag-and-drop, or by clicking on the transfer button (arrow). The red traffic light icon indicates that you can make an exclusion selection. This function reverses the selection logically and excludes the selected characteristics from the selection. Moreover, you can manipulate the sequence of the filters.

### Configuring Filters

In the following sections, you'll define your sample query based on the selected InfoProvider and restrict it by using filters. The goal of this example is to create a restriction for several company codes.

▶ Before you begin to create your sample query, you must activate the display of **Technical names** by clicking on the corresponding button (see Figure 7.5, Step 1).

[»]

▶ Click on the **Filters** button to display the filters area (Step 2).

Displaying the filters area

▶ To select a restricting characteristic, open the folder of the corresponding dimension in the field selection of the InfoProvider (in the example, that's Organization, Step 3).

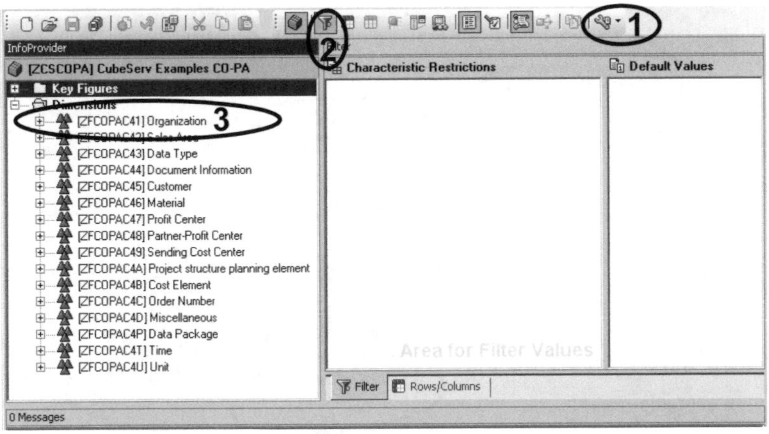

Selecting a characteristic

**Figure 7.5** Selecting the Filters

▶ The **Company Code** characteristic (0COMP_CODE) now displays (see Figure 7.6, Step 1).

▶ Drag the **Company Code** characteristic into the filters area. The characteristic is underlined in red, which indicates that the filter has been set but that it hasn't been restricted yet (Steps 1 and 2).

Selecting a
filter value

▸ Double-click on the **Company Code** item to open the filter popup
**Select Values For** [0COMP_CODE] Company code in the **Characteristic Restrictions** frame (Step 2). Alternatively, you can do this
by opening the context menu and selecting the Restrict item.

▸ Click on the company code [10] CubeServ Engines AG [Switzer-
land] to select it, and then click on the Transfer button (Steps 3
and 4).

▸ The selected value is then displayed in the Selection frame (Step 5).

▸ Transfer the selection into the query definition by clicking on **OK**
(Steps 6 and 7).

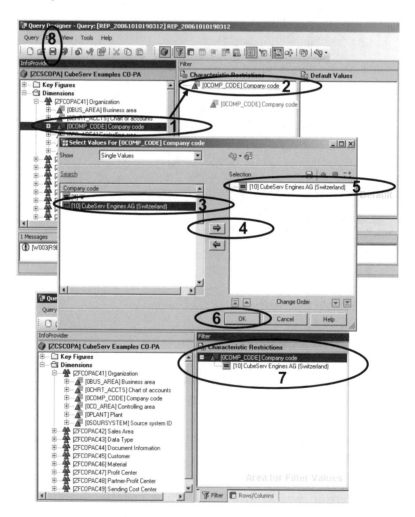

Figure 7.6  Selecting a Filter Value

▶ Save the query as **Profit Contribution Time Series** (ZCSCOPA0100) in your list of favorites via the **Save query** button (Step 8) by specifying the description and the technical name. Finally click on the **Save** button (see Figure 7.7, Steps 1 and 2).

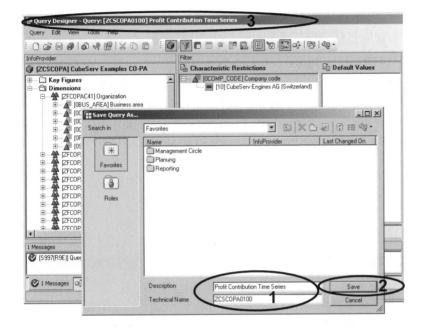

**Figure 7.7** Saving the Query

### 7.2.4 Rows and Columns

The structure of rows and columns represents the core of what is displayed as an analysis to the end user when the query is executed. Elements can be moved to the required position via drag-and-drop. We recommend that you combine key figures and characteristics into structures. In this way, you can, for example, move a group of key figures from the columns into the rows without encountering any problems.

The system allows you to create a total of two structures. Note that the key figures are already contained in a structure by itself. Structures are elements that can be stored as reusable elements so that they can be reused in other queries that are based on the same InfoProvider. Note, however, that changes to a global structure will

Structures

affect all queries that use this structure. Alternatively, you can detach a query, that is, to reconvert it into a local structure within a query.

### Configuring Rows and Columns

Now we want to configure the columns using key figures, while we use a time characteristic to configure the rows.

**[▪]**

▸ Click on the **Rows/Columns** button to display the **Free Characteristics**, **Rows**, and **Columns** areas (see Figure 7.8, Step 1).

Configuring the column structure

▸ To configure the column structure, open the key figures folder in the field selection of the InfoProvider and transfer the following key figures into the columns via drag-and-drop (see Steps 2 and 3 as an example):

▸ **Revenue** (0COPAREVEN)

▸ **CustDiscnt** (0CUST_DSCNT)

▸ **Manuf. Costs** (cons.) (ZFHKVKK)

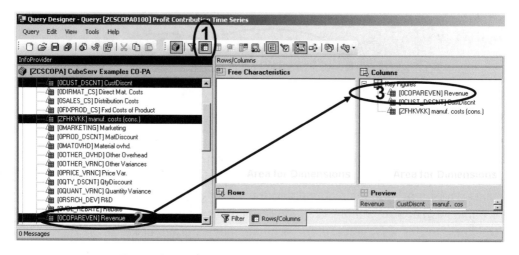

**Figure 7.8** Transferring Key Figures into Columns

Configuring the row content

▸ Configure the row contents as follows: In the field selection of the InfoProvider, click on the **Time** folder to open it and transfer the **Posting period** characteristic (0FISCPER3) into the rows via drag-and-drop (see Figure 7.9, Steps 1 to 3).

▸ Check the schematic display of the query in the preview (Step 4).

- If the display appears to be correct, save the configuration (Step 5).
- Execute the query by clicking on the **Execute** button (Step 6).

Executing the query

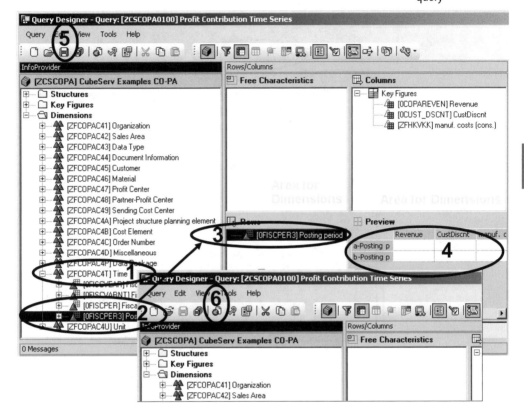

**Figure 7.9** Configuring the Row Characteristic to Be Displayed

- This starts the HTML browser that is set as the default browser in your system (such as Microsoft Internet Explorer), and the login screen for the SAP Enterprise Portal is displayed.

Displaying the query

- Enter your SAP BI user ID and password and click on the **Log on** button (see Figure 7.10, Steps 1 and 2).
- The query output is then displayed in the browser (Step 3).

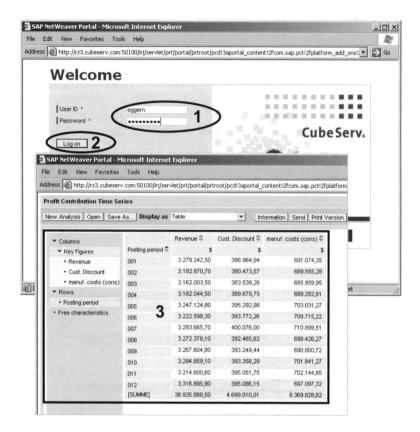

**Figure 7.10** Running the Query

### 7.2.5 Free Characteristics

Free characteristics enable navigation within the running query. Characteristics that have been included in the query as free characteristics do not appear in the initial drilldown of the query, but you can use them for other drilldowns and selections.

The difference between filters and free characteristics is that free characteristics enable a navigation from the selected dataset, whereas filters define the dataset.

#### Configuring Free Characteristics

You must now configure free characteristics that are to be used for navigation and selection purposes when the query is executed.

▶ Click on the **Rows/Columns** button to display the **Free Character-** **[⬛]**
istics, **Rows**, and **Columns** areas (see Figure 7.8, Step 1).

▶ To configure the free characteristics, open the folder containing   Configuring the
the characteristics to be transferred in the field selection of the   column structure
InfoProvider and transfer the characteristics via drag-and-drop
into the **Free Characteristics** frame: example of the **Fiscal Year**
characteristic (0FISCYEAR), see Figure 7.11, Steps 1 and 2.

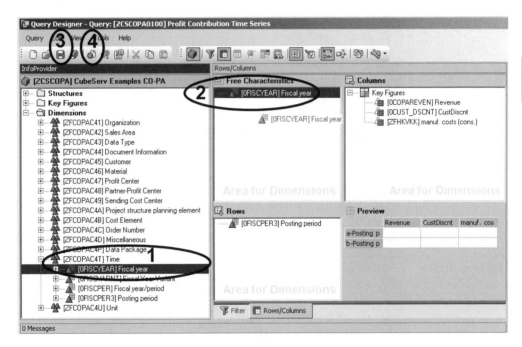

**Figure 7.11** Including a Free Characteristic in the Query

### 7.2.6 Formulas

You can use the key figures contained in a query to carry out formula
operations. Similar to the selection process, you must first select a
structure, then open the context menu, and select New Formula.
Within the formula, you can enter a fixed text or a variable as a
description.

To create the formula, you can use the formula editor. All available
operands are located in the lower left-hand area. These are the structure elements of the current structure, all formula variables, and specific cells from cell definitions.

The possible operators are located in the lower right-hand area. The operators can be divided into the following groups:

▸ Basic Functions

▸ Percentage Functions

▸ Data Functions

▸ Mathematical Functions

▸ Trigonometric Functions

▸ Boolean Functions

During the creation process, the syntax of the formula is permanently checked for accuracy. Errors are highlighted in red in the respective terms.

**[»]**    To avoid representing errors caused by non-defined calculation operations such as a division by 0, you can suppress such errors by using the operators NDIV0() and NOERR().

In our example, we now want to create a simple contribution margin scheme that's based on the basic key figures and carries out the following calculation:

Key figure scheme

*Gross sales*
*./. Discount*
*= Net sales*
*./. Full manufacturing costs*
*= Profit Contribution II*

The contribution margin is to be displayed in relation to net sales.

### Configuring Formulas

**[⬝]**    ▸ Click on the **Rows/Columns** button to display the **Free Characteristics**, **Rows**, and **Columns** areas (see Figure 7.8, Step 1).

Creating a formula    ▸ To configure the formulas, right-click on the icon next to a formula to be created in order to open the context-sensitive menu, and select the **New Formula** function (see Figure 7.12, Steps 1 and 2).

▸ This inserts a new item called **Formula nn** (Step 3).

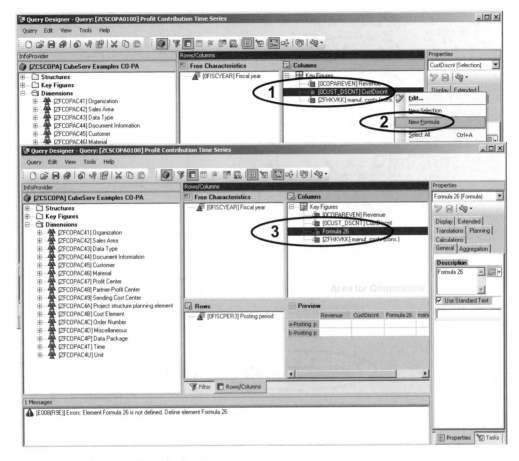

**Figure 7.12** Configuring a Formula, Part 1

▸ Double-click on the new item to start editing the **Formula nn** formula. This opens the **Change Formula** popup. Go to the General tab (see Figure 7.13, Step 1) and drag the key figures into the detail view (in the example: Revenue and CustDiscnt, Step 2). Then link the key figures to the required operators (Step 3).

▸ Deactivate the **Use Standard Text** property and enter the required description (in the example: Net Sales, Steps 4 and 5). Complete the configuration process by clicking on the **OK** button (Step 6).

Changing the description

▸ Then the formula is displayed with the new name in the **Columns** frame (Step 7).

▸ Proceed in the same way to configure the contribution margin.

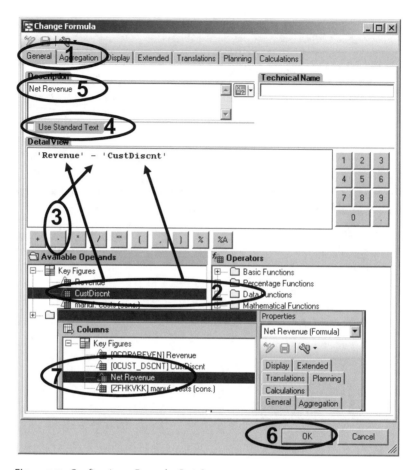

Figure 7.13  Configuring a Formula, Part 2

Percentage function

▶ You should also proceed in the same way when configuring the relative contribution margin. Here you must transfer the **Percentage** function from the **Percentage Functions** folder in the Operators frame via drag-and-drop (see Figure 7.14, Steps 1 to 6).

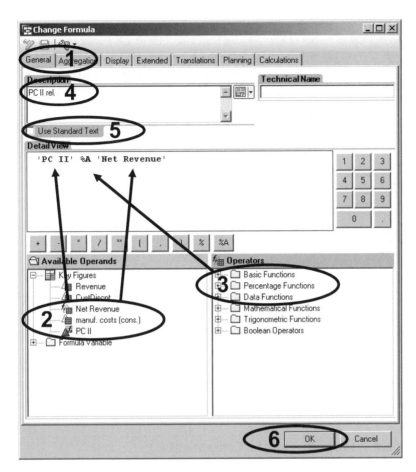

**Figure 7.14** Configuring a Formula with Percentage Function

▶ Once you have completed the key figure scheme, the column structure is displayed as shown in Figure 7.15 (circled section).

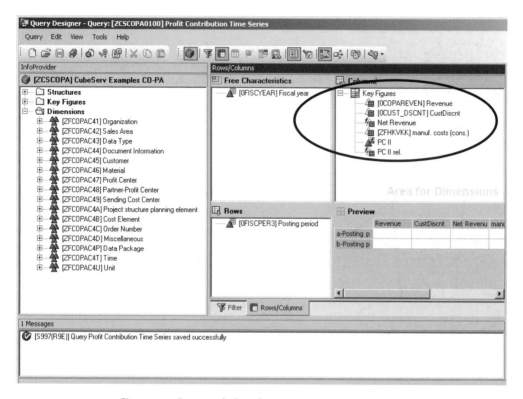

**Figure 7.15** Query with Complete Key Figure Structure

### 7.2.7 Properties of the Components

You can configure numerous properties of the row and column components.

Tabs   Within a component (selection), the tabs provide even more options to manipulate the component.

▶ **General**
This tab contains the definition of the selection, such as the name and formula definition or selection.

▶ **Aggregation**
This tab contains the set aggregation, that is, it provides information as to whether an exception aggregation is active that deviates from the totaling.

▶ **Display**
In this tab, you can find show and hide functions as well as scaling or highlighting settings.

- **Extended**
  This option enables you to activate the constant selection.

- **Translations**
  This tab allows you to set unit and currency translations.

- **Planning**
  This tab is relevant for integrated planning and is described in greater detail in Chapter 11, which deals with BI-integrated planning.

- **Calculations**
  These settings refer to results calculations. Here you can set both the totals calculation and the calculation of individual values. Moreover, you can define the direction of the calculation.

In this example, absolute amounts are to be displayed in .000 USD, while the relative contribution margin should be displayed as a percentage with one decimal place.

*Formatting*

### Configuring Component Properties

- Click on the **Rows/Columns** button to display the **Free Characteristics**, **Rows**, and **Columns** areas (see Figure 7.8, Step 1).

  [▪]

- To configure the display of key figures and formulas, proceed in the same way as when you configured the formulas (see description referring to Figure 7.16), that is, double-click on the row or column element to open the **Change Selection** popup.

  *Configuring the display*

- In the Change Selection popup and in the **Change Formula** popup, select the Display tab (see Figure 7.16, Steps 1 and 4).

- Select **0 Number of Decimal Places** (Step 2) and Scaling factor 1,000 (Step 3) for all elements except for the proportional key figure.

- Select **0.0 Number of Decimal Places** (Step 6) and Scaling factor 1 (Step 5) for the proportional key figure.

- Complete the configuration process by clicking on the **OK** button (Step 7).

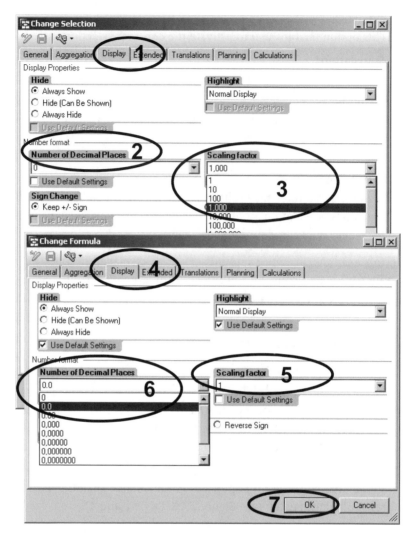

**Figure 7.16** Display of Key Figures and Formulas

### 7.2.8 Selections

Requirements Pure listings of values such as the posting period may not prove to be sufficient so that dedicated value compilations become necessary. To map this requirement, you must use selections of structure elements.

In addition to the restrictions, you can assign the aforementioned component properties to selections.

Properties of selections

### Configuring Selections

At this point, you must configure the selections. Note that instead of listing the posting periods in the example, you will map the following structure.

```
Row 1: January
Row 2: February
Row 3: March
Row 4 Quarter I
Row 5: April
Row 6 May
Row 7: June
Row 8: Quarter II

and so on up to

Row 15: December
Row 16. Quarter IV
Row 17: Entire year
```

The fiscal year is identical to the calendar year. In the example, you'll use two different variants to map the quarterly totals and the annual totals.

▶ Click on the **Rows/Columns** button to display the **Free Characteristics**, **Rows**, and **Columns** areas (see Figure 7.8, Step 1).

[■]

▶ To create a row structure, remove the drilldown characteristic **Posting period** (0FISCPER) from the **Rows** frame by dragging this item into the frame that contains the field selection.

▶ To initialize the configuration of the row structure, open the context menu by right-clicking into the **Rows** frame. Select the **New structure** function (see Figure 7.17, Step 1).

Creating a structure and inserting characteristic values

▶ This creates a new **Structure** folder in the **Rows** frame (Step 2).

▶ Then drag the required characteristic values, 001, 002, and 003 one after the other and in the correct sequence into the structure (in the example, this is shown for Posting period 003, Steps 3 and 4).

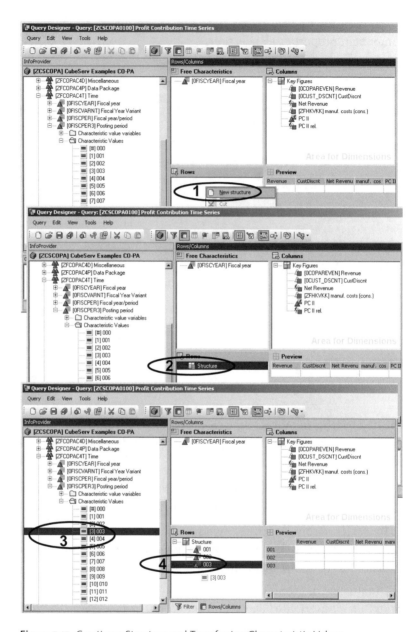

**Figure 7.17** Creating a Structure and Transferring Characteristic Values

### Inserting Calculations with Structure Elements

Similar to the above procedure for key figures, you can also insert calculations via characteristic values for structure elements.

▶ To do this, right-click on the structure element for which a calculation is to be performed to open its context-sensitive menu, and select the New Formula function (see Figure 7.18, Steps 1 and 2).  **[◄]**

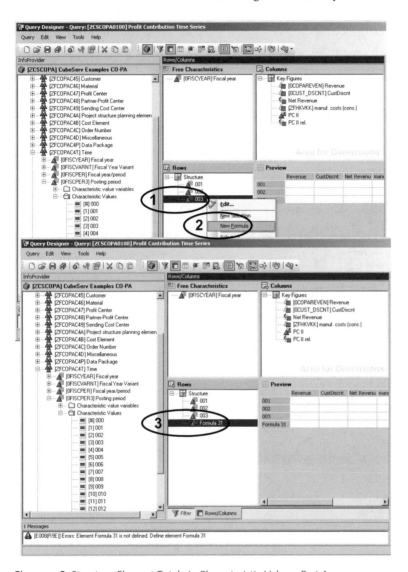

**Figure 7.18** Structure Element Total via Characteristic Values, Part 1

▶ This creates another item, **Formula nn**, in the structure (see Figure 7.18, Step 3).

▶ Double-click on it to open the **Change Formula** popup in which you can configure the formula.

Configuring the formula

▶ The configuration of the formula is similar to the configuration of the key figures: In the example you create the total for **Quarter I** by transferring the characteristic values 001, 002, and 003 from the **Available Operands** frame into the **Detail View** via drag-and-drop (see Figure 7.19, Steps 1 and 2). Then you must link the individual operands using the **+** operator by clicking on the **+** button (Step 3).

Entering a description

▶ To enter an individual description, deactivate the **Use Standard Text** option by clicking on it and enter the required text, **Quarter I**, in the **Description** frame (Steps 4 and 5).

▶ Complete the configuration process by clicking on the **OK** button (Step 6).

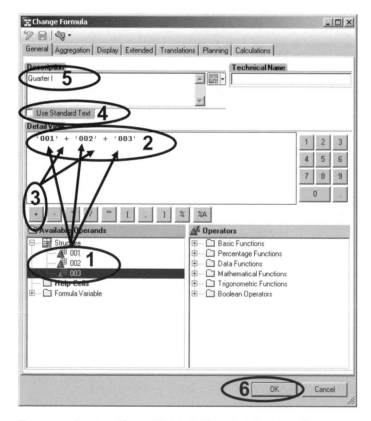

**Figure 7.19** Structure Element Total via Characteristic Values, Part 2

Completing the structure

▶ Complete the structure by transferring the posting periods 004 through 012 and configuring the quarterly totals II through IV.

▶ As an alternative to creating subtotals (which is recommended here), you can use a selection with several characteristic values. To do this, right-click on the structure element for which a calculation is to be performed to open its context-sensitive menu, and select the **New Selection** function (see Figure 7.20, Steps 1 and 2).

Selection with several characteristic values

▶ This inserts a new item, **Selection nn**, in the structure (Step 3).

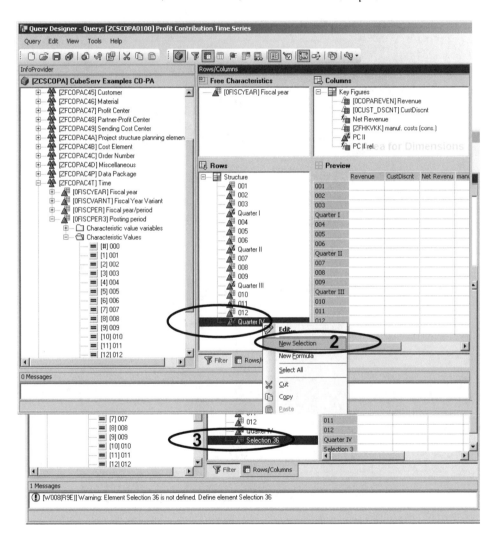

**Figure 7.20** Creating a Selection

▶ Double-click on the new item to open the **Change Selection** popup. In the field selection, click on the **Posting period** characteristic to highlight it. This characteristic serves as the selection

Configuring a selection

basis. Then transfer it via drag-and-drop to the Details of the Selection frame (see Figure 7.21, Steps 1 and 2).

▶ Next, right-click to open the context menu and select the **Restrict...** function (Step 3).

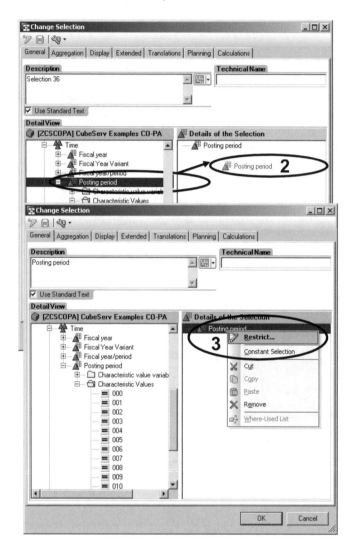

**Figure 7.21** Configuring a Selection, Part 1

▶ This opens the popup **Select Values For** [0FISCPER3] **Posting** period. Select the **Value Ranges** selection in the **Show** dropdown box and specify Between 001 and 012 as the interval to be used (see Figure 7.22, Steps 1 and 2).

- Click on the **Transfer** button to transfer the selection (Step 3).

- The selection is then displayed in the **Selection** frame (Step 4).

- Transfer the selection into the query definition by clicking on **OK** (Step 5).

- This activates the **Change Selection** popup once again. In this popup, click on the Use Standard Text option to deactivate it and enter **Entire Year** as description (Steps 6 and 7).

- Complete the configuration of the selection by clicking on the **OK** button (Step 8).

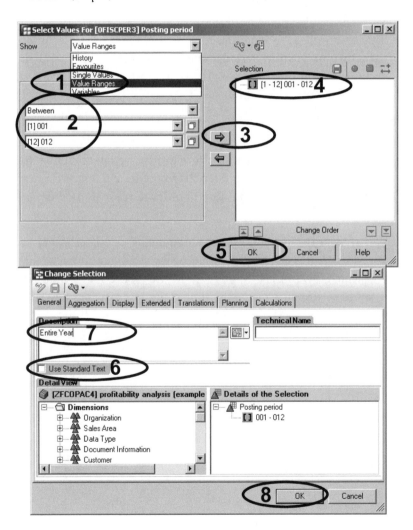

**Figure 7.22** Configuring a Selection, Part 2

▸ The system now displays the configuration of the query including the characteristic structure (see Figure 7.23, Step 1).

**Saving the Structure**

You can save the structure as a global structure so that it can be reused for the definition of other queries that are based on the same InfoProvider.

**[▪]** ▸ To do this, right-click on the **Structure** item in the **Rows** frame to open its context-sensitive menu, and select the **Save As...** function (see Figure 7.23, Steps 1 and 2).

▸ This opens the **Save Structure As...** popup. Enter the **Description**, **Structure of Posting Periods, Quarters & Entire Year**, and the technical name ZCSCOPAS0001. Then confirm your entries by clicking on **OK** (Steps 3 to 5).

▸ After that, the new structure description is displayed in the query definition in the **Rows** frame (Step 6).

▸ In addition, the new global structure is displayed in the frame that contains the field selection (Step 7) from where the structure can be transferred via drag-and-drop in order to reuse it in other queries.

Changing a global structure

If you change the structure or its components at a later stage, the changed structure is displayed with the new configuration in all queries in which it was used. In the example, this was done by adjusting the names of structure elements, similar to the procedure described in Figure 7.23.

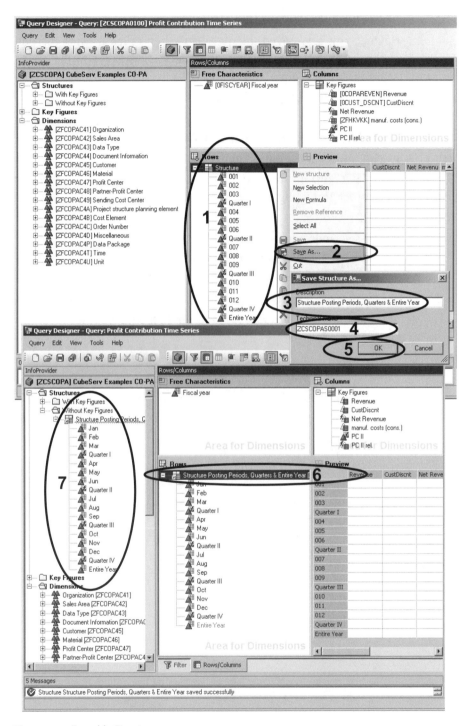

**Figure 7.23** Reusable Structures

**Executing a Query with Two Structures**

▶ Once you have saved the query and then called it using the buttons in the Query Designer, the query is displayed in the HTML browser (see Figure 7.24, Step 1).

▶ If you want to display a fiscal year, right-click on the free characteristic Fiscal year to open its context-sensitive menu and select the function **Filter · Select Filter Value** (Step 2).

▶ This opens the popup Input help for characteristic **Fiscal year** (0FISCYEAR). In this popup, click on the fiscal year to be selected in order to highlight it (in the example: 2005), and click on **Add** (Steps 3 and 4).

▶ The selected value is displayed in the **Selections** list, and the selection is applied to the query as soon as you click on the **OK** button (Steps 5 and 6).

This rather inconvenient selection method is supported by the variables technology that's described in the following section.

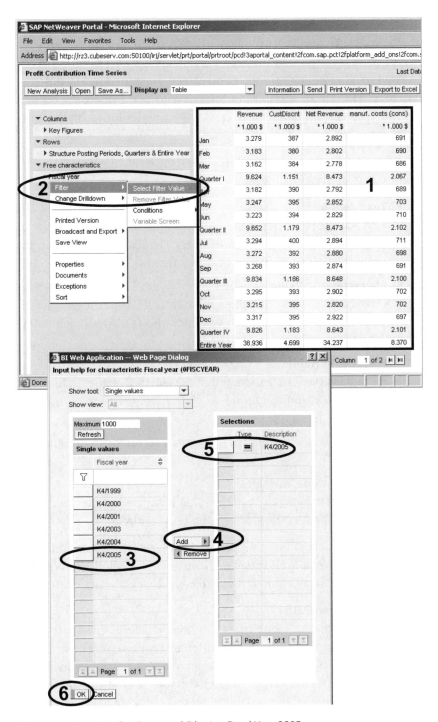

**Figure 7.24** Running the Query and Filtering Fiscal Year 2005

### 7.2.9    Variables

Variables are components of a query that are filled with relevant values at runtime so that they can parameterize a query. They are created as placeholders for an element and are processed in different ways. The use of variables enables you to use a query for various restrictions without having to create new queries for each value or to perform new selections at runtime.

Depending on the object to be replaced, the following different types of variables are available:

▶ **Text Variables**
Text variables replace descriptions within a query. They can be used within the description of query elements, as well as in the property dialogs of queries or selections.

▶ **Characteristic Value Variables**
Characteristic value variables fill a variable with a characteristic value. In addition to the text variables, this is the most commonly used variable type.

▶ **Formula Variables**
Formula variables are used within the Query Designer in formulas or exceptions and conditions.

▶ **Hierarchy Variables**
Hierarchy variables are used to restrict a hierarchy or presentation hierarchy.

▶ **Hierarchy Node Variables**
In contrast to hierarchy variables, hierarchy node variables display a node of the hierarchy or presentation hierarchy.

In addition to the different types of variables, there are also different ways of processing a variable. Note that not all the processing options are available for each variable type.

▶ **Replacement Path**
The variable is overwritten with a value at query runtime. Depending on the specific requirements, the replacement is carried out via a characteristic value, a query result, or by filling another variable. When another variable is used for filling, you must ensure that the variable represents a single value and that it has not been included yet.

▶ **Manual Input or Default Value**

A manual input enables the direct entry of a variable value immediately before the query is executed via the variable screen. If a default value exists, it is preassigned to the variable. You can suppress the variable screen for a web application, provided that you haven't implemented a variable that contains the Required property.

▶ **SAP Exit**

BI Business Content provides several predefined variables of this type. You must activate the Business Content in order to use these variables.

You cannot create any variables with this processing type by yourself.

▶ **Customer Exit**

The customer exit enables you to fill variables in any way. For example, you can include a logic. The implementation occurs via a function module, and once it has been implemented, it can be called via Transaction CMOD. This customer exit services all variables of this type; therefore, you don't need to create separate customer exits for all those variables. This processing type also enables you to access variables that have already been filled and to assign a value based on these variables.

To fill variables of this processing type, you must have ABAP/4 knowledge. [✎]

The required values are transferred to the internal table I_T_VAR_RANGE and are then available in the query. This structure must always be completely filled, even if the different variable types take different values from it.

Note that variables can be filled at different points in time. In the customer exit, you can do that by using I-STEPS that map the points in time from 0 to 3.

▷ I-Step 0: no call via the variable screen but from an external source such as the authorization check

▷ I-Step 1: prior to the variable input

▸ I-Step 2: call after the variable input, if it hasn't been filled in I-Step 1

▸ I-Step 3: call after I-Step 2 with the option to run the variable screen once again via an exception

▸ **Authorization**
If you have assigned authorizations to users, you can use a variable of this processing type to fill a hierarchy node or characteristic value with the authorizations of the user. In that case, the user can use only nodes and values pertaining to his or her authorizations in the initial status and for navigations.

Table 7.1 shows the possible combinations of variables and processing types.

| | Manual input | Replacement path | Customer exit | Authorization |
|---|---|---|---|---|
| **Characteristic value variable** | X | X | X | X |
| **Hierarchy variable** | X | X | X | |
| **Hierarchy node variable** | X | | X | X |
| **Text variable** | X | X | X | |
| **Formula variable** | X | X | X | |

**Table 7.1** Variables and Processing Types

Basically, you can use any number of variables to restrict a characteristic. Note, however, that the system does not accept all possible combinations. For instance, if you combined a customer exit variable with an authorization variable, the system would refuse this combination as being too complex.

**Configuring the Use of Variables**

In this example, you want to use a variable to filter the fiscal year.

[■] ▸ Click on the Filters button to display the filters area (see Figure 7.25, Step 1).

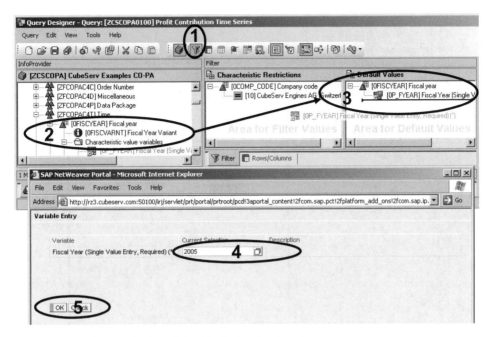

**Figure 7.25** Configuring the Use of Variables in Queries, Part 1

▸ In the field selection frame on the left, click on the **Time** folder to open it, then click on the folder pertaining to the **Fiscal year** characteristic (0FISCYEAR), and then on the Characteristic value variables folder (Step 2).

*Selecting the variable*

▸ If the SAP Business Content has been activated, the variable Fiscal Year (Single Value Entry, Required) (0P_FYEAR) is displayed, possibly among other things. Drag this variable into the **Default Values** frame and drop it below the (free) characteristic Fiscal year (Step 3).

▸ Once you have saved and executed the query, the new variable selection displays. Select the required characteristic value in the input field (in the example: 2005), and click on **OK** (Steps 4 and 5).

*Running queries with variables*

▸ Then the query result is displayed (Figure 7.26, Step 1).

▸ Click on the **Information** button so that a popup opens. Select the **Information** tab in this popup. The value selected for the fiscal year is displayed in this tab (Steps 2 and 3).

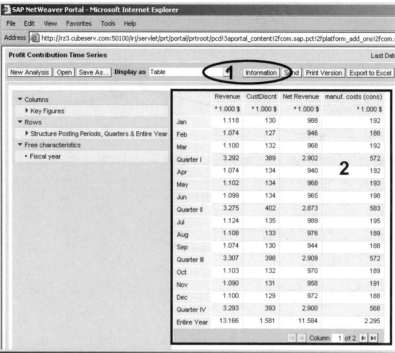

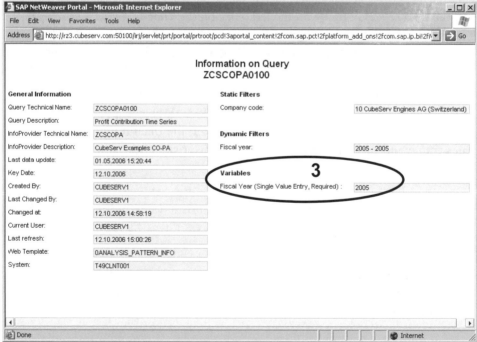

**Figure 7.26** Configuring the Use of Variables in Queries, Part 2

### 7.2.10 Conditions and Exceptions

Conditions allow you to hide data in the results area of the query, enabling you to display only specific sections of the results area.

Because conditions don't change any data or filter statuses and simply hide data that is not relevant, they have no influence on the total result. You can map several conditions within a query. You should note, however, that you can only display the data that meets all the conditions at the same time.

Conditions comprise the following functions:

▸ **Thresholds**
A value is displayed if it exceeds or falls short of a specific threshold value. The threshold value is specified in the condition.

▸ **Ranking List**
A ranking list displays the best or worst values, depending on the way you sort it. The sorting process is automatically based on the characteristic to which the condition refers. You can arrange the ranking list based on **Absolute** values, **Percentage** values, or **Absolute Total** values.

Exceptions describe the process of emphasizing values on the basis of defined rules. For example, critical objects are highlighted so that they immediately catch one's eye. Intervals and threshold values are assigned traffic light icons to indicate the current status. The status can be poor, critical, or good.

The relevant objects are determined at query runtime.

### 7.2.11 Exception Cells

Sometimes queries cannot be defined by the intersection of two axes, as is doable when you configure queries with lists of characteristic values or structures. An example of this is the share of a financial statement item in the balance sheet total, which is also referred to as a structural share or structural percentage. This item is usually presented with fixed structures. For this purpose, Business Explorer provides the function of exception cells.

Exception cells

If you define two structures within a query, you can implicitly create dedicated cell definitions at the intersections of the structure ele-

Prerequisites and functionality

ments. These cell definitions then determine the values to be presented in the cells. The cell definitions are created in the same way as formula and selection functions and they allow you to explicitly define formulas and selection criteria in addition to the implicit cell definitions. This allows you to override the implicitly created cell values.

Moreover, you can configure cells that have no direct relation to the respective structure elements. Those cells are not displayed and serve as a basis for auxiliary selections and formulas.

### 7.2.12 Table Display

Table display    The commonly used Business Explorer OLAP query automatically places the values defined in the Rows frame into the first column of the query results area displayed; however, this is not always suitable. For this reason, the table display function is available in Business Explorer (unless you use two structures).

The table display shows the characteristics and key figures in columns and doesn't provide any navigation options. Contrary to OLAP reporting, there are no free characteristics and rows available so that you cannot use the slice & dice function. You can use the filter in the table display to arrange characteristics, key figures, and attributes to meet your requirements. The column display is determined by the query definition, and unlike the OLAP query, it cannot be changed at runtime.

*The Business Explorer Analyzer enables the MS Excel-based presentation of data that is made available by the execution of Business Explorer queries. This component was also completely revised and complemented with new functions in SAP NetWeaver 2004s. This chapter describes some of these new functions.*

# 8    Business Explorer Analyzer

## 8.1    Introduction

Business Explorer Analyzer (BEx Analyzer) and the Business Explorer Query Designer (BEx Query Designer) are the two oldest Business Explorer components. Because the data is presented in MS Excel, BEx Analyzer is still used by many users despite its various drawbacks and the fact that it lacks the numerous options available with the Business Explorer web applications. One of the reasons for its popularity is certainly that one of the biggest target groups of data warehouse applications — the controllers — prefer Excel as their favorite tool for many tasks.

BEx Analyzer within the Business Explorer Suite

For this reason, SAP made a wise decision when it implemented various changes and enhancements in the new BEx Analyzer version in SAP NetWeaver2004s. The online documentation describes these changes[1], some of which will be critical for the user. In addition to technical changes such as

Changes and enhancements

▶ the support for entering and displaying Unicode texts,

it is predominantly the new functions such as

---

1  See the SAP documentation as available at the time this book was written:
   *http://help.sap.com/saphelp_nw04s/helpdata/de/f3/*
   *a75742330ad142e10000000a1550b0/content.htm,*
   *http://help.sap.com/saphelp_nw04s/helpdata/de/43/*
   *ec5e9085fc6befe10000000a11466f/content.htm,* and
   *http://help.sap.com/saphelp_nw04s/helpdata/de/43/*
   *f03ce0cec64c5de10000000a155369/content.htm.*

▶ the use of BI-integrated planning in the BEx Analyzer (see Chapter 11 on BI-integrated planning)

▶ the option to design Excel-based applications, for instance, in order to create planning applications

as well as new features in the operation of the tool such as

▶ the support of drag-and-drop when running BEx Analyzer applications

that represent a significant improvement of the user-friendliness of BEx Analyzer.[2]

## 8.2 Running a Query in BEx Analyzer

### 8.2.1 Starting BEx Analyzer

Like the other Business Explorer components, you can start BEx Analyzer from the programs menu in Windows.

[▪] ▶ To do that, activate the menu by clicking on the **Start** button (see Figure 8.1, Step 1) and open the **Programs** menu (Step 2).

▶ Click on the **Business Explorer** program group and select **Analyzer** (Steps 3 and 4).

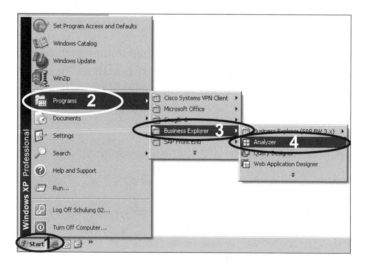

**Figure 8.1** Starting BEx Analyzer

---

2  See Footnote 1 in the SAP documentation for a complete list of new features.

▸ This starts MS Excel including the popup for the SAP BEx Analyzer macro. To use MS Excel as BEx Analyzer, click on the **Enable Macros** button (see Figure 8.2, Step 1).

▸ The macros are now activated and the toolbars **BEx Analysis Toolbox** and **BEx Design Toolbox** are displayed in Excel (Step 3).

### Opening a Query

▸ To execute a query in BEx Analyzer, click on the **Open** button and select the **Open Query** function from the menu (see Figure 8.2, Steps 2 and 4). If several SAP BW systems are available, the **SAP Logon** popup displays in which you can select the relevant SAP BW system.

[☞]

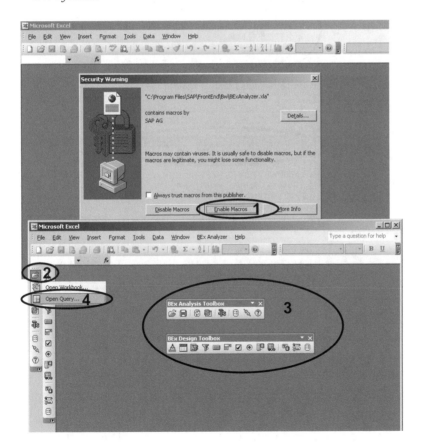

**Figure 8.2** Logging On and Selecting a Query, Part 1

▶ In the logon popup, **SAP Logon at ...**, enter the logon client, your user ID, password, and logon language, and click **OK** (Figure 8.3, Steps 1 and 2).

Selecting a query ▶ Then the **Open** popup displays in which you can select the preferred selection method (in the example: **History**) as well as a query (in the example: **Profit Contribution-Report per Country**) from the list (Steps 3 and 4).

▶ Click on the **Open** button to start the query in BEx Analyzer (Step 5).

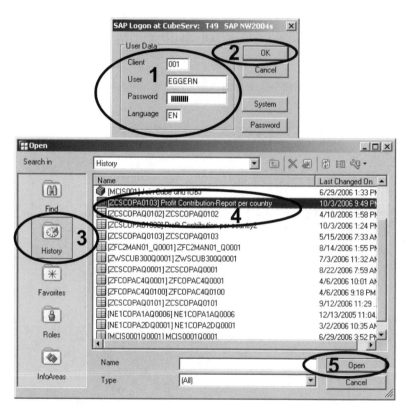

**Figure 8.3** Logging On and Selecting a Query, Part 2

Selecting variables ▶ If the BEx query contains variables with manual input, the popup of the new interface opens (see Figure 8.4, highlight 1).

▶ Enter or select the required variable value (in the example: **Fiscal Year 2005**, Step 2).

▶ Click on **OK** to confirm this. The query is now executed with the corresponding selections and displayed in the new style of SAP NetWeaver 2004s BEx Analyzer (Steps 3 and 4).

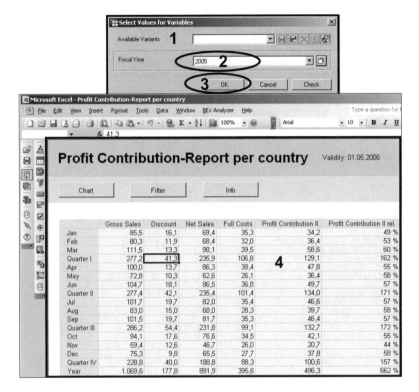

**Figure 8.4** Variable Selection and Query Display in BEx Analyzer

## 8.2.2 Using Filters in BEx Analyzer

In SAP NetWeaver 2004s BEx Analyzer, the user interface for carrying out filtering actions based on free characteristics has also changed. The new BEx Analyzer Workbook now contains a **Filter** button for this purpose.

*Using free characteristics as filters*

▶ If you click on this button (see Figure 8.5, Step 1), the relevant query components (free characteristics, key figures, and structures) are displayed on the left, next to the results table.

[✦]

▶ Right-click on the characteristic to be restricted to open the context-sensitive menu, and select the **Select Filter Value** function (Steps 2 and 3).

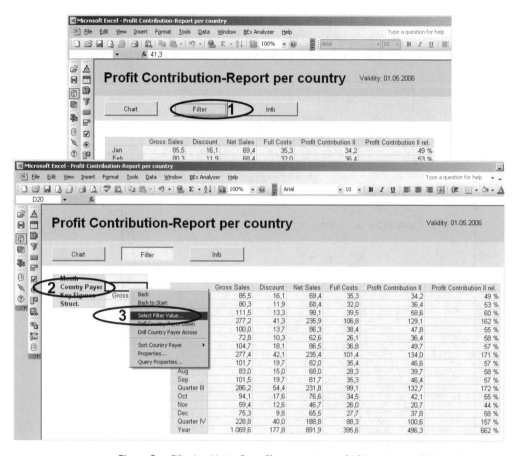

**Figure 8.5** Filtering Using Free Characteristics in SAP NetWeaver 2004s, Part 1

Selecting a
filter value

▶ This opens the popup **Select Values For Country** (in this example) in which you can click on the relevant value to select it (in the example: **Germany**) and confirm this selection by clicking on **OK** (see Figure 8.6, Steps 1 and 2).

▶ Once the query has been updated, the new filter value is displayed and the restriction is applied (Steps 3 and 4).

▶ To remove a filter, right-click on the relevant component to open the context-sensitive menu, and select the **Remove Filter** function (see Figure 8.7, Steps 1 and 2). *Removing a filter*

▶ After that, the query is updated and both the filter area and the results table are displayed without any restriction (Steps 3 and 4).

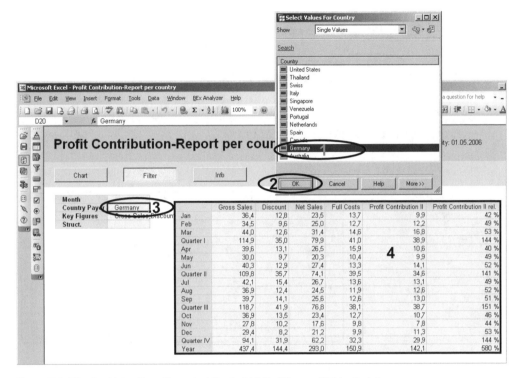

**Figure 8.6** Filtering Using Free Characteristics in SAP NetWeaver 2004s, Part 2

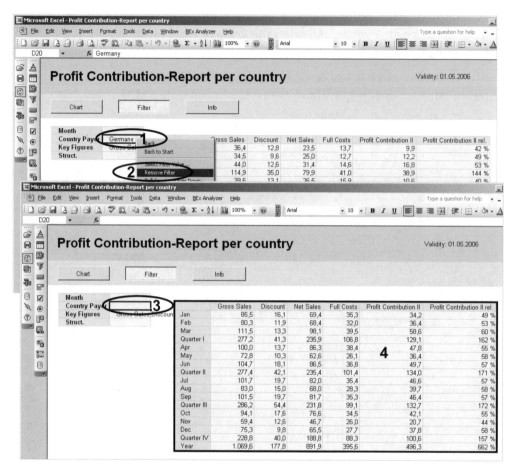

**Figure 8.7** Removing a Filter

### 8.2.3 Drag-and-Drop in BEx Analyzer

Drilldown via drag-and-drop

To drill down the query according to a characteristic, click on the characteristic and drag-and-drop it to the required position. In the example, you want to implement an additional drilldown by the sold-to country.

[.] ▸ To do that, select the sold-to country in the filter area and drag it into the column headers of the key figure structure (see Figure 8.8, Steps 1 and 2).

▸ After that, the drilldown status is displayed (Step 3).

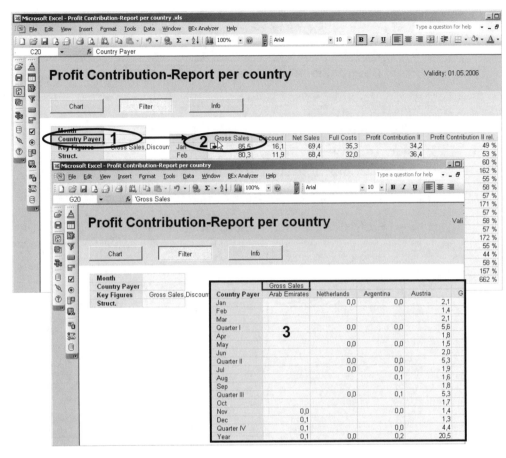

**Figure 8.8** Drilldown via Drag-and-Drop

Note that certain limitations exist in MS Excel (256 columns and 65,536 rows). This means that, depending on the drilldown status, a part of the results table can be truncated if you work with large drilldowns.

**[«]**

▸ As of SAP NetWeaver 2004s, you can use the drag-and-drop functionality to set filters on characteristic values and structure elements contained in the drilldown. To select the **Net Sales** element from the contribution margin scheme, click on the element and drag-and-drop it into the filter area (see Figure 8.9, Step 1).

Filtering via drag-and-drop

▸ The filter is then displayed in the filter area, and the results table is updated correspondingly (Steps 2 and 3).

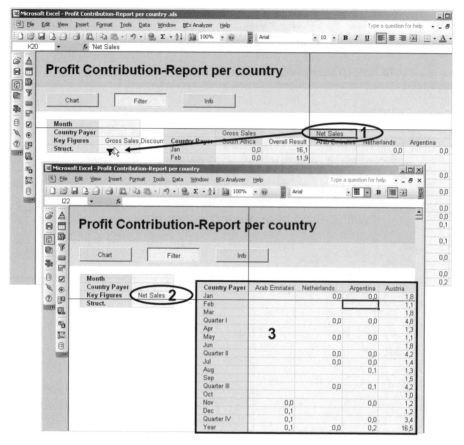

**Figure 8.9** Filtering via Drag-and-Drop

## 8.3 The Design Mode in BEx Analyzer

### 8.3.1 General Remarks

New design options

The design mode in SAP NetWeaver 2004s Business Explorer Analyzer provides completely new options for the design of workbooks. For example, you can integrate several components that you know from previous versions of SAP BW in BEx Analyzer workbooks. In addition, the BEx Analyzer design mode provides new design items such as a dropdown box, a radio button group, buttons, and so on. Therefore, the design mode in BEx Analyzer allows for the creation of more powerful applications without the need for any programming work. The formula mode, which is also new, facilitates the design of BEx Analyzer workbooks as well.

### 8.3.2 Creating an Application in the BEx Analyzer Design Mode

**Creating a New Workbook**

To create an application in the BEx Analyzer design mode, you must first create a new workbook.

▶ To do that, start BEx Analyzer and click on the Excel button **New** to create a new, empty workbook (see Figure 8.10, Step 1).

[**·**]

▶ In the empty spreadsheet, click on the cell into which you want to insert the analysis table (in the example: cell B7), and click on the **Insert Analysis Grid** button (Steps 2 and 3).

Inserting an analysis table

▶ If you haven't logged on yet, the **SAP Logon at ...** popup opens now. Here you must enter the logon client, your user ID, password, and your logon language. Confirm your entries by clicking on **OK** (Steps 4 and 5).

Logon

▶ Right-click on the design item to open the context-sensitive menu and select the **Properties** function (Steps 6 and 7).

Assigning a Data-Provider

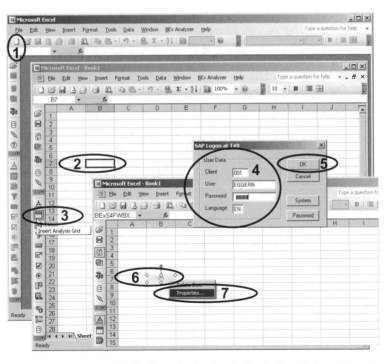

**Figure 8.10** Creating a BEx Analyzer Application in the Design Mode and Inserting an Analysis Table, Part 1

▶ This opens the **Analysis Grid Properties** popup. Click on the **Create DataProvider** button (see Figure 8.11, Step 1).

▶ In the **Create DataProvider** popup, click on the **Assign Query/Query View** button (Step 2) and select the required query in the **Open** popup (in the example: **Profit Contribution-Report per country** (ZCSCOPA0103), Steps 3 to 5).

▶ This transfers the selected query into the **Create DataProvider** popup (Step 6).

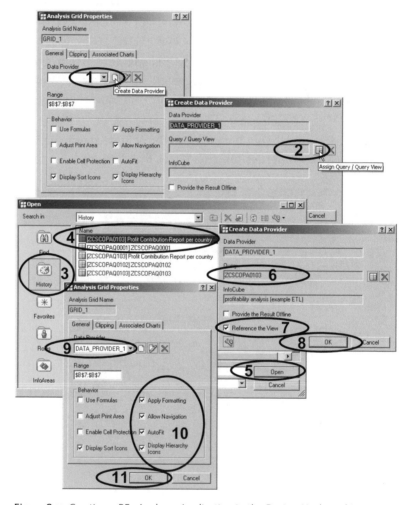

**Figure 8.11** Creating a BEx Analyzer Application in the Design Mode and Inserting an Analysis Table, Part 2

▶ Enable the **Reference the View** property and confirm this by clicking **OK** (Steps 7 and 8).

▶ In the **Analysis Grid Properties** popup, select the newly added **DATA_PROVIDER_1** and the properties, **Apply Formatting**, **Allow Navigation**, **AutoFit**, **Display Sort Icons**, and **Display Hierarchy Icons**. Complete the configuration process by clicking on **OK** (Steps 9 to 11).

### Execution

▶ Click on the **Exit Design Mode** button (see Figure 8.12, Step 1).  [■]

▶ Depending on the query, the data may not be displayed directly (Step 2).

▶ Click on the **Change Variable Values** button to open the selection popup of the query, enter the required variable values (in the example: **Fiscal Year 2005**), and click on **OK** (Steps 3 to 5).

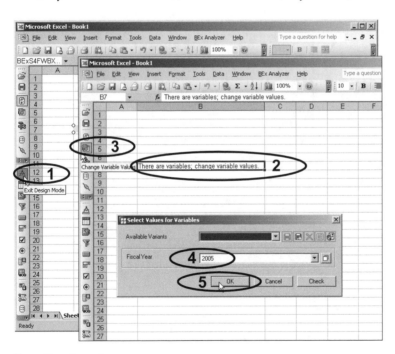

Figure 8.12 Execution

▶ The analysis table is now displayed in the correct position (see Figure 8.13, highlight 1).

377

### Saving the BEx Workbook

[●]
▸ To save your BEx workbook, click on the **Save** button and select the **Save Workbook as** function (see Figure 8.13, Steps 2 and 3).

▸ Enter the workbook name in the **Save Workbook** popup (in the example: **Profit Contribution-Report per country (Workbook)**, and click on **Save** (Steps 4 and 5).

▸ The workbook is now saved at the specified location in SAP BW (in the example that's the list of favorites), and the Windows title bar of BEx Analyzer now displays the name of the workbook (Step 6).

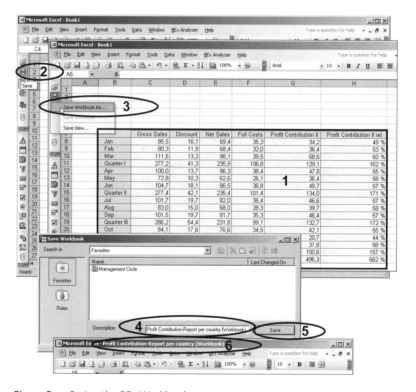

**Figure 8.13** Saving the BEx Workbook

### Inserting Text Elements: Query Description

In the next step, you want to display the query name, the static company code selection, and the selected year in the header of the BEx Analyzer workbook.

► Place the cursor in cell B1 and activate the **Design Mode** (see Figure 8.14, Steps 1 and 2). **[.']**

► Click on the **Insert Text** button (Step 3).

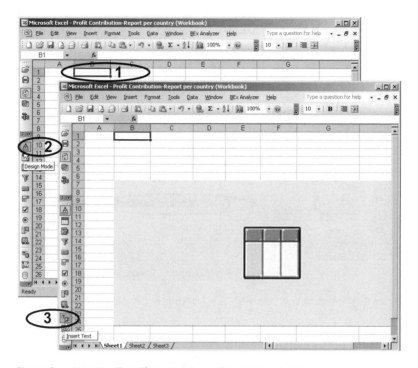

**Figure 8.14** Inserting Text Elements: Query Description, Part 1

► Right-click on the newly inserted design item to open the context-sensitive menu and select the **Properties** function (see Figure 8.15, Steps 1 and 2).

► In the **Text Properties** popup, go to the **General** tab and select **DATA_PROVIDER_1**. Then go to the **Constants** tab and select **Display Query Description** as the text element to be displayed (Steps 3 to 6).

► Complete the configuration process by clicking on the **OK** button (Step 7).

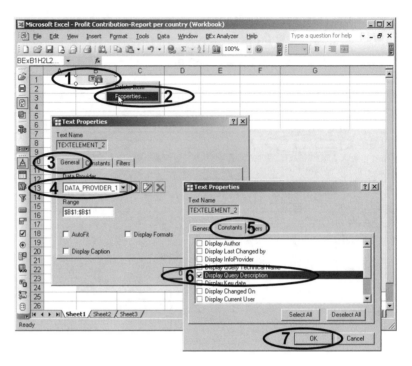

Figure 8.15 Inserting Text Elements: Query Description, Part 2

### Inserting Text Elements: Static Filter

Now you must insert the text element with information on the static filter, **Company code**, in the middle of the header. To do that, you must proceed in the same way as before.

[■]
- ▶ Place the cursor in cell D1 and click on the **Insert Text** button (see Figure 8.16, Steps 1 and 2).

- ▶ Right-click on the newly inserted design item to open the context-sensitive menu and select the **Properties** function (Steps 3 and 4).

- ▶ In the **Text Properties** popup, go to the **General** tab and select **DATA_PROVIDER_1**. Then go to the **Filters** tab and select **Display Company Code** as the text element to be displayed (Steps 5 to 6).

- ▶ Complete the configuration process by clicking on the **OK** button (Step 7).

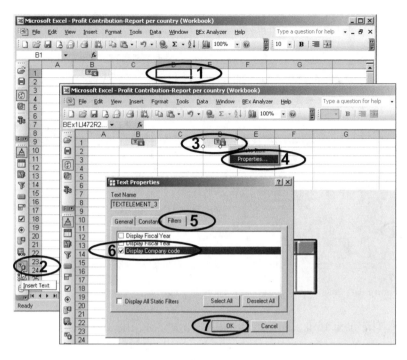

**Figure 8.16** Inserting Text Elements: Filters, Part 1

### Inserting Text Elements: Variable Value

Now you must insert the text element with information on the selected variable value, **Calendar year**, in the right-hand part of the header. To do that, proceed in the same way as you did before.

▶ Place the cursor in cell H1 and click on the **Insert Text** button (see Figure 8.17, Steps 1 and 2).                                              [◾]

▶ Right-click on the newly inserted design item to open the context-sensitive menu and select the **Properties** function (Steps 3 and 4).

▶ In the **Text Properties** popup, go to the **General** tab and select **DATA_PROVIDER_1**. Then go to the **Filters** tab and select **Display Fiscal Year** as the text element to be displayed (see Figure 8.17, Steps 5 and 6 as well as Figure 8.18, Steps 1 and 2).

▶ Complete the configuration process by clicking on the **OK** button (see Figure 8.18, Step 3).

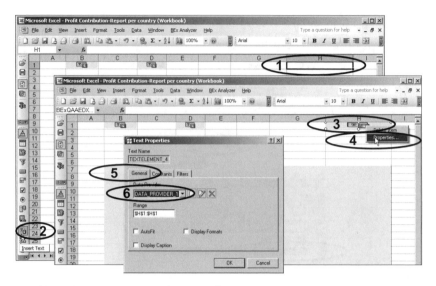

**Figure 8.17** Inserting Text Elements: Filters, Part 2

▸ The next time you run the BEx workbook, the analysis table and the inserted text elements will be displayed (Step 4).

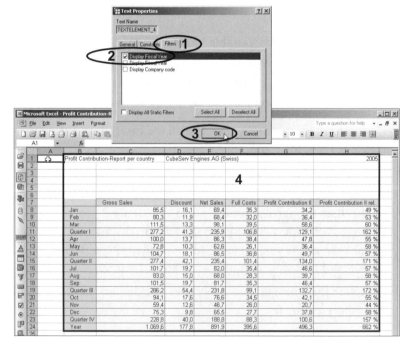

**Figure 8.18** Inserting Text Elements: Filters, Part 3

**Inserting a Dropdown Box for Characteristic Selection**

In the next step, you want to insert a dropdown box to be used for selections according to the free characteristic, **Sold-to Country**, in the BEx Analyzer workbook.

▶ Place the cursor in cell B4 and click on the **Insert Dropdown Box** [▪] button (see Figure 8.19, Steps 1 and 2).

▶ Right-click on the newly inserted design item to open the context-sensitive menu and select the **Properties** function (Steps 3 and 4).

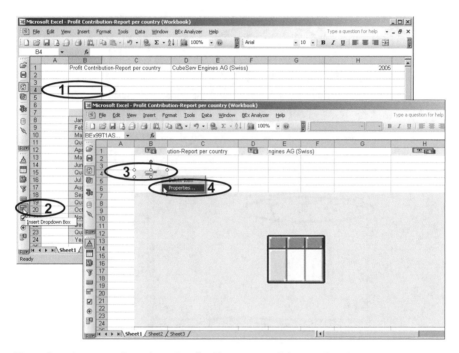

**Figure 8.19** Inserting a Dropdown Box for Characteristic Selection, Part 1

▶ In the **Dropdown Box Properties** popup, go to the **General** tab and select **DATA_PROVIDER_1** as well as the **Display Label** property (see Figure 8.20, Steps 1 to 3).

▶ Then go to the **Dimensions** tab and select the **Country Payer** characteristic as the dimension to be displayed (Steps 4 and 5).

▶ After that, go to the **TargetDataProvider** tab and select **DATA_PROVIDER_1** (Steps 6 and 7).

▶ Complete the configuration process by clicking on the **OK** button (Step 8).

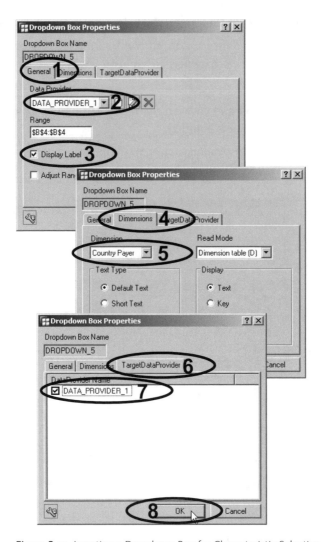

Figure 8.20 Inserting a Dropdown Box for Characteristic Selection, Part 2

### Inserting a Button

In the next step, you want to insert a button that will be used to update the BEx workbook after the selection of a sold-to country.

[▪] ▶ Place the cursor in cell H4 and click on the **Insert Button** button (see Figure 8.21, Steps 1 and 2).

▶ Right-click on the newly inserted design item to open the context-sensitive menu and select the **Properties** function (Steps 3 and 4).

► In the **Button Properties** popup, enter **Run** as the button text (Step 5).

► Select the **FILTER_IOBJNM** action and the value **DATA_PROVIDER_1** (Steps 6 and 7).

► Complete the configuration process by clicking on the **OK** button (Step 8).

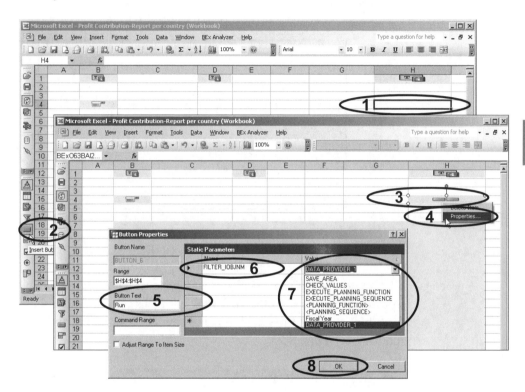

**Figure 8.21** Inserting a Button

### Executing and Selecting the BEx Workbook

When you execute the query, the dropdown box and the new button are displayed. If you select a value in the dropdown box (in the example: **Germany**) and then click on the **Run** button, the newly elected values are displayed in the BEx workbook (see Figure 8.22, Steps 1 to 3).

| | Gross Sales | Discount | Net Sales | Full Costs | Profit Contribution II | Profit Contribution II rel. |
|---|---|---|---|---|---|---|
| Jan | 36,4 | 12,8 | 23,5 | 13,7 | 9,9 | 42 % |
| Feb | 34,5 | 9,6 | 25,0 | 12,7 | 12,2 | 49 % |
| Mar | 44,0 | 12,6 | 31,4 | 14,6 | 16,8 | 53 % |
| Quarter I | 114,9 | 35,0 | 79,9 | 41,0 | 38,9 | 144 % |
| Apr | 39,6 | 13,1 | 26,5 | 15,9 | 10,6 | 40 % |
| May | 30,0 | 9,7 | 20,3 | 10,4 | 9,9 | 49 % |
| Jun | 40,3 | 12,9 | 27,4 | 13,3 | 14,1 | 52 % |
| Quarter II | 109,8 | 35,7 | 74,1 | 39,5 | 34,6 | 141 % |
| Jul | 42,1 | 15,4 | 26,7 | 13,6 | 13,1 | 49 % |
| Aug | 36,9 | 12,4 | 24,5 | 11,9 | 12,6 | 52 % |
| Sep | 39,7 | 14,1 | 25,6 | 12,6 | 13,0 | 51 % |
| Quarter III | 118,7 | 41,9 | 76,8 | 38,1 | 38,7 | 151 % |
| Oct | 36,9 | 13,5 | 23,4 | 12,7 | 10,7 | 46 % |
| Nov | 27,8 | 10,2 | 17,6 | 9,8 | 7,8 | 44 % |
| Dec | 29,4 | 8,2 | 21,2 | 9,9 | 11,3 | 53 % |
| Quarter IV | 94,1 | 31,9 | 62,2 | 32,3 | 29,9 | 144 % |
| Year | 437,4 | 144,4 | 293,0 | 150,9 | 142,1 | 580 % |

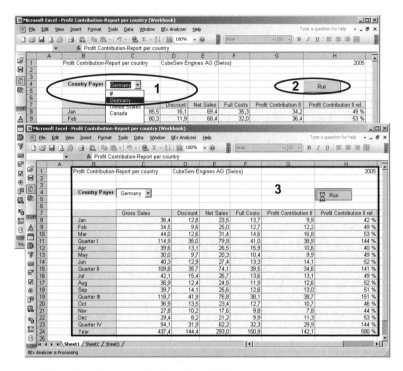

**Figure 8.22** Executing and Selecting the BEx Workbook

**Formattings** The familiar functions in MS Excel and Business Explorer enable you to add a header to the BEx workbook with a larger font and in bold type, hide the grid lines, column, and row headers, and include the toolbar (see Figure 8.23).

| | Gross Sales | Discount | Net Sales | Full Costs | Profit Contribution II | Profit Contribution II rel. |
|---|---|---|---|---|---|---|
| Jan | 36,4 | 12,8 | 23,5 | 13,7 | 9,9 | 42 % |
| Feb | 34,5 | 9,6 | 25,0 | 12,7 | 12,2 | 49 % |
| Mar | 44,0 | 12,6 | 31,4 | 14,6 | 16,8 | 53 % |
| Quarter I | 114,9 | 35,0 | 79,9 | 41,0 | 38,9 | 144 % |
| Apr | 39,6 | 13,1 | 26,5 | 15,9 | 10,6 | 40 % |
| May | 30,0 | 9,7 | 20,3 | 10,4 | 9,9 | 49 % |
| Jun | 40,3 | 12,9 | 27,4 | 13,3 | 14,1 | 52 % |
| Quarter II | 109,8 | 35,7 | 74,1 | 39,5 | 34,6 | 141 % |
| Jul | 42,1 | 15,4 | 26,7 | 13,6 | 13,1 | 49 % |
| Aug | 36,9 | 12,4 | 24,5 | 11,9 | 12,6 | 52 % |
| Sep | 39,7 | 14,1 | 25,6 | 12,6 | 13,0 | 51 % |
| Quarter III | 118,7 | 41,9 | 76,8 | 38,1 | 38,7 | 151 % |
| Oct | 36,9 | 13,5 | 23,4 | 12,7 | 10,7 | 46 % |
| Nov | 27,8 | 10,2 | 17,6 | 9,8 | 7,8 | 44 % |
| Dec | 29,4 | 8,2 | 21,2 | 9,9 | 11,3 | 53 % |
| Quarter IV | 94,1 | 31,9 | 62,2 | 32,3 | 29,9 | 144 % |
| Year | 437,4 | 144,4 | 293,0 | 150,9 | 142,1 | 580 % |

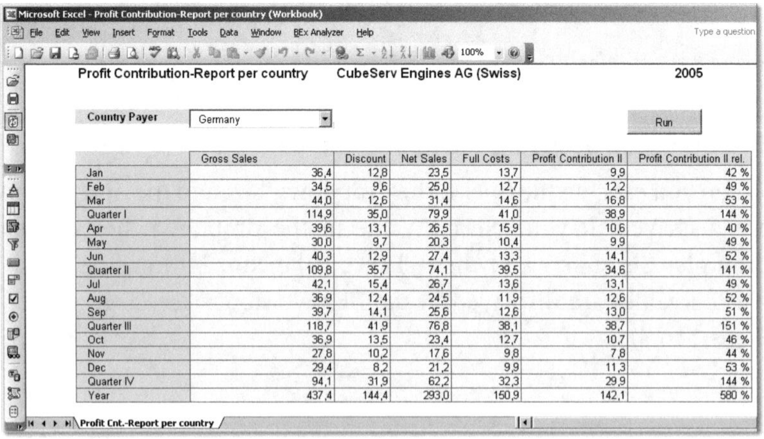

**Figure 8.23** The BEx Workbook with Configured Design Items and Formatting

*Compared to Excel-based reporting, web-based reporting using BEx Analyzer is much faster and provides better design options. The BEx Web Application Designer is a very valuable tool for the creation of web-based reporting applications. Unlike previous versions, the concept of this tool has been completely revised in SAP NetWeaver 2004s.*

# 9 BEx Web Application Designer

Contrary to SAP NetWeaver Visual Composer (see Chapter 12), which can also be used to create web-based applications, BEx Web Application Designer enables you to develop applications in the frontend and publish these applications to the SAP Enterprise Portal, a role, or the BEx Information Broadcaster. Moreover, you can run the applications directly in the browser without having to start a portal environment in the browser prior to that.

The following sections guide you step by step through the creation of a web application—a so-called *web template*—using the Web Application Designer.

## 9.1 Getting Started

Once you have logged in, the Web Application Designer displays on your screen. The screen is divided into three large areas (see Figure 9.1):

Three areas

▶ **Modeling area (highlight 1)**
This large area in the center of the screen is the part where you arrange the web items and the entire design. Here you can also use a limited preview to examine the web template being developed.

Furthermore, you can display the open template in three different views that can be changed using tabs. The **Layout** view is the default view that displays all items and elements you use. The lower part of the **Layout** view displays an overview of the Data-Providers that are known within the application.

In addition, you can use a view to display the source code by clicking on the **XHTML** tab. And finally, you can use the **Overview** tab to get a list of the items being used. The items are grouped by their type and sorted either by the place of their publication or in a hierarchy; however, the overview displays only existing web items and does not include extensions that you might have created manually.

▶ **Web item pool (highlight 2)**
The left-hand area of the screen displays the available elements, that is, the web items that you can integrate into the application, as well as their properties, in case you select a web item that has already been included.

The list contains all available web items, while the corresponding web item properties are displayed in the lower part of the screen. The properties area contains all properties that are available for each web item. There's only one exception to that, namely the chart, which uses a wizard to set its properties. This means that you can only make basic settings for the chart in the properties area.

▶ **Error and warning area (highlight 3)**
The area for error messages and warnings provides information on inconsistencies and errors that may exist in a web template.

Layout mode | For most applications, the **Layout** mode view is absolutely adequate. This is a kind of WYSIWYG editor, which you might be familiar with from having used similar authoring tools.

XHTML mode | Sometimes, however, it may be necessary to perform some fine-tuning action for which you should use the XHTML mode. This mode enables you to insert JavaScript code into the header area if necessary, for example.

For better readability, the elements are displayed in different colors in the XHTML mode.

▶ BI tags such as web items or DataProviders: dark red
▶ HTML elements: black
▶ Attributes: red
▶ Attribute values: blue
▶ Texts: green
▶ Comments: gray
▶ Hyperlinks: purple

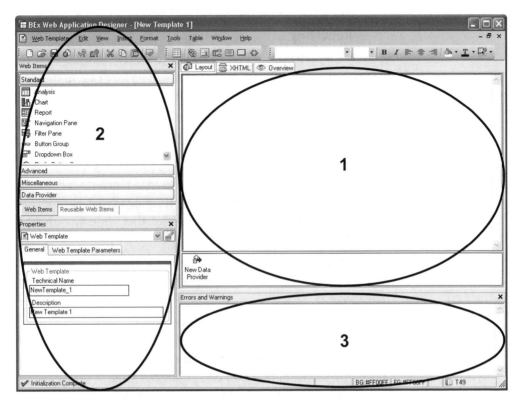

**Figure 9.1** Structure of BEx Web Application Designer

As in previous versions, you can use the data export of a template to edit templates that have been exported to a file system in an external HTML editor and to re-import the templates into the system afterwards.

When you leave the XHTML view and return to the **Layout** view, or when you save the web template, the system automatically verifies the source code. In this process, it checks the BI tags for syntax errors and displays errors in the warning area.

Verifying the source code

## 9.2 Simple Web Reporting

The first steps of web-based reporting are pretty easy. With its drag-and-drop interface, BEx Web Application Designer provides a simple tool that enables you to quickly achieve results.

### 9.2.1 Creating a Simple Web Template for Time Series Reporting

The first sample template that you want to create contains a simple table as a time series. Based on that, you will further extend the template in the subsequent steps until you obtain a complex reporting application at the end.

**Creating a Web Template**

▶ The first step consists of creating a new web template. When you launch BEx Web Application Designer and log in to it, the tool displays an overview of the web templates that were last opened. Select **Create New Web Template**.

▶ Use **Plan/Actual Sales** as the heading and write these words into the template. Then save the template in your list of favorites via **File • Save as**.

▶ The system requires both a technical name and a descriptive name. Choose **ZCSDEMO001** as the technical name and **Plan/Actual Sales Time Series** as the description. Save the template in your list of favorites (see Figure 9.2, Step 1). You can also save templates within specific roles in order to use the templates in future applications, which is also a good way of structuring your applications.

▶ Click on the **Run** button to view your first template in the browser (Step 2).

▶ The next step consists of adding a DataProvider. The DataProvider can either be a query or a query view. You want to use the query you created in Section 7.2, so you must select it. To do that, you must select the corresponding icon from the list of DataProviders (Step 3).

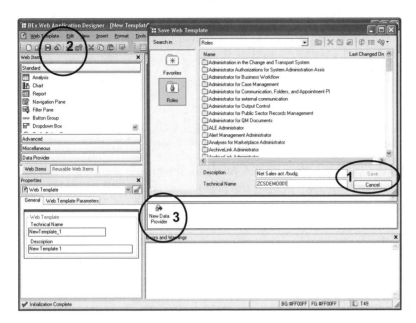

**Figure 9.2** Your First Web Template

## 9.2.2 Design of the Web Template

At this point, you should consider the basic design of your web template. Basically, there are two types of HTML design available. The first design type is controlled via Cascading Style Sheets (CSS), while the other type involves positioning within tables.

Because the table-based solution is easier to implement and is less confusing within BEx Web Application Designer, you will now create a table layout.

▶ Click on the button with the table icon and then select a table that consists of one row and three columns. When creating the table, enter the value **left** under the **align** attribute and enter **top** under **valign**. You will fill these three columns step by step during the course of this chapter (see Figure 9.3, Step 1). [⏴]

▶ Drag an **Analysis** web item from the web items pool and drop it into your template. This web item is automatically assigned DataProvider **DP_1**, which you have just selected (Step 2). This is necessary so that the web item is assigned a data source. Without a DataProvider, your analysis table would not display any data.

> ▶ In the **Properties** section, make sure that **Alternating styles for table rows** and **Visible table header** are activated, and that the **Full width** flag is checked (Step 3).

> ▶ Save the template once again and run it in the browser (Step 4).

The remaining fields will be filled with data in the subsequent chapters so that you'll have created a small web application by the time you reach the end of this book.

Analysis table

In the current version, the **Analysis table** web item replaces the familiar **Table** web item of the previous versions. This web item has been extended with planning functions and a function to display documents within cells. You can configure the web item according to your requirements in the **Properties** area. The properties contain default settings for width and height, but also table-specific properties such as the display of alternating styles for table rows.

A drag-and-drop function was mapped in the current version for the **Analysis table** and **Navigation Pane** web items.

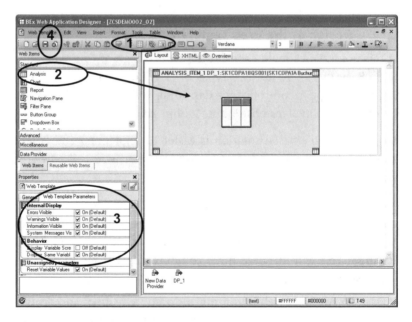

**Figure 9.3** Simple Web Template with Analysis Table

The navigation pane displays the current navigation status of the corresponding DataProvider and provides options to change this status. It displays all characteristics and structures of the DataProvider. This web item allows you to change the drilldown status via drag-and-drop by removing the characteristics from the relevant axes or by adding new characteristics. Moreover, you can interchange the axes.

Navigation pane

Language-independent text is used to incorporate continuous text in the web template. In addition to the default properties, you can define the color, design, and line breaks of the text in this context.

Language-independent text

As data source for this text, you can use a characteristic text, a general text element, or plain text. For the first two options, you must specify a DataProvider and a characteristic or text element respectively.

**Adding a Navigation Pane**

In the next step of the example, you'll add a navigation pane. To do that, you must first remove the label from the left-hand column and position it above the table by using the text icon.

► Drag a **Language-Independent Text** web item from the **Miscellaneous** tab and drop it above the table. Regarding the properties, you must ensure that you select the **Header 1** design and that line breaks are disabled (see Figure 9.4, Step 1). Set the width to 500 pixels. Select **Simple Text** as data binding method and enter **Net Sales act./budg.** in the window that displays under **Current Text Preview** (Step 3).

[.]

► Drag the **Navigation Pane** web item into the cell next to the **Analysis table** (Step 4).

► Place the cursor within a table cell. Right-click to open the context menu. Under **Tag <TD> Properties**, set the **Vertical Orientation** to **top**. Repeat this step for all three table cells.

► Save and execute your web template.

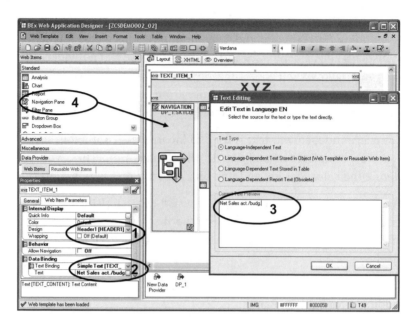

**Figure 9.4** Integrating a Navigation Pane and Text

### The Context Menu

The two web items you have just integrated both contain data. Moreover, they contain a context menu that you can open by right-clicking when you place the cursor in a table cell or the navigation pane.

Depending on the context, the web item, and the navigation status, the context menu allows you to execute several functions. In the current version, you can customize the context menu by using a separate web item. If this web item exists in the template, you can enable and disable the various functions in the properties area. Due to the large number of functions that are provided in one single menu, the context menu has become a powerful navigation tool, which is why we recommend your looking at the individual functions it provides.

The context menu contains the following functions (see Figure 9.5):

▸ **Back**

This function undoes the last navigation step on the DataProvider of the web item. You should use this function instead of the corresponding one provided by your browser in order to return to specific navigation statuses.

▶ **Filter**
This function enables you to filter the DataProvider. Not only can you fix, set, and remove filters, but also you can call the variable screen once again and create conditions. Such conditions, however, apply only for the current call and are not saved along with the query.

▶ **Change Drilldown**
This function manipulates the current drilldown of the DataProvider that's being executed. You can add and remove drilldowns, exchange axes and structures, and replace characteristics.

▶ **Hierarchy**
This function affects the presentation hierarchy of the DataProvider, if such a hierarchy exists. You can activate and deactivate hierarchies and expand or minimize nodes and levels.

▶ **Printed Version**
In the current version, you can produce a print version in PDF format from the web template that is being executed.

▶ **Broadcast and Export**
This function group contains functions for distributing the current web template via BEx Broadcaster to different recipients such as email or the Enterprise Portal. The BEx Broadcaster is described in Section 9.7. Moreover, this function group contains interfaces to other programs such as the export of data to MS Excel or as a comma-separated file (CSV). In addition, this group enables you to set bookmarks for each navigation status.

▶ **Save view**
This function saves the navigation status of the DataProvider as a query view, which you can then use, for instance, as a basis for a report in BEx Web Report Designer.

▶ **Properties**
Here you can change the properties of cells, DataProviders or web items at runtime. Note that the settings you make here do not overwrite the settings made at the time the objects were created. They only apply to the current execution.

▶ **Calculations and conversions**
This function group contains tools for the conversion of key figures as well as the settings for calculating single cells or results. Moreover, you can select a cumulative display here.

▶ **Exceptions**
Here you can create new exceptions. A wizard supports you in doing so.

▶ **Jump**
If you define jump targets via the report-report interface, you can jump to those targets from here.

▶ **Documents**
These functions are used for document management purposes. You can upload documents, view uploaded documents, and create a comment or formatted text.

▶ **Sort**
Depending on the cell type, you can sort by values or keys.

▶ **Key Figure Definition**
The key figure definition shows the structure of a key figure.

▶ **Personalized Web Template**
This function enables you to save the current status of the web template including drilldown and filter status as a personalized web template so that it is displayed in exactly the same way the next time it is called.

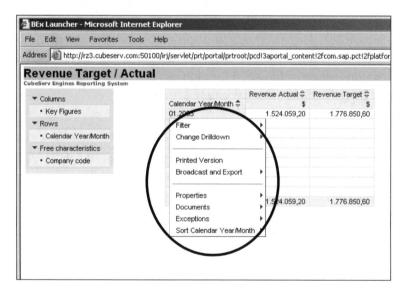

**Figure 9.5** Web Application with Context Menu

### 9.2.3    Design Based on CSS and MIME Objects

Up until now you have created a functioning but not very attractive web template. You already map functions such as navigation and drilldowns, but as mentioned earlier, one of the great strengths of web-based reporting is that you have more control over the design. In this context, there are two central elements: The option to integrate objects from the MIME Repository and the consistent use of cascading style sheets (CSS).

MIME (Multipurpose Internet Mail Extensions) objects are objects that are embedded in HTML pages. The MIME type defines the way in which the browser should display the object. In the SAP BW environment, MIME objects are stored in the MIME Repository from where they can be integrated in the web template. For graphics, the corresponding menu item is **Insert • Picture**. Other objects such as centrally managed JavaScripts can be integrated in the XHTML view. For objects to become available, you must first import them in the MIME Repository. Then you can integrate them in the web template by specifying the relevant navigation path.

*Embedded in HTML pages*

Cascading style sheets are MIME objects of the **Text** type. You can use them to define the formatting of fonts and other layout settings in one place within the HTML page. The advantage of a CSS is that each HTML element can be assigned a class, which, in turn, is centrally defined within the style sheet. In this way, you only need to make changes to the CSS instead of having to change each element individually. This method is extremely advantageous if you use complex reporting applications with several dozens of web templates. Although the standard version already contains several CSS files, we strongly recommend that you copy an existing style sheet and make changes only to the copy.

*Cascading style sheets*

To go to the style sheet entry, open the Edit menu and select **Edit Element <head> ....** If no entry is available here, the default style sheet will be used.

*Entering the style sheet*

You can also assign a CSS class or HTML attribute directly to the HTML elements. To do this, a dialog exists that you can call via the context menu of the respective item or HTML tag. The settings you make there apply to the selected object.

### Adjusting the Design of the Sample Template

In this section, you'll assign a CSS class to several elements and align the orientation of the elements.

[•] ▸ Create a `<DIV>` tag below the heading text by using the corresponding icon (see Figure 9.6, Step 1).

▸ Enter the text **CubeServ Engines Reporting System** in the tag.

▸ Right-click to open the context menu and select **Tag <DIV> Properties**. Go to the **CSS Style** tab.

▸ Under **fontFamily**, select **Verdana**, then select **bold** under **fontStyle**, finally select **#00005B** under **Color**. The text element will now be displayed in bold and dark blue Verdana font (Step 2).

▸ Transfer these settings and confirm your selection.

▸ Then save and execute your web template.

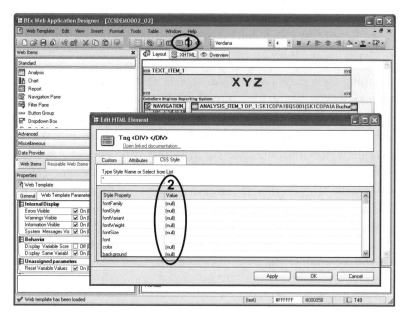

**Figure 9.6** Entering the CSS Properties

The text within BEx Web Application Designer automatically adjusts itself to your CSS changes.

### 9.2.4 Integrating Charts

A chart processes the information from a DataProvider and stages it graphically. To create a chart, a chart designer is available that contains a preview function and provides numerous chart types and setting options. In contrast to other web items, charts are controlled using a wizard that displays the changes in real time. Once you have decided on a basic design, the wizard can generate a complete chart; however, usually, you must make certain additional settings via the **Refine** button.

The setting options are divided into different categories.

▶ **Global Settings**
The global settings are used to make basic settings such as the chart type, dimensionality, color palette, and font. These settings apply to the entire chart. You can either define the color palette by yourself, or you can choose a color palette from various existing ones.

▶ **Layout**
The **Layout** category controls the arrangement of chart elements across the entire graphic. You can arrange all elements individually or use the automatic arrangement function.

▶ **Background**
Here you can define the background including the frame.

▶ **Drawing Area**
Similar to the setting options for the background, the drawing area category controls the drawing area of the graphic.

▶ **Chart Type**
This category provides settings for the different chart types. In a bar chart, for example, you can define the distances and instances of overlapping between the individual bars.

▶ **Category Axis, Value Axis**
The axis properties describe values such as the display of the smallest and biggest values. If automatic scaling is not required, you can assign two different scalings to the value axis, and you can also assign data series to different axes.

▶ **Title, Subtitle**
If a title has been specified, you can format it here.

▶ **Legend**
If the chart contains a legend, you can use settings for orientation, distance, separator signs, or sequence.

▶ **Series, Points**
You can define different chart types for different data series. By
default, the main chart type is set for all data series. Moreover,
you can change the appearance of data series and points.

▶ **Structures**
This category does not allow you to make any changes.

The chart wizard reminds you of the setting options available in MS
Excel so that all those options are also available in the Web Application Designer.

**Integrating a Bar Chart**

In the following exercise, you will integrate a bar chart into the application. The bar chart is based on the table that you created earlier.

[▪] ▶ Drag a **Chart** item from the selection list into the blank cell at the
right margin of the table and make sure that **DP_1** has been
selected as DataProvider (see Figure 9.7, Step 1). Under certain circumstances it is useful to have two separate DataProviders for the
table and the chart because a chart typically contains data that is
aggregated at a higher level. Moreover, the chart should not contain more than five data series.

▶ To obtain a clearer display, interchange the **Axes** of the DataProvider in the properties area.

▶ Adjust the width of the element to the free space within the HTML
table. Make sure that you use up the space in such a way that it
still fits into a screen in order to avoid using scroll bars.

▶ Left-align the chart at the upper margin of the cell.

▶ Ensure that the legend is displayed below the chart.

▶ Change the property for **Category Axis** · **Line** · **Text Properties** ·
**Direction** to **down** (Step 2).

▶ Change the bar colors for **Actual Sales Revenues** to dark green and
those for **Planned Sales Revenues** to dark blue. You can find this
setting in the **Series** group. The easiest way to access the series is
to click on it in the legend (Step 3).

▶ Save and execute your web template.

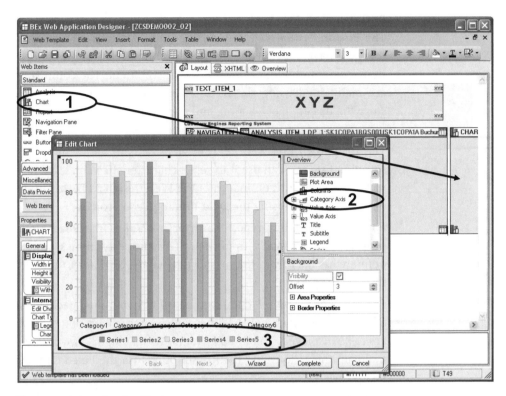

**Figure 9.7** Integrating the Chart

## 9.2.5 Other Web Items

Of course, the web items described up until now are definitely not all web items that are available. The following list briefly describes all the remaining web items.

▶ **Report**
The **Report** web item inserts a report that has been created in BEx Web Report Designer. You can access BEx Web Report Designer either by starting the standalone application or via the context menu of the web item. Then you must select the relevant report via the **Report Design** property.

▶ **Filter Area**
The **Filter area** web item enables you to filter single characteristics by characteristic values. The characteristics are arranged in dropdown boxes and are made available in one place. The **Characteristic quantity** property allows you to define the initial pool of characteristic values to be made available.

▶ **Button Group**

The **Button Group** web item enables you to organize commands that you have previously created using the Web Design application programming interface (API) via a web item. The commands are maintained using the **Button List** property. There you can store the design, label, action, and a tooltip.

▶ **Dropdown Box**

The **Dropdown Box** web item provides content and actions as a selection list. You can use it to select characteristic values, a query view, or to execute commands of the Web Design API. The differentiation is made using the **Data Binding Type** property.

For the data binding type, **Characteristic Value**, the **Read Mode** property is specifically important. This property allows you to define what data from the master data table you want to transfer into the dropdown box.

For the query view selection, on the other hand, the **Specific List of Query Views** parameter defines which query views of the query are to be displayed. To bind data to the Web Design API, you must maintain the actions and their descriptions via the **Fixed Options List** property.

▶ **Radio Button Group**

The **Radio Button Group** web item represents characteristic values as a list with radio buttons. If you activate a radio button, the associated DataProvider is filtered by this characteristic. For the purpose of simplification, you should use this filtering method only for characteristics that don't contain more than 10 values. Again, the **Read Mode** property is important here as it enables you to manipulate the read mode of the master data table.

▶ **Checkbox Group**

Similar to the **Radio Button Group** web item, you can use the **Checkbox Group** web item to list characteristic values as a group of checkboxes. The difference between the radio button group and the checkbox group is that the latter enables you to include more restrictions so you can check and uncheck different characteristics. Again, note the **Read Mode** property.

▶ **Listbox**

The **Listbox** web item displays the values of the set characteristic in a listbox. Multiple selections are possible here. Again, note the **Read Mode** property.

▶ **Hierarchical Filter Selection**
The **Hierarchical** web item enables you to filter a presentation hierarchy by hierarchy nodes and leaves. When navigating within the hierarchy, you can expand and collapse nodes. Moreover, you can perform a search through the entire hierarchy.

▶ **Web Template**
The **Web Template** web item allows you to embed other, previously defined web items into the current one. The implementation occurs at runtime.

▶ **Container Layout**
The **Container Layout** web item arranges the web items it contains as would occur in an HTML page. Additionally, aspects such as accessibility are also considered. The **Row List** property allows you to define the exact position of items. A prerequisite for this functionality is that you must first drag the web items into the container layout.

▶ **Container**
You can use the **Container** web item to group HTML code or web items and to display them within other items, such as **Tabs**.

▶ **Tabs**
The **Tabs** web item is used to arrange different web items. For example, you can assign a web item to each tab so that the web items only display when you click on the associated tab. The **Tab List** property enables you to define which web items you want to assign to which tab.

▶ **Group**
A **Group** web item is a syntactically coherent entity within a web application.

▶ **Single Document**
The **Single Document** web item displays a document from knowledge management in the web template. To do that, you must first transfer the document into SAP BW via the master data maintenance or the Data Warehousing Workbench. In addition to the **Document Type** and **List of Documents** properties, you can also define a **Default Screen** that displays when no corresponding document is found.

▶ **List of Documents**
A **List of Documents** web item displays the documents that belong to the navigation status. The presentation includes the characteristics that have been set in the Development Workbench.

▶ **Map**

The **Map** web item can display geographical information in the form of a map. You can implement geographical data using the external ArcView (ESRI) tool. This web item enables you to display regional information at different levels of detail. Map levels can be defined and maintained via properties.

▶ **System Messages**

The **System Messages** web item displays system messages such as errors, warnings, and notes.

▶ **Info Field**

The **Info Field** web item displays various kinds of information, for instance, on users, connected DataProviders, or the web template itself. You can define what kind of information you want to display via the properties.

▶ **DataProvider Information**

The **DataProvider Information** web item generates XML data at query runtime, which contains information on the navigation status of the DataProvider or the query results of the DataProvider. Note that the generated XML data is not displayed in the frontend, since it is merely generated into the source text.

▶ **Text**

The **Text** web item displays a language-dependent text in the logon language of the user. This can be a plain text, a characteristic value, or a general text element.

▶ **Link**

The **Link** web item generates a language-dependent link to any command; for example, this can be a command of the Web Design API.

▶ **List of Exceptions**

The **List of Exceptions** web item lists all exceptions that are available in the query or query view. In this context, it doesn't matter whether or not the exception is active.

▶ **List of Conditions**

The **List of Conditions** web item lists all conditions that are available in the query or query view.

▶ **Menu Bar**

The **Menu Bar** web item enables a simple display of menus. You can group commands via the **Menu** property and trigger an action, for example, a Web Design API action. The individual items to be included in menu groups can be created using the **Menu Item** property.

▶ **Ticker**
The **Ticker** web item enables you to display the content of a query as a ticker. The ticker is a good means of displaying data that changes quickly, such as share prices.

▶ **Property Area**
The **Property Area** web item allows you to display the properties of the web template. You can define the display of specific properties using the **Property Definition** property. The **Debug Mode** property that displays the technical names of the displayed objects provides a diagnosis functionality.

▶ **Context Menu**
In the current version, you can define the context menu by using the **Context Menu** web item. If the web item does not exist in the template, the system uses a default context menu. You can show and hide the different functions of the context menu by specifying the corresponding settings in the properties.

These brief summaries don't describe the full functionality of the web items and should simply be regarded as a short outline of the available options.

At this point, we should mention that you can also mark web items with existing settings as reusable. To do that, open the context menu and select **Save item as reusable**. The system then prompts you to enter a technical name and description. Once you have entered this information, you can reuse the web item.

## 9.3    Complex Web Reporting

Complex web reporting deals with the more difficult tasks of web reporting such as the language-dependent maintenance of texts. But even these tasks have become easier due to the redesign of BEx Web Application Designer.

The Web Design API is the central tool to use for complex web reporting. But, do not mistake this tool with the tool for customizing BI tables in Version 3.x, which has the same name. The central tools

Web Design API

within the Web Design API are commands and command sequences that are executed via command wizards.

The command wizards replace the manual entry of commands, which should be familiar to you if you have used previous versions. You can assign the generated commands to different web items. Another new web item is the option to group different web items and arrange them, for example, in a menu. Nevertheless, you can still carry out the final step of the template creation by inserting Java-Script code or by fine-tuning the code.

This section describes the techniques involved in complex reporting and explains the functionality on the basis of an example. You will create a new application containing this functionality.

### 9.3.1 Basic Template

**Creating a Basic Template**

Your first task consists of creating a basic template, which will then be extended in the subsequent steps.

**[◼]**
- ▶ Create a new web template via **Web Template · New**.
- ▶ Define **NESKCOPA01** as a new DataProvider, **DP_1**.
- ▶ Create an HTML table that consists of three rows and one column.
- ▶ Drag a new **Analysis** web item into your web template. Position this item in the bottom row and set the **Full Width** property.
- ▶ Drag a new **Text** web item into the top row to use it as the title of the application. Enter **CubeServ Engines Reporting** as the text. Make sure that the **Design** property is set to the value, **Header1**.
- ▶ Check if your analysis table is assigned to DataProvider **DP_1**.
- ▶ Define **NESKCOPA02** as a new DataProvider, **DP_2**.
- ▶ Drag the **Context Menu** web item into your application to obtain access to the context menu functions. Although the position of this web item doesn't really matter, you should make a habit of always placing it in the same position, for example, as the last web item.
- ▶ Save your work.

You'll use this web template as a basis for all subsequent steps. This template that you just created contains a heading, a data area, and context menu. You'll use the area that has been left blank for navigation purposes.

### 9.3.2 Menu Structure

Not only does a menu structure enable the user to execute different commands and actions in a clear and straightforward way, it also provides a certain degree of modularization, which enables the developer to structure the application.

Enables modularization

The current version provides the **Menu Bar** web item that allows you to implement commands as actions in order to obtain a menu-driven control. Therefore, complex programmings, for instance, in JavaScript, are a thing of the past. A menu, however, must still be well planned; otherwise, the users would get lost within the application. For this reason, you should carefully consider at which points within the application an overall navigation should take place and whether it makes sense to separate the navigation within the application from the navigation based on filters within individual templates. For applications with large filter areas, it may be useful to use tabs to separate the filters from the display.

If you want to navigate across several web templates, you must ensure that the navigation always occurs in the same place. This gives users the impression that they are working within one application, although they are combining technically separate applications with each other. Menu bars typically start with a few items and grow continuously over time, along with the application.

#### Creating a Menu Bar

In the following example, you'll implement a menu bar and define the first two items.

- ▸ Drag the **Menu Bar** web item into the blank area in the middle of your HTML table (see Figure 9.8, Step 1). You can find this web item in the **Miscellaneous** category. **[⚡]**
- ▸ Add another item to the menu bar (Step 2).
- ▸ Select **Trigger Action** for the first menu item and launch the detail view by clicking on the corresponding icon (Step 3). The parameter wizard opens.

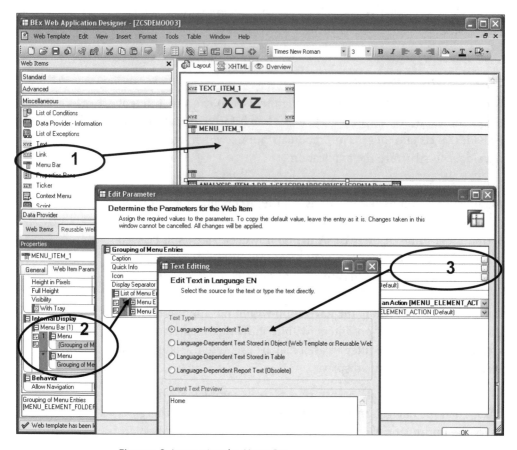

**Figure 9.8** Integrating the Menu Bar

▶ In the wizard, assign the **Home** name to the **Label** and **Tooltip** properties (see Figure 9.9, Step 1).

▶ Select **CHANGE_TEMPLATE** from the **Commands for Web Templates** subfolder, and specify the name of the current template as target template. This command opens a new template. Later on, you will integrate a title page, which you can access from any point within the application.

Commands   You have integrated a web template command in your web template. Such commands affect DataProviders or even entire web templates. Those of you who have already worked with previous versions should remember this technique from the so-called command URLs. The functionality has also been integrated in the graphical user interface.

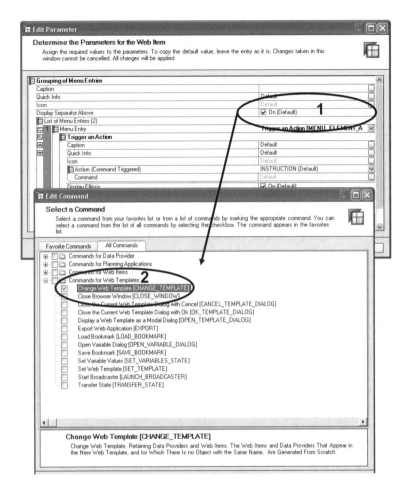

**Figure 9.9** Setting the Action

The commands are arranged in different groups.

▶ **Commands for DataProvider**
The commands for DataProviders contain actions to manipulate the status of the DataProvider. These actions include commands to interchange the axes or to filter by characteristics.

▶ **Commands for Planning Applications**
These commands can be used with planning applications.

▶ **Commands for Web Items**
The commands for web items modify the properties of web items being used. You can use these commands, for example, to change the parameters of a web item or to open the properties dialog.

► **Commands for Web Templates**
These commands include actions that refer to the web template being executed. These include the setting of bookmarks and the closing of the current template.

### Creating the Menu Item "Functions"

In the next step, you'll include two more actions into your menu bar. For this purpose, you must first create a new menu item, **Functions**, which will then contain the commands.

**[⬝]**

► Select the menu bar and generate a new menu item.

► Select **Grouping of Menu Entries** as the relevant function (see Figure 9.10, Step 1).

► Open the wizard.

► Enter **Functions** as label and tooltip text.

► Create two more menu items in the window that opens now (Step 2).

► Select **Action** for both menu items.

► Create the first item using the label **Export to MS Excel** and the command, **EXPORT**. Select **MS EXCEL** as the export format to be used and enter your analysis table in the **Data Binding** section (Step 3).

► Create the first item using the label **Print to PDF** and the command, **EXPORT**. Select **PDF** as the export format to be used and enter your analysis table in the **Data Binding** section (Step 4).

► Then save and execute your web template.

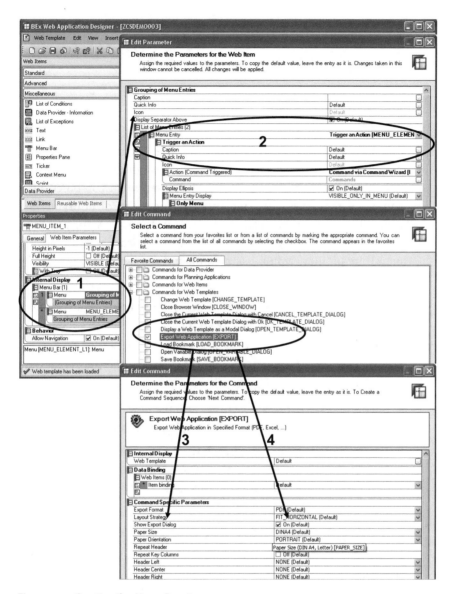

**Figure 9.10** Creating the Menu Functions

### 9.3.3 Export Function

The web application now contains a grouped function menu with two functions. The **Export** function is a powerful tool to make the data available to other applications. Printing into the popular PDF format enables you to also transfer page formattings. The **Export to MS Excel** is provided for users who want to post-edit the data.

[»] You should note that, however, the connection to the server no longer exists and that you cannot carry out any OLAP operations such as filterings or drilldown changes.

### Bookmarking

Bookmarking describes the process of storing a navigation and drilldown status in the system in order to retrieve it at a later stage. The bookmark is stored in the system. You can call the bookmark at a later stage via a bookmark ID. Furthermore, when combined with command sequences, bookmarks are a good way of notifying end users about certain navigation statuses. In the next step, you'll set bookmarks and define a bookmark call for which you'll use a command. In addition, you'll use a command sequence to describe the printout into a PDF file via a bookmark.

[▪] ▸ Create a new menu group in the **Menu Bar** web item of your template and assign the name **Hot Spot** to it.

▸ Within the menu group, create an item called **Set Bookmark**. Assign the **SAVE_BOOKMARK** action from the **Web Template Commands** group to this item.

▸ Save and restart your application. Run the new command. The system returns a bookmark ID. Write down this bookmark ID.

▸ Create another menu item in the **Hot Spot** menu group, and call it **Hot Topic**. Assign the **LOAD_BOOKMARK** action from the **Web Template Commands** group to this item.

▸ Save and execute your web template.

You can now set bookmarks, and the bookmark you just created guides the users to a setting defined by yourself. To enable your users to directly print out your analysis, you will now define a command sequence, which first calls the bookmark and then exports the analysis into a PDF file.

[▪] ▸ Add another menu item to the **Hot Spot** menu group under the **Menu Bar** web item, and call it **Hot Spot Printable**. Assign the **LOAD_BOOKMARK** action to this new item. Select the bookmark you created in the previous step as data binding.

▸ Select **Next Command** to create a command sequence. This takes you to the **Command List Editing** screen (see Figure 9.11, Step 1).

- ▶ Select the **EXPORT** command from the **Commands for Web Templates** group.

- ▶ Select **PDF** as the export format and save the command sequence. The new command is listed in the command sequence (Step 2).

- ▶ Save and execute your web template.

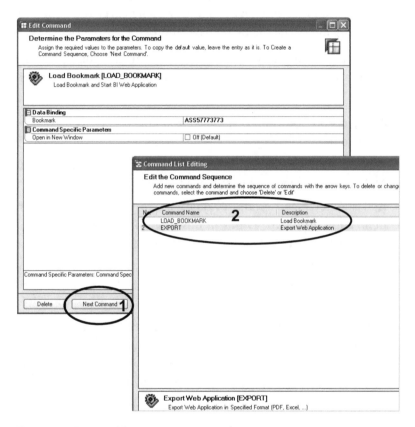

**Figure 9.11** Command Sequences

## Command Sequences

Command sequences enable you to link any number of actions to each other that are to be performed in a specific sequence. You can maintain and manage the actions separately and independent of each other. This way you can implement BI statements via the command sequences, irrespective of the complexity of the statements. Note that the sequence of the commands can affect the functionality of your application. Therefore, for example, filter actions should be carried out at the beginning of the sequence, whereas the closing of the application should, of course, occur at the end of the sequence.

### Integrating Other Templates

Typically, complex applications consist of several templates that are linked to each other and have a common home page. The templates are logically linked via the menu navigation.

In the next section, you'll create a second template, link this to the first one via the menu bar, and then create a **Home** page that welcomes the user.

[■]
- ▶ Create a copy of your current web template and assign a new name to it.
- ▶ Remove the **Analysis** web item and replace it with a **Bar Chart**. Make sure the axes are interchanged for the display.
- ▶ Add another menu group, **Evaluations**, to your **Menu Bar** web item, and create two actions in this group that contain the command **CHANGE_TEMPLATE**. Therefore, each action refers to one of your web templates.
- ▶ Arrange your **Menu Bar** in such a way that the functions are positioned at the end. **Home** should occur in the first place.
- ▶ Create a new template. Place a **Text** web item into this template and use **Welcome!** for the text. Save this web template as **ZCSHOME**. Change the setting for the action in the **Home** menu item in such a way that it refers to the newly created page.

### 9.3.4 Multiple Languages

Web applications can output content in the logon language of the user. In this context, you must consider several aspects.

The master data on which the queries are based must be maintained in all the languages you need. If that is the case, you must prepare the query itself for the use of multiple languages. This means that you must maintain text elements in all logon languages. You must also consider the language dependency of text variables of the customer exit type, because these variables are not caught using standard SAP tools.

Finally, you must translate the web application. There are several ways to do this.

▶ **Language-dependent report texts, Text program**
Users of Version 3.x will certainly remember the text program. You create a program in Transaction SE38 where you maintain text icons. The text icons are assigned sequential numbers as keys, which, in turn, are used to call the text icons in BEx Web Application Designer. For compatibility reasons, this option is also available in the current version. Note, however, that it is marked as being outdated. The input process has been redesigned and is now more convenient as you can select the key in the properties of a **Text** type web item. Note also that those texts require a separate transport as they belong to a separate program.

▶ **Language-dependent texts, stored in the object**
These texts are stored as language-dependent in the selected object and depend on the logon language in BEx Web Application Designer. The object can be a web item or a web template. Texts that are stored in this way can be post-edited in the BEx Web Application Designer.

▶ **Language-dependent texts, stored in the table**
These texts are stored within the text table for BEx objects. Texts that already exist can also be displayed, provided that translated versions are also available. These texts are not bound to BEx Web Application Designer and are therefore also available in other components of the BEx Suite.

**Using Multiple Languages**

In the following exercise, you'll welcome the users in different languages on your home page.

▶ Open your web template **ZCSHOME**.                              [✓]

▶ Edit the text properties.

▶ Select **Language-Dependent Text Stored in Object** as text type (see Figure 9.12, Step 1), and create a new text. Enter **Welcome to the Reporting Cockpit!** as the label (Step 2).

▶ Save the text element.

▶ Re-logon to the system. Select **German** as the **Logon Language**.

‣ Repeat the steps for the German translation. Select **Edit** in the text element to edit it (Step 3).

‣ Save and execute your web template.

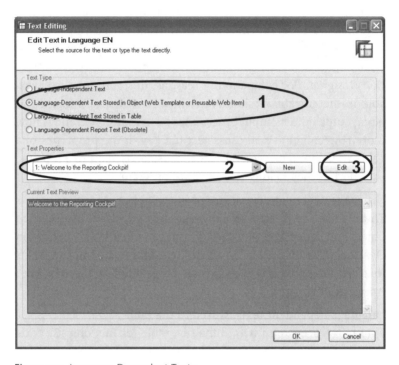

**Figure 9.12** Language-Dependent Texts

### Maintaining Language-Dependent Texts

In the previous step, you integrated a language-dependent text into your application. If a user logs on in the respective logon language, the system displays the texts in that language. Basically, all web items are prepared for the use of multiple languages so that in the next step, you can enter language-dependent texts in the entire application to ensure consistency.

[■] ‣ Open the web templates **ZCSCOPA002** and **ZCSCOPA003**, and edit the **Menu Bar** web item.

‣ Set the description to the **Language-Dependent Text Stored in Object** text type for each menu item.

‣ Repeat this procedure for the logon language German.

‣ Save your work.

### 9.3.5   Links

Finally, you must link the **Home** page with the other components of the application. For this purpose, you must create a link for each template and the **Hot Spot** and create a short welcome text.

▶ Open the **ZCSHOME** template and insert an HTML table that con-   [.]
sists of one row and two columns underneath the text.

▶ Drag three **Link** type web items into the right-hand column.

▶ Assign an **Action** to each of the links Two links should reference the web templates you created previously, while one link is supposed to run the Hot Spot bookmark.

▶ Fill the left-hand area with a **Text** web item that contains a short welcome text, or perhaps even some current news. Format the text using the **Label** property.

### 9.3.6   Preliminary Result

Up until now, you have written a small but rather powerful web application. In summary, your web application contains the following features:

▶ Language dependency
▶ Menu navigation
▶ DataProvider command
▶ Bookmarking
▶ Export function to MS Excel
▶ Printing into PDF format
▶ Focusing of users to a specific navigation status
▶ Home page
▶ Context menu
▶ Modular structure

As you can see, it is possible to quickly and easily obtain useful results. You can also further extend this web application whenever you like.

## 9.4    Structure of Web Templates

This section describes the source code of web templates and is intended for users who know XHTML and how to create web templates.

XHTML view The basic structure of a web template does not differ from that of a static HTML page. When you open a new template and go to the XHTML view, you'll see the following source code:

```
<bi:bisp  xmlns="http://www.w3.org/TR/REC-html40"
xmlns:bi="http://xml.sap.com/2005/01/bi/wad/bisp"
xmlns:jsp="http://java.sun.com/JSP/Page" >
    <html >
        <head >
            <title >NetWeaver BI Web Application</title>
            <meta http-equiv="Content-Type"
content="text/html; charset=utf-8" />
        </head>
        <body >
            <bi:TEMPLATE_PARAMETERS name="TEMPLATE_
PARAMETERS" />
<!--
 insert data providers, items and other template content
here -->
        </body>
    </html>
</bi:bisp>
```

BI-specific tags On the one hand, the source code contains standard HTML tags such as <head> and <body>; on the other hand, it also contains *BI-specific tags* that designate the web items. The <bi:bisp> tag forms the framework of the web template. It defines the communication path via Java Server Pages (JSP) and XML.

If you integrate a web item, the following code displays for the web item (here: an analysis table).

```
<bi:ANALYSIS_ITEM name="ANALYSIS_ITEM_1" designwidth="400"
designheight="200" >
    <bi:DATA_PROVIDER_REF value="DP_1" />
    <bi:FULL_WIDTH value="X" />
</bi:ANALYSIS_ITEM>
```

The item is opened and closed by a tag. These tags enclose the definition of the DataProvider. As in previous versions, the properties are maintained as combinations of a property and a value.

## 9.5 Portal Integration

You can integrate the BI content you created with the Business Explorer Suite into the SAP Enterprise Portal. In this way, you can merge different types of content from the Internet and intranet in one place.

The integration enables closer collaboration, even across the boundaries of the BI system. Because you can also connect other systems to the SAP NetWeaver Portal, you can combine tasks such as a workflow, for instance, at one maintenance point. The integration into the portal is based on the role concept, which means that the end user can view and navigate the reports and content for which his or her role is authorized.

As of the latest version, the web applications are processed entirely by the engine of the SAP NetWeaver Portal. The following options are available:

- Integration as iView
- Integration as document via Knowledge Management
- Web Analyzer link
- Direct link
- Business Planning and Simulation (BW-BPS) web interface

If you choose an integration via iViews, you can arrange several web applications in parallel within the portal.

## 9.6 Migrating 3.x Web Templates

Since there are already countless web applications available in the BI environment and the changes in the current version are based on a different technology, the BEx Web Application Designer contains a migration tool that supports the migration of web templates of earlier versions. If you don't carry out a migration, you cannot use the new features; however, note that SAP NetWeaver 2004s fully supports 3.x web templates.

You can access the migration tool by selecting **Tools • Migration Tool** from the menu. To carry out the migration process, you must define the following:

▸ The web template that you want to migrate (see Figure 9.13, highlight 1)

▸ The conversion settings (highlight 2)

The migration process then consists of the following steps:

▸ Select the web template to be migrated

▸ Create an export XML

▸ Transformation process based on an XML schema

▸ Possible correction

▸ Completion and saving of the web template

**[»]**   Note that you cannot carry out an automatic correction in all cases. The more proprietary developments your web template contains, the more manual corrections you will have to perform.

During the migration process, a progress bar informs you about the current status of the migration (highlight 3).

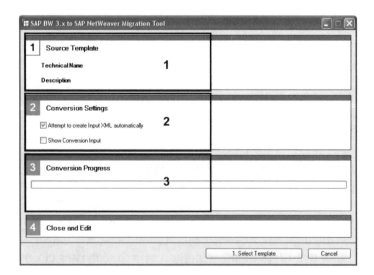

**Figure 9.13** Migration Tool for 3.x Web Templates

## 9.7    BEx Broadcaster

Broadcasting describes the distribution of previously calculated content to different recipients. This enables you to make a specific piece of information available to a wide range of users. The tool to be used for broadcasting is the BEx Broadcaster, which now performs the tasks of the familiar Reporting Agent. The Reporting Agent is still available (Transaction REPORTING_AGENT), but it is no longer supported.

You can schedule queries, query views, reports, or entire workbooks or web templates for broadcasting and dispatch them via email, publish them into SAP NetWeaver Portal, or print them. You can also just send a link to an application via email.

Therefore, the BEx Broadcaster is a tool that enables power users or system administrators to dispatch reports on a regular or event-driven basis. The functions include the following:

▶ **Dispatch of Emails**
The dispatch via email enables you to distribute precalculated objects such as reports or workbooks, or links to a specific template to a large number of users. You can combine this function with a specific user's profile. The prerequisite for the email dispatch is the correct maintenance of the assignment of user names to email addresses in the user master data.

▶ **Precalculating the Value Set**
Precalculated value sets fill variables of this type with characteristic values that are then available in BEx queries.

▶ **Filling the Precalculation Storage**
This option performs a precalculation (for example, for web templates) and stores the precalculated versions in the portal structure. The precalculated versions can then be accessed in the portal structure.

▶ **Filling the OLAP Cache**
The OLAP cache is filled with the defined queries, which significantly reduces the workload of the application server at query runtime. Because the cache is a temporary storage, it is not filled completely and permanently.

▸ **Filling the MDX Cache**
The filling of the Multi-Dimensional Expressions (MDX) cache enables you to cache query results for the downstream delivery to non-BW applications.

▸ **Dispatch (Several Channels)**
The dispatch through several channels enables the simultaneous distribution in different ways by using only one broadcasting setting. The type of data to be distributed determines the way in which the distribution occurs.

▸ **Dispatch Exception Specifically**
This function monitors queries containing exceptions in the background. When a defined threshold value is reached, a document is created and distributed to the recipients.

You can call BEx Broadcaster in the following ways:

▸ BEx Query Designer: menu bar

▸ BEx Report Designer: menu bar

▸ BEx Web Application Designer: menu bar

▸ BEx Analyzer: analysis toolbar

▸ Web application: context menu of a web item; the context menu must be configured correspondingly

▸ Web Analyzer: context menu of a web item; the context menu must be configured correspondingly

▸ Standard web report: **Send** button

The broadcasting setting that contains criteria for a preferred process is the basis for each broadcasting process.

Once you have specified the BI object and the distribution type, including the preferred settings, the object is distributed according to the settings.

You will now have a template precalculated, which you can then send to your email address. Note that email addresses must be contained in the user master record.

**[▪]**  ▸ Run a web template in the browser. The template must contain at least one web item and an activated context menu.

▸ Start BEx Broadcaster via the context menu, **Distribute and Export • Send E-Mail**.

▶ Select **Online Links to Current Data** as output format (see Figure 9.14, Step 1).

▶ Then enter your email address, a subject, and a descriptive text (Step 2).

▶ Assign the technical name **ZCSDEMO01** to the planning and use **Broadcaster** as a description (Step 3).

▶ Select the **Direct Scheduling in the Background Processing** option (Step 4).

▶ Confirm your entries by clicking on the **Schedule** button.

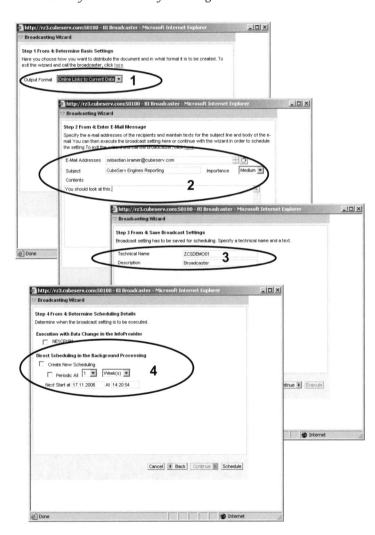

**Figure 9.14** BEx Broadcaster

*The Report Designer is an entirely new component within SAP Business Explorer. This tool enables you to create formatted reports for online and print applications. This chapter provides you with an overview and instructions on using the basic functions of the Report Designer.*

# 10 Report Designer

## 10.1 Introduction

With regard to the use of analysis tools, there are two predominant types of usage: Whereas one of the two types needs the tools mainly for analysis and research purposes, the second type of usage requires formatted tools that are optimized for screen and/or print output. Since its inception, SAP BW has supported the analysis with many useful functions. For formatted, print-optimized reporting, however, third-party frontends or very advanced, customized solutions were frequently used.

Formatted reporting as a usual requirement

With its Enterprise Reporting concept, SAP provides formatted, output-optimized reports in SAP NetWeaver 2004s. These reports are created using the Business Explorer component, Report Designer (see Figure 10.1 and the SAP documentation).[1]

A tool for formatted reporting

The BEx Report Designer uses Business Explorer queries as data sources. The reports are presented through a web browser (for example, Microsoft Internet Explorer). Reports that have been created using BEx Report Designer can be integrated in Business Explorer web applications. For this purpose, the design tool for Business Explorer web applications—the BEx Web Application Designer—provides a corresponding web item. A PDF file is generated for print output via the Adobe server.

Data source and output medium

---

1 See also: *http://help.sap.com/saphelp_nw04s/helpdata/de/4b/ 157e41ec0d020de10000000a1550b0/content.htm*

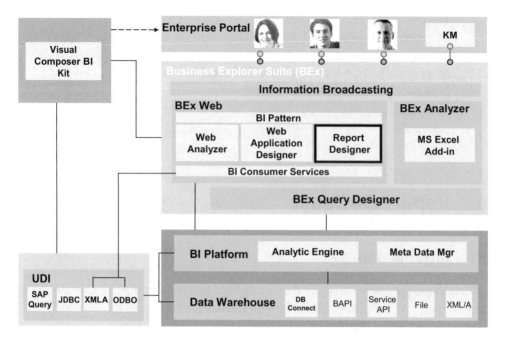

**Figure 10.1** The Report Designer as a Component of the Business Explorer Suite (Source: SAP AG)

## 10.2 Enterprise Reporting—Sample Application

Query as a data source

We now want to create a sample report that displays the data of the query CubeServ Engines Profit Contribution (ZCSCOPAQ0101) (see Figure 10.2).

▶ The columns of the query contain a simple contribution margin scheme with amounts displayed in terms of million euros. The rows display a structure with calendar months and subtotals per quarter as well as the annual total amount.

▶ We will exactly define the formatting of columns, rows, and cells (see Figure 10.3).

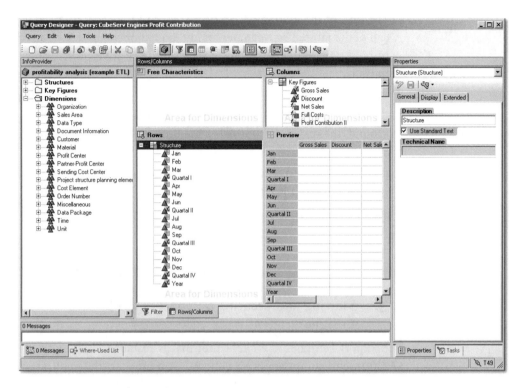

**Figure 10.2** Query "Profit Contribution (Time Series)"

| in Mio EUR | Gross Sales | Discount | Net Sales | Full Costs | PC II | PC II rel. |
|------------|------------|----------|-----------|-----------|-------|-----------|
| Jan | 27,7 | 4,0 | 23,8 | 10,0 | 13,7 | 57,7 % |
| Feb | 27,4 | 4,0 | 23,4 | 9,9 | 13,5 | 57,6 % |
| Mar | 27,5 | 4,0 | 23,5 | 9,9 | 13,6 | 58,0 % |
| **Quartal I** | **82,6** | **11,9** | **70,7** | **29,8** | **40,8** | **57,8 %** |
| Apr | 27,7 | 3,9 | 23,7 | 9,8 | 13,9 | 58,5 % |
| May | 27,9 | 4,0 | 23,9 | 10,0 | 14,0 | 58,4 % |
| Jun | 27,6 | 4,0 | 23,6 | 9,9 | 13,7 | 58,1 % |
| **Quartal II** | **83,2** | **11,9** | **71,3** | **29,7** | **41,6** | **58,3 %** |
| Jul | 27,8 | 4,0 | 23,8 | 10,1 | 13,7 | 57,5 % |
| Aug | 28,3 | 4,1 | 24,2 | 10,1 | 14,1 | 58,3 % |
| Sep | 28,4 | 4,0 | 24,3 | 10,3 | 14,1 | 57,8 % |
| **Quartal III** | **84,5** | **12,1** | **72,4** | **30,5** | **41,9** | **57,9 %** |
| Oct | 28,4 | 4,1 | 24,4 | 10,2 | 14,2 | 58,2 % |
| Nov | 28,6 | 4,0 | 24,5 | 10,1 | 14,4 | 58,6 % |
| Dec | 28,0 | 4,0 | 23,9 | 10,1 | 13,9 | 58,0 % |
| **Quartal IV** | **84,9** | **12,1** | **72,8** | **30,4** | **42,4** | **58,3 %** |
| **Year** | **335,2** | **48,0** | **287,2** | **120,4** | **166,7** | **58,1 %** |

CubeServ Engines Profit Contribution

**Figure 10.3** Standard Print Output of Query "CubeServ Engines Profit Contribution" Using Standard PDF Printing

- The unit of the amounts is to be displayed in the upper left-hand cell of the table. The **Net Sales** and **PC II** columns will be formatted in bold type, while we want to italicize the relative profit contribution.

- The totals (quarters and year) are to be displayed in bold type in the rows. The individual months are assigned a light gray background, the quarterly subtotals a medium gray color, and the total amount is to be assigned a dark gray background.

- For better readability, we want to separate the lead column and the **Net Sales** and **PC II** columns from the other columns.

- The query description is to be formatted as the report title.

## 10.3 Installing and Executing BEx Report Designer

### 10.3.1 Starting and Creating a Report in the Report Designer

The Report Designer is a client tool that is installed along with the SAP frontend components on your PC. You can start the application from the program menu of your PC.

**Starting the Report Designer**

[■]
- To start the Report Designer — provided the installation of the SAP frontend components on your PC hasn't been modified — click on the **Start** button to open the **Programs** menu. Then select the **Business Explorer** group and then **Report Designer** (see Figure 10.4, Steps 1 to 4).

Logging onto SAP NetWeaver 2004s BI
- This opens the **SAP Logon at ...** popup. Enter the logon client (**Client**), the user ID (**User**), the password (**Password**), and the required logon language (**Language**) (Step 5).

- Complete the logon process by clicking on the **OK** button (Step 6).

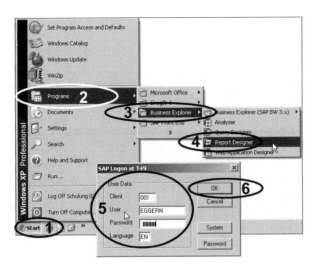

**Figure 10.4** Starting Business Explorer Report Designer

### Adding a Query as Data Source

▶ Once you have logged on, the Report Designer opens.  [▪]

▶ To define a data source, click on the **Add Data Provider** button (see Figure 10.5, Step 1).

▶ In the **Open** popup, go to the search method **History** and select the required query (in the example: Query **ZCSCOPAQ0101**) by clicking on it. Then click on the **Open** button (Steps 2 to 4).

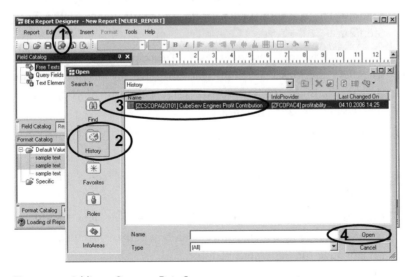

**Figure 10.5** Adding a Query as Data Source

429

▶ This transfers the query into the report (see Figure 10.6, Step 1).

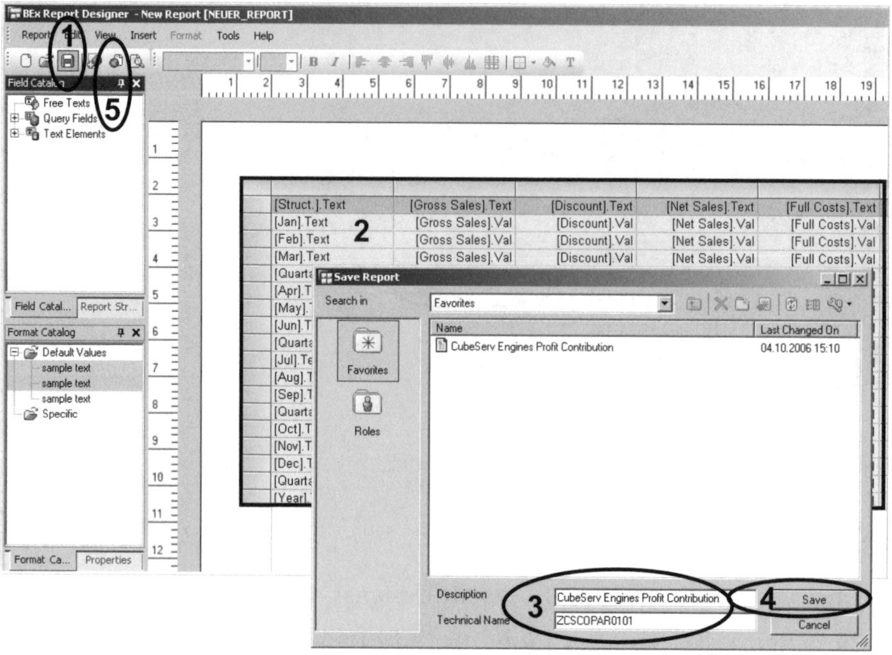

**Figure 10.6** Transferring the Data Provider into the Report

### Saving, Starting, and Printing a Report

[■] ▶ You can now already save the report with the settings you have made so far. To do this, click on the **Save** button (see Figure 10.6, Step 2).

▶ In the **Save Report** popup, enter the **Description** (in the example: **CubeServ Engines Profit Contribution**) and the **Technical Name** (in the example: **ZCSCOPAR0101**) (Step 3). Confirm your entries by clicking on **Save** (Step 4).

Running the report ▶ Start the report by clicking on the **Run** button (see Figure 10.6, Step 5).

▶ The report now opens in the HTML browser (see Figure 10.7, Step 1).

Printing the report ▶ Click on the **Print Version** button to open the **File Download** popup (Step 2) in which you can select whether you want to display or save the generated PDF file.

▶ Click on the **Open** button to display the PDF output (Step 3).

▶ This opens the program for PDF output (e. g., Adobe Reader) and the report is displayed as print output (Step 4).

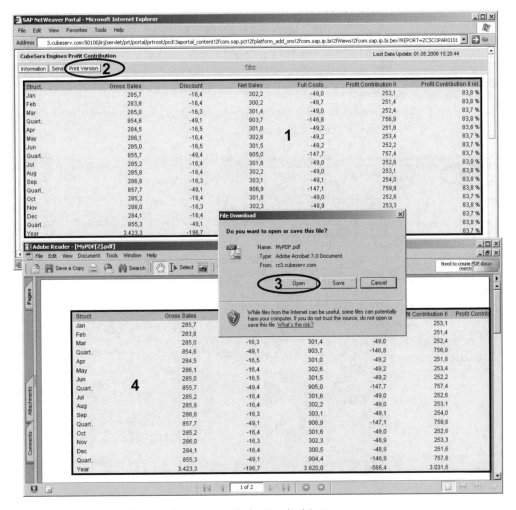

**Figure 10.7** Running and Printing the Report with the Standard Settings

431

### 10.3.2 Setting Up a Page in the Report Designer

[▪] ► To adjust the page orientation of the print output, click on the **Report** menu in the Report Designer and select the **Set Up Page** function (see Figure 10.8, Steps 1 and 2).

► This opens the **Set Up Page** popup. Click on the **Landscape** option to select it and confirm this setting by clicking on **OK** (Steps 3 and 4).

► Once you have saved the setting, it is used from the next execution of the report onwards.

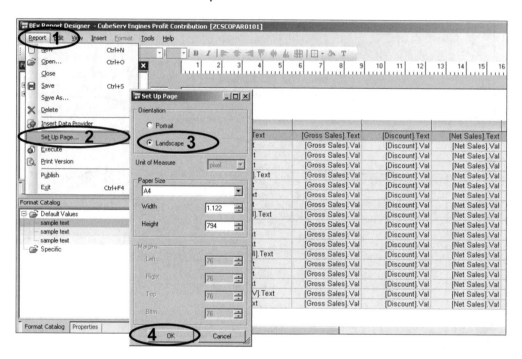

**Figure 10.8** Set Up Page in the Report Designer

### 10.3.3 Forcing a Variable Selection at Report Runtime

When you execute reports that have been created using the Report Designer, they are executed using a standard web template. Consequently, the general Business Explorer web application parameters apply to the reports.

Business Explorer web applications enable you to either activate the setting for mandatory variable input in the web template or the parameterization via the URL. If you complement the URL with the

&VARIABLE_SCREEN=X

string, you can force the variable input, provided that variables exist (see Figure 10.9, Step 1).

Parameters for mandatory variable input

#### Running a Report with Variable Input

- ▸ Once you have called the report with the URL complement, the selection screen for variables displays.

[▪]

- ▸ Enter the required fiscal year and click on **OK** (see Figure 10.9, Steps 2 and 3). Then the report is run using the specified calendar year.

- ▸ In accordance with the configuration of the print output described in Section 10.3.2, the output is displayed in A4 landscape format (Steps 4 to 6) so that the **PC II rel.** column is no longer truncated (Step 7).

Displaying A4 landscape print version

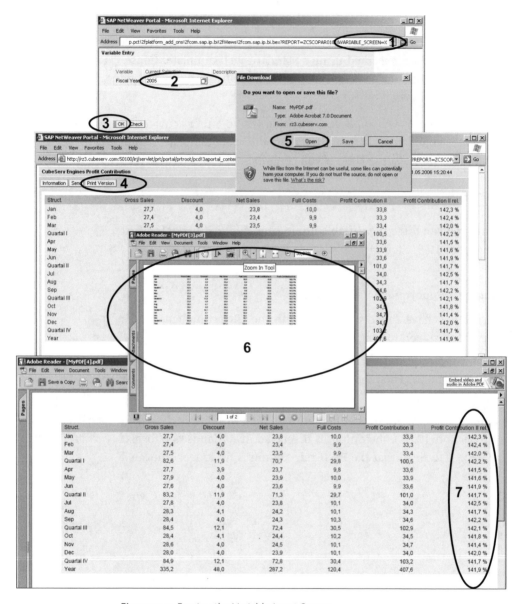

**Figure 10.9** Forcing the Variable Input Screen

## 10.4 Formatting in BEx Report Designer

### 10.4.1 Report Designer General Settings via Portal Theme

Similar to the HTML style sheet technology, the Report Designer allows you to modify general settings such as colors, fonts, and so on by using portal themes.

▶ To do that, click on the **Tools** menu in the Report Designer and select the **Portal Theme** function (see Figure 10.10, Steps 1 and 2).  [◦]

▶ There you can select the required formatting from the portal themes provided.

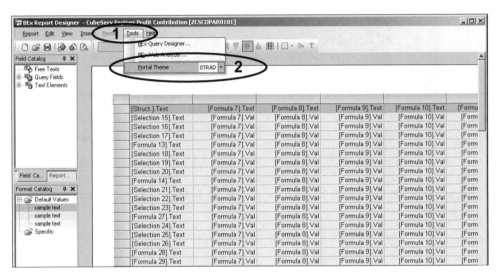

**Figure 10.10** General Settings via Portal Theme

### 10.4.2 Formatting Columns

You can use the Report Designer to format single columns, rows, and cells with any combination of fonts, font sizes, font styles, and so on.  *Formatting single columns*

In this example, you want to format the columns **Net Sales** (**[Formula 9].Text** column) and **PC II** (**[Formula 11].Text** column) in bold type.

▶ Click on the column header of the **Net Sales** column (**[Formula 9].Text** column) to highlight the column, and then click on the **B** button (bold).  [◦]

▶ Repeat this step for the **[Formula 11].Text** column (see **Italicizing the column** and

▸ Figure 10.11, Steps 1 to 4)

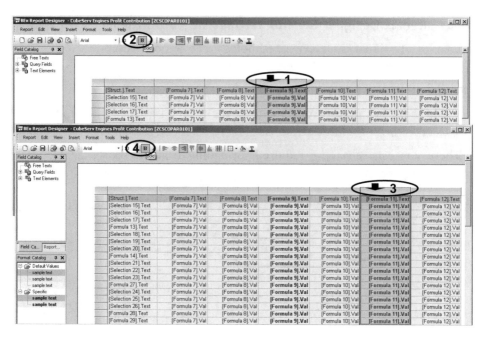

**Figure 10.11** Formatting the Net Sales and Profit Contribution II Columns in Bold Type

Italicizing the column

▸ Now you must italicize the **PC II rel.** column ([**Formula 12].Text** column).

▸ Click into the row header to highlight the **PC II rel.** column ([**Formula 12].Text** column) and then click on the **I** button (italics, see Figure 10.12, Steps 1 and 2).

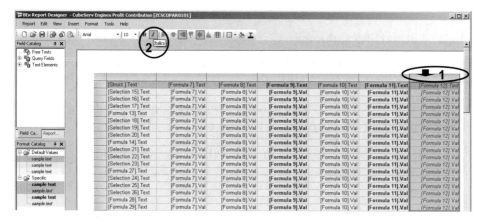

**Figure 10.12** Italicized Column "PC II rel."

### 10.4.3  Formatting Rows with Different Font Styles

In the next step, you want to format the following rows in bold type: Quarter I ([Formula 13].Text row), Quarter II ([Formula 14].Text row), Quarter III ([Formula 27].Text row), Quarter IV ([Formula 28].Text row), and Year ([Formula 29].Text row).

**Formatting a Column in Bold Type**

▶ Format the rows by clicking in the respective row header to high-  **[▪]**
light it and then click on the **B** button (bold). See for example Figure 10.13, Steps 1 and 2, where the row **Year** (**[Formula 29].Text**) has been bolded.

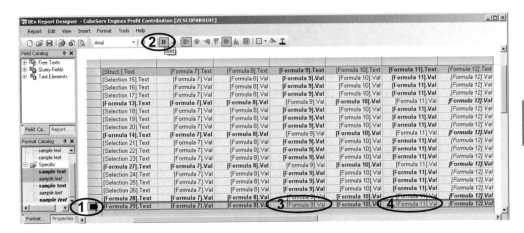

**Figure 10.13**  Formatting Rows in Bold Type

However, you should note that the intersections of previously bolded col-  **[«]**
umns are reset with the rows that have just been bolded. You can correct these formattings at cell level.

### 10.4.4  Formatting Cells with Different Font Styles

The rows with intersections of bolded cells that have been reset due to the duplicate bolding must also be displayed in bold type.

**Formatting a Column in Bold Type**

▶ Format the cells by clicking in the respective cell to highlight it  **[▪]**
and then click on the **B** button (bold). See for example Figure

10.14, Steps 1 and 2, where the cell **Year/PC II ([Formula 11].Val)** has been bolded.

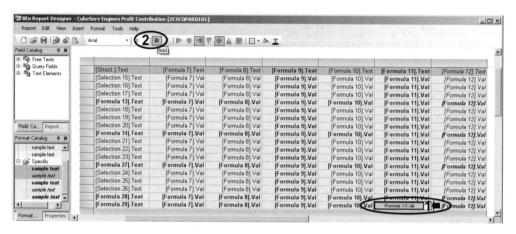

**Figure 10.14** Formatting the Year/PC II Cell in Bold Type

> ► Similarly, you can format the cells of the column headings in bold type (see Figure 10.15, Step 1).

**Manual Entry of Cell Content**

Next you want to replace the contents of cell [].Text (column 1, row 1) with the text: in Mio EUR.

[•]
> ► Highlight the cell by clicking on it and right-click to open the context-sensitive menu (see Figure 10.15, Step 2).

> ► Select the **Delete Field** function (Step 3).

> ► The field is then displayed as empty (Step 4).

> ► If you double-click on the field to activate it, it becomes ready for input and the text **[Custom Text]** is displayed (Step 5).

> ► Then enter the text **in Mio EURO** in the cell. Click somewhere outside the edited cell to reset the cell so that you can no longer make any entries (Steps 6 to 8).

> ► Format the cell in bold type similar to the procedure described above (Steps 9 and 10).

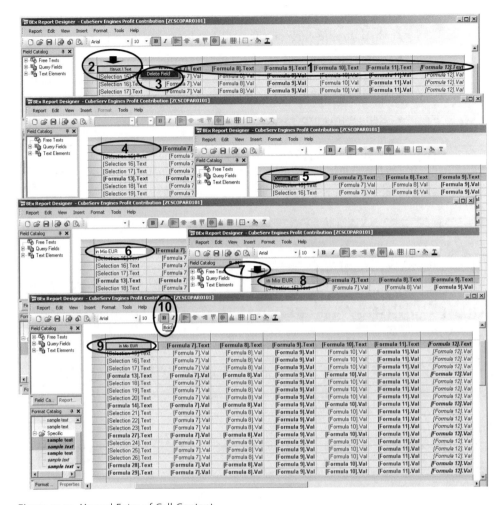

**Figure 10.15** Manual Entry of Cell Content

### Concatenating Cell Content

Now you want to attach the percent sign (%) to the PC II rel. values transferred from the query without any indication of the unit.

▸ Click on the relevant cells to activate them (in the example: **Jan/PC**  **[▪]** **II rel. ([Formula 12].Val)**, right-click in the empty area to the right of the data-containing contents (**[Formula 12].Val**) to open the context-sensitive menu, and select the **Insert Free Text** function (see Figure 10.16, Steps 1 and 2).

▸ The system displays the placeholder for free text **[Custom Text]** (Step 3).

▸ To activate the placeholder, click into the cell to be edited and then double-click on the placeholder (Steps 4 and 5).

▸ Enter the required value (in the example: %), and click somewhere outside the cell you are editing. This displays the concatenation between the query result and the entry (Steps 6 and 7).

▸ Repeat this process for all cells.

[»] As you can see, it takes a lot of work and time to edit many cells individually, so it is highly recommended that you transfer as much content as possible directly from the query.

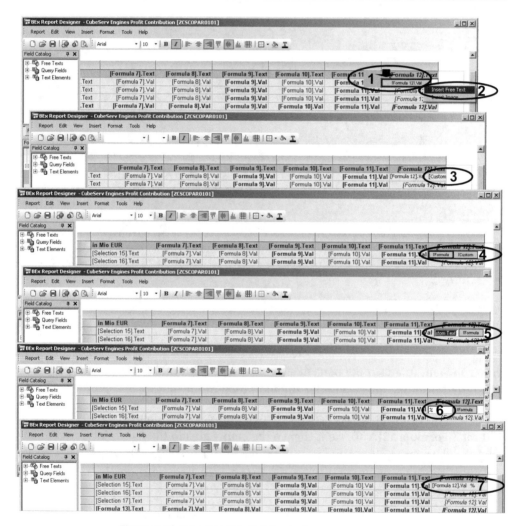

**Figure 10.16** Concatenating Cell Content

## 10.4.5 Changing the Background Color

You now want to change the background color of the standard template. The rows containing the monthly values are supposed to be displayed in light gray, while the rows containing quarterly subtotals and the total annual value are to be assigned darker tones of gray.

### Changing the Default Values

To change the background colors, you must first change the default value for the data rows.

▶ Right-click on the default value of the data rows to open the context-sensitive menu and select the **Format · Background Color** function (see Figure 10.17, Step 1). **[▪]**

▶ Then you can either choose a color in the **Color** popup or click on the **Define Custom Colors >>** button to define your own color values (Step 2).

▶ If you define your own color value in the advanced **Color** popup (Step 3), you can transfer the color value into the color palette by clicking on the **Add to Custom Colors** button (Steps 4 and 5).

▶ Complete the entry by clicking on the **OK** button (Step 6).

▶ This transfers the new color setting into the default value (Step 7), and the components that are assigned this formatting will be changed accordingly (Step 8).

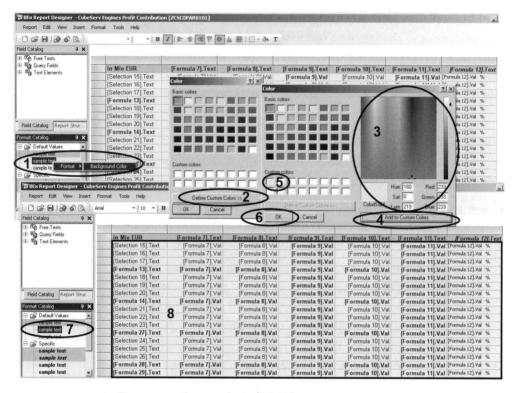

**Figure 10.17** Changing the Default Values

### Changing the Background Colors of Single Rows

**[»]**

▶ To change the background colors of single rows, click on the row header to highlight it (see Figure 10.18, Step 1).

▶ Then click on **Background Color** (Step 2) and either select an existing color or click on the **Define Custom Colors** >> button (Step 3).

▶ If you define your own color value in the advanced **Color** popup (Step 4), you can select this value by highlighting one of the available placeholders for user-defined colors (Step 5) and transfer your own color to the color palette by clicking on the **Add to Custom Colors** button (Step 6).

▶ Complete the configuration process by clicking on the **OK** button (Step 7).

▶ This transfers the new color setting for the row that you're currently editing (Step 8).

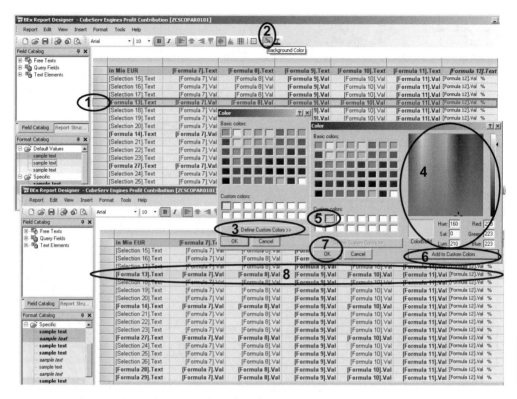

**Figure 10.18** Changing the Background Colors of Single Rows, Part 1

You can now directly transfer the user-defined color for the other quarterly subtotals.

▶ Click on the relevant row to highlight it (for example, see Figure 10.19, Step 1).

▶ Then click on the **Background Color** button (Step 2) and select the previously defined user-defined color by clicking on it (Step 3).

▶ Complete the entry by clicking on the **OK** button (Step 4). This transfers the new color setting for the row that you're currently editing.

▶ Repeat this process also for the **Year** row with a color of your choice (Step 5).

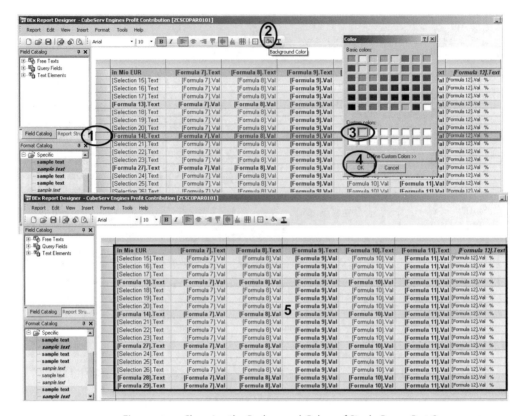

**Figure 10.19** Changing the Background Colors of Single Rows, Part 2

### 10.4.6 Adjusting the Column Width and Row Height

You want to set the column widths to fixed values.

[•] ▸ Change the column width by moving the column borders in the column header via drag-and-drop in such a way that the required width is reached (see Figure 10.20, Step 1).

▸ If necessary, you can use the ruler for that. Repeat this process for all columns in question (Step 2).

▸ The newly set column widths are used the next time the query is executed (Step 3).

Adjusting the
row height ▸ You can change the height of rows in a similar way.

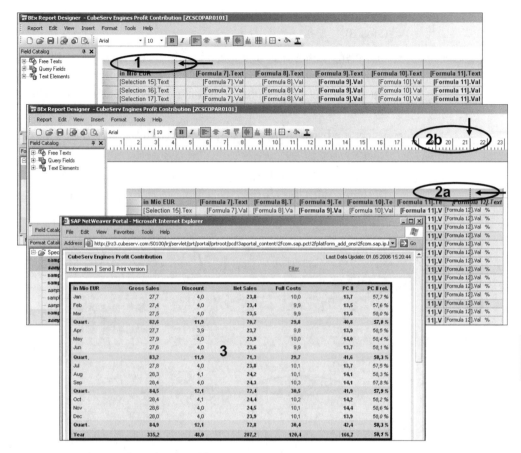

**Figure 10.20** Adjusting the Column Widths

### 10.4.7 Inserting Spacing Columns and Rows

We now need to separate the lead column, the Net Sales column, and the PC II column from the other columns. Similarly, we want to insert an empty row below the column heading and above the Year row.

#### Inserting Columns

First you must insert some blank columns.

▶ Right-click on the column header of the lead column to open the context-sensitive menu and select the **Insert Column (right)** function (see Figure 10.21, Steps 1 and 2).  **[⦁]**

▸ The new blank column displays to the right of the lead column (Step 3).

▸ The blank column is to appear in white color, corresponding to the background color. To implement that, highlight the column header of the blank column and click on the **Background Color** button (Steps 3 and 4).

▸ Select the background color by clicking on it and confirm with **OK** (Steps 5 and 6).

▸ The newly inserted column is now displayed in the Report Designer with the correct background color (see Figure 10.22, Step 1).

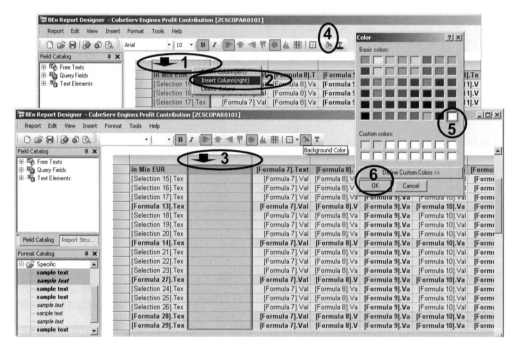

**Figure 10.21** Inserting a Spacing Column, Part 1

Defining the width
of the blank
column

Adjust the width of the blank column using the procedure described above (see Figure 10.22, Steps 2 and 3).

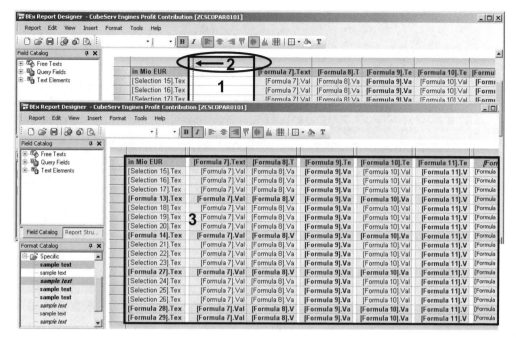

**Figure 10.22** Inserting a Spacing Column, Part 2

### Inserting Rows

Now you must insert the blank rows.

▶ Right-click on the row header of the header row to open the context-sensitive menu and select the **Insert Row** function (see Figure
10.23, Steps 1 and 2).

[▪]

▶ A new row displays below the header row (Step 3).

▶ The blank row is also to appear in white color. To implement that,
highlight the row header of the blank row and click on the **Background Color** button (Steps 3 and 4).

Defining a color for
the blank row

▶ Select the background color by clicking on it and confirm with **OK**
(Steps 5 and 6).

▶ The newly inserted row is now displayed in the Report Designer
with the correct background color (see Figure 10.24, Step 1).

▶ Adjust the height of the blank row using the procedure described
above (see Figure 10.24, Step 2).

Defining the
height of the
blank row

▶ Once you have saved these settings, the formatted report is displayed accordingly (Step 3).

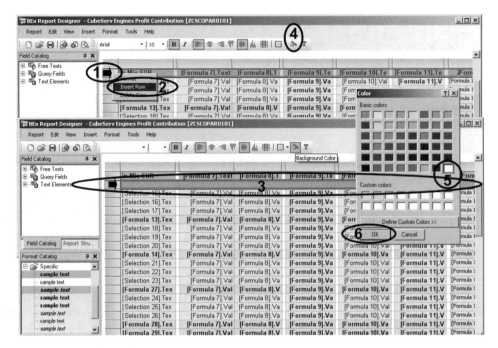

**Figure 10.23** Inserting Blank Rows, Part 1

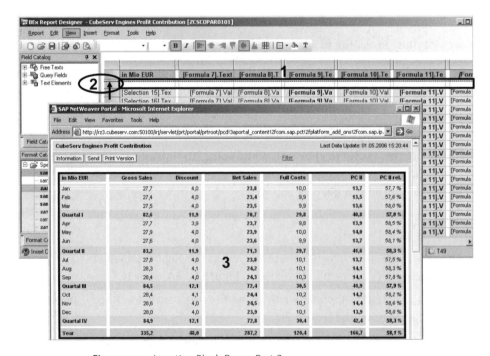

**Figure 10.24** Inserting Blank Rows, Part 2

### 10.4.8  Inserting the Report Title as Page Header

The report should contain the query description as its title.

For this purpose, you'll insert a page header.                    [**⬚**]

▶ Activate the **Insert** menu and select the **Page Header** function (see Figure 10.25, Step 1).

▶ This inserts a page header area (Step 2).

▶ Then open the **Text Elements** folder in the **Field Catalog** frame and drag-and-drop the **Query Description** into the header area (Steps 3 and 4).

▶ The placeholder for the query description now displays in the page header (Step 5).

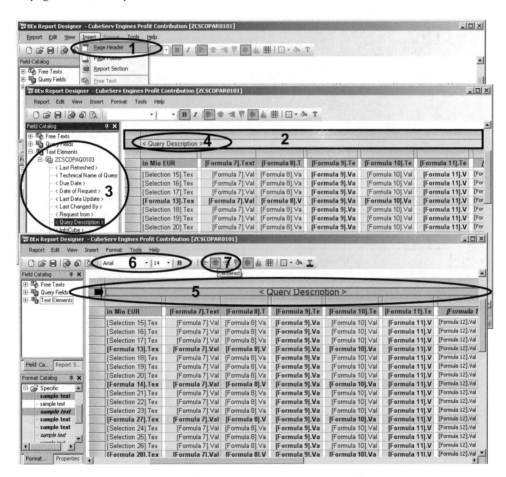

**Figure 10.25**  Inserting and Formatting the Query Description as Report Title

449

Fromatting the
query description

▶ To format the query description, highlight the row in the page header (Step 5) and assign the **Arial** font to it as well as font size **14** and type **bold** (Step 6).

▶ Center the report title by clicking on the **Centered** button (Step 7).

▶ For better readability, you should insert a spacing row into the page header (see Figure 10.26, Steps 1 to 3) and adjust the row height and background color similar to the procedure for the spacing column described above.

▶ Once you have saved the settings, the report is displayed accordingly (Step 4).

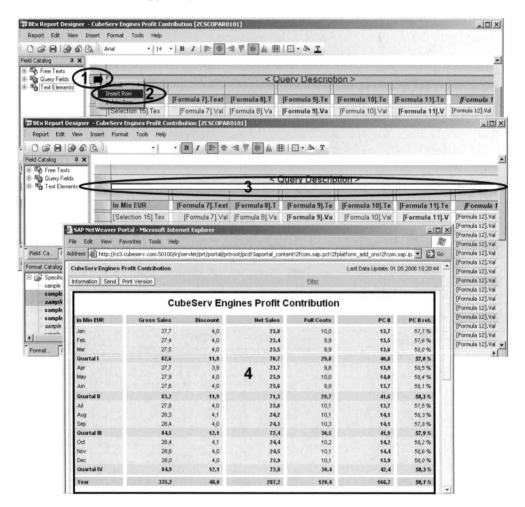

**Figure 10.26** Inserting a Spacing Row in the Page Header and Executing the Report

*What is BI-integrated planning and what benefits can a company derive from this SAP component? What technical architecture is the BI-integrated planning environment based on, and how can professional planning cockpits appear in Excel or on the web? We will address all of these questions in this chapter using our sample model company "CubeServ Engines." We will also provide you with implementation guidelines.*

# 11 BI-Integrated Planning

## 11.1 Introduction

The term *BI-integrated planning* describes the complete integration of planning and BI functions with a uniform user interface and design environment, as well as a commonly used analysis engine and data basis. BI-integrated planning marries the requirements of the planning freedom and flexibility users are accustomed to from using spreadsheets with a high level of system integration, so that the technical and operational business requirement for a "single point of truth" is also met.

In particular, BI-integrated planning comprises the following requirements:

- Uniform user interface for analysis and planning
- Uniform process and modeling logic for analysis and planning (e. g., the use of hierarchies, variables, calculated key figures, etc.)
- Uniform and consistent design tools for analysis and planning (e. g., Query Designer, Web Application Designer, etc.)
- Uniform and consistent data basis for analysis and planning
- Flexible planning modeling using simple or complex multiple aggregation levels, a versioning concept, use of hierarchies, etc.
- System-supported, web-based modeling environment for planning applications (Planning Wizard and Planning Modeler)

- Planning on the web and in MS Excel
- Support for Excel-based planning through user-specific auxiliary ledgers in Excel workbooks, without losing the connection to the central planning model
- Support for planning through delivered, customer-specific planning functions
- Support for the planning process through
  - Single point of entry
  - Information broadcasting
  - Status and tracking system

**Excursus: BI-integrated planning vs. BW-BPS**

With SAP BW 3.5, SAP also delivered the planning module Business Planning and Simulation (BPS) with SAP BW for the first time.[1] Following the market release and introduction of SAP NetWeaver 2004s, both BW-BPS and the BI-integrated planning are delivered together to customers. Both planning components must be delivered concurrently so that the customers who are already using SAP BW-BPS are not forced to migrate to the BI-integrated planning. You can continue to operate your planning applications already created with BW-BPS in the usual way. Nevertheless, in implementing new planning scenarios, you are recommended to use the functions of the BI-integrated planning, particularly since only these functions will be further developed by SAP in the future.

**General Information on BI-Integrated Planning and BW-BPS**

- Both planning tools use the same data basis and can be operated in parallel in a single system. There is no need to migrate existing planning applications.
- Some functions such as blocking procedures and formulas are used jointly both by the BW-BPS and by the BI-integrated planning.
- In the BI-integrated planning, most of the BEx and OLAP functions from the analysis are also available for planning applications. You need fewer objects in comparison with the use of the BW-BPS (e. g., since you can use the same variables in analysis and planning) and tools (Query Designer and Web Application Designer).

---

1 Prior to SAP BW 3.5, BPS was a component of SEM (Strategic Enterprise Management).

▶ Since many BW-BPS concepts are also used in a similar or modified form in the BI-integrated planning (e. g., planning levels, functions, and sequences, characteristic relationships, and data slices), the planning applications created with BW-BPS can be converted to the BI-integrated planning if necessary.

Table 11.1 provides a brief overview of both planning applications.

| Functionality | BW-BPS | BI-Integrated Planning |
|---|---|---|
| Planning on transactional/ real-time InfoProvider | X | X |
| Connection and simultaneous use by several InfoProviders | X | X |
| Characteristic derivations | X | X |
| Data slices | X | X |
| Variables | X | X |
| Planning functions | X | X |
| Planning profile | X | No longer necessary |
| Planning application executed on the web | X (via Web Interface Builder) | X (via Web Application Designer) |
| Planning applications executed in Excel | X (only limited, Excel-in-place functionality/ BPS-Excel) | X (full Excel support via a Microsoft Excel add-in) |
| Support for Excel-based planning through user-specific auxiliary ledgers in Excel workbooks, without losing the connection to the central planning model | | X |
| ALV frontend | X | |
| Uniform user interface for analysis and planning | | X |
| Uniform process and modeling logic for analysis and planning (e. g., the use of hierarchies, variables, etc.) | | X |
| Web-based modeling environment for planning applications | | X |

Table 11.1  SAP BW BPS and BI-Integrated Planning

| Functionality | BW-BPS | BI-Integrated Planning |
|---|---|---|
| Single point of entry | | X |
| Information Broadcasting | | X |
| Status and tracking system | X | X |

Table 11.1 SAP BW BPS and BI-Integrated Planning (cont.)

The above table highlights the functional differences between BW-BPS and the BI-integrated planning. The differences between both planning components at a system level are again somewhat greater.

Selective approach    If one were to try to illustrate all of the new functions and enhancements of BI-integrated planning by way of an example, this would certainly far exceed the scope of this book. We can therefore only look at some selected functions at this point. Therefore, this chapter focuses primarily on the new planning environment delivered with SAP NetWeaver 2004s, the Planning Modeler and Wizard, the creation of planning cockpits on the web and in Excel, and all key functions and innovative enhancements. On the other hand, this book will focus on a small number of functions in the specific area of automatic planning functions.

## 11.2    Sample Scenario

Now that our model company "CubeServ Engines" has already succeeded in fully mapping its planning requirements with SAP BW-BPS under SAP BW 3.5,[2] the management of CubeServ Engines plan to convert to BI-integrated planning—following a release switch towards SAP NetWeaver 2004s—in particular, to leverage the many advantages such as the parallel execution of the planning applications on the web and in Excel, uniform user interface, process- and modeling logic for analysis and planning, and single point of entry, etc. The company is striving to implement the switch to BI-integrated planning as quickly as possible, to be able to perform future planning applications directly with the BI-integrated planning.

With SAP NetWeaver 2004s, there is no need to migrate the existing planning applications, because both BW-BPS planning applications

---

2  See Egger, Fiechter, Rohlf, Rose, Weber, 2005 (available only in German).

and the BI-integrated planning applications can be operated in parallel within SAP NetWeaver 2004s. CubeServ Engines nevertheless would like to migrate its BW-BPS application, to gain experience for new planning requirements and planning applications. Furthermore, CubeServ Engines already enjoys substantial BW-BPS knowledge and planning-specific expertise. It should therefore be easier to migrate an existing application into a new planning environment than to develop an entirely new planning application in a planning environment that is also new, as represented by the BI-integrated planning.

### Planning Requirements

The rolling planning developed in the first implementation step with an integrated sales-, operations- and profit contribution planning and a transfer to the planned income statement is to be migrated from the BW-BPS planning environment to the BI-integrated planning environment during a migration project. Initially, the sales planning for the planning point of June 2006 will be considered. The data slice technology will be used to set the periods from January to June as not ready for input, and the period from July 2006 as ready for input. Within our planning scenario, the focus will then shift to the transfer of actual data as default values for the planned data. Primarily, we will show the various modeling possibilities with the Planning Wizard and the Planning Modeler, as well as the web and Excel-based user interfaces. Based on these implementations and the experience gained, the management would then like to assess the overall advantages of the BI-integrated planning.

As far as possible, SAP Business Content (SAP BCT) is used. If it is possible to apply it, this must then be taken into account during the implementation planning. The Business Content is used unmodified to ensure ease of release and application of the SAP Business Content. If changes are required to the SAP Business Content, these are made following more detailed checks. If it does not make sense to transfer the Business Content, the required objects are created in the customer-specific namespace.

*Use of SAP Business Content*

Integrated data retrieval with extractors is used to link upstream SAP R/3 systems.[3] For the ETL process from the SAP R/3 upstream sys-

*Extraction methods*

---

3  See also Chapter 4, *Data Retrieval.*

tems, the extraction method for the application-specific extraction of the results and market segment calculation at the level of the individual items is used:

▸ Application-specific extraction of the results and market segment calculation at the level of **individual items**

▸ Application-specific extractor of the logistics extract structure customizing cockpit at document level

▸ Business content extractors in the area of the transaction data of the general accounting and master data

▸ The SAP R/3 source data not mapped by the Business Content and application-specific extractors is mapped with generic Data-Sources

SAP BW data targets
SAP BW reporting components generally use InfoCubes and Multi-Providers. The planning applications write their data back into real-time-enabled[4] InfoCubes.

Reporting tools
The Business Explorer Web Applications are used during analysis and reporting. For additional, specific requirements, the Business Explorer Analyzer is used.

Planning interface
Web interfaces are generally used as the standard medium for mapping the planning requirements. However, since SAP NetWeaver 2004s allows Excel-based planning, the planning requirements are also shown in this medium. Preferably, those SAP BW-BPS standard functions that can be implemented without programming will be used to map the planning functions (even if the exit function may offer better performance).

### 11.2.1 Planning Application Requirements

**Providing the Required SAP BW Data Model**

The required components of the SAP BW data model are provided to depict the requirements for the BI-integrated planning application. The data from the planning applications is saved in the InfoObjects (characteristics and key figures) and the InfoCubes (see Table 11.2).

---

4 With SAP NetWeaver 2004s, the terminology has changed. The original *transactional InfoCubes* are now referred to as *real-time-enabled InfoCubes*.

| InfoCube | Usage |
|---|---|
| ZFCOPAC1 actual data: Profitability analysis | Transfer is in planning |
| ZFCOPAC2 planned data: Profitability analysis | Storage of planned data |
| ZFCOPAC3 planned price & planned HK | Prices & cost rates |
| ZFCFIGLC2 CubeServ Engines planned data: Balance sheet/P&L | Transfer of data to planned profitability statement |

Table 11.2 InfoCubes of the Planning Applications

These InfoProviders are based on the planning example that was developed as part of the SAP BW compendium. Within this chapter, the InfoProviders in particular will find **ZFCOPAC1 actual data: profitability analysis** and **ZFCOPAC2 planned data: profitability analysis** usage.

### Providing the Planning Environment

The required planning environment must be provided to map the planning functions and data-entry layouts and web interfaces required for the planning process:

▶ To copy the actual profitability analysis data as the planning basis

▶ To store the planned profitability analysis data

Unlike BW-BPS, no planning areas are created in the BI-integrated planning. Instead, *aggregation levels* are created at the level of the InfoProvider or the MultiProvider. An aggregation level is a virtual InfoProvider that allows data to be planned manually or changed using planning functions (see also Section 11.3). Because an aggregation level constitutes a selection of characteristics and key figures of the underlying InfoProvider, it is also used to set the granularity of the planning.

Variables are employed to design the planning applications as flexibly as possible. The variable control applies both to the parameterization of the functions to change the values of the key figures and to the selection of characteristic values.

The cumulative values at annual level are distributed using seasonal factors. Planned sales and planned manufacturing costs are determined based on manually prepared planned sales volumes and the

InfoCubes

Planning areas

Variables

457

planned prices and planned manufacturing cost unit rates. Revenue reductions are determined using devaluation percentages.

## 11.3    The Planning Environment

### 11.3.1    Introduction

The planning environment forms the basic framework and the central working environment for each planning application. With the implementation of BI-integrated planning, the planning environment that is already familiar from SAP SEM-BPS and SAP BW-BPS was entirely newly designed and developed. It is now fully integrated into the BI system. The planning environment within the BI-integrated planning comprises the components shown in Figure 11.1.

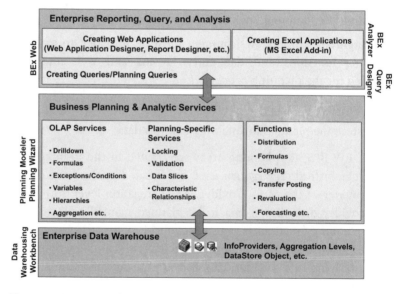

**Figure 11.1** BI-Integrated Planning Environment (according to SAP AG)

As you can see from this diagram, the BI-integrated planning environment primarily consists of the three components *Enterprise Data Warehouse, Business Planning & Analytic Services,* and *Enterprise Reporting, Query, and Analysis*.

### Enterprise Data Warehouse

The Enterprise Data Warehouse forms the basis for all planning applications. Here, InfoProviders form the data basis for the BI-integrated planning. InfoProviders accepting planned data, which was still described as transactional data under BPS, are now flagged as real-time-enabled InfoCubes. Virtual InfoProviders of the type **aggregation level** are created on such a real-time-enabled InfoCube or on a MultiProvider that contains such an InfoCube. These aggregation levels allow for the manual planning or changing of data using planning functions.

An aggregation level is described using many characteristics and key figures of the underlying InfoProvider and is itself in turn an Info-Provider within the planning application. It represents the basis for a query that is ready for input for manual planning and also for the planning functions in the automatic planning. The aggregation level establishes at what granularity the data is entered and stored. The key figures contained in the aggregation level are aggregated via the characteristics contained in the InfoProviders situated below the aggregation level. In the simplest case, an aggregation level lies on a real-time-enabled InfoCube. Aggregation levels can also be created on MultiProviders.[5] Different levels can be modeled in the planning using several aggregation levels.

*Aggregation level*

All InfoProviders, and the InfoObjects required for a planning application, are modeled via the Data Warehousing Workbench.

### Business Planning & Analytic Services

The Business Planning & Analytic Services component represents a key element of BI-integrated planning. It enables, using the OLAP services, the functions such as drilldown, variables, aggregation, etc. that we are already familiar with from the reporting. However, planning functions are also provided. These include distribution, FOX formula functions, exit functions, re-evaluation, copying, deleting, etc. All planning data is buffered in the planning cache, before it is updated into real-time-enabled InfoCubes.

---

5  See also the SAP NetWeaver 2004s online help.

This second component of the BI-integrated planning environment, with the web-based tools *Planning Modeler* and *Planning Wizard*, which are installed on the J2EE Engine, enables the actual backend planning applications to be created. These are no longer created via the SAP GUI, but rather using a Web Dynpro Interface. The Planning Wizard allows a simpler introduction to the modeling of planning applications ; however, in so doing, it only provides a reduced scope of functions. On the other hand, the Planning Modeler offers all of the following functions:

▸ Choice of an InfoProvider

▸ Assigning of characteristic relationships[6]

▸ Assigning of data slices[7]

▸ Selection, changing or creation of an InfoProvider of the type **aggregation level**

▸ Creation and changing of filters, where a filter is an object that describes the multi-dimensional extraction of data from a data set. A filter defines the selection for the data with which a planning function operates. These filters are available both in the planning and in the reporting.

▸ Creation and changing of planning functions and planning sequences. A planning sequence is composed of several planning functions. Provision is currently not made for a linking of planning sequences, as was possible under BPS. Nevertheless, the created planning sequences can be included in process chains with SAP NetWeaver 2004s (Transaction RSPC, **Process chain maintenance**).

▸ Creating and changing variables

**Enterprise Reporting, Query, and Analysis**

The final component in the context of BI-integrated planning is formed by Enterprise Reporting, Query, and Analysis. With the BEx Query Designer, this enables queries that are ready for input to be

---

6  Characteristic relationships are used to model relationships between characteristics (such as product-product group). Characteristic relationships are created for InfoCubes.

7  Data slices protect specific areas of data globally against changes.

created, which are used for manual data entry. These queries can subsequently be provided as a web application to users using the Web Application Designer. The enhanced functional scope of the Web Application Designer delivered with SAP NetWeaver 2004s allows professional and user-oriented web-based planning applications to be created.

Another possibility is to provide the queries that are ready for input to the planning user via the BEx Analyzer as an Excel frontend or as a workbook.

### 11.3.2 Planning Environment Objects

The planning environment of the BI-integrated planning comprises the following objects:

▶ **InfoProvider**
These can be standard- or real-time-enabled InfoCubes, MultiProviders, DataStore objects and InfoObjects.

▶ **Aggregation Level**
Virtual InfoProviders that serve as a basis for manual and automatic planning functions.

▶ **Filter**
These restrict the characteristic values of the characteristics provided with the aggregation level.

▶ **Planning Function**
These may be manual or automatic functions for entering or changing planned values.

▶ **Planning Sequence**
Summary of planning functions that are processed sequentially based on technical or operational business requirements.

Figure 11.2 describes the relationships between the individual objects in the planning environment.

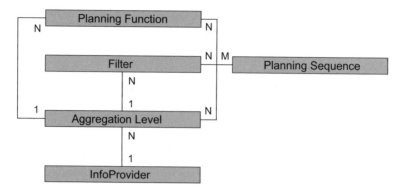

**Figure 11.2** Planning Environment Objects

Figure 11.2 shows that the functionality of the profiles that is familiar from BW-BPS is currently no longer available. In BW-BPS, profiles represented a user-oriented selection of planning objects to
structure the planning objects represented in the SAP GUI and allow
the developer a better overview. Due to the increased comfort and
the context-sensitive management within the Planning Modeler and
Planning Wizard, it was possible to avoid using the planning profiles,
which was sometimes unfavorable.

In order to create a planning application, you need the transactions
listed in Table 11.3.

| Transaction | Description | Explanation |
|---|---|---|
| RSPLAN | Modeling BI-Integrated Planning | Central initial transaction for modeling planning applications |
| RSPLF1 | Start: Processing function type | Creation/editing of function types that represent parameterizable procedures, to change movement data in the context of the BI-integrated planning. This also includes all planning functions. Function types replace the exit functions known from BW-BPS.[8] |
| RSPLSA | BI Planning: Starter Settings | Enables the URL prefix to be defined to start the Planning Modeler |
| RSPLSE | BI Planning: Lock management | Basic setting and monitoring possibilities within the lock management |

**Table 11.3** Transactions for the Planning Application

BI-Integrated
planning
transactions

---

8  However, you can now also integrate function modules from the FOX formula editor.

Transaction RSPLAN is used to call the initial page of the BI-integrated planning (see Figure 11.3).

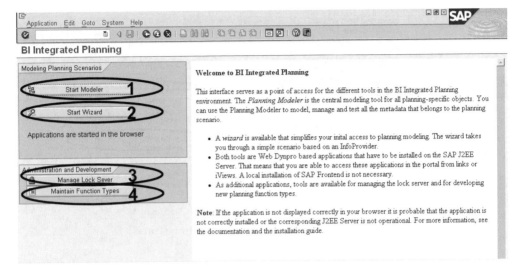

**Figure 11.3** Calling the Initial Cockpit for BI-Integrated Planning

Here you can call the *Planning Modeler* (see Figure 11.3, highlight 1), the *Planning Wizard* (highlight 2), the *Manage Lock Server* (highlight 3) and the *Maintain Function Types* (highlight 4) directly.

### 11.3.3    Business Planning with the SAP Enterprise Portal

Since the web-based components Planning Modeler and Planning Wizard are installed on the SAP J2EE Server, you can also call them directly from the SAP Enterprise Portal. To do this, you simply have to assign the relevant user the authorization **com.sap.ip.bi.business_ planning_showcase** (see Figure 11.4).

You can then access the required components directly. The following access options are available to you here:

▶ Planning Modeler (see Figure 11.4, highlight 1)

▶ Planning Wizard (highlight 2)

▶ BEx Web Analyzer (highlight 3)

▶ Quick access for all planning-relevant objects (highlight 4)

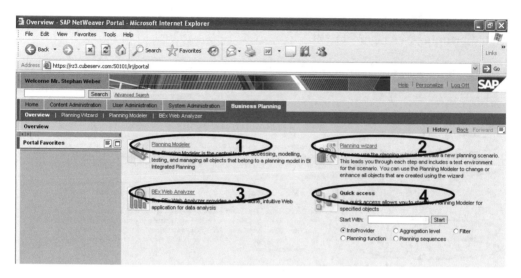

Figure 11.4 Business Planning in the SAP Enterprise Portal

### 11.3.4 Lock Concept

Lock algorithm

The basis of all planning applications is formed by the real-time-enabled InfoCubes in which the planning data is saved and stored. Furthermore, the lock concept of the BI-integrated planning, which was entirely newly developed, represents a key component of a planning application. To ensure that only one user can change data, his or her data is blocked against any third-party changes. Depending on the expected load (which is determined by the number of parallel users and by the complexity of the selection), one of several lock behaviors provided can be preset. The lock algorithm is used both by BW-BPS and by the BI-integrated planning.[9]

Lock management

Transaction RSPLSE is used to call the lock management, which enables all of the settings of the lock server for the planning and monitoring of the current lock entries. The initial screen allows the relevant lock table to be managed (see Figure 11.5).

---

9 See also the SAP online help.

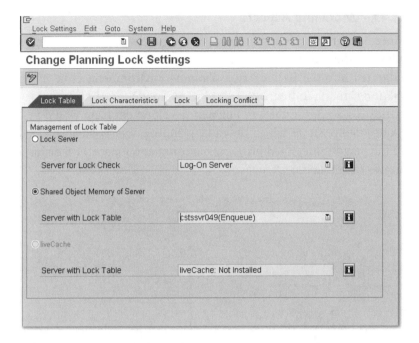

**Figure 11.5** Initial Screen of the Lock Management

▸ Depending on the number of parallel planning users and the complexity of the lock queries caused by the modeling, different technologies can be used to administer the lock table:[10]

▸ **Lock Server (Previous Implementation in BPS)**
Particularly suitable for small and medium-sized installations

▸ **Shared Object Memory of Server**
Better Performance than the Lock Server

▸ **SAP liveCache**
Appropriate for very large installations. A SAP liveCache Server
must be installed for this.

The CubeServ Engines configures the lock management as a Shared
Object Memory to benefit from the performance advantages over
the previous lock server.

---

10 See also the corresponding information in the SAP Reference IMG and the icons
in Transaction RSPLSE.

### 11.3.5 Modeling Aspects

Since, in the context of the project that CubeServ Engines is trying to achieve, the existing planning application under BW-BPS is to be migrated into the BI-integrated planning environment, basic information is required first with regard to the modeling of planning scenarios. To do this, CubeServ Engines' development team would first like to demonstrate which previous planning objects have changed in the new BI-integrated planning environment. Figure 11.6 demonstrates the modeling changes.

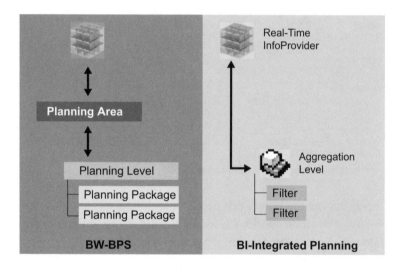

**Figure 11.6** Comparison of the Planning Objects

Aggregation levels  In principle, you can develop an aggregation level on a real-time-enabled InfoCube. Aggregation levels can also be created on Multi-Providers, so that the concept of the planning areas (standard-, multi-planning area) is no longer required. Figure 11.7 describes a possible scenario.

Thanks to the integrated approach, MultiProviders can be used instead of multi-planning areas. The same MultiProviders can therefore be used both in reporting and in planning.

466

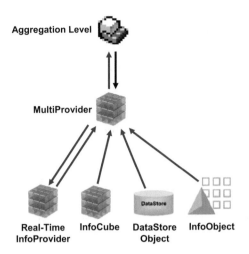

**Figure 11.7** Aggregation Level Based on a MultiProvider

The following illustration (see Figure 11.8) shows another possible example. Generally, you should note that aggregation levels (just as for MultiProviders) cannot be nested.

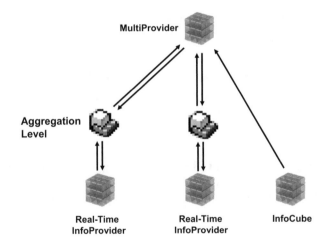

**Figure 11.8** Aggregation Levels Directly on Real-Time InfoProvider

Based on this information, CubeServ Engines plans to proceed as follows:

    Possible migration scenario

▶ Each InfoProvider used in the original scenario is copied, as the existing planning application is to remain unmodified as a fallback solution.

▸ To model its planning scenarios, CubeServ Engines uses the instruments *Planning Modeler* and *Planning Wizard* provided by the BI-integrated planning. Since both tools are Web-Dynpro-based applications, a local installation of the SAP frontend for the modeling of the planning application is not necessary.

▸ Within your sample scenario, you must therefore first copy actual data into the planning application. CubeServ Engines would first like to consider the key figure **Sales Quantities**.

### 11.3.6 InfoProviders

Standard InfoCube

Unlike in BW-BPS, there are no planning areas in the BI-integrated planning. The InfoProvider, apart from the actual InfoObjects, thereby forms the smallest unit of a planning application. The actual data of this model company is in the InfoProvider **Actual Data: Profitability Analysis** (ZFCOPAC1). This InfoProvider is a standard Info-Cube that supports parallel write accesses and is optimized for read processes.

### Creating a Real-Time-Enabled InfoCube

The planned data is stored in a real-time-enabled InfoCube.[11] Real-time-enabled InfoCubes are different from standard InfoCubes in that they are optimized for read processes. Several users can therefore write data to the real-time-enabled InfoCube at the same time. Real-time-enabled InfoCubes can also be switched, enabling data to be loaded via BI-staging.

**[+]**  However, your goal should not be to switch real-time-enabled InfoCubes due to modeling aspects.[12] A planned and a loading InfoProvider are always preferable, making it unnecessary to switch a real-time-enabled InfoCube.

**[■]**  ▸ Real-time-enabled InfoCubes are created in the same way as standard InfoCubes. However, they must additionally be described as real-time-enabled (see Figure 11.9, highlight).

---

11 In BW-BPS, those InfoProviders were referred to as *transactional*.
12 See also Egger, Fiechter, Rohlf, Rose, Weber, 2005 (available only in German), on this subject.

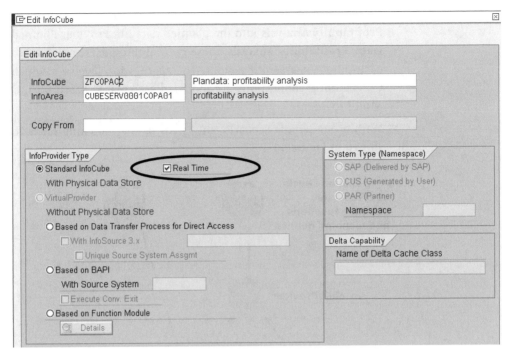

**Figure 11.9** Creating a Real-Time-Enabled InfoCube

You can convert an InfoProvider defined as a standard InfoCube into a real-time-enabled InfoCube at a later time. To do this, you must execute the SAP_CONVERT_NORMAL_TRANS program in the background. This report also guarantees that the transaction data already contained in the InfoProvider will be preserved. **[«]**

▸ Figure 11.10 shows the initial screen of this program.

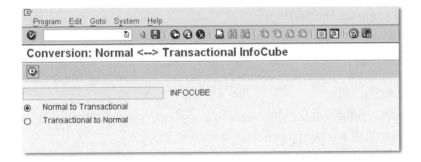

**Figure 11.10** Converting an InfoProvider into a Real-Time-Enabled InfoCube While Retaining the Transaction Data

▶ To allow the data to be copied from the InfoProvider **Actual Data: Profitability Analysis** into the planned data InfoProvider **Planned Data: Profitability Analysis**, these two InfoProviders are linked to each other via a MultiProvider. The aggregation levels on which the planning applications are modeled are created based on this MultiProvider.

▶ Within our sample scenario, this gives us the modeling scenario shown in Figure 11.11.

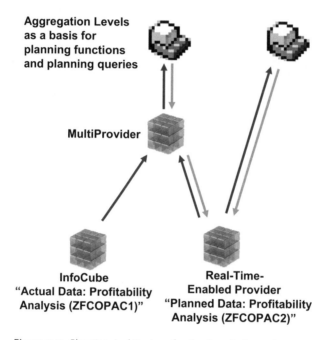

**Aggregation Levels as a basis for planning functions and planning queries**

**MultiProvider**

**InfoCube "Actual Data: Profitability Analysis (ZFCOPAC1)"**

**Real-Time-Enabled Provider "Planned Data: Profitability Analysis (ZFCOPAC2)"**

**Figure 11.11** Planning Architecture for the Sample Scenario

### Configuring the Settings

▶ Once all the necessary InfoProviders have been created, the first settings are then made for the planning model using Transaction RSPLAN. The image shown in Figure 11.12 shows the transaction being called.

▶ The **InfoProvider** view (see Figure 11.12, Step 1) allows you to display all real-time-enabled InfoProviders.

▶ A more precise selection is possible using the generic search (Step 2).

▸ Using the **ZFC\*** string and clicking on the **Start** button (Step 3) displays all of CubeServ Engines' relevant real-time-enabled InfoProviders.

▸ If a real-time-enabled InfoProvider is also selected (Step 4), the additional tabs **Characteristic Relationships**, **Data Slices**, and **Settings** (Step 5) open.

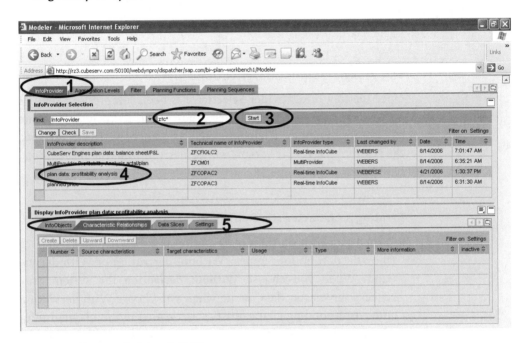

**Figure 11.12** Planning Modeler—Initial Screen

▸ The initial screen first shows everything in display mode. You need to use the **Change** button (see Figure 11.13, Step 1) to be able to make settings at the level of a selected InfoProvider.

▸ You can also use the **Compress Tray** button (Step 2) to show or hide the corresponding tray.

471

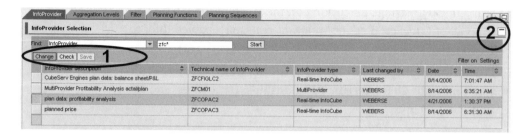

Figure 11.13 Changing Settings

### 11.3.7 Characteristic Derivations

Once the tray **InfoProvider Selection** has been compressed, settings are made for the characteristic derivation.[13] Due to the fact that some of CubeServ Engines' company codes use other fiscal year variants, the relevant fiscal year variant will be derived from the master data, based on the company code.

#### Creating a Characteristic Derivation

[◆] ▸ When you click on the **Create** button (see Figure 11.14, Step 1), the selection options appear **Without derivation** or **With derivation**. When you choose **Without derivation** the system only checks the master data, while when you choose **With derivation** the corresponding characteristics are loaded in the planned Info-Cube, without the corresponding characteristic needing to be present in the aggregation level.

▸ Because the fiscal year variant is derived from the master data of the company code, CubeServ Engines' implementation team opts to choose the **With derivation** option (Step 2).

▸ Due to the selection that has been made, the next input option opens to establish how the derivation is to run (Step 3).[14]

---

13 See Egger, Fiechter, Rohlf, Rose, Weber, 2005 (available only in German), on the functionality and the areas of application of a characteristic derivation.

14 The selection options do not depend on the characteristic combination check and proposal.

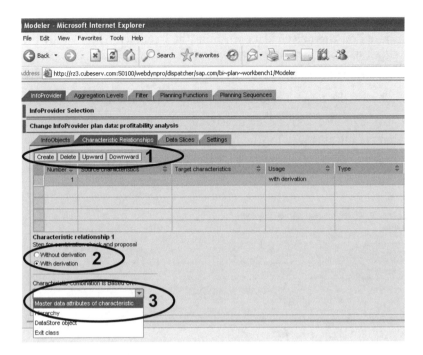

**Figure 11.14** Creating a Characteristic Relationship

There are also fundamental changes here compared with BW-BPS. As with BW-BPS, you can perform the derivation based on the master data or based on a characteristics hierarchy. However, with the BI-integrated planning, you can also store the derivation logic in a DataStore object and access it through the characteristic derivation. The derivation via an exit function familiar under BW-BPS has also changed. With BI-integrated planning, you can now address not only function modules, but entire exit classes. The classes listed in Table 11.4 form the basis for this new functionality.

**Changes compared to BW-BPS**

| CL_RSPLS_CR_EXIT_BASE | Characteristic relationships: exit |
| --- | --- |
| CL_RSPLS_CR_EXIT_BPS | Characteristic relationships: exit |
| CL_RSSEM_CR_EXIT | Characteristic relationships: exit |

**Table 11.4** Exit Superclasses

For each of these superclasses, you can create separate subclasses in which the corresponding coding is stored for characteristic combination checks and derivation.

**[■]**
- In our example, we are working with a characteristic derivation based on the master data attributes of a characteristic. Following the selection, an input window appears to define the source characteristic **Company Code** (see Figure 11.15, Step 1).
- Choose the target characteristic **Fiscal Year Variant** (Step 2).
- You can also activate or deactivate the characteristic derivation created in this way for the InfoProvider (Step 3).
- Finally, save the entire characteristic derivation (Step 4).

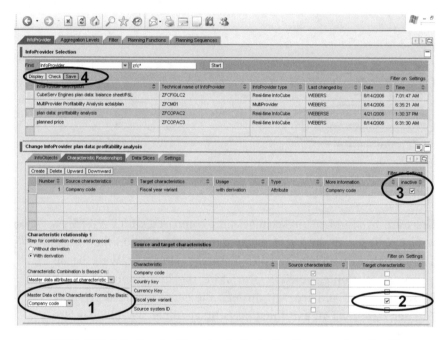

Figure 11.15  Activating the Characteristic Derivation Company Code-Fiscal Year Variant

**[»]**
In addition to the characteristic relationships mentioned above, the BI-integrated planning automatically supports the characteristic relationships for BI time characteristics, unlike BW-BPS. If redundant time characteristics, for example, are contained in a real-time-enabled InfoCube (such as **0FISCPER** and the pair **0FISCPER3** and **0FISCYEAR**), the system applies these relations between time characteristics[15] for combination checking or derivation. Missing characteristic values for time characteristics are therefore filled automatically by the system.

---

15 The time characteristics derivation via an exit function required in BW-BPS is not necessary here. See also Egger, Fiechter, Rohlf, Rose, Weber, 2005 (available only in German).

## 11.3.8 Data Slices

In the next step, you will create a data slice. This will ensure that once a planning round of CubeServ Engines is completed, no more planned data can be changed.

> Data slices are a concept for centrally protecting data of a real-time-en-     **[«]**
> abled InfoCube against changes. This protection affects queries that are
> ready for input and all planning functions that use this InfoCube.[16]

### Creating Data Slices

You can create data slices in very much the same way as you create characteristic derivations.

► First, switch to the corresponding InfoProvider on the **Data Slices**     **[▪]**
   tab (see Figure 11.16, Step 1).

► When you click on the **Create** button, you can enter an explanatory text for a sequential number (Step 2).

► In the third step, the basis for the data slice is specified. This can be a selection as in the case shown, or an exit class. The classes listed in Table 11.5 are available for selection.

| | |
|---|---|
| CL_RSPLS_DS_EXIT_BASE | Data slices: Exit |
| CL_RSSEM_DS_EXIT | EXIT class for check data slice |
| CL_RSPLS_DS_EXIT_BASE | Data slices: Exit |
| CL_RSPLPPM_LOCK_DATA-SLICE | Data slice for PPM |
| CL_UPS_LOCK_DATASLICE | Data slice for locking |

Table 11.5 Classes Available

> The exit class must implement the IF_RSPLS_DS_EXIT interface. It is     **[+]**
> recommended that the customer class should inherit from the template
> class CL_RSPLS_DS_EXIT_BASE. Re-implement the method IS_PROTEC-
> TED. You should also note the deactivated sample source text in the template class, which offers an infrastructure for a buffering, for example.

---

16 See also the SAP help on BI-integrated planning-data slices.

▶ In our example, the definition of a data slice is performed by selection (see Figure 11.16, Step 3).

▶ Finally, the characteristic that is to be restricted is selected (Step 4).

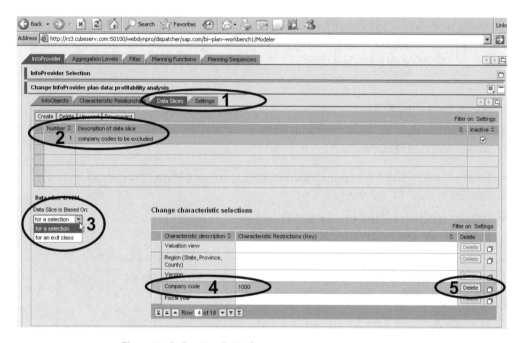

**Figure 11.16** Creating Data Slices

▶ Individual company codes or intervals of company codes can be selected using a selection screen. When you choose the input help (see Figure 11.16, Step 5), you reach the following input screen (see Figure 11.17).

▶ Here you can first select whether you want to choose individual values or entire value ranges.

▶ You can also access history values or previously defined favorites. Since CubeServ Engines wants to create a data slice for the company code **1000 (CubeServ Vertriebs GmbH (Germany))**, this company code is selected (Step 2) and then displayed among the chosen selections (Step 3) using the **Add** button.[17]

---

17 During the course of the project, the implementation team of CubeServ Engines will also create a data slice for the months from January through June 2006 so that only the values as of July 2006 can be changed.

▶ In a similar way to the Query Designer, you can also make exclusive selections by selecting the chosen characteristic value using the mouse. In the menu window that opens, you can exclude the characteristic value.

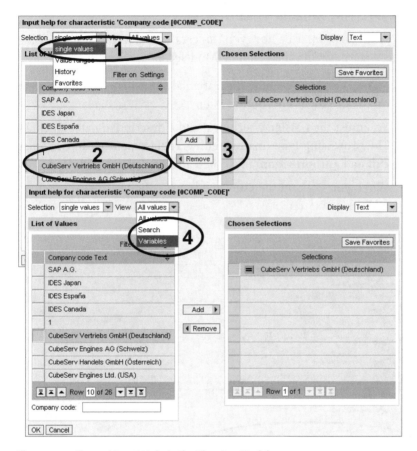

**Figure 11.17** General Input Help in the Planning Modeler

> You are recommended to design all planning applications as flexibly as **[+]**
> possible. Here it is useful to use variables because, for instance, variables
> of the type **Exit** can be maintained centrally and are thus available for the
> entire planning application on an ongoing basis and with the desired characteristic values.

▶ To be able to use variables you can switch the selection from **All values** to **Variables** (see Figure 11.17, Step 4). If the desired variable is not defined yet, the Variable Wizard allows you to create a corresponding variable. This variable created for a characteristic is then available not only in the BI-integrated planning, but also in the reporting.

### 11.3.9 The Variable Wizard

We will now describe how you can create or change variables using the Wizard, within the Planning Modeler.[18]

[.]
- ▶ Figure 11.18 shows how the Variable Wizard is called by clicking on the **Create** or **Edit** button (Step 1).

- ▶ You must then assign a technical and a descriptive name (Step 2). The processing type (**manual entry, replacement path, customer exit** and **authorization**) must then also be defined.

- ▶ When you click on the **Continue** button, the next variable screen is displayed (Step 3).

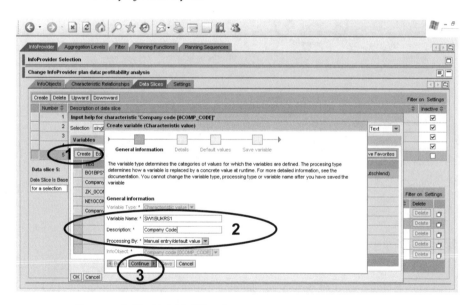

**Figure 11.18** The Variable Wizard

- ▶ Figure 11.19 shows that further entries (Steps 1 and 3) are required.

---

18 The procedure for creating variables does not differ from the procedure within the Query Designer which is why we'll describe it only briefly here.

▸ The **Continue** button will bring you to the next respective definition view (Steps 2 and 4).

▸ When the definition has been fully completed using the Wizard, you can save the new variable (Step 5).

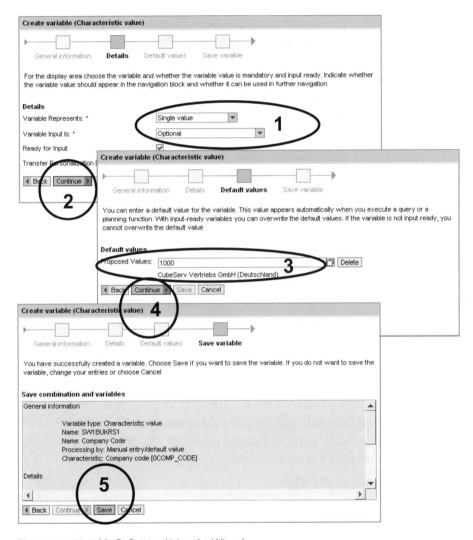

**Figure 11.19** Variable Definition Using the Wizard

▸ The data slice can be saved using a characteristics selection or by choosing a variable and is available within the planning process.

## 11.4  Planning Functions

### 11.4.1  Creating a Delete Function Using the Planning Wizard

General
requirements

The management of CubeServ Engines wants to migrate its sales planning already created with BW-BPS into the new BI-integrated planning environment.[19] Because of these requirements, and in order to provide a planning basis, the CubeServ Engines development team will first implement a delete function. To provide a complete planning basis, the actual data will be copied as planned data (default values) in a further step.

Definition

We recommend using a delete function during the initialization of a planning round, or for the specific deletion of invalid characteristic combinations.

**Creating the Delete Function**

CubeServ Engines' implementation team wants to use the delete function as part of the initialization of the planning rounds. All data records are to be deleted that are located in the real-time-enabled InfoProvider **Planned Data: Profitability Analysis** (ZFCOPAC2) at the current planning point. For this reason, an aggregation level and the delete function are created directly on this InfoProvider. The implementation team opts to use the Planning Wizard here.

[⚫]

▶ The Wizard is called using Transaction RSPLAN. Figure 11.20 shows the Wizard's initial screen. In the top area, you can see a navigation help that supports the implementer in his or her work (Step 1). This shows that the following components are required to create a planning function or application:

  ▶ Aggregation Level

  ▶ Filter

  ▶ Planning Function (Function in the actual sense or manual input layout )

▶ In the next step (Step 2), the provider for which an aggregation level is to be created is selected.

19  See also Egger, Fiechter, Rohlf, Rose, Weber, 2005 (available only in German), for a more detailed description of the example and the requirements.

▶ You can use the navigation support **Filter on** (Step 3) to search selectively through the components displayed in the tray.

▶ **Settings** allows you to define the characteristic selection, the sorting sequence, and the rows to be displayed for each specific user. Nevertheless, the settings do not globally affect all of the trays of the Wizard, but instead depend on the relevant tray.

▶ Using the **Continue** or **Back** button allows you to navigate between the individual components in the Wizard (Step 4).

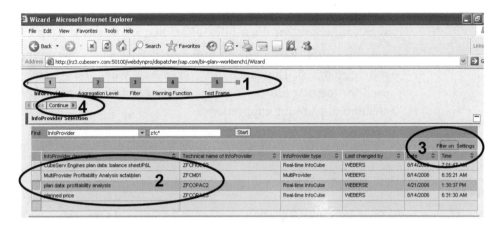

**Figure 11.20** Initial Planning Wizard Screen

▶ Figure 11.21 shows that you are in the definition area of the aggregation level (Step 1).

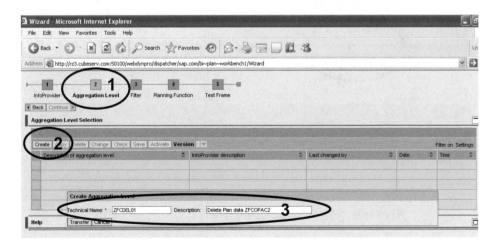

**Figure 11.21** Creating an Aggregation Level

▸ An aggregation level is created using the **Create** button (Step 2).

▸ Another window opens where you can enter the technical and the descriptive name of the aggregation level (Step 3).

▸ You can click on the **Copy** button to open another tray where the InfoObjects belonging to the aggregation level are specified (see Figure 11.22).

▸ The button **Select all** defines all characteristics of the InfoProvider for the aggregation level as well (Step 1).

▸ Here you can display **All** InfoObjects, or only those **Used** in the aggregation level, or those InfoObjects that are **Not used** (Step 2).

▸ You can also click on a specific button to display a help text on the settings (Step 3). This function is very useful when the system is used for the first time as it guides the user smoothly through the creation of planning applications.

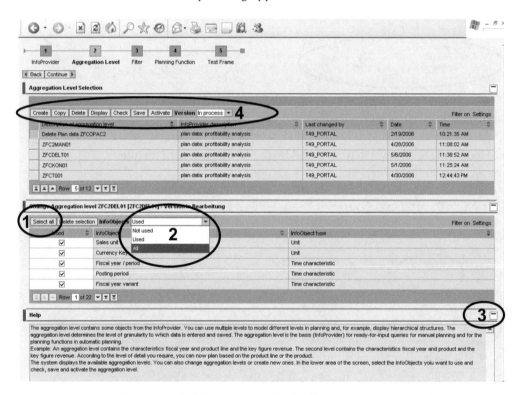

Figure 11.22 Defining an Aggregation Level

▶ Once all necessary settings have been made, the aggregation level can be checked, saved, and activated (Step 4).

▶ Since an aggregation level also involves an InfoProvider, the same saving and activation functions are available here as those that you are already familiar with from the Data Warehousing Workbench. Furthermore, the aggregation level is also listed in the Data Warehousing Workbench (see Figure 11.23, Step 1).

▶ You can branch directly into the Planning Modeler using the context-sensitive menu (Step 2) or use the **Change** function (Step 3).

▶ The successful activation is notified to the implementation team in the Planning Wizard (see Figure 11.24, Step 1).

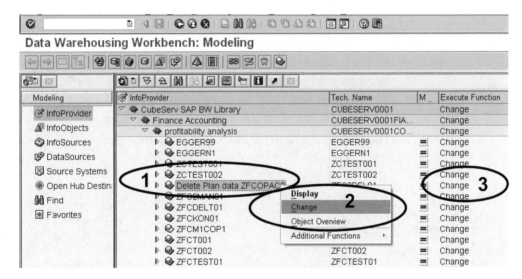

**Figure 11.23** Aggregation Level Within the Data Warehousing Workbench

**Creating a Filter**

▶ Via the **Continue** button, you will then reach the setting component **Filter** (Step 2).

[✶]

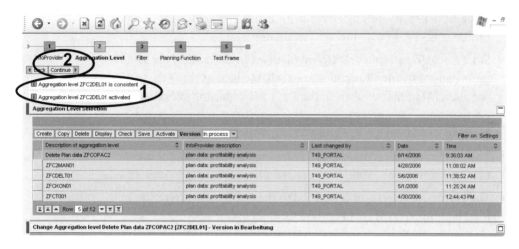

Figure 11.24 Fully Activated Aggregation Level

Filter ▸ Filters are always created for an aggregation level. In the application component **Filter** (see Figure 11.25, Step 1), by clicking on the **Create** button (Step 2), you'll open a screen in which you can set the technical name and describe the filter (Step 3).

▸ The **Transfer** button (Step 4) will open another tray for setting the filter values.

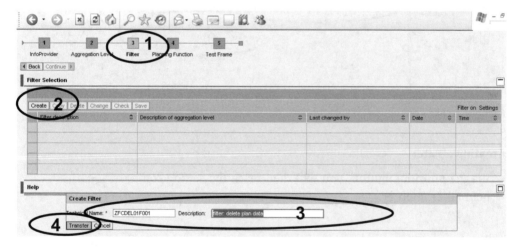

Figure 11.25 Creating a Filter for the Aggregation Level

▸ Here the user is first offered all of the characteristics that are also contained in the aggregation level (see Figure 11.26, Step 1). Since only the planned data for a particular planning point is to be deleted, this is selected.

► When you click on the **Add** button, the selected characteristic from the aggregation level is assigned to the filter (Step 2).

► You can also choose to display only the text, the keys, or both the text and the keys for the individual characteristics (Step 3).

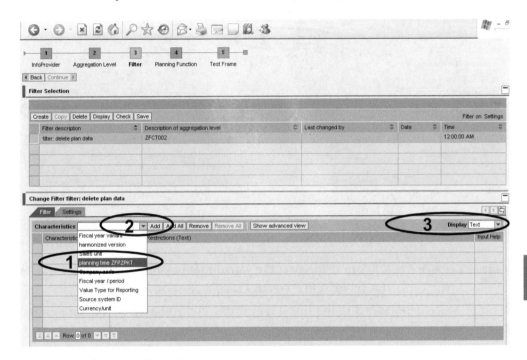

**Figure 11.26** Defining the Filter Values

► Once the **Planning point** characteristic has been added, it is specified more precisely for the selection through the value help (*see* Figure 11.27, Step 1).

**Specifying the planning point**

► Since the planning point changes from one planning round to the next, the selection will be made using a variable (Step 2).

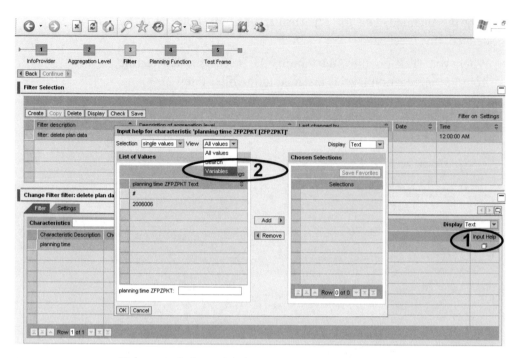

**Figure 11.27** Defining the Planning Point Using a Variable

Adding a variable

▶ You can then select the variable and add it, or create it if it does not yet exist (see Figure 11.28, Steps 1 and 2).

▶ Step 3 shows that it is available in the **Chosen Selections** area and can be copied (Step 4).

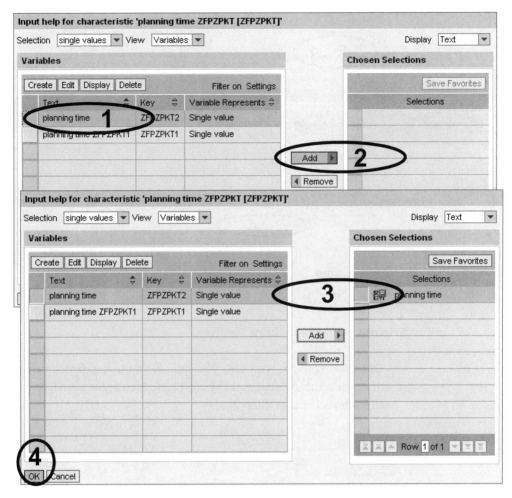

**Figure 11.28** Variable Selection

### Defining a Planning Function

► Once you save the filter, the **Continue** navigation button brings [◄]
you to the actual definition of the **Planning Function** (see Figure
11.29, Step 1).

► The **Create** button (Step 2) opens another dialog window in which
you can specify the type of planning function (in this example, the
**Delete** function was selected, Step 3) and the technical and descriptive name of the planning function (Step 4).

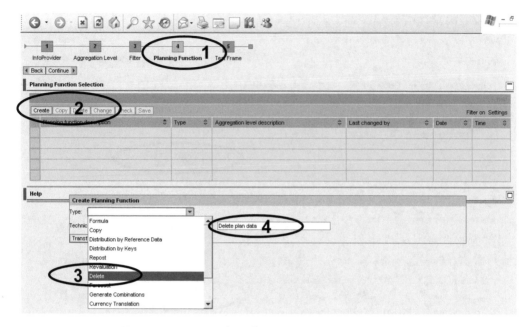

**Figure 11.29** Creating the Delete Function

▶ Once you confirm with **OK**, you can select the key figure values that you want to delete (see Figure 11.30, Step 1), or switch to the characteristic usage (Step 2).

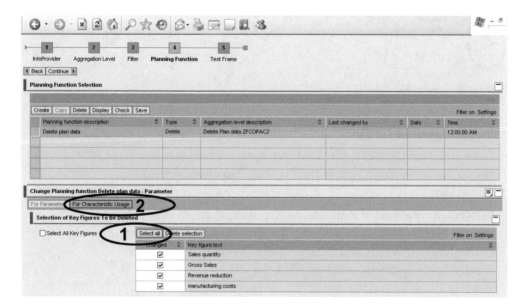

**Figure 11.30** Delete Function—Selecting Characteristics

▶ In the characteristic usage, you can define whether conditions for the values to be deleted should be taken into account. The Cube-Serv Engines implementation team decides to delete all transaction data from the planned InfoCube. The **Delete** function therefore no longer needs to be restricted through additional selections (see Figure 11.31, Step 1).

Characteristic usage

This procedure of deleting all data records from the planned InfoProvider is useful if all transaction data of a previous planning round has first been copied or updated into a separate InfoProvider. This should be recommended in the context of implementation projects, because it also offers performance benefits in addition to making the planned InfoProvider easier to administer.

**[+]**

▶ Support helps are also available here for the implementer (Step 2).

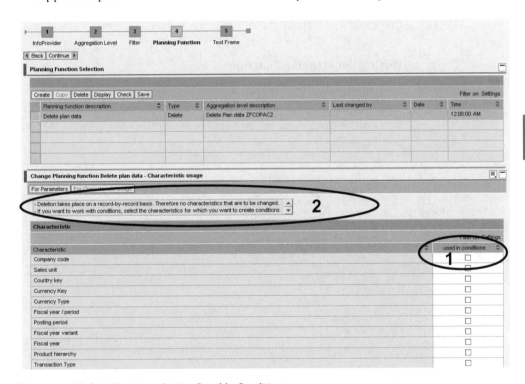

**Figure 11.31** Delete Function—Setting Possible Conditions

▶ Now that the **Delete** function has been created, it can be saved in a further step (see Figure 11.32, highlight).

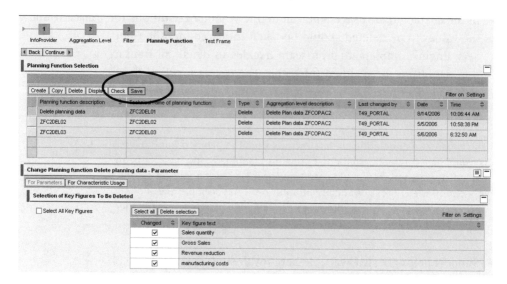

**Figure 11.32** Delete Function—Saving

### Testing the Planning Function

Test frame This first planning function within the BI-integrated planning has now been completed and needs to be tested. The **Continue** navigation button brings you to the **Test Frame** within the Planning Wizard (see Figure 11.33).

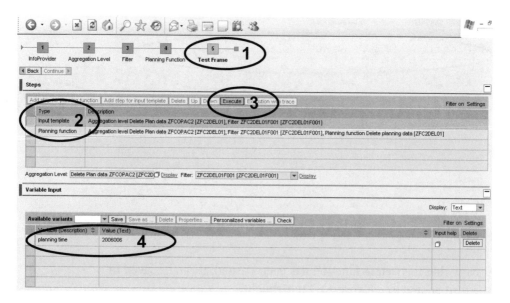

**Figure 11.33** Executing the Test Frame

Generally the relevant planning functions created for an aggregation level are shown within the test frame. The system also automatically creates a planning function of the type **Input template**. Input templates allow the implementer to display all of the data of an aggregation level, giving an overview of the existing InfoObjects of an aggregation level and the corresponding transaction data.

Input screen

Since the input template contains the granularity and the corresponding transaction data, it can be very helpful in creating planned queries.

[«]

When a planning function (planning function in the narrower sense and input template) is selected (see Figure 11.33, Step 2), it can be executed using the button **Execute** or **Execution with trace** (Step 3). At the same time, the variables used are displayed (Step 4) whose default values can still be adjusted if necessary.

Trace mode

If a planning function is executed in trace mode (see Figure 11.34, Step 1), related transaction data is grouped into *block records* and displayed (Step 2). Selecting a block record shows the transaction data before and after the planning function is executed (Step 3).

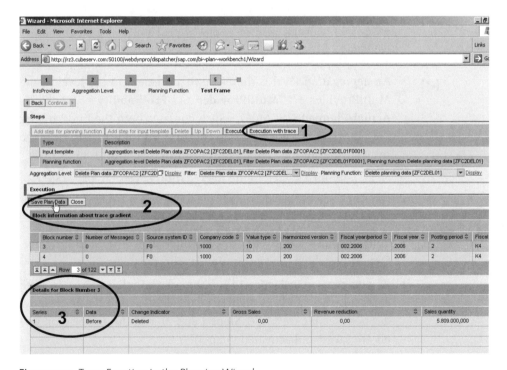

**Figure 11.34** Trace Function in the Planning Wizard

### 11.4.2 Creating a Copy Function Using the Planning Modeler

Now that the delete function has been fully created, the planning process should be supported in such a way that actual data from the data InfoProvider will be provided as the basis for a planning round. To do this, the actual data is first copied from the InfoProvider **Actual Data: Profitability Analysis** (ZFCOPAC1) into the planned InfoProvider.

Further implementations will now only be made with the Planning Modeler, because it provides the extensive functions.

**Creating an Aggregation Level**

Since the actual data is located in the InfoProvider **Actual Data: Profitability Analysis** (ZFCOPAC1) and it is to be stored in the InfoProvider **Planned Data: Profitability Analysis** (ZFCOPAC2), the copy function must be built on an aggregation level located on a MultiProvider.

[»]     Due to the BI-integrated approach, this procedure is possible via Multi-Providers without the need to employ the multi-planning areas known from the BW-BPS world.

[■]    ▸ An aggregation level is therefore first created on the level of the MultiProvider **MultiProvider Profitability Analysis Actual/Planned** (ZFCM01), which contains both the InfoProvider ZFCOPAC1 and ZFCOPAC2. To do this, you must first select the InfoProvider in the Planning Modeler (see Figure 11.35, Step 1).

▸ Next, you must switch to the **Aggregation Levels** tab page (Step 2).

▸ Here you can choose both the technical and the descriptive name of the new aggregation level to be created (Steps 3 and 5).

▸ You must also specify the InfoProvider (here the MultiProvider, Step 4) on which the aggregation level is created.

▸ As you can see in Figure 11.36, the relevant characteristics, time characteristics, and key figures of the aggregation levels are now defined (see Figure 11.36, Steps 1 and 2), and the aggregation levels are saved and activated (Step 3).

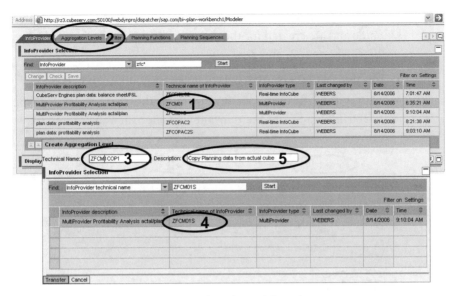

Figure 11.35  Creating an Aggregation Level on the MultiProvider

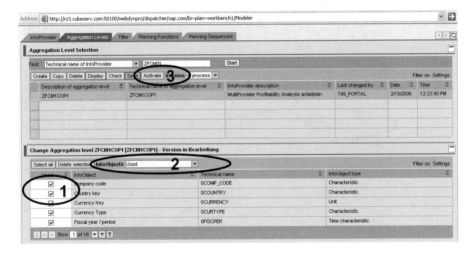

Figure 11.36  "Copy" Aggregation Level Definition

### Navigation in the Planning Modeler

The Planning Modeler does not guide you through the Customizing of planning applications quite so smoothly as does the Planning Wizard; however, the Planning Modeler does allow you to orient yourself using the tabs. This helps you to create filters after creating aggregation levels.

[■] ▸ These must first be specified using the technical and descriptive name and are created for the relevant aggregation level (see Figure 11.37, Steps 1, 2, and 3).

▸ Clicking on the **Transfer** button creates the filter (Step 4).

▸ This is then further specified through the characteristics to be selected (Step 5) and the relevant characteristic values (Step 6).[20]

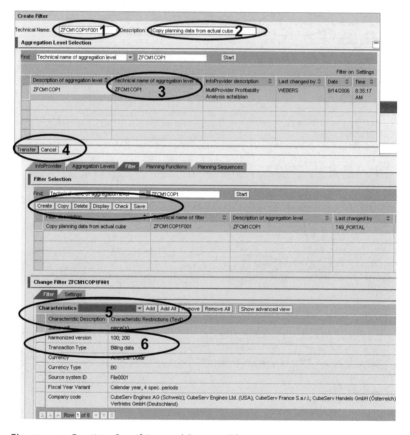

**Figure 11.37** Creating, Specifying, and Saving a Filter

▸ Since now both the aggregation level and the required filter have been created, the actual planning function can be created. Switching to the **Planning Functions** tab now creates the copy function of the type **Copy**. This corresponds to the copy function from the already familiar area of BW-BPS.

---

20 As the handling does not differ from the procedure within the Planning Wizard, we'll describe it only briefly at this point.

▸ Once the relation to the aggregation level has been created by selecting the level (see Figure 11.38, Step 1), you select the function type (here: **Copy**) (Step 2).

▸ A technical and a descriptive name are also issued (Steps 3 and 4).

▸ Finally, by clicking on the **For Characteristic Usage** button (Step 5), you can set the characteristic values to be changed as part of the copy functions (Step 6).

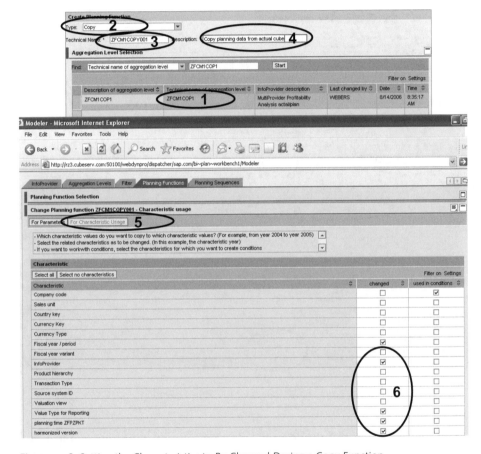

**Figure 11.38** Setting the Characteristics to Be Changed During a Copy Function

### Defining a Copy Operation

CubeServ Engines intends to copy the actual transaction data for fiscal year 2005 to the new planning year 2006. This data will serve as planned default values. Since the entire year is to be included for the

**Sales Quantity** key figure, all actual monthly values for the year 2005 are stored as planned monthly values for 2006.

Figure 11.39 shows the changes to the relevant characteristic values: For the **Sales Quantity** key figure (highlight 1), both the **From...** values and the corresponding **To...** values are maintained (highlights 2 and 3). Once these activities have been finished, the copy function is complete.

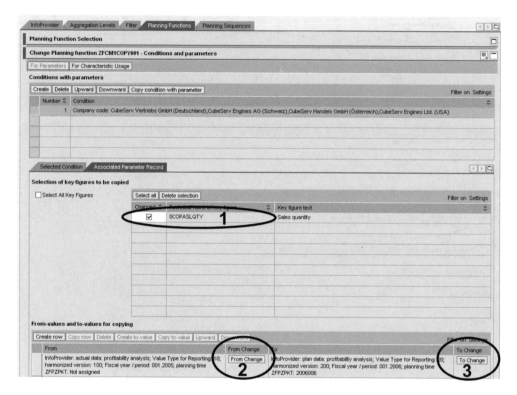

**Figure 11.39** From and To Values for the Copy Operation

**[»]**  Each function should be tested to ensure you that the system is functioning correctly. You can test in the Planning Modeler in the same way as in the Planning Wizard; however, no test frame is available here. Nevertheless, you can use the **Planning Sequence** function for test purposes. More specifically, planning sequences serve to group several planning functions collectively, according to operational business aspects or technical aspects. But, since the Planning Modeler also allows you to process a planning sequence in trace mode, this function is ideally suited for testing planning functions that you have created.

▶ To do this, switch to the **Planning Sequences** tab in the Planning   **[»]**
Modeler (see Figure 11.40).

▶ To create a planning sequence (Step 1), you must specify the technical name and descriptive name (Steps 2 and 3).

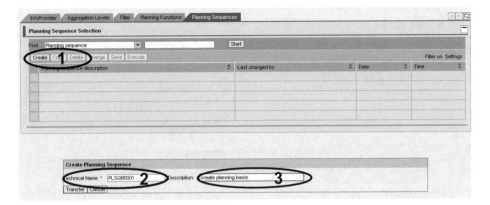

**Figure 11.40** Creating a Planning Sequence to Initialize the Planning Basis

▶ Then you simply select the required aggregation levels, filters, and
planning functions to be contained in the planning sequence (see
Figure 11.41, Steps 1, 2, 3, and 4).

▶ You can also determine the sequence in which the planning functions should be processed (Step 5).

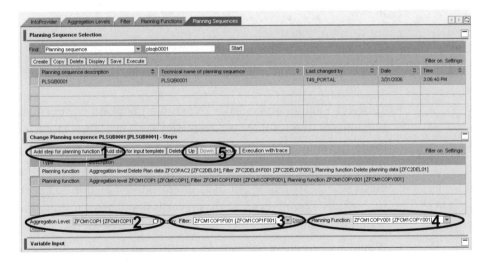

**Figure 11.41** Initialization Planning Sequence with Two Functions

▶ Once the planning sequence is saved, you can execute the individual planning functions or execute them via trace (see Figure 11.42, Step 1).

▶ You can also execute the entire planning sequence (Step 2).

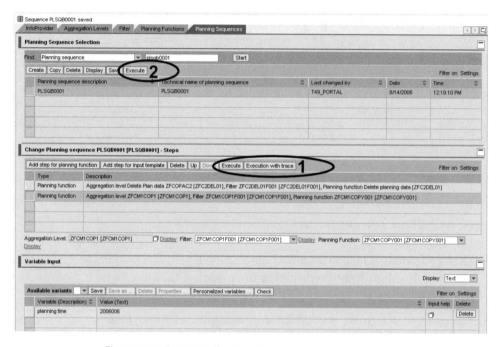

**Figure 11.42** Executing Planning Sequences

> **[+]** To perform a sound analysis of a planning function, we recommend that you perform the planning function via a trace. Data comparisons are then possible here (i. e., data before and after the planning is executed).

▶ Cubeserv Engines also decides to execute the planning functions individually, the result of which is displayed in Figure 11.43 for the initialization of the planned values.

▶ When you click on the **Execution with trace** button (Step 1), a message appears telling you that the planning function has been successfully executed and 12 data records have been copied to the planning version (Step 2).

▶ When you execute in trace mode, another analysis area also opens in which the user can select the block information and produce a data comparison.

498

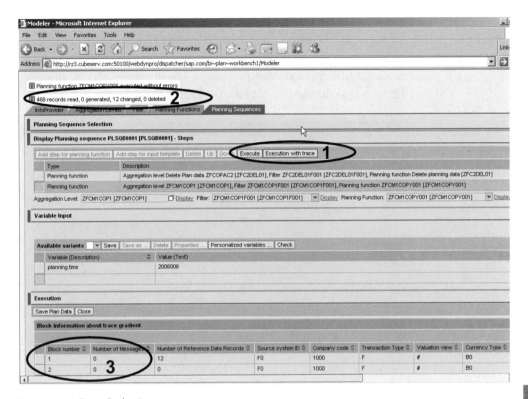

**Figure 11.43** Trace Evaluation

### 11.4.3 Delete and Copy Functions in the Planning Cockpit

Since the delete and copy functions have already been created, the CubeServ Engines implementation team wants to integrate these functions into both a web-based and an Excel-based planning cockpit. To meet these requirements, you first need to create a query that is ready for input (see Section 11.5), as well as the corresponding web planning cockpit (see Section 11.6) or an Excel-based planning cockpit (see Section 11.7). The implementations for these planning components will be described at the appropriate places within this chapter; therefore, only the planning cockpits to be completed at this time will be displayed.

The planning cockpit completed with the Web Application Designer is designed as shown in Figure 11.44. You can see that the planning application created can be arranged using tabs (for example, for **Documentation**, **Planning,** and **Reporting**) (highlight 1). Also shown is a planning query that allows you to enter planned values (highlight 2), as well as allowing for the display of key figures that are not ready for input or calculated (highlight 3). In the BPS world, this calculation of key figures was possible only by using very broad planning functions, so this application represents a key improvement of the functional scope that SAP NetWeaver 2004s offers.

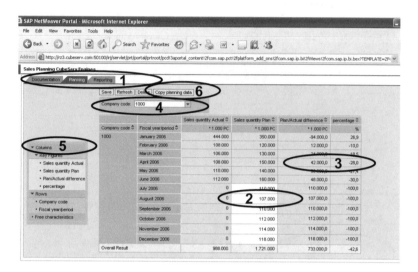

**Figure 11.44** Web-Based Planning Cockpit

With the move to BI-integrated planning, you can use simple query definitions to create informative planning layouts quickly and easily. This way, you save costs in the creation and maintenance of planning layouts. Furthermore, the switch to BI-integrated planning also offers an enhanced functional scope.

Enhanced functional scope

The planning cockpit in Figure 11.44 has also been enhanced with additional reporting functions such as a filter, for example (highlight 4), and a navigation block (highlight 5). The planning functions have also been added to the planning cockpit, so that the planner can be provided with a high-performance and informative planning tool.

In addition to a web-based planning cockpit, the CubeServ Engines Controlling department also requires an Excel-based solution. The creation of an Excel-based planning cockpit is described in Section 11.7. Figure 11.45 shows an example of this cockpit.

This figure also shows the interactive layout of reporting and planning requirements. The planning cockpit contains a planning query that is ready for input with the advantages listed above (highlight 1). It also offers purely reporting-specific functions such as selections and graphics (highlights 2 and 3). It also has planning-relevant functions. These are illustrated here in the form of the planning functions (highlight 4).

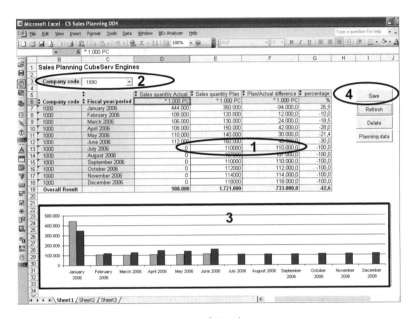

**Figure 11.45** Planning Cockpit in Microsoft Excel

### 11.4.4 Copying with the FOX Formula Function

Due to the excellent experience to date, the CubeServ Engines implementation team decides, using a FOX formula function, to also store the original data of the ZFCOPAC1 InfoProvider (actual data:profitability analysis) as actual data in the planned InfoProvider. The FOX formula function is a very powerful formula language that was already available in the BPS world.

FOX formulas can be used to implement different calculation functions that can be used for value assignments in formulas. You can also use the FOX formula language to model complex process controls.

The handling and functional scope of the FOX formula language have once again significantly improved for the BI-integrated planning environment. It is much simpler to create formulas thanks to help

Improvements for the FOX formula language

texts, process control, additional selection possibilities, and input helps. Additional program elements are now also available. For example, you now can call self-defined function modules from the formula language. This signifies a huge expansion of the functional scope, because now an additional process logic and other enhancements, in terms of the master data information, are possible. Moreover, there have been many enhancements in character strings and operators, for example; however, it would not make sense, or even be possible, to list and describe all of the enhancements here.

### Creating a FOX Formula Function

Bearing these considerations in mind, we will now create a FOX formula function based on the aggregation level **Copy Planned Data from ActualCube** (ZFCM1COP1), which was already created in Section 11.4.2.

[▪] 
- To do this, first you must branch in the Planning Modeler to the tab page **Planning Functions** (see Figure 11.46, Step 1).

- In the next step, choose the aggregation level **ZFCM1COP1** (Step 2).

- The function type of a planning function is set in the dropdown box **Type**. Choose the entry **Formula** here (Step 3).

- Next, define the technical and descriptive name of the FOX formula function to be created (Step 4).

- Once these settings have been made, you must select the characteristics to be changed within the function, and the characteristics that are to be used in the conditions for the planning function (see Figure 11.47).

- First, switch to the characteristic usage (Step 1).

- Then, the characteristics to be changed and those to be used in the conditions are selected (Steps 2 and 3).

- The parameters for the conditions are also maintained by clicking on the tab **For Parameters** (see Figure 11.48, Step 1).

- You must now make a corresponding characteristic selection (Step 3) for each parameter group (Step 2).

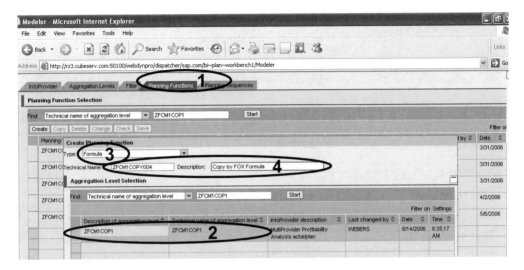

**Figure 11.46** Creating the FOX Function for the Aggregation Level

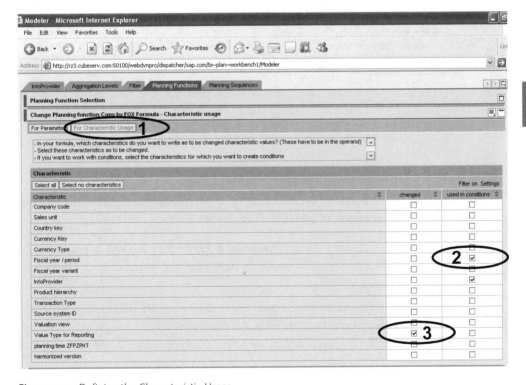

**Figure 11.47** Defining the Characteristic Usage

[»] You should also note that an existing parameter group is very easy to copy and can serve as a basis for further settings.

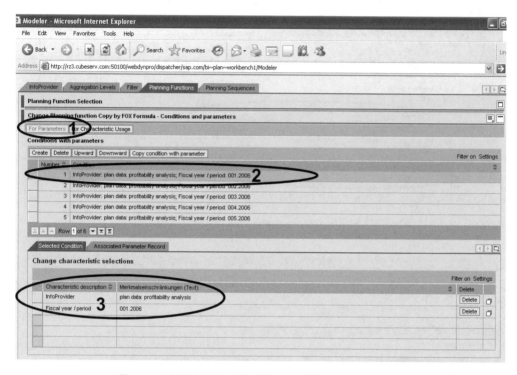

Figure 11.48 Maintaining Conditions and Parameters

**Maintaining Parameter Records**

The parameter records belonging to a parameter group that contain the actual FOX formula components are then maintained.

[■] ▸ By clicking on the **Associated Parameter Record** tab (see Figure 11.49, Step 1), you can open the corresponding maintenance screen.

▸ Here SAP provides you with a user-friendly means of support for implementing formulas. As shown in Figure 11.49, you can now first select the key figure to be changed (Steps 2 and 3).

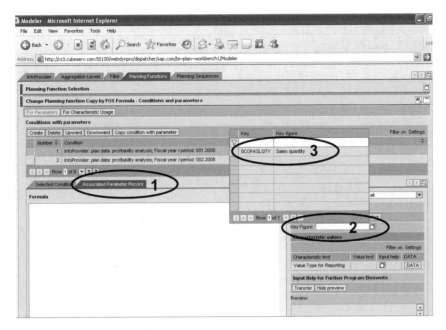

**Figure 11.49** Selecting the Relevant Key Figures

▶ You can then set the characteristic values to be changed for each characteristic to be changed (see Figure 11.50, Step 1) and copy it using the **Transfer** button into the **Formula** window (Step 2).

▶ In Step 3, you'll see that both the transfer of the key figure (Sales quantity) and the value for the characteristic **Value Type** has been successful.

▶ The FOX formula must be completed in the same way (see Figure 11.51, Step 1). The case shown here is a very simple example in which another value type is simply assigned to the **Sales quantity** key figure. This is a copy operation.

▶ The FOX formula function also makes additional program elements available (Step 2), which are simply selected with a mouse-click and then displayed in the preview window located above. The implementer is also given system-side support here, for example, because when the program element VARV is selected, another window appears where the variables from the aggregation level are offered for selection.[21]

---

21 The acronym VARV stands for *variable value*. Here the language element of the formula language reads the variable value and provides it to the planning function.

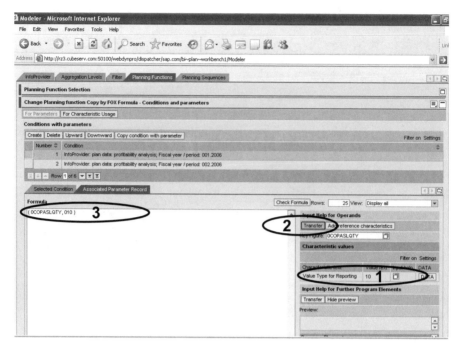

**Figure 11.50** Definition of the FOX Formula

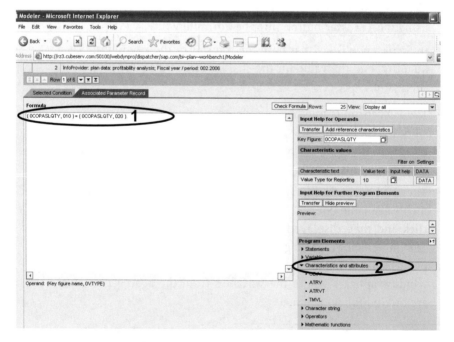

**Figure 11.51** Completed FOX Formula

Once the planning function has been completed, it is added to the Excel-based planning layout of the sales planning and is available in the planning process there (see Figure 11.52, highlights 1 and 2). You can also tell that the planned sales quantities have only been ready for input since July 2006, because CubeServ Engines decided to lock previous periods using data slices.

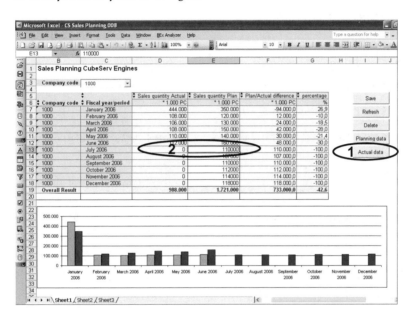

**Figure 11.52** Enhanced Planning Layout

## 11.5 Manual Planning

Unlike BW-BPS, manual planning layouts are not created in the context of the planning environment. Using the BI-integrated planning allows ready-for-input queries to be created that the user can employ to maintain planned values. There is no need to laboriously create planning layouts, and the corresponding maintenance effort involved has also been dispensed with. Thanks to the approach of using reporting tools, the integrative requirement for BI-integrated planning has been entirely fulfilled, because, in addition to InfoProviders that are already used within the reporting, you can now also use the reporting queries and their components (structures, variables, selections, etc.) for planning purposes.

**Simplifications**

Thanks to this integrative approach, the following functions are also available within the planning:

- Drilldown
- Hierarchical structures in rows and columns
- Calculated key figures
- Structures
- Alerts
- Conditions
- Support for the planning process through graphics
- Currency conversions, etc.

We will now describe how CubeServ Engines creates an initial ready-for-input query to use on the web or in Excel.

First, the CubeServ Engines implementation team develops an aggregation level located directly on the planned InfoProvider **Planned Data: Profitability Analysis** (ZFCOPAC2). Since ready-for-input planned queries are not created directly on an InfoProvider, but instead—like all other planning functions within the BI-integrated planning must be created—on so-called aggregation levels, this development step is required first.

[»]   Generally, with these aggregation levels, you should take into account, in the context of planned queries, that the granularity of the aggregation level also determines the granularity of the manual planned values stored in the InfoProvider.[22] Furthermore, the planned values entered via a query must be unique to ensure consistent data management. The query must therefore store the planned values under clear characteristic values in each case. If this cannot be ensured, a planning query is not ready for input even though the respective key figures are flagged as being ready for input. You should also note that the following InfoProviders are suitable for defining a ready-for-input query:

- Aggregation levels (see aggregation level)
- MultiProviders containing at least a simple aggregation level

---

22 In BW-BPS it was the planning levels that determined the data granularity.

### Creating a Planning Query That Is Ready for Input

The first aggregation level is arranged as follows (see Figure 11.53):

▸ The aggregation level **Aggr. level for query** (ZFC2MAN01) was cre-  [▪]
ated with a technical and descriptive name (Step 1) and contains
the corresponding InfoObjects defined by the implementation
team (Step 2).

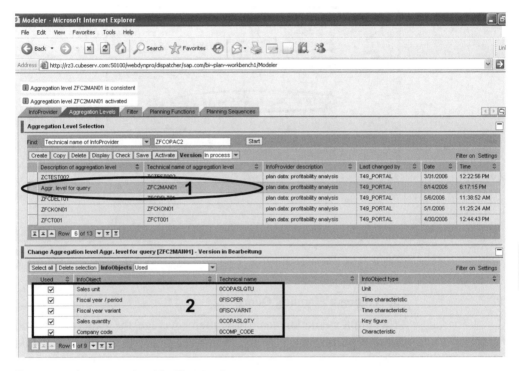

**Figure 11.53** Aggregation Level for Planning Query

▸ Aside from this aggregation level, no additional settings are
required at first in the Planning Modeler, so that the ready-for-
input planning query can be created using the SAP Query
Designer based on this aggregation level.

▸ To do this, as in the Reporting you also first select the InfoProvider **Aggr. level for query** (see Figure 11.54, Steps 1 and 2).

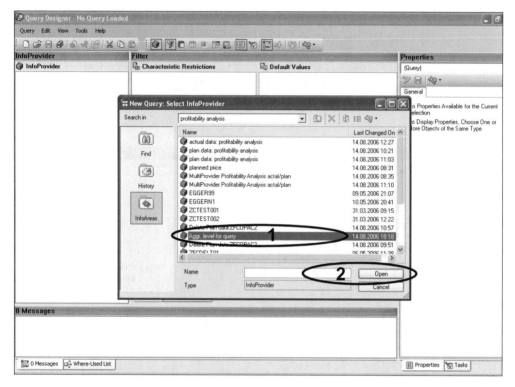

**Figure 11.54** Creating a Planning Query

### Specifying a Planning Query

The implementation team can then leverage the expertise gained from reporting projects and define the query in an often-practiced way.

**[»]** Still, we must state that, contrary to the realization of reporting queries, not all dimensions of the InfoProvider can be enhanced with InfoObjects in the InfoProvider overview. Because the query is defined on an InfoProvider of the type **Aggregation Level**, all dimensions of the actual InfoProvider are shown, but only the InfoObjects of the aggregation level appear (see Figure 11.55, Step 1).

**[■]** ▶ Within the actual query creation, first all filters are defined (Step 2). Here you must explicitly ensure that the definition for a ready-for-input planning query is unique.

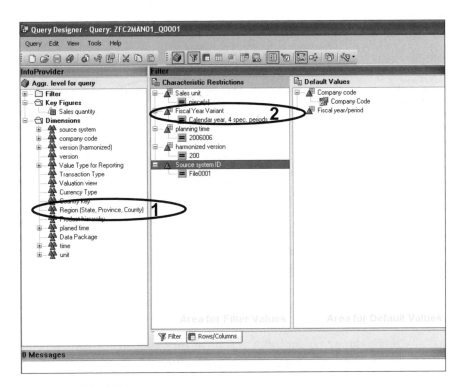

**Figure 11.55** Filter Values

▸ In Figure 11.56, Step 1, you can see the row and line definition made.

▸ To define a query as ready for input, the key figures must be set in such a way that changes can be done manually or via a planning function (see Figure 11.56, Steps 2 and 3).

These settings in Step 3 are imperative in order to make changes through a planning function or to make manual entries. So you can set here that the query is only started in display mode. At runtime, the users can activate the ready for input status to use the query to manually input planned data or to execute planning functions. In this way, you can ensure that users do not mutually lock each other in using the query in planning applications.

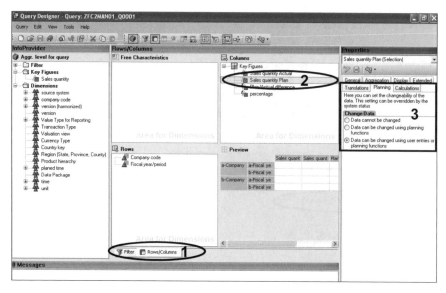

**Figure 11.56** Definition of Key Figures

Queries are ready for input as soon as they contain a structural component with one of the following attributes:[23]

▶ Data can be changed by planning functions: The data is locked from a technical point of view and can be changed by planning functions; however, it is not ready for input for the manual planning.

▶ Data can be changed through user entries or planning functions: The data is locked from a technical point of view and ready for input for manual planning. Planning functions can also be applied.

**[»]** In addition to entering planned values, the Query Designer also allows the already familiar query functions to be included in a planning layout. In the BW-BPS environment, this was very difficult, or was even impossible with many functions.

### Extending the Planning Layout

Below we will show you an example of how a planning layout can be expanded using simple arithmetic functions.

**[⟋]** ▶ This can be a subtraction, for example, or the determining of percentage deviations (see Figure 11.57, Steps 1 and 2).

---

23 See also the SAP online documentation.

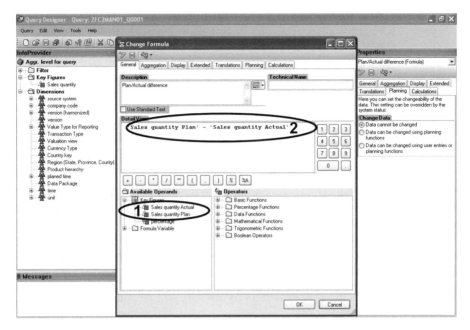

**Figure 11.57** Expanding the Planning Query with Formulas

▶ Once the simple query example has been completed, the execution on the web is assessed by the CubeServ Engines implementation team (see Figure 11.58).

▶ It is clear that the planned sales values are ready for input (Step 1) and that the actual sales values are not ready for input (Step 2). This corresponds to the settings that were made in the query.

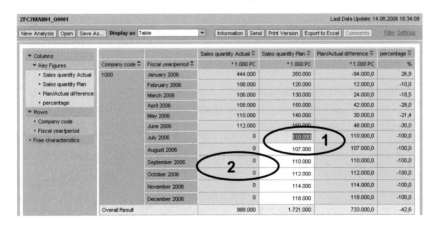

**Figure 11.58** Planning Query Executed on the Web

## 11.6    Planning on the Web

Once planning functions and a ready-for-input planning query have been created, we want to create a simple, web-enabled planning cockpit in a further step. This is done using the SAP Web Application Designer, which now has much more extensive functionality with SAP NetWeaver 2004s.[24]

To create a web-enabled planning cockpit, you must perform the following steps:

▸ Create the layout regarding the DataProviders, tab pages, and navigation options to be used.

▸ Specify the layout (settings for the heights and widths of the relevant objects, assigning the objects to tab pages, header definitions, etc.).

▸ Assign the DataProviders to the data sources/queries.

▸ Set the planning functions.

To create a planning cockpit, the following components, among others, are provided in the Web Application Designer:

▸ Tables, graphics

▸ Buttons for executing planning functions and sequences

▸ Dialog boxes for parameterizing planning functions

▸ Navigation block

▸ Variable selection via dropdown lists, radio buttons, and input fields

### Creating a Planning Cockpit

Based on these advantages, we will therefore now create a simple planning cockpit; however, it must also be expandable for future planning applications.

[▪]    ▸ First, you create a new template in the Web Application Designer (see Figure 11.59, Step 1).[25]

---

24  See also Chapter 9, *BEx Web Application Designer*.
25  See Section 9.3.1, *Basic Template*, for further information.

▸ Then we add a *container*, which allows any content that is to be displayed or that is not visible to be grouped together, to the web template via drag-and-drop (Step 2), to group together the planning layout with all corresponding planning components (such as planning functions, navigation block for the planning query).

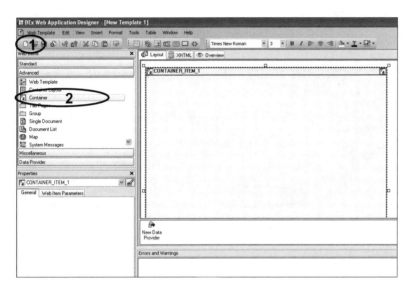

**Figure 11.59** Inserting a Container via Drag-and-Drop

▸ The actual table is stored in this container by selecting the **Analysis** web item and storing it in the layout area of the Web Application Designer (see Figure 11.60, Steps 1 and 2).

▸ To further specify the **Analysis** web item, it is vital that you specify a DataProvider including the data source (Step 3).

▸ In the case of CubeServ Engines, the ready-for-input planning query **Q0001** (ZFCMAN01_Q0001) must be selected here (Steps 4 and 5).

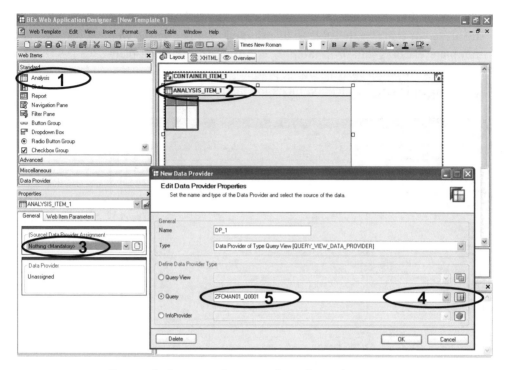

**Figure 11.60** Inserting a Query into the Web Template

### Using a Button Group

First, the SAP standard planning functions **Save** and **Update** and the self-created planning functions **Delete** and **Copy Planned Data** will now be provided in the planning cockpit. A so-called *button group* is required for this.

**[»]**    The web item **Button Group**, which represents a group of buttons, allows you to execute one or several commands from the Web Design API if the user selects accordingly. This web item supports the smooth integration of commands from the Web Design API into a web application. For this function to operate in this way, a command or a command sequence is stored behind each button.

**[■]**    ▸ Place the button group into the web template (see Figure 11.61, Steps 1 and 2).

▸ Parameterize the button group by storing a planning function for each function button to be implemented (Step 3).

▸ In order to do this, you must first select the desired action (Step 4).

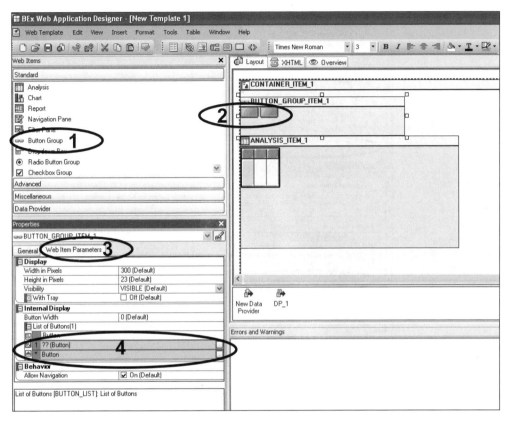

**Figure 11.61** Button Group for Planning Functions

▶ The parameterization is performed with an Edit Command Wizard, which supports the creation of a function bar (see Figure 11.62).

▶ In this figure, you can see that both a function button for saving (Step 1) and a button for refreshing data (Step 2) are created.

We recommend that you create a function button for the update, because this function ensures that query results (determining absolute or percentage deviations) are correctly displayed in the planning cockpit, for example. **[+]**

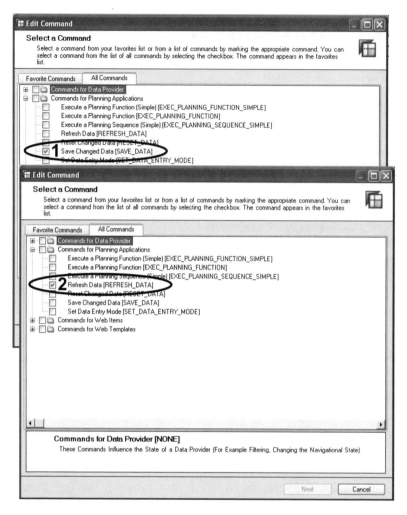

**Figure 11.62** Creating an Update and Save Button

▶ Furthermore, another button is created for the delete function. To do this, you must first choose the entry **Execute a Planning Function** in the Edit Command Wizard (see Figure 11.63, highlight).

▶ The wizard will then bring you to the selection of the planning function to be stored (see Figure 11.64).

▶ To do this, you must first select the DataProvider to be considered and also the planning function (Steps 1 and 2).

▶ A selection box will assist you in choosing the planning function (Step 3).

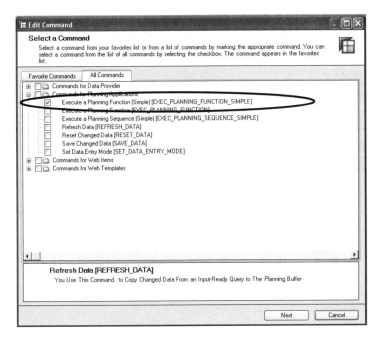

Figure 11.63 Defining a Button for a Planning Function

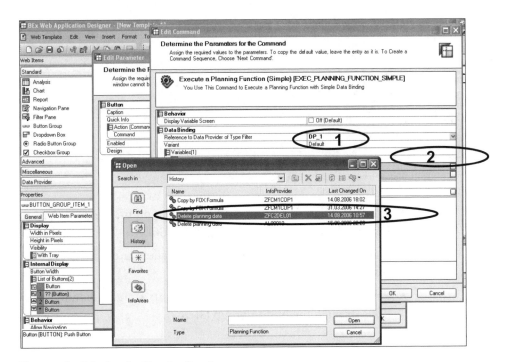

Figure 11.64 Selecting the Planning Function

▶ In the same way, a function button must also be created to provide the planned data, so that the button group initially provides the four functions **Save**, **Refresh**, **Delete**, and **Copy planning data** (see Figure 11.65, Step 1).

▶ Once you save this web template, you have now created a rudimentary planning layout (Step 2).

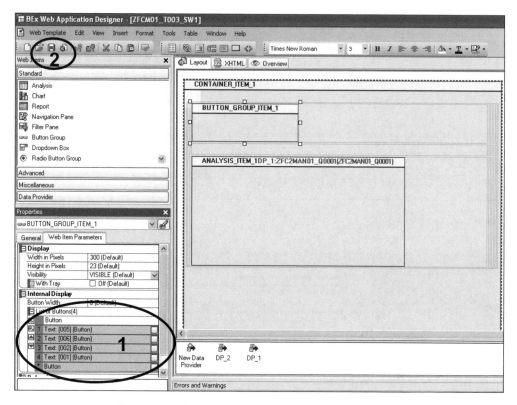

**Figure 11.65** Saving and Executing the Template

▶ If this template is executed on the web, you first receive the following planning cockpit (see Figure 11.66).

▶ Figure 11.66 shows that the planning query provides the values ready for input (Step 1).

▶ Furthermore, the user is offered the four stored planning functions through the button group (Step 2).

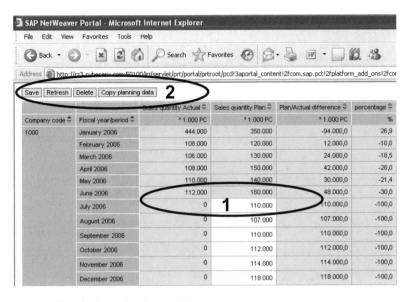

**Figure 11.66** Executing the Planning Layout

### Creating the Planning Cockpit

You will now expand this planning screen to form a simple planning cockpit. This cockpit will be arranged by using tabs in order to bring the user through the planning application and to simplify the navigation within an application.

▶ The **Tab Pages** web item allows planning cockpits to be created. [↵]
  Figure 11.67 (Step 1) shows that this web item must also be placed in the web template (Step 2) by drag-and-drop.

▶ Finally, the tabs to be created must be defined by first determining the labeling and the relevant content of each tab. The web item supports the implementer in doing this by offering all web items that are already used in the web template in a selection box (Steps 3 and 4).

Here you can recognize the advantage of first grouping the planning functions and the planning query in a container, because you can only select one web item per tab. [«]

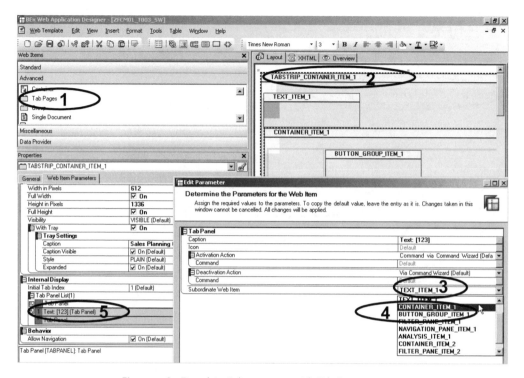

**Figure 11.67** Template Enhancement with Tab Pages

▸ After you select the relevant web item, you must also define a qualifying name for each tab. Once the web template has been saved and executed on the web, you get the following planning cockpit (see Figure 11.68).

▸ You can see that two tabs have been added to the planning cockpit (Step 1). The first tab contains a documentation part (controlled through the web item **Text**). The above example only gives a sample test.

[+]   However, in the course of numerous planning projects, it has always proven very useful to supply the user within a planning cockpit with detailed information, or with user documentation regarding the planning application. This makes a vast difference in boosting user acceptance.

▸ In the **Planning** tab, you will note that a navigation block was also added to the planning layout (see Figure 11.68, Step 2). However, even without this navigation block, you can use the right mouse button to further navigate (in the same way as reporting queries).

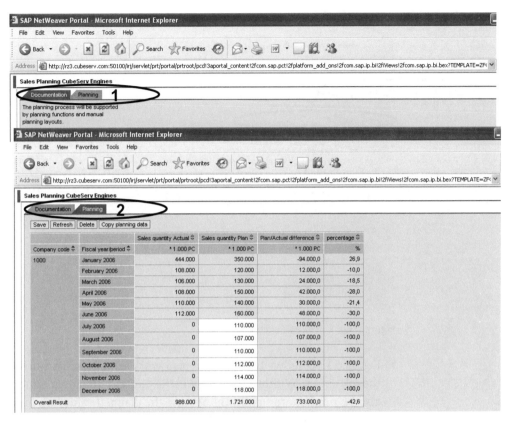

**Figure 11.68** Planning Application Executed on the Web

▸ Figure 11.69 also illustrates an example in which a **Reporting** tab was added to the number of tabs (Step 1).

▸ The user is also supported by a filter during the planning process, that is, the user can select the characteristic values that are relevant, which produces a clearer planning layout (Step 2).

▸ Additionally, the locking of the period January to June using the data slice technology is shown.

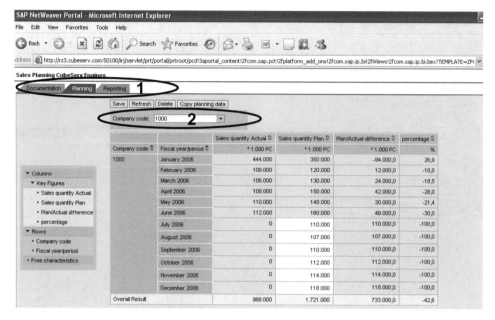

Figure 11.69 Enhanced Functions

▶ Figure 11.70 shows that you can also work with graphics during the planning. Within this context, the **Refresh** function button also becomes more significant because the planned values are only updated when you click on this button in the graphic.

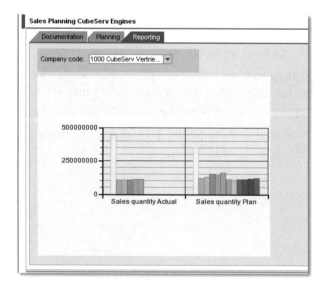

Figure 11.70 Reporting in the Context of the Planning

## 11.7    Planning in Microsoft Excel

Until BW-BPS, you could use Excel-in-place functions to perform a type of Excel-based planning with all the known advantages and disadvantages. With SAP NetWeaver 2004s and the BI-integrated planning, complete Excel integration has now been achieved. This offers the following important advantages:

▶ Creation of complete Excel workbooks using the planning and reporting functions of SAP NetWeaver 2004s

▶ Possibility of creating local versions containing enhancements and auxiliary ledgers. Nevertheless, data consistency and integrity are guaranteed because each workbook can be synchronized by refreshing the query with the BW system.

▶ Complete consistency and integrity of transaction data and master data

▶ Planning scenarios can be mapped more simply and flexibly in Excel workbooks and be made available centrally to all planners. In this way, the advantages of Excel's flexibility and BW's integrity (single point of truth, etc.) can be merged and exploited.

▶ Previously used Excel-based planning books can be expanded with functions from the BI-integrated planning.

▶ Advantages of purely Excel-based functions in planning workbooks (such as formulas, graphics, and pivot tables, for example)

▶ Enhancement of the planning applications through Visual Basic programming

▶ Creation of highly-developed, formatted, and individual workbooks

▶ Support for the planning process through automatic and manual data entry and changes

▶ Exploitation of BEx Analyzer functionalities (drilldown, filters, sorting, drag-and-drop, etc.)

▶ The operational planning processes often supported by Excel in the past can continue to be supported by Excel in the future, and also by SAP NetWeaver 2004s in the background. In this sense, there is no actual system change for the end users (because they can continue to plan in Excel), which will lead to an increased user acceptance.

### Mapping the Planning Application in Excel

Due to these persuasive advantages, our model company "CubeServ Engines" also plans to map the planning application to be created in Excel as well for a certain user group.

**[∎]**  ▸ To do this, first a new workbook is created in Excel (see Figure 11.71).

**[»]**  Note that each user must set the flag for **Trust Access to Visual Basic Project** under **Extras • Macro • Security** in the **Trustworthy Editors** tab. The BI-integrated functions to be used in the Excel workbook require this setting as a prerequisite.

▸ This created Excel sheet can be given a title for the planning application. The CubeServ Engines team opts for **Sales Planning CubeServ Engines** and makes the corresponding formatting such as the font family, font style, and font size.

▸ The cell in which the ready-for-input query is to be placed is then selected (see Figure 11.71, Step 1).

▸ To implement such a query in the workbook, you must click on the **Insert Analysis Grid** button from the BEx Design Toolbox (Step 2).

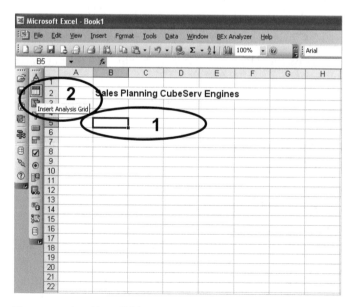

**Figure 11.71** Inserting a Table

▶ It is therefore initially fixed that a ready-for-input query should be used in the workbook. Nevertheless, the assignment to this precise query is missing. This setting is performed in the next step, that is, the implementer clicks on the symbol for the analysis grid (see Figure 11.72, Step 1).

▶ In the window that opens in which the characteristics of the analysis table are defined, a DataProvider is first created (Step 2) that is assigned to a query (Step 3; here the planning query **Q0001** (ZFC2MAN01_Q0001) that is already defined and used in other chapters in the book is used).

▶ In Figure 11.72, you can already see the extensive possibilities such as, for example, settings in the area of sorting and hierarchy functions and size adjustments and cell settings.

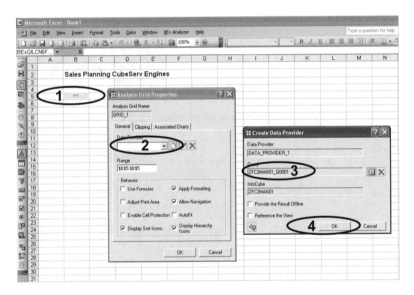

**Figure 11.72** Assigning a DataProvider to the Table

### Adding Function Buttons

However, since the planning cockpit is not intended to support just one ready-for-input query, function buttons will also be added to it.

▶ To do this, you must first select the cell in which the function button is to be placed (see Figure 11.73).

▶ Then, from the BEx Design Toolbox, you must select the **Insert Button** icon (Step 1).

▶ When you click on the newly created button (Step 2), a dialog box to define the button properties opens.

▶ The function button is given a descriptive name (Step 3).

▶ Next, you assign the static parameters. This refers to the command functions and the assignment of the command values (Step 4).

▶ Lastly, you confirm the definition (Step 5).

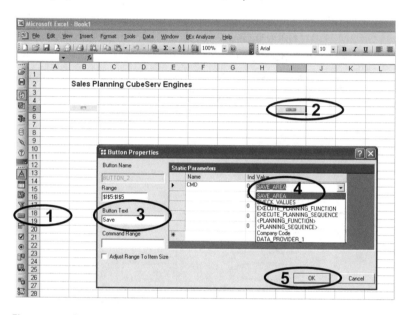

**Figure 11.73** Creating a Save Button

▶ Once the **Save** button is created (as described above), a **Refresh** button is created in the same way (see Figure 11.74).

▶ Here, you first select the button function (Step 1), and then you set the button properties by clicking on the button symbol (Step 2).

▶ When defining the properties, first the button name (Step 3) and then the static parameters must be maintained (Step 4).

▶ Lastly, you confirm the settings (Step 5).

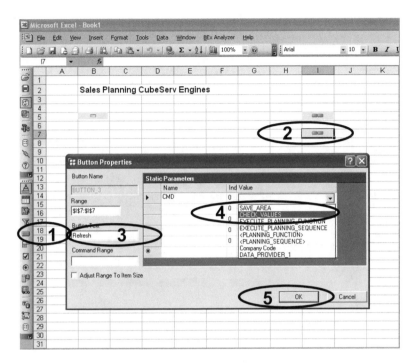

**Figure 11.74** Creating an Update Button

Figures 11.75 and 11.76 describe the creation of a button for deleting and copying the planning data. The procedure is always identical:

▶ **Step 1**
Fix the Excel cell and click on the button for creating function buttons from the BEx Design Box.

▶ **Step 2**
Click on the newly created symbol for a function button.

▶ **Step 3**
Define a button text.

▶ **Step 4**
Set the static parameters and confirm the settings made using the **OK** button.

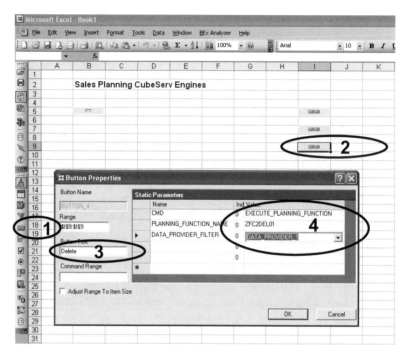

Figure 11.75 Creating a Delete Button

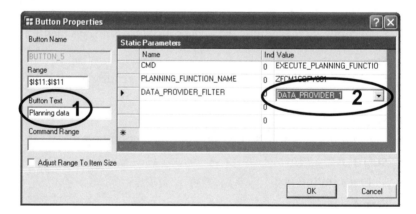

Figure 11.76 Creating a Button to Copy Planning Data

### Displaying Notifications in Excel

To also inform the end user of success, or of warning or error messages while planning is underway, you can display notifications generated by the BW system in Excel.

▶ Here you must first select the Excel cell in which the error messages should be displayed. **[✒]**

▶ Furthermore, from the BEx Design Box, the user clicks on the button for messages so that a corresponding symbol appears in the Excel sheet (see Figure 11.77, Step 1). To make the settings for this message box, you must click on the corresponding symbol.

▶ You can now set the message properties in the dialog box that appears, that is, you can define which BW messages (warnings, success messages, information) are displayed (Step 2).

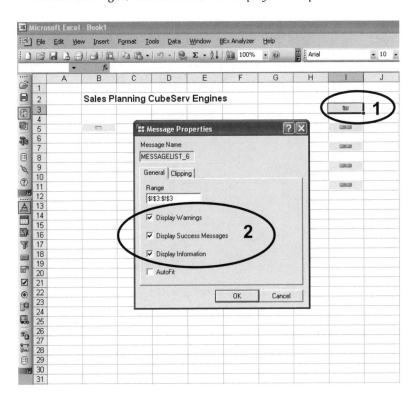

**Figure 11.77** Adding a Message Box

▶ Once these activities have been performed, the definition of a simple, Excel-based planning cockpit is already completed. When you leave the design mode, the query is executed automatically and you get the following planning cockpit (see Figure 11.78).

▶ You can tell that the cells for the planned sales quantities are ready for input (Step 1), while the actual sales quantities and the query calculations (see **Plan/Actual difference** and **percentage**) are grayed out and thus not ready for input. This corresponds exactly to the query definition that was made with the SAP Query Designer (see Section 11.6).

▸ Furthermore, the created function buttons that are required during the planning process are provided in the planning cockpit (Step 2).

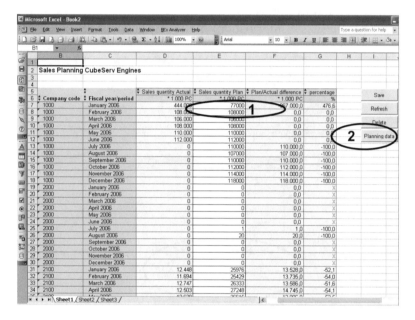

**Figure 11.78** Executing an Excel-Based Planning Layout

## Additional Settings

The layout and functional scope of the above-described planning cockpit can be further enhanced. For example, it would also be useful to have a filter function at the **company code** level, while a graphic support would also be desirable. Similarly, the grid shown in Excel does not particularly simplify the recognition and processing of planned values.

[▪] ▸ For this reason, first a dropdown box is selected for filtering from the BEx Design Box, so that a filtering is possible through the **Company code** characteristic (see Figure 11.79).

▶ Clicking on the dropdown box symbol (Step 1) opens the dialog box to make the required settings.

▶ In the example, it is specified that the dropdown box should refer to the **Company code** attribute (Step 2).

▶ Furthermore, it is defined through the read mode that not all values of the **Company code** characteristic should be displayed, but rather only the **Posted values**.

▶ Finally, the settings made are confirmed using the **OK** button (Step 3).

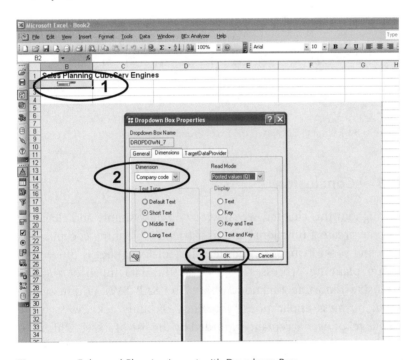

**Figure 11.79** Enhanced Planning Layout with Dropdown Box

▶ Additionally, the implementation team also includes a graphic in this Excel workbook. Since this involves a purely Excel activity, it will not be described any further. Furthermore, the grid lines are also hidden via **Extras • Options • View • Grid Lines**.

▶ Once all the settings have been made, you receive the following Excel planning cockpit (see Figure 11.80).

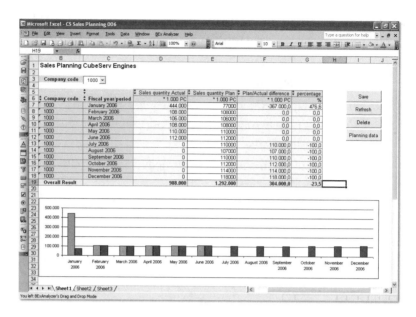

**Figure 11.80** Planning Cockpit in the Excel Workbook

## 11.8 Conclusion

Throughout this chapter, we showed you how simply and elegantly you can create a functional and user-friendly planning cockpit. This planning cockpit supports the flexibility of Excel that is often used within planning processes, as well as the data integrity and the extensive reporting functions offered by SAP BW. Within operational business applications, you must certainly acknowledge the high level of user acceptance afforded by the use of Excel, which can allow for a planning-driven implementation project to be successful. However, you can also attest to the fact that the web planning cockpits that can be built with the support of BI-integrated planning have become much more powerful with the use of SAP NetWeaver 2004s, and allow user-friendly, functional, and high-performance planning.

*With SAP Analytics, SAP moves towards integrating Business Intelligence solutions with any other applications within the scope of SAP NetWeaver 2004s. The Visual Composer serves as the user interface for SAP Analytics applications. This model-based tool enables the integration of data from the most different systems and the creation of professional frontends. Furthermore, this powerful design tool enables users to achieve high productivity. This chapter introduces the capabilities of Visual Composer.*

# 12 SAP NetWeaver Visual Composer

## 12.1 Sample Scenario

For our model company, CubeServ Engines, a composite application will be created in the field of Customer Credit Management:

- **Central Selection**
  The entire application will be controlled by a central selection. This specifies the credit control area for which the customers should be displayed and the currency in which to present the amount key figures.

  As an example, a static and a dynamic selection list are created:

  - The admitted currencies are provided as a static dropdown list, while the credit control areas are made available in a dynamic dropdown list as master data posted in the SAP BW.

  - When the selection changes, the application should not be updated with the new selection parameters until the **Execute** button has been clicked.

  - For the condition, the number of customers to be displayed should be controlled via an input field **Top N Customers**.

- **Application Help**
  It should be possible to call the documentation directly from the application via a button.

▶ **Overview Accounts Receivables by Customer**
As the initial view, the table top n — **Overview of accounts receivables by customer** — is to be displayed with **open receivables, credit limit, limit utilization/overdraft** as well as the **date of the last payment**. For a better identification of the customers, their **country, zip code**, and **town** are also displayed. The number of customers to be displayed is determined based on the receivables by the top n condition mentioned above.

▶ **For the Selected Customer: Second-level Report of the Payment History**
For a customer selected in the overview table, the payment history will be presented in a rolling form, both as a table and as a chart. The table should display the payments without **cash discount, the payments with cash discount,** as well as the **number of payments** for the current 12 periods (i. e., the current period and the 11 previous periods). A stacked bar chart should present the payment total (with and without cash discount) for the specified periods.

▶ **Display and Maintenance of Credit Management Data**
For the customer selected in the overview table, the status data of the credit management will be displayed. It should be possible to edit and save the presented status data back to the SAP R/3 OLTP system. A message should be displayed for success and failure of the update.

▶ **Display of the Customer Data Sheet**
For the customer selected in the overview table, the customer data sheet, a document containing unstructured data, is to be integrated.

## 12.2    Basis Components

### 12.2.1    SAP BW

The analytic data basis is created by SAP BW.

Object "Credit Management Control Area Data"

The data model is formed by the SAP Business Content DataStore object Credit Management Control Area Data (0FIAR_O09). Data is retrieved via the SAP Business Content object Customers: Credit Management Control Area Data (0FI_AR_9). This is where the Data-

Source, the InfoSource, and the update rules of the same name are implemented (see Figure 12.1).

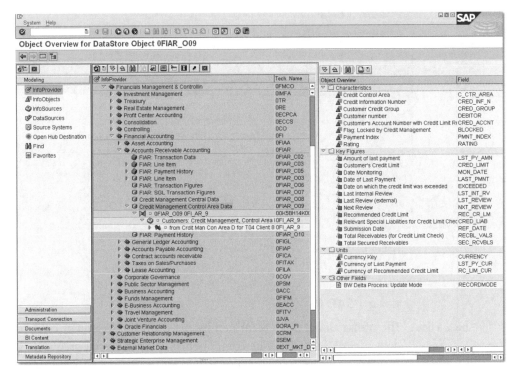

**Figure 12.1** Data Model and ETL Process for DataStore Object "Credit Management, Control Area Data" (0FIAR_O09)

Because this chapter is not intended to provide SAP BW EDW basics (see the *SAP BW Library*, Volume 1–4), these data model objects are used unchanged.

This also applies to the second data basis, the SAP Business Content InfoCube FIAR: Payment History (0FIAR_C05). Data is retrieved via the SAP Business Content object Payment History (0FI_AR_5). This is where the DataSource, the InfoSource, and the update rules of the same name are implemented (see Figure 12.2).

**Payment history of the customer**

537

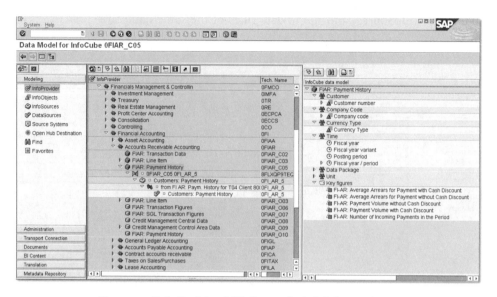

Figure 12.2 Data Model and ETL Process for InfoCube "FIAR: Payment History" (0FIAR_C05)

### 12.2.2 SAP R/3 (ERP)

OLTP transaction The transactional basis is formed by the credit management component in SAP R/3 (ERP). The components of the customer credit management status view (Transaction FD33) are used in data maintenance.

▶ The data in the SAP OLTP system is stored per **Customer** and **Credit control area**[1] (see Figure 12.3, Step 1).

▶ After selecting the values and the view (in this case, the **Status** view), the display is called via the **Enter** button (Steps 2 and 3).

▶ The customer settings to be used in the composite application are **Risk category**[2], **Credit rep. group**[3], and the **Blocked** indicator (by Credit Management)[4] (Step 4).

---

1 Organizational unit that defines and controls a credit limit for customers. A credit control area can include one or more company codes.

2 A customer can be assigned to a credit risk class. The credit risk class controls all credit checks.

3 A customer can be assigned to an agent group for credit control. This agent group is included in the request and can be used as the selection criterion for validations and release functions.

4 This causes a customer to be blocked from all business transactions (order receipt, delivery, goods issue) by credit management. However, the posting of invoices for goods already delivered is still possible.

538

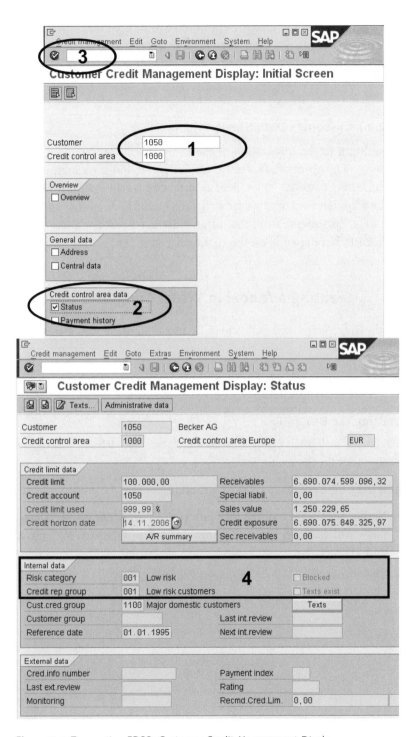

**Figure 12.3** Transaction FD33: Customer Credit Management Display

OLTP data basis The data basis for the analytic application to be created is formed by the master data tables **Customer master (general part)** (KNA1) and **Customer master Credit management: Control area data** (KNKK), as well as their check tables.

### 12.2.3 Customer Data Sheet

In addition to the integration of the analytic and transactional components, a customer data sheet is also integrated in the example scenario. This customer data sheet is intended as an example of the embedding and integration of structured and unstructured data. In this case, documents from the intranet are used that are addressable via a URL that depends on the customer's number.

## 12.3 Creating a Model in Visual Composer

In the next step, you will create a model and its corresponding iView.

### 12.3.1 Creating a Model

**Starting the Design Tool**

To create a Visual Composer model, start the Visual Composer design tool (in the example):

*http://rz1.cubeserv.com:51000/VC/default.jsp*

[◦] ▸ In the logon screen of the SAP Enterprise Portal, enter user ID and password and click on the **Log on** button (see Figure 12.4, Steps 1 and 2).

▸ The Visual Composer design tool is now opened.

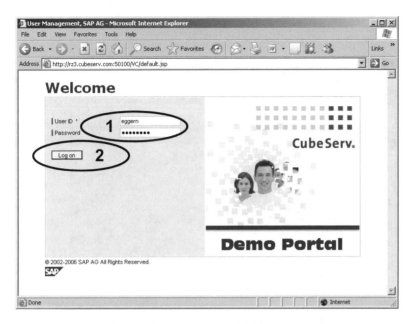

**Figure 12.4** Starting the Visual Composer Design Tool

### Creating a Folder

You should first create a folder for the generally available objects.

▶ Activate the **Model** menu, and select the **Manage Models** function (see Figure 12.5, Steps 1 and 2).  **[◂]**

▶ This opens the **Model Browser** popup. Highlight the **Public** folder and click on the **New Folder** button (Steps 3 and 4).

▶ A new folder called **New Folder** is created below the selected folder. The name of the folder can be changed accordingly (in this case: **CubeServDebitorCreditManagement**, Step 5).

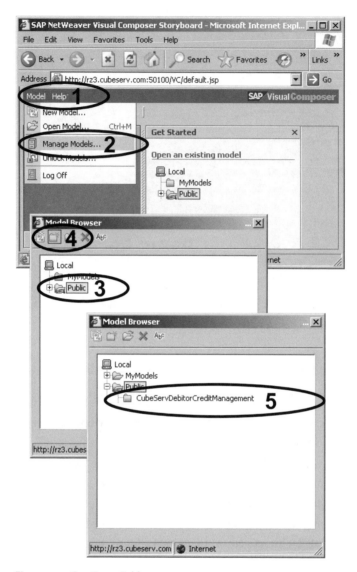

**Figure 12.5** Creating a Folder

**Creating a Model**

▶ In the folder structure, highlight the new folder, activate the **[.]**
Model menu, and select the **New Model** function (see Figure 12.6,
Steps 1 and 2).

▶ Enter the name of the model (in this case,
**CubeServDebitorCreditManagement0001**), and click on the **OK**
button (Steps 3 and 4).

▶ An empty model is created.

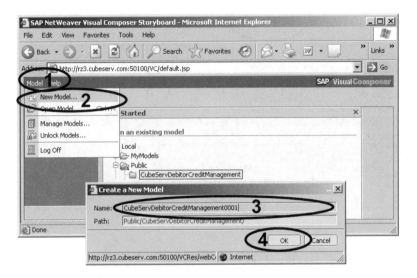

**Figure 12.6** Creating a Visual Composer Model

## 12.3.2 Creating an iView

In the next step, you will create and name an iView in the previously
created model.

▶ Click on the **Compose** button, and move the **iView** component **[.]**
type via drag-and-drop into the model (see Figure 12.7, Steps 1 to
4).

▶ Enter the name of the iView (in this case, **CubeServDebitorCredit-
ManagementStatus**, see Step 5).

▶ The name is accepted after you click into the work area outside the
created object.

▶ To edit the model, double-click to go to the iView model (Step 6).

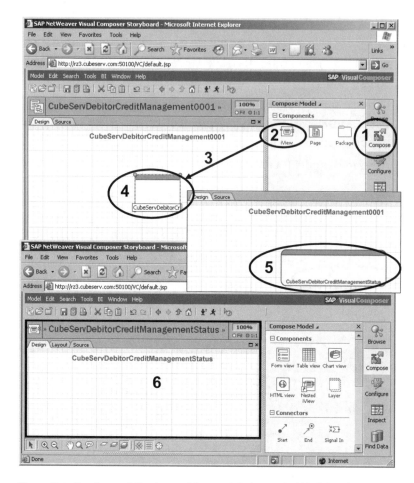

**Figure 12.7** Creating and Naming an iView and Going to the Work Level

## 12.4 The "Accounts Receivables by Customer" Overview

### 12.4.1 Underlying SAP BW Components

The entry point is a top n overview of accounts receivables by customer.

Top n overview query

Because there is no corresponding Business Content query, the **CubeServ: Credit Management Open Receivables, Credit Limit** query (ZF0FIAR_O09Q0002) was created based on the DataStore object Credit Management, Control Area Data (0FIAR_O09).

It shows the following data, sorted by receivables in descending order:

▶ The selected top n customers (InfoObject **0DEBITOR**) with the display attributes **Country** (InfoObject **0COUNTRY**), **Postal Code** (InfoObject **0POSTAL_CD**) and **City** (InfoObject **0CITY**) from the customer master (general part)

▶ The identifiers **Receivables** (InfoObject **0RECBL_VALS**), **Credit Limit** (InfoObject **0CRED_LIMIT**), the difference between open receivables and credit limit, as well as the **Date of the Last Payment** (InfoObject **LAST_PMNT**)

The top n presentation and the sorting are implemented by the top n customers condition that operates based on the top n formula variable (ZFTOPNF0).

*Top n condition and selection*

Among others, the credit control area (InfoObject 0C_CTR_AREA) is available as a free characteristic. It should be used for filtering in the application to be created.

*Filtering by free characteristic*

The amounts are presented in a currency to be selected. For this purpose, the currency translation for the key figures Receivables (0RECBL_VALS) and Credit Limit (0CRED_LIMIT) is performed via the BEx variable Currency (ZFCURRP0) using the average rate currency translation key on the current date (0MEANTODAY).

For the credit control area, a dynamic selection takes place based on the master data texts. It is based on the function module CubeServ Visual Composer: Selection Credit Control Area (ZCS_SELECT_0C_CTR_AREA), which reads the texts of the active credit control area master data that are available in SAP BW, and provides texts and attributes in two internal tables. The function module is created immediately with the characteristics Remote-Capable Module and Start:

*Dynamic selection via function module*

```
FUNCTION ZCS_SELECT_0C_CTR_AREA.
*"----------------------------------------------------------------
*"*"Local interface:
*"  TABLES
*"      IC_CTR_AREA_TEXT STRUCTURE  /BI0/TC_CTR_AREA
*"      IC_CTR_AREA_ATTR STRUCTURE  /BI0/PC_CTR_AREA
*"  EXCEPTIONS
*"      NODATA
```

```
*"------------------------------------------------------------
constants cOBJVERS type RSOBJVERS value 'A'.
select * from /BIO/PC_CTR_AREA into IC_CTR_AREA_ATTR
where OBJVERS   = cOBJVERS
and   C_CTR_AREA <> ' '.
append IC_CTR_AREA_ATTR.
select single * from /BIO/TC_CTR_AREA into IC_CTR_AREA_TEXT
where C_CTR_AREA = IC_CTR_AREA_ATTR-C_CTR_AREA
and   LANGU       = sy-langu.
if sy-subrc = 0.
    append IC_CTR_AREA_TEXT.
else.
    IC_CTR_AREA_TEXT = IC_CTR_AREA_ATTR-C_CTR_AREA.
    append IC_CTR_AREA_TEXT.
endif.
endselect.
ENDFUNCTION.
```

### 12.4.2 Creating Selections for the Top N Overview in Visual Composer

Requirements For the top n overview to be created, there should be the possibility to select the credit control area, display the key figure currency and the top n customers. After specifying the settings, there should be the possibility to update the display by clicking on a button. There should be default values for the initial display.

### Configuring the Selection

[▪] ▸ To configure the selection, while the **Compose** button is active, drag a form view from the component selection to the working area and name it **SelectValues** (see Figure 12.8, Steps 1 to 4).

▸ Right-click to open the context-sensitive menu, and select the **Configure Element** (Step 5).

Creating the input field for "Top N Customers" ▸ Click on the **Add** button, and in the **New UI Control** popup select the **Input Field** control type (see Figure 12.8, Step 6, and Figure 12.9, Step 1).

▸ As the **Field name**, enter **sel_TopN** and confirm by clicking on **OK** (see Figure 12.9, Steps 2 and 3).

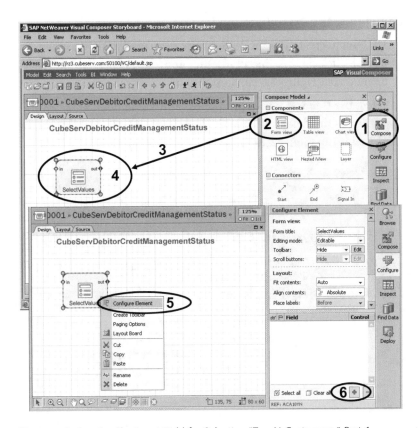

**Figure 12.8** Creating the Input Field for Selecting "Top N Customers," Part 1

**Figure 12.9** Creating the Input Field for Selecting "Top N Customers," Part 2

### Configuring the Default Setting for "Top N Customers"

▶ The newly created input field is now displayed in the field list. By double-clicking on the field, the **Control Properties** popup is opened (see Figure 12.10, Step 1).

▶ Select the **General** tab and in the **Default value** field, enter a value of **"10"** as the default setting (including quotes). Then, click on the **Close** button (Steps 2 to 4).

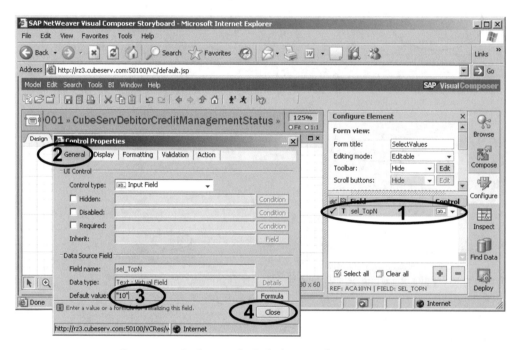

**Figure 12.10** Configuring the Default Setting for "Top N Customers"

### Configuring a Currency Parameter

Configuring a selection

▶ Click on the **Add** button again, and in the **New UI Control** popup, select the **Drop-down List** control type (see Figure 12.11, Steps 1 and 2).

▶ As the **Field name**, specify **sel_Currency** and confirm your entry by clicking on **OK** (Steps 3 and 4).

▶ The newly created dropdown list is then displayed in the field list (Step 5).

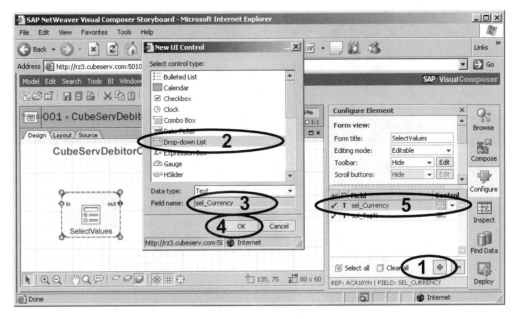

**Figure 12.11** Configuring the Dropdown List for Selecting the Currency to Be Displayed, Part 1

▶ A double-click on the field that you just created opens the **Control Properties** popup.

*Configuring selection values and default settings*

▶ Select the **General** tab, and in the **Default value** field enter a value of **"EUR"** as the default setting (including the quotes, see Figure 12.12, Steps 1 and 2).

▶ The values for this dropdown list should be provided statically. Next, select the **Entry List** tab.

▶ Check a value of **Static** for the **List scope** selection. Click three times on the **Add entry** button to manually insert three entries (Steps 3 and 4).

▶ Enter the desired selection list in the input lines:

```
USD    American Dollar
EUR    Euro
CHF    Swiss Franc
```

▶ Then click on the **Close** button (see Figure 12.12, Steps 5 and 6).

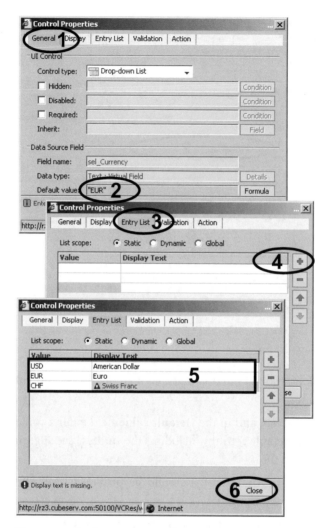

**Figure 12.12** Configuring the Dropdown List for Selecting the Currency to be Displayed, Part 2

### Configuring the Credit Control Area Parameter

Configuring a selection

▶ Click on the **Add** button again, and in the **New UI Control** popup, select the **Drop-down List** control type (see Figure 12.13, Steps 1 and 2).

▶ As the **Field name**, specify **sel_C_CTR_AREA** and confirm your entry by clicking on **OK** (Steps 3 and 4).

▶ The newly created dropdown list is then displayed in the field list (Step 5).

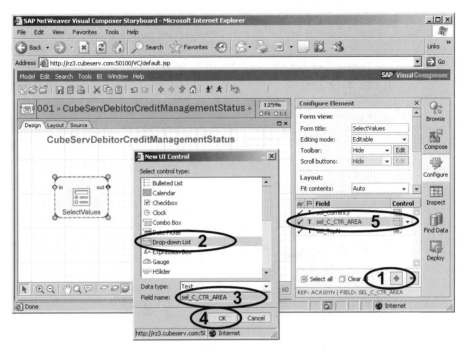

**Figure 12.13** Create a Dropdown List with Dynamic Selection of the Credit Control Area, Part 1

▶ A double-click on the newly created field opens the **Control Properties** popup.

▶ Select the **General** tab, and in the **Default value** field (for the Europe credit control area) enter a value of **"1000"** as the default setting (including the quotes, see Figure 12.14, Steps 1 and 2).

▶ The values for this dropdown list should be provided dynamically. Next, select the **Entry List** tab.

▶ Change the **List scope** selection to **Dynamic**.

▶ Click on the **Find Data Service** button (Steps 3 to 5).

▶ Another popup, **Find Data Service**, opens. In the **Look for** search field, enter a generic portion of the name or the entire name of the function module ZCS_SELECT_0C_CTR_AREA and click on the **Search** button (Step 6).

▶ The function module is then available for selection in the **Select data service** selection list. Highlight the module, select **IC_CTR_AREA_TEXT** as the **Output port** to support the master data text display, and click on **OK to confirm** (Steps 7 to 9).

Configuring selection values and default settings

551

▶ The function module and the output port are transferred to the **Entry List** tab of the **Control Properties** popup (Step 10).

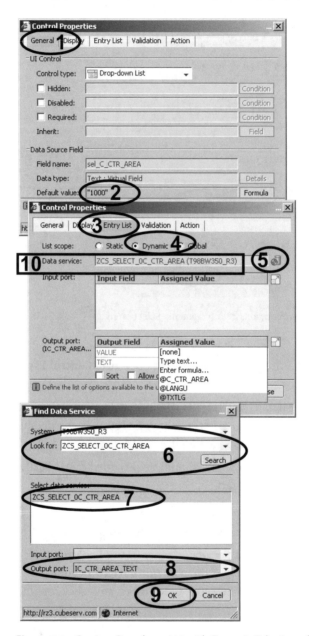

**Figure 12.14** Create a Dropdown List with Dynamic Selection of the Credit Control Area, Part 2

▶ First activate the menu by clicking on the **fx** icon. For the **Output Field VALUE**, select the key of the credit control area (**@C_CTR_ AREA**). Then, activate the menu using the same **fx** icon, and for the **Output Field TEXT**, select the name of the credit control area (**@TXTLG**) of the selected output table of the selected function module (see Figure 12.15, Steps 1 and 2).

▶ Click on the **Close** button (Step 3).

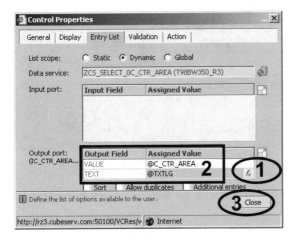

**Figure 12.15** Create a Dropdown List with Dynamic Selection of the Credit Control Area, Part 3

### Creating a Button for Executing the Application Using the Set Selections

In the next step, you will create a button that you can later use to run the application with the set selections.

▶ Click on the **Add** button again, and in the **New UI Control** popup, select the **Pushbutton** control type (see Figure 12.16, Steps 1 and 2).

▶ As the **Field name**, specify **BTN1_execsel** and confirm your entry by clicking on **OK** (Steps 3 and 4).

▶ The newly created button is then displayed in the field list (Step 5).

553

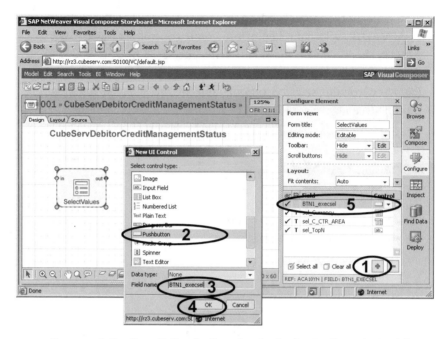

**Figure 12.16** Creating a Button for Executing the Application Using the Set Selections, Part 1

▸ A double-click on the field opens the **Control Properties** popup. Select the **Action** tab and specify the option **System action: Submit form Apply to: Self** as the **Action type** (see Figure 12.17, Steps 1 to 3).

▸ Confirm these settings by clicking on the **Close** button (Step 4).

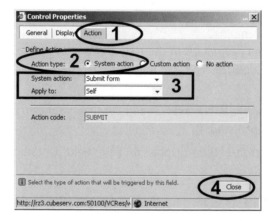

**Figure 12.17** Creating a Button for Executing the Application Using the Set Selections, Part 2

### Creating a Button for Calling the Application Help

A help document is to be integrated in the example application to be created.

▶ As shown in Figure 12.18, create another button with a **Field** **[•]** **name** of **BTN2_help** (see Figure 12.18, Steps 1 to 7).

▶ Then select the **System action: Hyperlink Apply to: Self** option (Step 8).

▶ As the **Hyperlink address**, specify the URL of the documentation to be linked[5] and click on the **Close** button (Steps 9 and 10).

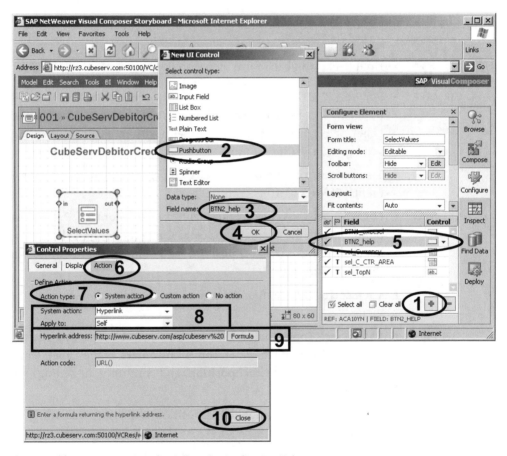

**Figure 12.18** Creating a Button for Calling the Application Help

---

5 In the example: *http://www.cubeserv.com/asp/cubeserv%20demo/VisualComposer/ CubeservVisualComposerDemoDocumentation1.htm*.

**Editing Components of the Form View**

Layout

The components that are automatically arranged by configuring the components via the Visual Composer design tool can then be arranged using the WYSIWYG technology.

[■]

▶ Select the **Layout** tab (see Figure 12.19, Step 1).

▶ Use drag-and-drop to change the size of the **SelectValues** form view to the desired width (in this example: 1248) or height (in this example: 832, see Steps 2 and 3), and move the objects to the desired position (in the example they are aligned horizontally, see Step 4).

Names and positions

The names of the form view components are edited as well:

[■]

▶ Double-click on each form view component to modify it.

C_CTR_AREA

▶ For the **C_CTR_AREA** component, in the **Control Properties** popup, select the **Display** tab, enter **"Credit control area"** as the **Label**, select **Long label** as the **Label position**, and confirm your settings via the **Close** button.

▶ Then correct the component's position according to your requirements (Steps 5 to 10).

sel_Currency

▶ For the **sel_Currency** component, in the **Control Properties** popup, select the **Display** tab, enter **Currency** as the **Label**, leave **Label before** as the **Label position**, and confirm your settings via the **Close** button.

▶ Then correct the component's position according to your requirements.

sel_TopN

▶ For the **sel_TopN** component, in the **Control Properties** popup, select the **Display** tab, enter **Top N Customers** as the **Label**, leave **Label before** as the **Label position**, and confirm your settings via the **Close** button.

▶ Then correct the component's position and width according to your requirements.

BTN1_execsel

▶ For the **BTN1_execsel** component, in the **Control Properties** popup, select the **Display** tab, enter **Run** as the **Label**, and confirm the settings using the **Close** button.

- Then correct the component's position and width according to your requirements.

- For the **BTN2_help** component, in the **Control Properties** popup, select the **Display** tab, enter **Documentation/Help** as the **Label**, and confirm the settings using the **Close** button.

    BTN2_help

- Then correct the component's position and width according to your requirements.

Now set the frame style of the form view:

Frame style

- To configure the frame style, double-click on the form view to activate the editing of properties, and use the dropdown list to set the frame style from **Default** to **Transparent** (see Figure 12.19, Steps 11 and 12).

**Saving and Testing**

- Save the current model state using the appropriate button (see Figure 12.20, Step 1).

    [■]

- On demand, you can test the current status by clicking on the **Deploy** button and again selecting the **Deploy** button (Steps 2 to 3).

- If the deployment was successful, the log contains the entry **Run "[model name]"**.

- Start the provided model by clicking on the **Run** log entry (Step 4).

- After logon to the SAP Enterprise Portal, the current development status is shown (Step 5).

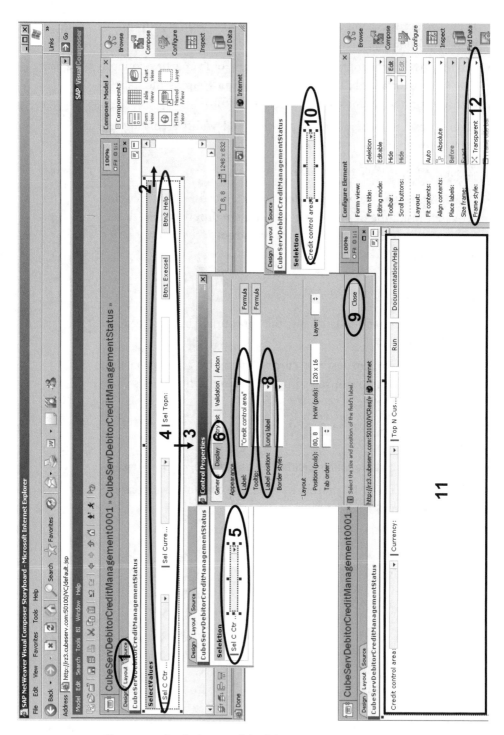

**Figure 12.19** Set the Layout of the Selection Form View

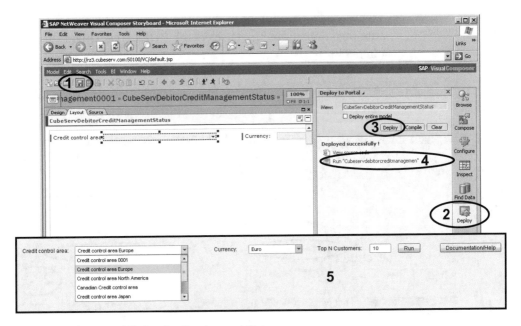

**Figure 12.20** Saving and Testing the Development Status

### 12.4.3 Creating the Top N Overview in Visual Composer

To create the top n overview, in the Visual Composer design tool, select the **Design** tab (see Figure 12.21, Step 1).

**Inserting a Query as the Data Source**

The data for the top n overview is provided via the query documented above (see Section 12.4.1). To integrate this query as the data source, perform the following steps:

▶ Click on the **Find Data** button (see Figure 12.21, Step 2) and under **System** select the SAP BW system that provides the desired query (in the example, **T98CLNT100**, see Step 3).

▶ For the search option, select **Look for a query**, enter the entire technical name of the desired query or a generic portion of it in the **Query** input field (in this case, **ZF0FIAR_O09Q0002**), and click on the **Search** button (Steps 4 to 6).

▶ The query is then displayed in the list of found objects (Step 7).

▶ Using drag-and-drop, drag the query to the Design area (Step 8).

Providing data columns of the query

▶ To make all data columns of the query available, right-click to activate the context menu and select the **Define/Test Query** function (Step 9).

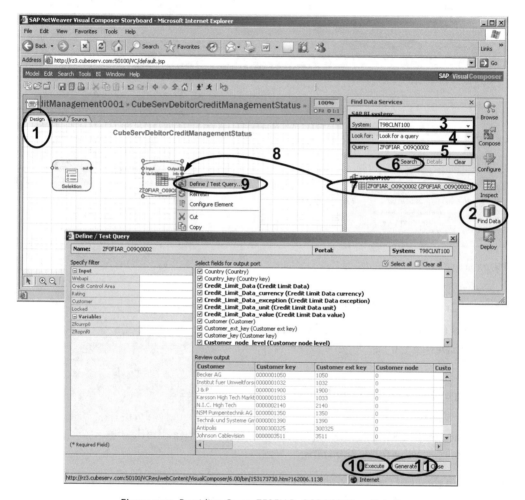

**Figure 12.21** Providing Query ZF0FIAR_O09Q0002 as Data Source

▶ The **Define/Test Query** popup opens. Click on the **Execute** button and then on the **Generate** button (Steps 10 and 11).

▶ All data columns of the query are now available, and the **Define/Test Query** popup closes automatically.

### Determining the Start Point

Because this is the first data source in the application, a start point is defined for the query ZF0FIAR_O09Q0002.

▶ Keep the mouse button pressed while dragging the mouse pointer from the **Input** flag (see Figure 12.22, Step 1) to a free space in the Design area, and in the displayed context menu, select the **Start Point** function (Step 2). [**.**]

▶ Close the **Select Input Fields** popup via the **OK** button (Step 3).

▶ The **start** point is displayed in the Design area (Step 4).

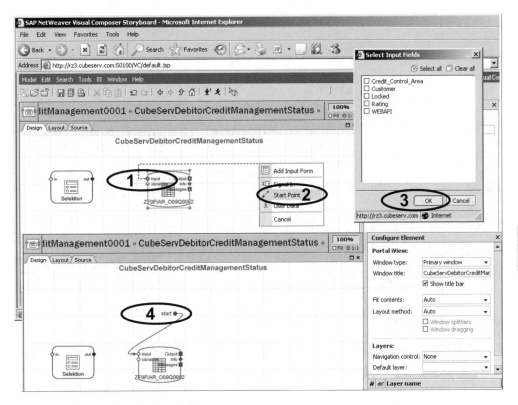

**Figure 12.22** Determining the Start Point

### Transferring Values to the Query Variables

For a data source of the type "Query with Variables," you should use the following selections:

> ► Click on the **Variables** flag of the query, keep the mouse button pressed, and drag the pointer to the **out** flag of the selection form view (see Figure 12.23, Step 1).

> ► After both interface points have been connected, the connection line is displayed as dashes and marked with the **submit** flag (Step 2).

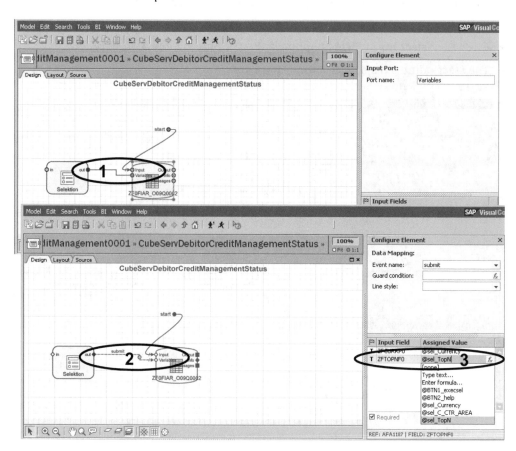

**Figure 12.23** Filling Variables of the Query ZF0FIAR_O09Q0002

> ► The lower right part of the design tool shows the variables. The query uses two variables: The **ZFCURRP0** variable is a characteristic value variable that expects the currency into which the amount fields of the query need to be translated. The **ZNTOPNF0** variable is a formula variable that expects the number for the top n condition of the query.

► Using the menu via the **fx** button, you can select the available components of the selection form view: For the **ZFCURRP0** variable, select the form view component **@sel_Currency**, and for the **ZNTOPNF0** variable, select the form view component **@sel_TopN** (Step 3).

### Filtering by Free Characteristics

For the given data source of the Query type, you'll create the credit control area by automatically filtering the free characteristic of the same name via setting a default value.

► Click on the **Input** flag of the query, keep the mouse button pressed, and drag the pointer to the **out** flag of the selection form view (see Figure 12.24, Steps 1 and 2).      **[♪]**

► After both interface points have been connected the connection line is displayed dashed and marked with the **submit** flag (Step 3).

► In the lower right part of the design tool, the **Input** fields (and the free characteristics contained therein) are displayed. Activate the menu via the **fx** button and select the **@sel_C_CTR_AREA** component of the selection form view as the source for filtering the free characteristic **Credit Control Area** (Step 4).

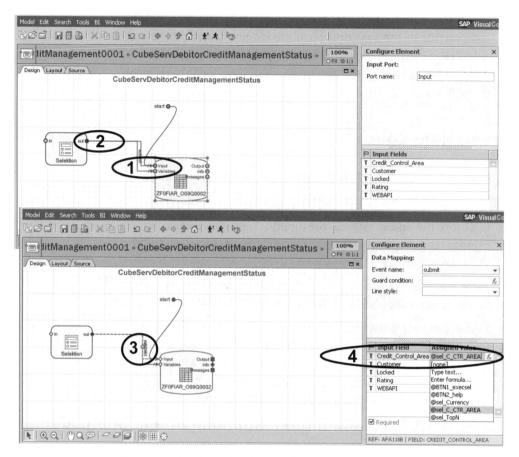

**Figure 12.24** Presetting the Filtering of Free Characteristics Via Form View Components

### Configuring and Editing the Output Table

In the next step, you will configure the output table of the ZF0FIAR_O09Q0002 query.

[■] ▸ Keep the mouse button pressed while dragging the mouse pointer from the **Output** flag of the query (see Figure 12.25, Step 1) to a free space in the Design area, and in the displayed context menu select the **Add Table View** function (Step 2).

The **Select Display Fields** popup is displayed, providing the data columns of the query for selection. Select the following fields by clicking on them:

- ▸ **Customer**
- ▸ **Receivables**
- ▸ **Receivables____Credit Limit** (stands for Receivables ./. Credit Limit)
- ▸ **Credit Limit**
- ▸ **Country**
- ▸ **Last Payment**
- ▸ **City_key**
- ▸ **ZIP_key**

▸ Confirm your selection via the **OK** button (Steps 3 and 4).

▸ A table is added in the Design area, the description of which you can maintain.

▸ After you have entered the description and clicked on a free space in the Design area, the table description is displayed (Steps 5 and 6).

The output table that is automatically arranged by configuring the components via the Visual Composer design tool can then be edited using the WYSIWYG technology.

▸ Select the **Layout** tab. Change the position (in the example: 0 pixels from the left edge and 40 pixels from the top, see Figure 12.26, Step 1) and the size of the output table (in the example: 840 x 272 pixels) via drag-and-drop (Step 2).

Editing the layout

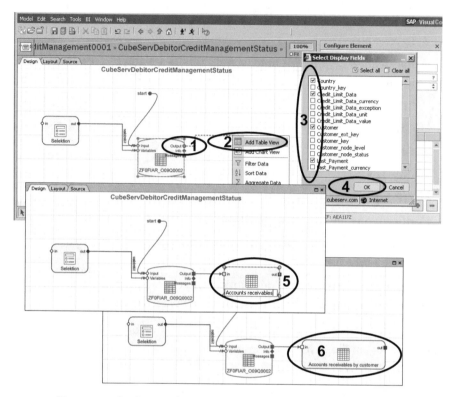

**Figure 12.25** Configuring the Output Table

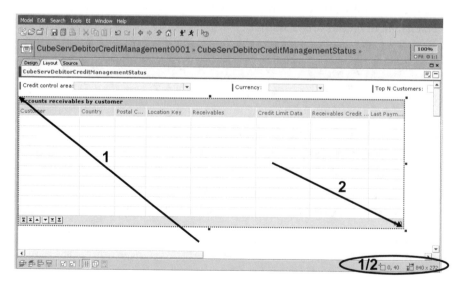

**Figure 12.26** Configuring Position and Size of the Output Table of Query
ZF0FIAR_O09Q0002

▶ Select those columns in the output table the width of which you want to adapt, and change their width via drag-and-drop (see Figure 12.27, Step 1). **Column widths and column headers**

▶ Right-click those columns the headers of which you would like to change (e. g., the **Postal Code Key** column) to activate the context menu, and select the **Edit Label** function (Step 2).

▶ The column header now accepts input (Step 3).

▶ Change the column header (in the example: **Postal Code**, see Step 4), and confirm the changed header via the Enter key.

▶ The changed column header is shown in the table (Step 5).

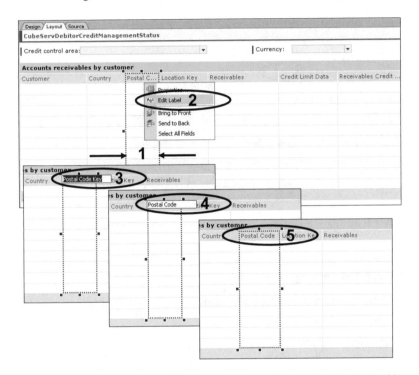

**Figure 12.27** Configuring Column Widths and Column Headers of the Output Table of Query ZF0FIAR_O09Q0002

▶ For the amount columns, a right-aligned arrangement increases readability. Therefore, the alignment is configured for all amount columns. For the amount column, right-click to activate the context menu, and select the **Properties** function (see Figure 12.28, Step 1). **Aligning columns**

▶ The **Control Properties** popup is opened. Change to the **Display** tab, for the **Text align** property select **Right**, and click on the **Close** button (Steps 2 and 3).

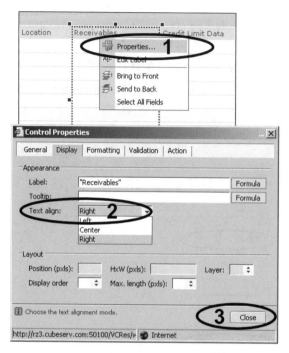

**Figure 12.28** Configuring the Alignment of Output Table Columns of Query ZF0FIAR_O09Q0002

### Saving and Testing

[▪] ▶ Save the current model state using the appropriate button (see Figure 12.20, Step 1).

▶ If required, you can test the current status following the steps described in Figure 12.20 in Section 12.4.2. The selections, as well as the top n overview, are displayed according to the configuration.

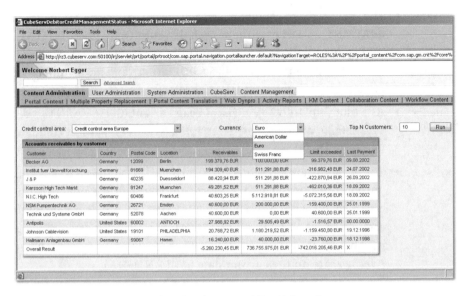

**Figure 12.29** Running the Model With Selection and Top N Overview

## 12.5 Development of the Payment History of a Selected Customer

### 12.5.1 Underlying SAP BW Components

The detail data of a selected customer is displayed based on an SAP BW query.

Because there was no appropriate Business Content query, the query **CubeServ: Customer Payment History (Credit Management)** (ZF0FIAR_C05Q0001) was created based on the Business Content InfoCube FIAR: **Payment History** (0FIAR_C05):

Query "Payment History (Credit Management)"

▶ For a selected customer (free characteristic: InfoObject **0DEBITOR**), this shows the 12 periods before the current period in a rolling form (InfoObject **0FISCPER**). The current period is determined based on the SAP Business Content variable **current fiscal year/period (SAP exit) (0FPER)**. The 12 rolling periods are mapped via a variable offset.

▶ The row headers are created from the determined values for fiscal year and posting period using the text variables **ZFFYPPT0** and **ZFFYPYT0**, which provide the respective posting period with two digits and the respective fiscal year with four digits.

Columns

569

Filter ▸ The key figures **Payment without cash discount** (InfoObject **0PAYMNT_2**), **Delay without cash discount** (InfoObject **0DELAY_2**), **Payment with cash discount** (InfoObject **0PAYMNT_1**), **Delay with cash discount** (InfoObject **0DELAY_1**) and the **Number of payments** (InfoObject **0NUM_PAYMNT**).

Currency translation ▸ As a filter, the InfoObject **Fiscal Year Variant** (0FISCVARNT) is set as a default value using the variable **Fiscal Year Variant (hidden) K4** (ZFFIYVH0).

▸ The amounts are presented in a currency to be selected. For this purpose, the currency for the amount key figures **Payment without cash discount** (InfoObject **0PAYMNT_2**) and **Payment with cash discount** (InfoObject **0PAYMNT_1**) is translated via the BEx variable **Currency** (ZFCURRP0) using the currency translation key **Average rate on the current date** (0MEANTODAY).

### 12.5.2 Creating the Table "Payment History" in Visual Composer

To create the detailed display including the payment history development of a selected customer, in the Visual Composer design tool, select the **Design** tab (see Figure 12.30, Step 1).

**Inserting a Query as Data Source**

The data for the payment history development of a selected customer is provided by the query documented above (see Section 12.5.1). To integrate this query as the data source, perform the following steps:

[✷] ▸ Click on the **Find Data** button (see Figure 12.30, Step 2) and under **System** select the SAP BI system that provides the desired query (in the example, **T98CLNT100**, see Step 3).

▸ For the search option, select **Look for a query**, enter the entire technical name of the desired query or a generic portion of it in the **Query** input field (in this case, **ZF0FIAR_C05Q0001**), and click on the **Search** button (Steps 4 to 6).

▸ The query is then displayed in the list of found objects (Step 7).

▸ Using drag-and-drop, drag the query to the Design area (Step 8).

▶ To make all data columns of the query available, right-click to activate the context menu and select the **Define/Test Query** function (Step 9).

Providing data columns of the query

▶ The **Define/Test Query** popup opens. Click on the **Execute** button and then on the **Generate** button (Steps 10 and 11).

▶ All data columns of the query are now available, and the **Define/Test Query** popup closes automatically.

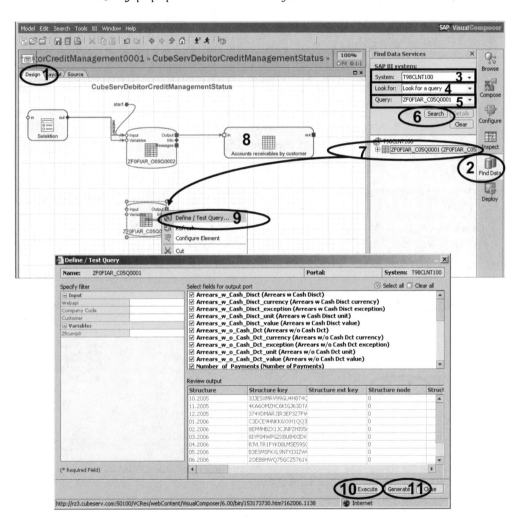

**Figure 12.30** Providing Query ZF0FIAR_O05Q0001 as Data Source

**Transferring the Selected Currency "Values" to the Query Variable**

For a data source of the type **Query with Variables**, you should use the following selections:

[•] ▸ Click on the **Variables** flag of the query, keep the mouse button pressed, and drag the pointer to the **out** flag of the selection form view (see Figure 12.31, Steps 1 and 2).

▸ After both interface points have been connected, the connection line is displayed as dashes and marked with the **submit** flag.

▸ The lower right part of the design tool shows the variable. The query uses the characteristic value variable **ZFCURRP0** and expects the currency into which the amount fields of the query need to be translated.

▸ Using the menu via the **fx** button, you can select the available components of the selection form view: For the **ZFCURRP0** variable, select the form view component **@sel_Currency** (Step 3).

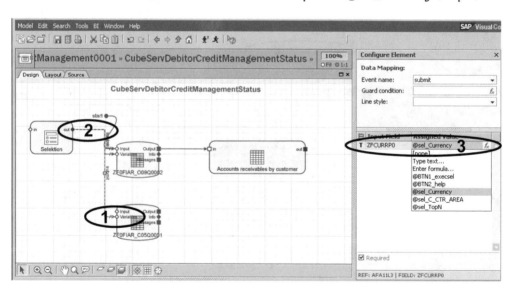

**Figure 12.31** Transferring the Variable for Currency and Filter Value for the Free Characteristic "Customer," Part 1

Filtering by free characteristic

For the given data source of the Query type, the customer selected in the overview table should additionally be transferred to the free characteristic of the same name as an automatic filter.

▶ Click on the **out** flag of the table **Accounts receivables by customer**, keep the mouse button pressed, and drag the pointer to the **Input** flag of the query ZF0FIAR_C05Q0001 (see Figure 12.32, Steps 1 and 2).

▶ After both interface points have been connected, the connection line is displayed as dashes and marked with the **submit** flag. In the lower right part of the design tool, the **Input** fields (and the free characteristics contained therein) are displayed.

▶ For the **Customer** input field, the field **@Customer_key** (not **@Customer**) now needs to be assigned as the **Assigned Value** (Step 3). For this purpose, activate the menu using the **fx** button.

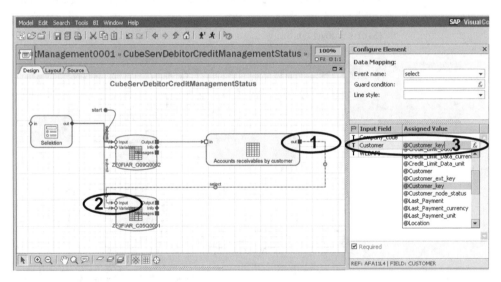

**Figure 12.32** Transferring the Variable for Currency and the Filter Value for the Free Characteristic "Customer," Part 2

### Configuring the Output Table

In the next step, you'll configure the output table of the ZF0FIAR_C05Q0001 query.

▶ Keep the mouse button pressed while dragging the mouse pointer from the **Output** flag of the query (see Figure 12.33, Step 1) to a free space in the Design area, and in the displayed context menu, select the **Add Table View** function (Step 2).

▶ The **Select Display Fields** popup is displayed, providing the data columns of the query for selection.

▶ Select the following fields:

  ▶ **Number_of_Payments**

  ▶ **Period_Year**

  ▶ **Payment_w_Cash_Discnt**

  ▶ **Payment_w_o_Cash_Dist**

  by clicking on them.

▶ Confirm your selection via the **OK** button (Steps 3 and 4).

▶ A table is added in the Design area, the description of which is deleted for this example.

▶ After you have deleted the description and clicked on a free space in the Design area, the table is displayed without a description (Steps 5 and 6).

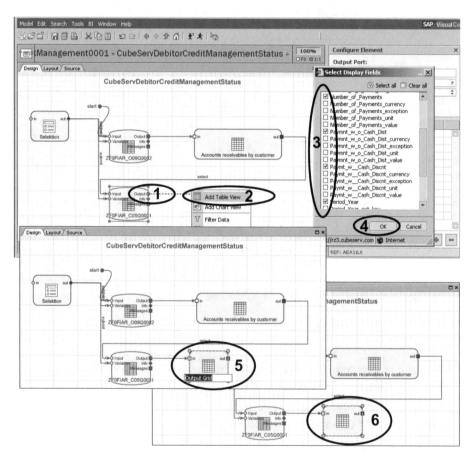

Figure 12.33 Configuring the Output Table for Query ZF0FIAR_C05Q0001

The output table that is automatically arranged by configuring the components via the Visual Composer design tool can then be edited using the WYSIWYG technology.

*Editing the layout*

► Select the **Layout** tab.

► Change the position (in the example: 0 pixels from the left edge and immediately below the table **Accounts receivables by customer**, see Figure 12.34, Step 1) and the size of the output table (in the example: 392 x 288 pixels) using drag-and-drop (Step 2).

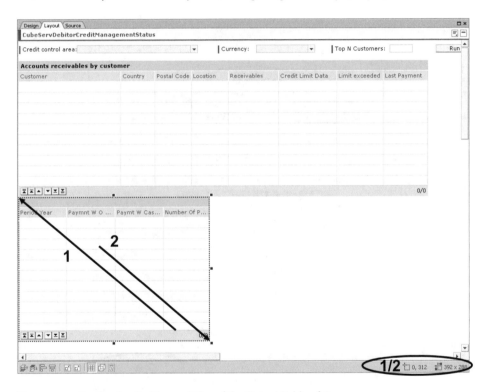

**Figure 12.34** Configuring Position and Size of the Output Table of Query ZFOFIAR_C05Q0001

► Select those columns in the output table the width of which you want to adapt, and change their width via drag-and-drop (see Figure 12.35, Step 1).

*Setting up column widths and column headers*

► Right-click on those columns, the headers of which you would like to change (e. g. the **Payment With Cash Discount** column), to activate the context menu, and select the **Edit Label** function (Step 2).

► The column header now accepts input.

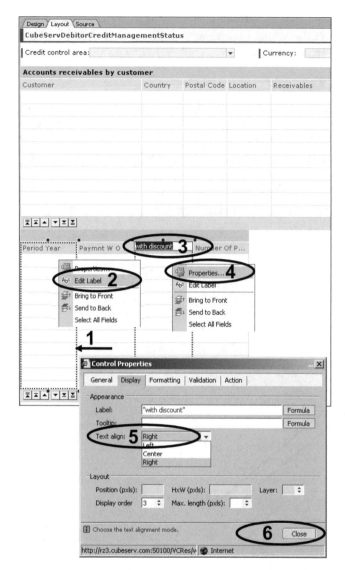

**Figure 12.35** Configuring Column Widths, Column Headers, and Alignment of the Output Table of Query ZF0FIAR_C05Q0001

▶ Change the column header (in the example: **with discount,** see Step 3), and confirm the changed header via the Enter key.

**Setting up the column alignment**

▶ For the numeric columns, a right-aligned arrangement increases readability. Therefore, the alignment is configured for all numeric columns. Right-click on the numeric columns to open the context menu and select the **Properties** function (Step 4).

- The **Control Properties** popup opens.

- Select the **Display** tab, and for the **Text align** property, select **Right**, and click on the **Close** button (Steps 5 and 6).

### 12.5.3 Creating the "Payment History" Chart in Visual Composer

To create a chart showing the payment history development, select the **Design** tab.

#### Configuring a Chart Showing the Payment History

- To create the chart, keep the mouse button pressed while dragging the mouse pointer from the **Output** flag of the query (see Figure 12.36, Step 1) to a free space in the Design area, and in the displayed context menu, select the **Add Chart View** function (Step 2).   **[▪]**

- Change the name of the chart according to your requirements (in the example: **Time series payment history**), and click on another place in the **Design** area. The changed chart name is displayed (Steps 3 and 4).   Renaming a chart

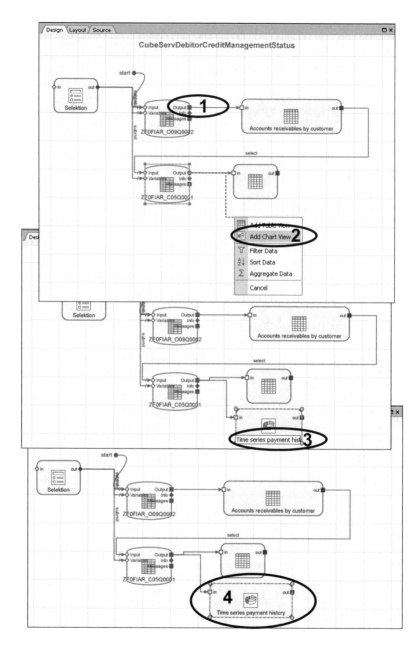

**Figure 12.36** Adding and Renaming a Chart View

Adding key figures to the chart

▶ To select the key figures to be presented in the chart, activate the chart configuration by double-clicking on the Chart icon in the Design area, and click on the **Add** button (see Figure 12.37, Steps 1 and 2).

- Select the required key figure (in the example: **@Paymnt_w_o_Cash_Dist_value**) in the **Formula** selection list (Step 3), and enter the description in the **Data Series** column (in the example: **without discount**).

- Repeat these actions for every other key figure (in the example: **@Paymt_w_Cash_Discnt_value** with the description **with discount**, see Step 4).

- The properties of the chart can be edited in the **Configure Element** area.

  Configuring the chart

- As the **Chart Type**, select **Column** with a stacked arrangement of the Data Series (selection **Stacked**, Steps 5 and 6).

- As the **Category Axis**, select the field **Period_Year,** and delete the **Axis label** (Steps 7 and 8).

- As the Flash **Data Animation**, select the **Interpolate** setting (Step 9).

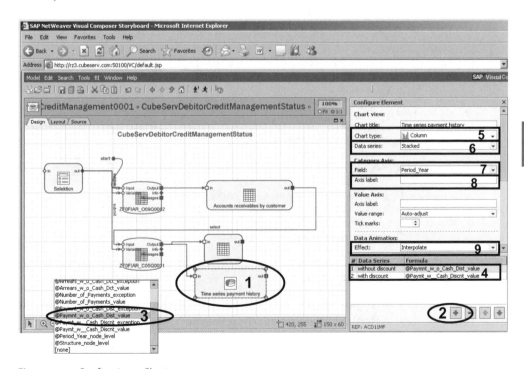

**Figure 12.37** Configuring a Chart

### Editing the Layout of the Output Table

[■] ▶ Follow the procedure above for changing the position and size of the chart using drag-and-drop (see Figure 12.34) so that it is displayed directly below the overview table and to the right of the table showing the payment history development, at the same height and aligned with the overview table (in the example: position 392, 312, size 448 x 288, see Figure 12.38, selections 1 and 2).

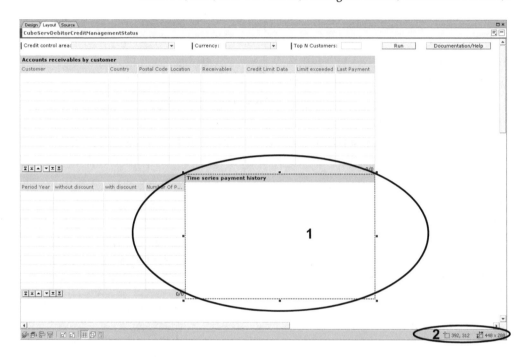

**Figure 12.38** Configuring the Chart Position and Size

### Saving and Testing

[■] ▶ Save the current model state using the appropriate button (see Figure 12.20, Step 1).

▶ If required, you can test the current status following the steps described in Figure 12.20 in Section 12.4.2.

▶ The selections, the top n overview, as well as the detailed table and chart are displayed according to the configuration.

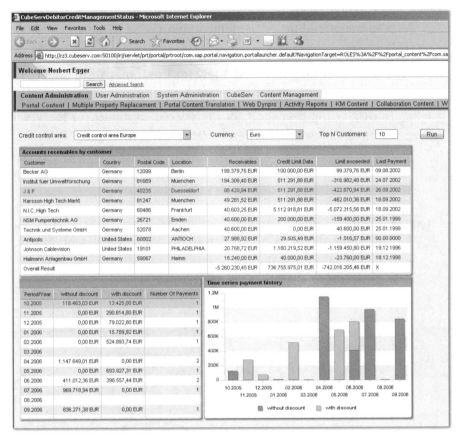

**Figure 12.39** Application with Selection, Overview Table and Details About the Payment History per Period, Table, and Chart

## 12.6 The Customer Data Sheet

### 12.6.1 Underlying Documents

The customer data sheet display should show the additional information about the respective customer according to the customer selections.

For this simple model, the data sheets per customer are provided as HTML documents in a web directory.[6] These data sheets are to be displayed in the application using selection-based functions. All data

---

6 In the example: *http://www.cubeserv.com/ASP/Cubeserv Demo/VisualComposer.*

sheets are named according to the convention **Customer [nnnnnnnnnn].htm**, where **nnnnnnnnnn** is the customer number.

### 12.6.2 Creating an HTML View for Customer Data Sheets in Visual Composer

To display the data sheet for the selected customer, in the Visual Composer design tool select the **Design** tab (see Figure 12.40, Step 1).

**Inserting the HTML View**

[.] ▸ Then activate the **Compose** button (see Figure 12.40, Step 2), and use drag-and-drop to move an HTML View component onto the Design area (Steps 3 to 5).

▸ Enter a description for the HTML View, and click in the Design area (Steps 6 and 7).

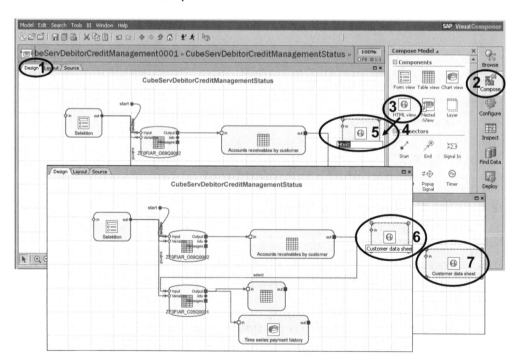

**Figure 12.40** Inserting the HTML View

### Configuring a Dynamic Document Assignment

▶ To transfer the selected customer to the HTML View component, **[◆]** use drag-and-drop from the output port (**out**) of the overview table to the input port (**in**) of the HTML View (see Figure 12.41, Step 1).

▶ Activate the selection list by clicking on the **fx** edit function, and select the **Enter formula ...** function (Steps 2 and 3).

▶ The **Assign Value** formula popup opens. Specify the function for the data-driven selection of the respective customer data sheet:

"**http://www.cubeserv.com/ASP/Cubeserv** Demo/VisualComposer/Debitor**" & @Customer_key & ".htm"**

▶ The "**&**" in this formula links the first part containing the path to the directory and the constant name portion (**"http://www.cubeserv.com/ASP/Cubeserv** Demo/VisualComposer/Debitor"**) to the customer number selected in the overview table (**@Customer_key**) and the file extension (.htm), and transfers this URL to the HTML View (Steps 4 to 6).

▶ Confirm your selection by clicking on **OK** (Step 7).

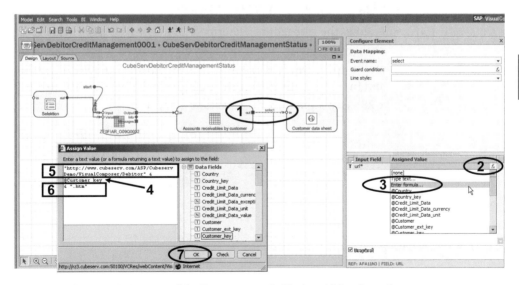

**Figure 12.41** Dynamic Assignment of the Documents to Be Displayed (Via a Formula Function), Part 1

Setting a default
URL ▶ Click on the HTML View component and specify a default URL (in the example: *http://www.cubeserv.com*, see Figure 12.42, Steps 1 and 2).

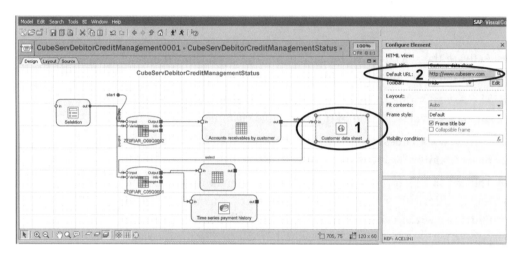

**Figure 12.42** Dynamic Assignment of the Documents to Be Displayed (Via a Formula Function), Part 2

### Editing the Layout of the Output Table

[⬛] ▶ Follow the procedure described above (see Figure 12.34) to change the position and the size of the HTML View using drag-and-drop so that it is displayed to the right of the overview table and in full page height (in the example: position 840, 40, size 408 x 784, see Figure 12.43, selections 1 and 2).

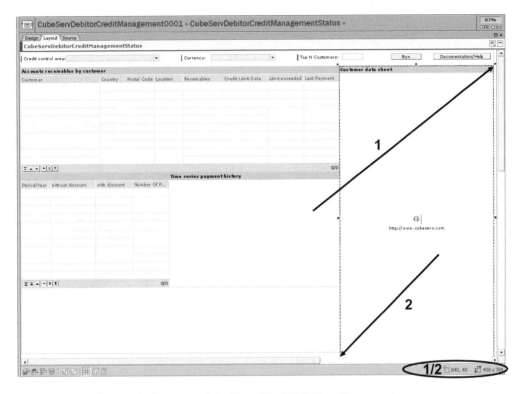

**Figure 12.43** Configuring the Position and the Size of the HTML View Component

### Saving and Testing

▸ Save the current model state using the appropriate button (see Figure 12.20, Step 1). [■]

▸ If required, you can test the current status following the steps described in Figure 12.20 in Section 12.4.2. The selections and the top n overview are displayed together with the detailed table, the chart, and the customer data sheet according to the configuration.

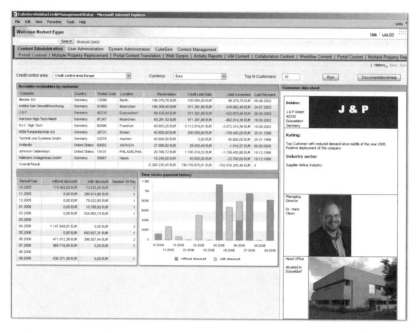

**Figure 12.44** Application with Selection, Overview Table, and Details About the Payment History per Period, Table, Chart, and Customer Data Sheet

## 12.7 Changing Customer Credit Management Data in the OLTP System

### 12.7.1 Underlying Components in the OLTP System SAP R/3 for Updating the Customer Credit Management Data

The last part of the composite application that still needs to be implemented is the part for changing and updating the customer credit management data. The existing master data of the customer selected in the overview report should be displayed for data maintenance in Visual Composer.

### Transferring Data From SAP R/3 Via Function Module

This task is carried out by the function module **Transfer CubeServ Credit Management Data From SAP R/3** (Z_CS_CREDITCONTROL_READ).[7]

---

7   This example function module was *exclusively* created for demonstrating the functioning of Visual Composer. It is *not* intended for productive use.

At the same time, the function module provides the permitted characteristic values for the field **Credit management: risk class** (field **CTLPC**):

```
FUNCTION Z_CS_CREDITCONTROL_READ.
*"----------------------------------------------------------
*"*"Local interface:
*"  IMPORTING
*"     VALUE(IKUNNR) LIKE  KNKK-KUNNR
*"     VALUE(IKKBER) LIKE  KNKK-KKBER
*"  TABLES
*"      IKNKK STRUCTURE  KNKK
*"      IMESSAGE STRUCTURE  ZCS_MESSAGE1
*"      VCTLPC STRUCTURE  T691T
*"----------------------------------------------------------


***************Data KNKK **********************
select single * from knkk into iknkk
where KUNNR = iKUNNR
and   KKBER = iKKBER.

if sy-subrc = 0.
  IMESSAGE-TEXT = Customer credit control data read'.
  append iknkk to iknkk.
else.
  IMESSAGE-TEXT = 'No customer credit control data found'.
endif.

append  IMESSAGE.

******************** Texts for CTLPC  **************
select  * from T691T into VCTLPC
where SPRAS = sy-langu
and   KKBER = iKKBER.
append VCTLPC.
endselect.

ENDFUNCTION.
```

## Update Via Function Module

The last part of the composite application that still needs to be implemented is the part for changing and updating the customer credit management data. This requires a function module in the SAP R/3 system that provides the SAP default update functions.

The function module **Credit Limit Update** (Z_CS_CREDITLIMIT_CHANGE_NE1) is such a module. This function module has the characteristics "remote-capable module" and "start immediately."

**Global data (function pool)** The global data is provided via the function pool ZCUBESERV_VC01A:

```
FUNCTION-POOL ZCUBESERV_VC01A.          "MESSAGE-ID ..
CONSTANTS:
*      Credit activities all start with CR
       ACTIVITY_CREDIT(2)              VALUE 'CR',
*      Credit activities in detail
       ACTIVITY_CREDIT_RECHECK(4)  VALUE 'CRCH',
       ACTIVITY_CREDIT_
AUTHORI(4)  VALUE 'CRAU', "complete check
       ACTIVITY_CREDIT_
AUTHPRE(4)  VALUE 'CRAP', "internal check
       ACTIVITY_CREDIT_RELEASE(4)  VALUE 'CRRL',
       ACTIVITY_CREDIT_REJECT(4)   VALUE 'CRRJ',
       ACTIVITY_CREDIT_FORWARD(4)  VALUE 'CRFW'.
CONSTANTS:             CHARX TYPE C VALUE 'X',
                       TRUE TYPE C VALUE 'X'.
tables: T100.
```

Essentially, the example function module[8] accesses the SAP update function module UPDATE/INSERT of the credit limit (CREDITLIMIT_CHANGE) and writes the changes back to the table **Customer Master Credit Management: Control Area Data** (KNKK). The result of the update is checked and returned:

```
FUNCTION Z_CS_CREDITLIMIT_CHANGE_NE1.
*"-------------------------------------------------------
*"*"Local interface:
*"  IMPORTING
*"     VALUE(I_KUNNR) TYPE  KNKK-KUNNR
*"     VALUE(I_KKBER) TYPE  KNKK-KKBER
*"     VALUE(I_CTLPC) TYPE  KNKK-CTLPC OPTIONAL
*"     VALUE(I_SBGRP) TYPE  KNKK-SBGRP OPTIONAL
```

---

8  This example function module was *exclusively* created for demonstrating the functioning of Visual Composer. It is *not* intended for productive use.

```
*"     VALUE(I_CRBLB) TYPE  KNKK-CRBLB OPTIONAL
*"  TABLES
*"      MSG STRUCTURE   T100
*"- - - - - - - - - - - - - - - - - - - - - - - - - - - - - - - - - - - - - - -
  DATA: lv_knka       TYPE knka,
        lv_knkk       TYPE knkk,
        check_knkk    TYPE knkk,
        lv_upd_knka TYPE cdpos-chngind,
        lv_upd_knkk TYPE cdpos-chngind,
        lv_xneua      TYPE rf021-xneua,
        lv_xrefl      TYPE rf021-xneua,
        lv_yknka      TYPE knka,
        lv_yknkk      TYPE knkk.

* Determine values before update
  SELECT SINGLE * INTO lv_yknka
    FROM knka
    WHERE kunnr = i_kunnr.

  SELECT SINGLE * INTO lv_yknkk
    FROM knkk
    WHERE kunnr = i_kunnr
    AND   kkber = i_kkber.

* Determine new values
  lv_knka = lv_yknka.
  lv_knkk = lv_yknkk.
  lv_knkk-ctlpc = i_ctlpc.
  lv_knkk-sbgrp = i_sbgrp.
  lv_knkk-crblb = i_crblb.
  lv_upd_knkk = 'U'.

  CALL FUNCTION 'CREDITLIMIT_CHANGE'
    EXPORTING
      i_knka        = lv_knka
      i_knkk        = lv_knkk
      upd_knka      = lv_upd_knka
      upd_knkk      = lv_upd_knkk
      yknka         = lv_yknka
      yknkk         = lv_yknkk.

COMMIT WORK.

* Update check (due to update module)
select single * from knkk into check_knkk
    WHERE kunnr = i_kunnr
    AND   kkber = i_kkber.
```

```
if sy-subrc = 0 and check_knkk = lv_knkk.
  select single * from T100 into T100
  where SPRSL = sy-langu
  and   ARBGB = '/SAPDMC/LSMW'
  and   MSGNR = '000'.
  if sy-subrc <> 0.
    MSG-TEXT = 'ERROR NO MESSAGE FOUND IN T100'.
  else.
    MSG-TEXT = T100-TEXT.
  endif.
else.
  select single * from T100 into T100
  where SPRSL = sy-langu
  and   ARBGB = '1J'
  and   MSGNR = '123'.
  if sy-subrc <> 0.
    MSG-TEXT = 'ERROR NO MESSAGE FOUND IN T100'.
  else.
    MSG-TEXT = T100-TEXT.
  endif.
endif.

append MSG.

ENDFUNCTION.
```

### 12.7.2 Components for Updating the Customer Credit Management Data in Visual Composer

Requirements  For a selected customer, the properties of the KNKK database table that are relevant to credit management, like the following, can be displayed and changed:

▸ **Flag: Locked by credit management?** (Field **CRBLB**)[9]

▸ **Credit management: risk class** (Field **CTLPC**)[10] and

▸ **Agent group for credit management** (Field **SBGRP**)[11]

---

9  **Flag: Locked by credit management?** causes a customer to be blocked from all business transactions (order receipt, delivery, goods issue) by credit management. However, the posting of invoices for goods already delivered is still possible.

10  **Credit management: risk class:** A customer can be assigned to a credit risk category. The credit risk category controls all credit checks.

11  **Agent group for credit management:** A customer can be assigned to an agent group for credit control. This agent group is included in the request and can be used as the selection criterion for validations and release functions.

The data is maintained in the SAP R/3 system via the Transaction Change Customer Credit Management (FD32), **Status** view.

**Inserting a Function Module**

To display the existing master data of the selected customer, integrate the function module **Transfer CubeServ Credit Management Data From SAP R/3** (Z_CS_CREDITCONTROL_READ) in the application:

▸ In Visual Composer, select the SAP R/3 system containing the master data and the function module (in the example: **T04CLNT800_R3**), and set the search method to **Look for a service by name** (see Figure 12.45, Steps 1 and 2).    [▪]

▸ Specify the entire name of the function module or a generic portion of it, and start the search by clicking on the **Search** button (Steps 3 and 4).

▸ The function module is then displayed in the results list (Step 5).

▸ Using drag-and-drop, drag the function module to the Design area (Step 6).

▸ The **Define Data Service** popup opens. Select the **Output Ports**, and click on the **OK** button (Steps 7 and 8).

▸ Confirm the **Confirmation** popup via the **Yes** button.

▸ The function module is then displayed in the Design area (Steps 9 and 10).

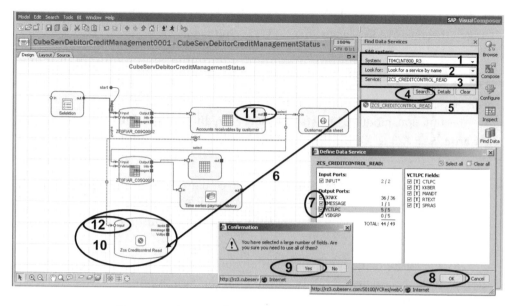

**Figure 12.45** Inserting the Function Module from SAP R/3 to Transfer the Data to the Composite Application

### Preparing Transfer Parameters

To transfer the selected customer, configure the parameter transfer in the next step:

[■] ▸ Using drag-and-drop, move the mouse pointer from the output port (**out**) of the overview table (see Figure 12.45, Step 11) to the **Input** of the function module **Transfer CubeServ Credit Management Data from SAP R/3** (Z_CS_CREDITCONTROL_READ) (Step 12).

*Configuring the Parameter Transfer* ▸ To configure the transfer parameters, activate the connection between the output table and the function module on the **submit** selection (see Figure 12.46, Step 1).

▸ The transfer parameters are then made available for configuration in the field list. The **Credit Control Area** should receive the value of the general selection; and the **Customer** parameter should get the value of the customer selected in the overview table.

*Parameter Transfer for Credit Control Area* ▸ To activate the menu for the **IKKBER** parameter (credit control area), click on **fx**, and select the **Enter formula ...** function (Steps 2 and 3).

▸ The **Assign Value** popup opens.

- In the field list, open the **Data Fields** folder and the **Selection** sub-folder, and use drag-and-drop to move the **sel_C_CTR_AREA** entry into the formula area (Steps 4 to 6).

- The transfer definition is transferred to the field list via the **OK** button (Step 7).

- To activate the menu for the **IKUNNR** parameter (customer), click on **fx**, and select **@Customer_key** (Steps 8 and 9).

Parameter transfer for customer

- This transfer definition is transferred to the field list now as well.

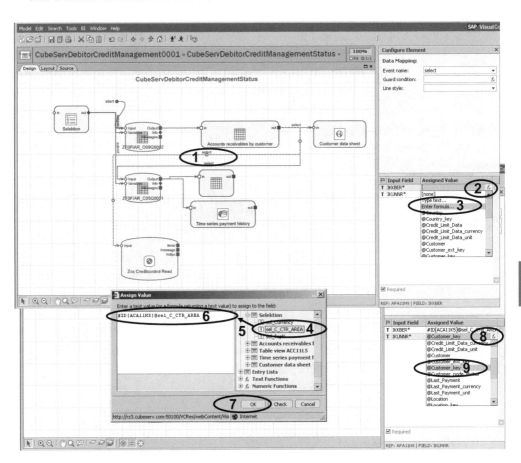

**Figure 12.46** Configuring the Parameter Transfer

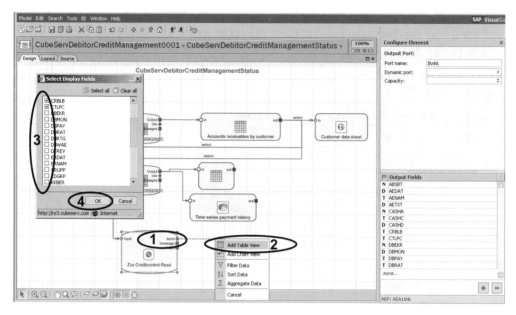

**Figure 12.47** Output Table for Customer Credit Management Data, Part 1

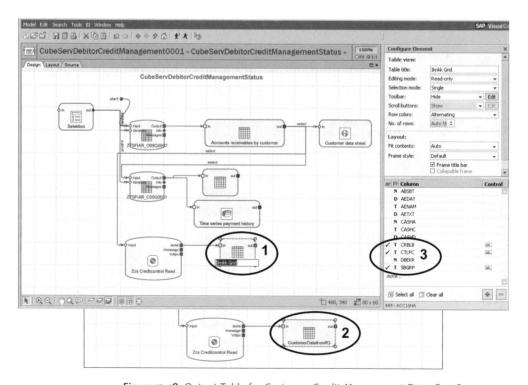

**Figure 12.48** Output Table for Customer Credit Management Data, Part 2

### Preparing the Maintenance Table

The output table just created is to be extended to present a maintenance table at the same time.

▶ For this purpose, the three fields of input fields are changed to **[⟐]** dropdown lists (see Figure 12.49, Steps 1 and 2).

▶ The properties for all of the three maintenance fields are then to be maintained.

### Identifier: Locked by Credit Management

▶ For the field **CRBLB** (**Flag: Locked by credit management**), open the context menu (Step 3), and select the **Properties** maintenance (Step 4).

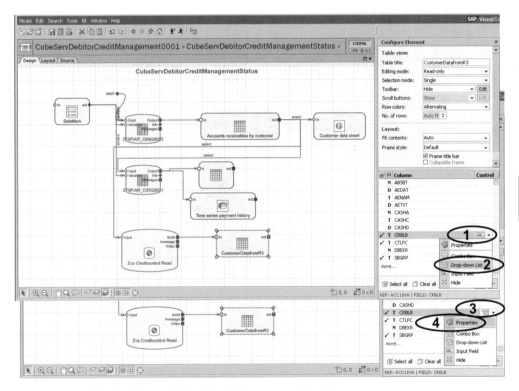

**Figure 12.49** Field "Identifier: Locked by Credit Management," Part 1

▶ The **Control Properties** popup opens. In the **General** tab in the **Default value** input field, click on the **Formula** button (see Figure 12.50, Step 1).

▶ The **Default Value** popup opens.

▶ Open the folder structure so that the **CRBLB** field is displayed (folder **Data Fields**, subfolder **CustomerDatafromR3**).

▶ Using drag-and-drop, move the field to the formula window and confirm the button via **OK** (Steps 2 to 5).

▶ The dynamic default value is thus transferred to the input field (Step 6).

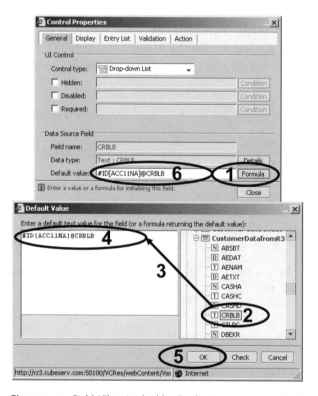

**Figure 12.50** Field "Flag: Locked by Credit Management," Part 2

▶ Then select the **Entry List** tab, and click twice on the **Add entry** button (see Figure 12.51, Step 1).

▶ Enter the following admissible values (Step 2):

  ▶ " " for **not blocked**

  ▶ "**X**" for **blocked**

▶ Click on the **Close** button (Step 3).

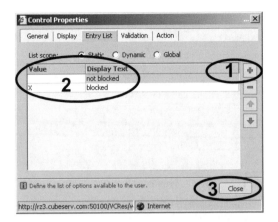

**Figure 12.51** Field "Flag: Locked by Credit Management," Part 3

**Agent Group for Credit Management**

▶ Use the procedure described for the field **Flag: Locked by credit management**, and use the **SBGRP** field as the dynamic default setting (folder **Data Fields**, subfolder **CustomerDatafromR3**, see Figure 12.52, Step 1).

▶ Enter the following admissible values (Step 2):

  ▶ **001** for low risk customers

  ▶ **002** for high risk customers Credit Management: Risk Class

▶ Use the procedure described for the field **Flag: Locked by credit management**, and use the **CTLPC** field as the dynamic default setting (folder **Data Fields**, subfolder **CustomerDatafromR3**, see Figure 12.53, Steps 1 and 2).

▶ Select the **Entry List** tab, and click on the **Find data service** button (Steps 3 and 4).

▶ In the **Find Data Service** popup, enter the SAP R/3 system and the entire or a generic portion of the function module name for master data maintenance, and click on the **Search** button (Steps 5 and 6).

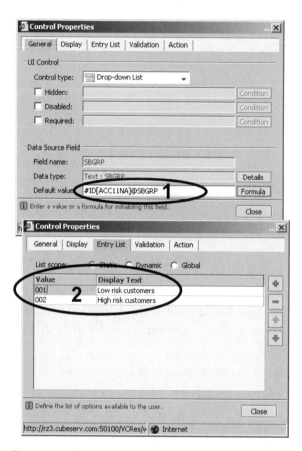

**Figure 12.52** Dynamically Presetting and Manually Filling the Selection Options for the Field "Agent Group for Credit Management"

- ▶ After the function module has been found, the **Input** and **Output Ports** are provided for selection.

- ▶ As the **Output Port**, select **VCTLPC,** and confirm your selection with **OK** (Steps 7 to 9).

- ▶ The function module and the selected ports are transferred to the **Control Properties** popup (Step 10).

- ▶ The input and the output port now provide the fields for linking. Activate the menu by clicking on **fx**, and for both **Input Port** fields select the **Enter formula ...** function (Step 11).

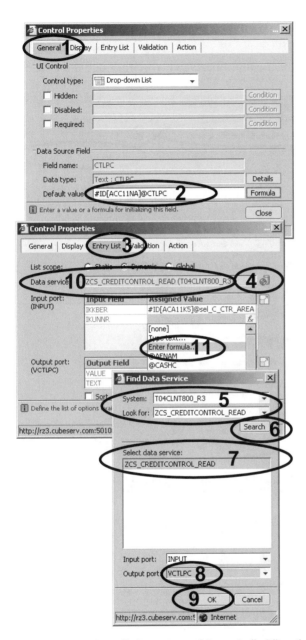

**Figure 12.53** Dynamically Presetting and Dynamically Filling the Selection Options for the Field "Credit Management: Risk Class," Part 1

▶ For the field **IKKBER**, transfer the source field **#ID[ACA11K5]@sel_C_CTR_AREA** from the subfolder **Selection**, or for the field **IKUNNR**, transfer the source field **#ID[ACC11KT]@Customer_key** from the subfolder **Accounts receivables by customer**(see Figure 12.54, Steps 1 to 8).

▶ The parameters for the input ports fields are thus defined (Step 9).

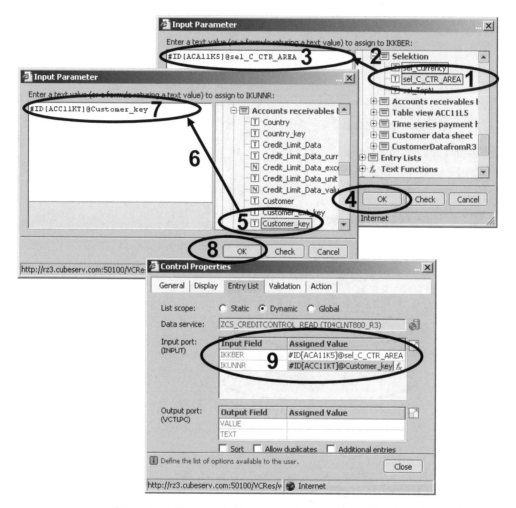

**Figure 12.54** Dynamically Presetting and Dynamically Filling the Selection Options for the Field "Credit Management: Risk Class," Part 2

▶ Click on **fx** to activate the menu for the **Output Ports** fields, and from the selection list for the **VALUE** field, select the source field **@CTLPC**, or for the **TEXT** field, select the source field **@RTEXT**, respectively (see Figure 12.55, Steps 1 and 2).

▶ Complete the configuration by clicking on the **Close** button (Step 3).

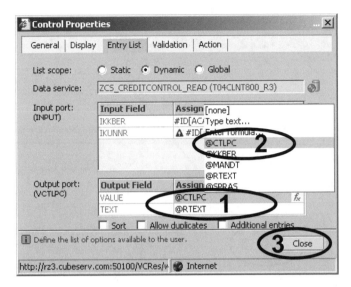

**Figure 12.55** Dynamically Presetting and Dynamically Filling the Selection Options for the Field "Credit Management: Risk Class," Part 3

**Form View Using "Run" Button**

In the configured table, the provided customer credit management data can be changed. In the next step, you must transfer the data (i. e., if it is changed) to the update function module.

▶ Using drag-and-drop, move a form view to the Design area, and change the form view name to **Edit customer** (see Figure 12.56, Steps 1 to 4).

[▪]

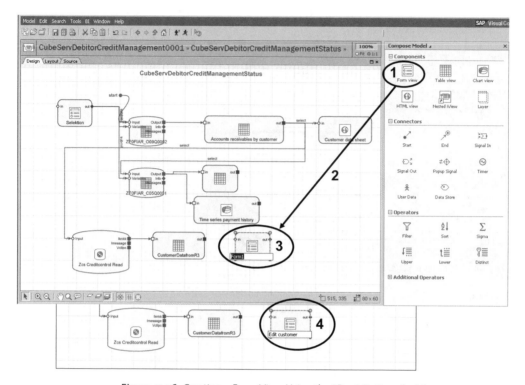

**Figure 12.56** Creating a Form View Using the "Run" Button, Part 1

▸ Using drag-and-drop, move the connection from the output port (**out**) of the table **CustomerDatafromR3** to the input port (**in**) of the form view **Edit customer** (see Figure 12.57, Step 1).

▸ Click on the form view to activate it, and click on the **Add** button (see Figure 12.57, Steps 2 and 3).

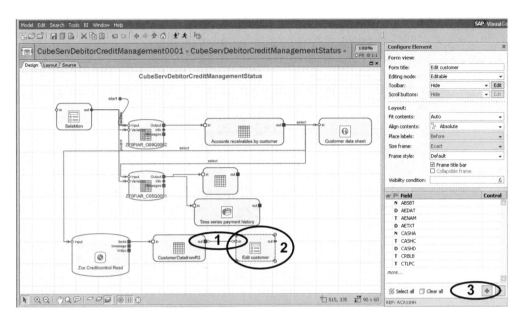

Figure 12.57  Creating a Form View Using the "Run" Button, Part 2

▶ The **New UI Control** popup opens. Select the **Control Type push-button**, use **BTN1_update** as the **Field Name,** and click on the **OK** button (see Figure 12.58, Steps 1 to 3).

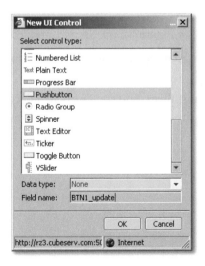

Figure 12.58  Creating a Form View Using the "Run" Button, Part 3

▸ The field list now includes the new field **BTN1_update**. Click on the control icon of this field to open the context menu, and select the **Properties** function (see Figure 12.59, Steps 1 and 2).

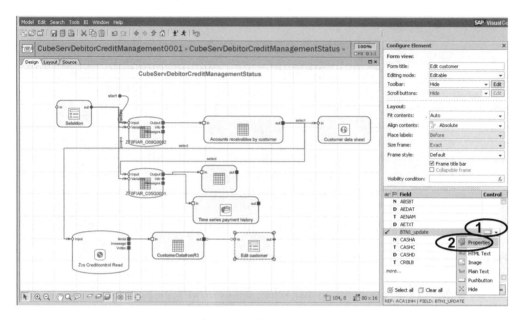

**Figure 12.59** Configuration of the "Update Changes" Button, Part 1

▸ The **Control Properties** popup opens. Select the **Display** tab, and for **Label** enter **Update changes** (see Figure 12.60, Steps 1 and 2).

▸ Next, select the **Action** tab, and specify **System action** for **Action type** (Steps 3 and 4).

▸ As the **System action**, select **Submit form**, and for **Apply to** select **Self**. Then confirm these settings by clicking on the **Close** button (Steps 5 and 6).

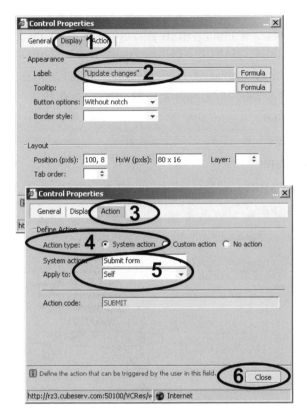

**Figure 12.60** Configuration of the "Update Changes" Button, Part 2

### Inserting an Update Function Module

In the next step, you will insert the update function module.

▶ Select the **Find Data** button and the appropriate SAP R/3 system   [▪]
   (in the example: **T04CLNT800_R3**). Then, set the search method to
   **Look for a service by name,** and enter the entire function module
   name or a part of it in the **Service** input field (in the example: **Z_
   CS_**, see Figure 12.61, Steps 1 to 4).

▶ After clicking on the **Search** button, the found function modules
   are displayed in the results list (Steps 5).

▶ Per drag-and-drop, move the function module you just created, Z_
   CS_CREDITLIMIT_CHANGE_NE1, to the Design area (Steps 6 to
   8).

605

Configuring
the parameter
transfer

▶ Use drag-and-drop to connect the output port (**out**) of the form view **Edit customer** to the input port (**Input**) of the function module **Z_CS_CREDITLIMIT_CHANGE_NE1** (see Figure 12.62, Step 1).

▶ The list of input fields is displayed. From the selection list of every field, transfer the corresponding source field (Steps 2 and 3):

**@CRBLB for I_CRBLB**

**@CTLPC for I_CTLPC**

**@KKBER for I_KKBER***

**@KUNNR for I_KUNNR***

**@SBGRP for I_SBGRP**

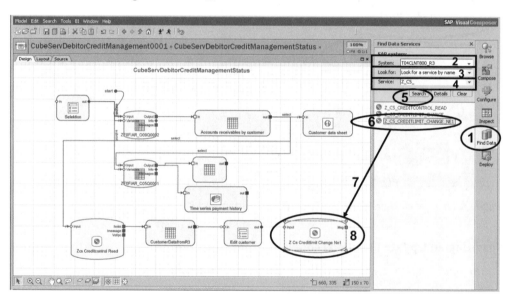

**Figure 12.61** Inserting the Update Function Module Z_CS_CREDITLIMIT_CHANGE_NE1, Part 1

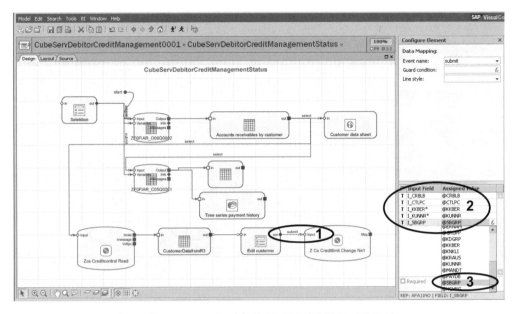

**Figure 12.62** Inserting the Update Function Module Z_CS_CREDITLIMIT_CHANGE_
NE1, Part 2

## Inserting a Message Table

The success or failure of an update, respectively, is reported to the
composite application via a message table.

▶ To insert this table in the application, push and drag the mouse **[»]**
button from the output port **Msg** of the function module Z_CS_
CREDITLIMIT_CHANGE_NE1 to the Design area.

▶ In the displayed context menu, select the **Add Table View** function, and change the table name to **Messages** (see Figure 12.63,
Steps 1 to 4).

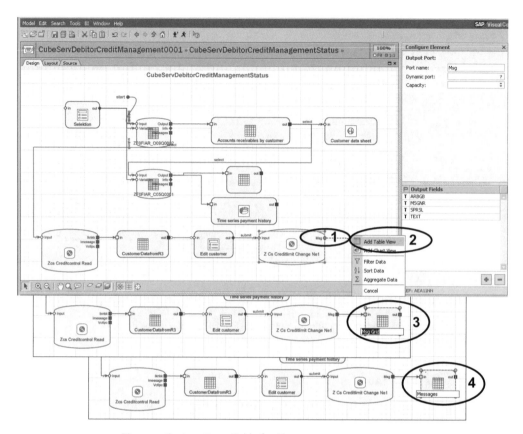

**Figure 12.63** Inserting a Table for Messages

▶ The technical information of the message table is not to be displayed. Therefore, double-click on the checkmark icon of the **ARBGB**, **MSGNR**, and **SPRSL** columns to disable these so that only the **TEXT** column is still activated (see Figure 12.64, Steps 1 and 2).

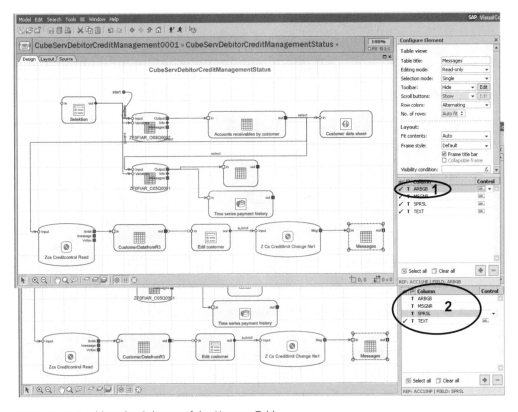

**Figure 12.64** Disabling the Columns of the Message Table

### Adapting the Layout for Update Components

▶ To finalize the layout, select the **Layout** tab (see Figure 12.65, Step 1).          **[■]**

▶ Drag the **Edit customer** form view directly below the components with the **Time series payment history**. Increase the width of the form view so that it aligns with the **Time Series** chart (Steps 2 and 3). This leads to a position of 0, 600 and a size of 840 x 224.

▶ Move the **Update Changes** button and change the size of the button accordingly (in the example: position 0, 104, size 144 x 16, see Step 4).          Update Changes button

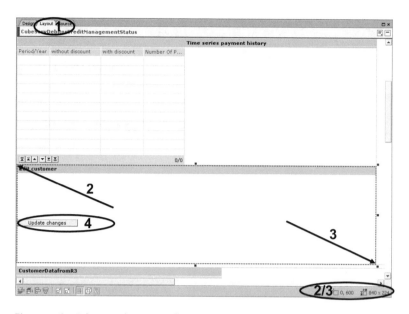

**Figure 12.65** Adapting the Layout for Data Maintenance (1)

### CustomerDatafromR3 Table

In the next step, edit the data maintenance table. Because the different editing components should be nested, the data maintenance table must be positioned in the foreground.

[➥] ► Therefore, select the table and click on the **Bring to front** button (see Figure 12.66, Steps 1 and 2).

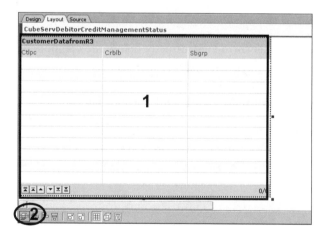

**Figure 12.66** Positioning the Data Maintenance Table in the Foreground

▶ Change the size of the table **CustomerDatafromR3** to a height of two rows and a width of 832 pixels by moving the edge of the table accordingly (see Figure 12.67, Steps 1 and 2).

▶ Then move the table to the form view **Edit customer** to a position above the **Update Change** button (in the example: position 832 x 88, Figure 12.67).

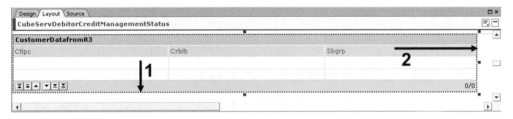

**Figure 12.67** Changing the Column Headers and Column Widths, Part 1

▶ Then change the column headers

- ▶ **Ctlpc** to **Credit management: risk class**
- ▶ **Crblb** to **Flag: Blocked by credit management?** and
- ▶ **Sbgrp** to **Agent group for credit management**

by right-clicking on every column to open its context menu and selecting the **Edit Label** function (see Figure 12.68, Step 1).

▶ The column header now accepts input (Step 2).

▶ Change the respective column header (Step 3).

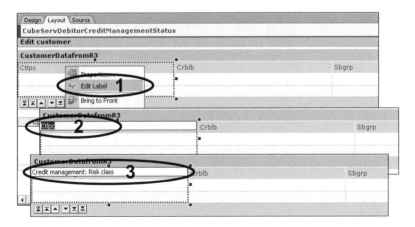

**Figure 12.68** Changing the Column Headers and Column Widths, Part 2

▸ Then change the column widths using drag-and-drop so that the column headers are completely displayed (see Figure 12.69, Steps 1 and 2).

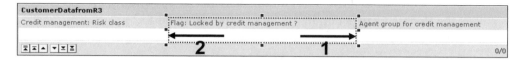

**Figure 12.69** Changing the Column Headers and Column Widths, Part 3

Configuring the Appearance

▸ Now configure the appearance of the table: Select **Hide** to hide the toolbar (see Figure 12.70, Step 1).

▸ Disable the **Frame title bar** (Step 2).

▸ Select **Editable** as editing mode (Step 4).

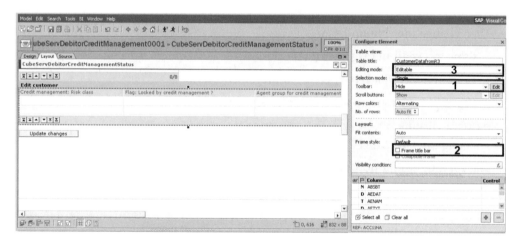

**Figure 12.70** Configuring the Appearance of the Table, Part 1

The data maintenance table is now presented differently (see Figure 12.71, selections 1 and 2).

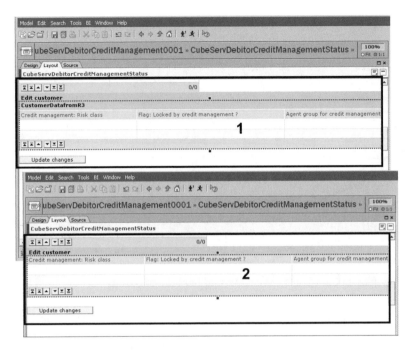

**Figure 12.71** Configuring the Appearance of the Table, Part 2

### Message Table

You will now edit the message table.

▶ Use drag-and-drop to reduce the table height, and move the table to the foreground by clicking on the **Bring to front** button (see Figure 12.72, Steps 1 and 2). **[▪]**

▶ Then move the table to the form view **Edit customer** directly below the **Update Changes** button (in the example: position 0, 744, size 480 x 80, see Steps 3 and 4).

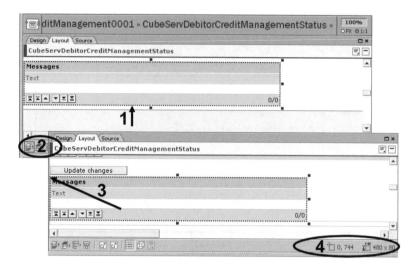

**Figure 12.72** Configuration of the Message Table, Part 1

▶ Hide the toolbar (**Hide** setting), and disable the **Frame title bar** (see Figure 12.73, Steps 1 and 2).

▶ The message table is now presented differently (see Figure 12.73, selection 3).

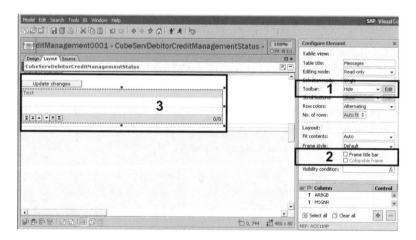

**Figure 12.73** Configuration of the Message Table, Part 2

▶ Change the column header of the message table by right-clicking to open the context menu and selecting the **Edit Label** function.

▶ Follow the procedure described in Figure 12.74 to change the column header to **Messages** (see Figure 12.74, Steps 1 and 2)

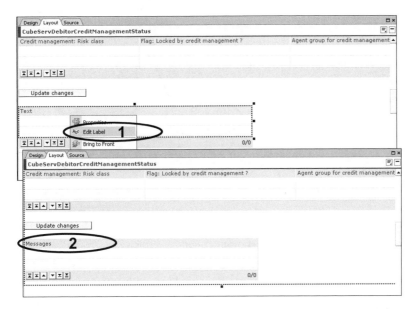

**Figure 12.74** Changing the Column Header of the Message Table

## 12.8 Creating a Header Field

In the configuration above, the header of the table showing the payment history development of the selected customer was removed.

### Configuring a Header Field

In the last configuration step, you will configure a header field based on a form view.

▶ Select the **Compose** button, and use drag-and-drop to move a form view to the Design area (see Figure 12.75, Steps 1 to 4).    [◾]

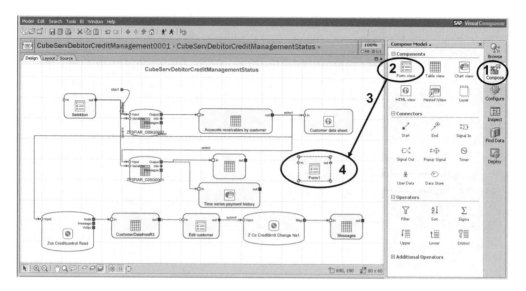

**Figure 12.75** Configuring a Header Field, Part 1

▶ Activate the **Form1** form view by clicking on it (see Figure 12.76).

▶ An empty field list is displayed. Click on the **Add** button to define a field (see Figure 12.76, Step 1).

▶ The **New UI Control** popup opens. Select **Plain Text** as the **Control type** and click on the **OK** button (Steps 2 and 3).

▶ The field **LBL1** is now available in the field list. Click on the **Text** control type to activate the function selection list, and select the **Properties** function (Step 4).

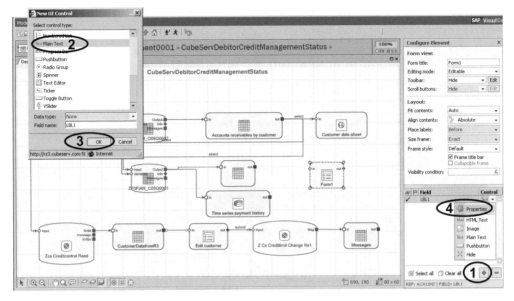

**Figure 12.76** Configuring a Header Field, Part 2

▸ In the **Display** tab, click on the **Formula** button. The **Dynamic Label** popup opens (see Figure 12.77, Step 1).

▸ Specify a combination of texts and data fields (**Customer** and **Customer_key**), transferring the field contents using drag-and-drop (Step 2 to 4):

```
"Customer " &
#ID[ACC11KT]@Customer &
" (" &
#ID[ACC11KT]@Customer_key &
")"
```

▸ A header is created with the following structure:

**Customer [CustomerName] ([CustomerNumber])**

(Steps 2 to 4).

▸ When you click on the **OK** button, the application transfers the label configuration to the **Control Properties** popup (**Display** tab, see Steps 5 and 6).

▸ Change the **Text Style** to **Bold** and close the popup via the **Close** button (Steps 7 and 8).

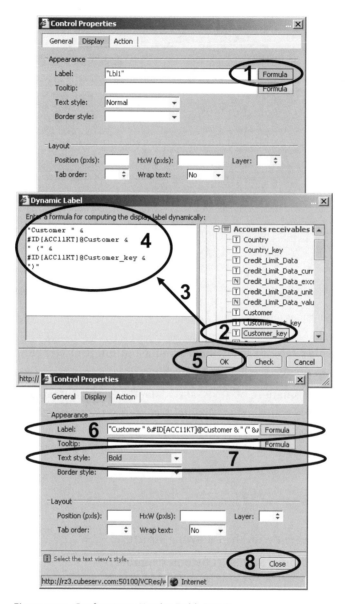

Figure 12.77  Configuring a Header Field, Part 3

**Processing the Header Field in the Layout**

[■] ▸ Select the **Layout** tab, and change the height and width of the header field **[Formula]** (size 384 x 16) (see Figure 12.78, Step 1 to Step 3).

618

▶ Then reduce the height of the form view **Form1** (size 392 x 48). Position the form view in the foreground by clicking on the **Bring to Front** button (Step 4).

▶ Drag **Form1** form view to the header of the tables **Time series payment history.** Change the frame style to **Transparent** (and thus without a **Frame title bar**) (Step 5 to Step 8).

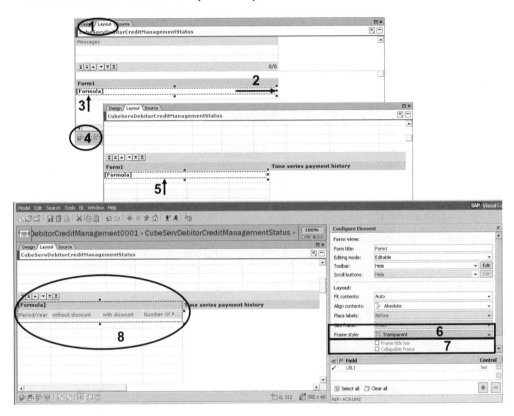

**Figure 12.78**  Editing the Layout of the Header Row

### Saving and testing

▶ Save the current model state using the appropriate button (see Figure 12.20, Step 1).     [▪]

▶ If required, you can test the current status following the steps described in Figure 12.20 in Section 12.4.2. The complete application with selections, top n overview, detailed table and chart, the customer data sheet, and the components for maintaining the customer credit management data is displayed according to the configuration.

## 12.9 Integrating the Composite Application in the SAP Enterprise Portal

At deployment time, the Visual Composer design tool places the models directly in the SAP Enterprise Portal (see Figure 12.79, highlight).

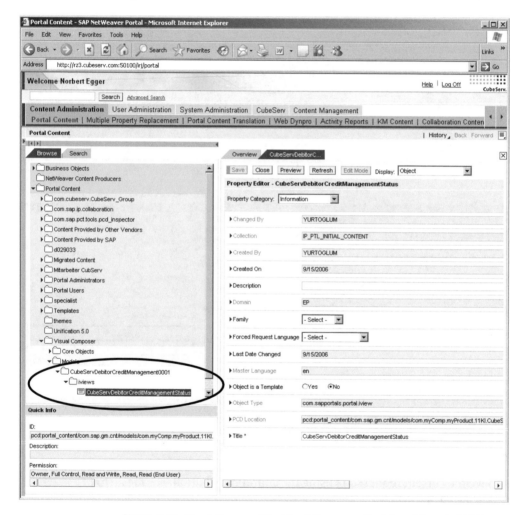

**Figure 12.79** Direct Storage of the Visual Composer Models as iViews in SAP Enterprise Portal at Deployment Time

620

### Assigning VC-iView to the Portal Role

The applications can therefore be very easily assigned to the various portal roles via an SAP Enterprise Portal standard function.

▶ In the SAP Enterprise Portal, open the editing of the **Portal Con-** **[▪]**
   **tent** in the role **Content Administration** (see Figure 12.80, Steps 1
   and 2).

▶ Double-click on the folder structure of the **Portal Content** to open
   it so that the target role is activated for editing (in the example: the
   **CubeServ** role, Steps 3 and 4).

▶ Select the position to which the Visual Composer iView is to be
   assigned (In the example: folder **CubeServ CustomerCredit Man-**
   **agement**, see Step 5).

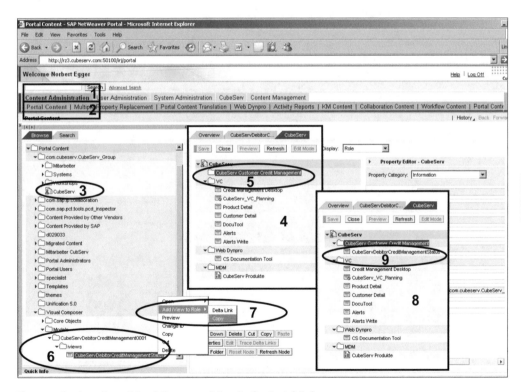

**Figure 12.80** Inserting a Visual Composer iView in the Portal Role

▶ Then continue opening the Portal Content folder structure until
   the iView to be integrated in the role is displayed (in the example:
   **CubeServDebitorCreditManagementStatus**, see Step 6).

► Select the iView using the right mouse button, and in the context menu select the **Add iView to Role** function. In the example, it was added using the **Copy** function (see Step 7).

► The iView in the selected folder is thus added to the role being edited (Step 8 and 9).

When this role is called in the SAP Enterprise Portal, this iView is now available for execution (see Figure 12.81, highlight)

## 12.10   Running the Application

**Start the application**

When you start the application by clicking on the role entry in the SAP Enterprise Portal, the components are activated with the initial selection (see Figure 12.81, highlight).

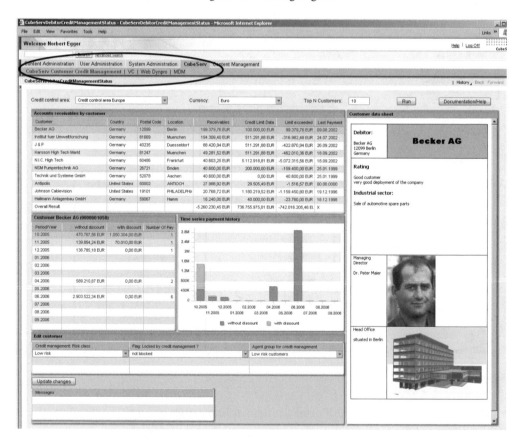

**Figure 12.81** Running the Visual Composer iView as an SAP Enterprise Portal Role

## Changing and Running the Selection

▶ When changing the selections (in the example, amounts are pre-  [◦]
sented in the currency **American Dollar**, the display is not
refreshed until the **Run** button is clicked (see Figure 12.82, Steps 1
to 3).

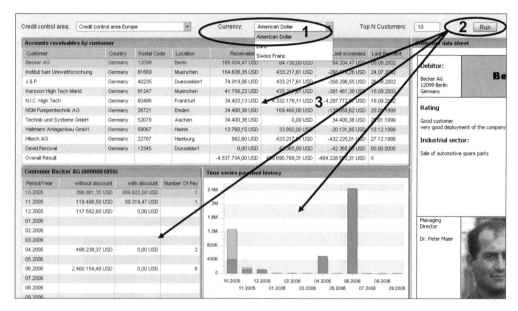

**Figure 12.82** Changing and Refreshing the Selection After Clicking on the Run Button

▶ To change the top n customers of the displayed customers, you       Changing "Top N
need to change the number shown in the **Top N Customers** input    Customers"
field and to either click on the **Run** button or to press the **Enter**
key (see Figure 12.83, Steps 1 and 2).

**Figure 12.83** Changing "Top N Customers"

▶ To obtain detailed information about a specific customer, click on the corresponding entry in the **Accounts receivables by customer** table (see Figure 12.84, Step 1). This will update

  ▶ the table **Time series payment history**

  ▶ the chart **Time series payment history**

  ▶ the customer data sheet and

  ▶ the customer credit management data (status)

  for the selected customer (Step 2)

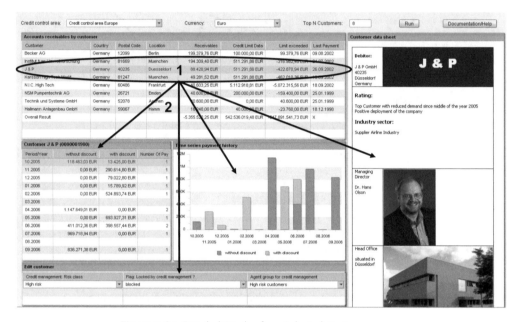

**Figure 12.84** Detailed Display for a Selected Customer

## Data Maintenance

▶ Customer credit management status data can be maintained by switching the dropdown lists (see Figure 12.85, Steps 1 to 3).

▶ After the update has been performed by clicking on the **Update Changes** button (Step 4), a message describing the update result is displayed (Step 5).

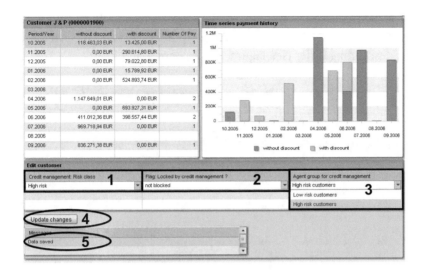

**Figure 12.85** Maintenance of Customer Credit Management Status Data

## General Table Functions

Visual Composer provides automated table functions that can be applied in this example as well.

▸ The column width can be changed per drag-and-drop by moving [•] the column borders (see Figure 12.86, Step 1).

**Accounts receivables by customer**

| Customer | Country | Postal Code | Location | Receivables | Credit Limit Data | Limit exceeded | Last Payment |
|---|---|---|---|---|---|---|---|
| Antipolis | United States | 60002 | ANTIOCH | 23.715,01 USD | 25.000,00 USD | -1.284,99 USD | 00.00.0000 |
| Johnson Cablevision | United States | 19101 | PHILADELP | 17.597,34 USD | 1.000.000,00 USD | -982.402,66 USD | 19.12.1996 |
| Chinese Garden Restaurant | United States | 19103 | PHILADELP | 7.276,00 USD | 1.000.000,00 USD | -992.724,00 USD | 02.01.2001 |

**Accounts receivables by customer**

| Customer | Country | Postal Code | Location | Receivables | Credit Limit Data | Limit exceeded | Last Payment |
|---|---|---|---|---|---|---|---|
| Antipolis | United States | 60002 | ANTIOCH | 23.715,01 USD | 25.000,00 USD | -1.284,99 USD | 00.00.0000 |
| Johnson Cablevision | United States | 19101 | PHILADELPHIA | 17.597,34 USD | 1.000.000,00 USD | -982.402,66 USD | 19.12.1996 |
| Chinese Garden Restaurant | United States | 19103 | PHILADELPHIA | 7.276,00 USD | 1.000.000,00 USD | -992.724,00 USD | 02.01.2001 |
| Philadelphia Security Inc. | United States | 19132 | PHILADELPHIA | 6.826,60 USD | 1.000.000,00 USD | -993.173,40 USD | 02.01.2001 |
| BMC Associates Incorporated | United States | 19133 | PHILADELPHIA | 5.350,00 USD | 1.000.000,00 USD | -994.650,00 USD | 02.01.2001 |
| Thomas Bush Inc. | United States | 60153 | MAYWOOD | 5.300,00 USD | 1.000.000,00 USD | -994.700,00 USD | 20.09.2002 |
| Havers Inc. | United States | 60002 | ANTIOCH | 3.309,13 USD | 100.000,00 USD | -96.690,87 USD | 00.00.0000 |
| Beck Sports | United States | 19113 | PHILADELPHIA | 2.368,90 USD | 1.000.000,00 USD | -997.631,10 USD | 02.01.2001 |
| Computer World | United States | 19124 | PHILADELPHIA | 2.152,51 USD | 1.000.000,00 USD | -997.847,49 USD | 02.01.2001 |
| Office Supplies Incorporated | United States | 19145 | PHILADELPHIA | 1.934,56 USD | 1.000.000,00 USD | -998.065,44 USD | 21.12.2000 |
| Overall Result | | | | 80.740,74 USD | 162.894.100,00 USD | -162.813.359,26 USD | X |

**Figure 12.86** Changing the Column Width and the Sorting, Part 1

▶ If you click on a column header, the corresponding column is sorted in ascending order. After another click, it is sorted in descending order (see Figure 12.87, Steps 1 and 2).

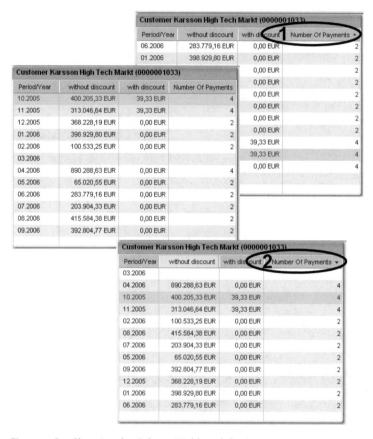

**Figure 12.87** Changing the Column Width and the Sorting, Part 2

## Documentation

When you click on the **Documentation/Help** button, the user documentation integrated via a URL is displayed (see Figure 12.88, Steps 1 and 2).

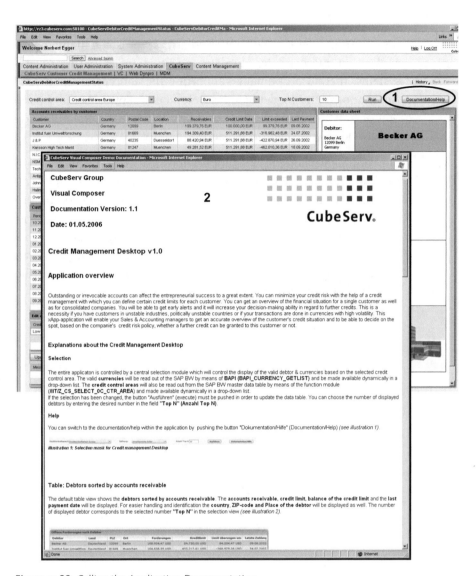

**Figure 12.88** Calling the Application Documentation

## 12.11 An Interim Result

With the Visual Composer, SAP provides a new generation of frontend technology.

The design tool greatly supports modeling even for complex applications. Compared to earlier technologies, the productivity of applica-

Visual Composer
design tool

627

tion development has increased. The access to very different applications (SAP and non-SAP) is supported just as well as the simultaneous application-internal access to data and functions stored on several systems, therefore optimally supporting the concept of Composite Applications. The model-based development allows for the separation of functionality/data flows and layout. Most of application layout development is performed according to WYSIWYG.

**Visual Composer applications from the user's point of view**

The runtime version provides applications that are fully integrated in the SAP Enterprise Portal. In the deployment from the design tool, the runtime stores iViews directly as Portal Content. In addition to classical HTML views, the Adobe Flash technology is also provided as a presentation method. Therefore, applications are made available with powerful data flows, a freely designable functionality, and an appealing appearance. In short, the Visual Composer enables the deployment of user-friendly applications.

# Appendix

# A   Abbreviations

| | |
|---|---|
| **ABAP** | Advanced Business Application Programming |
| **ADK** | Archiving Development Kit |
| **ALE** | Application Link Enabling |
| **ALV** | SAP List Viewer |
| **API** | Application Programming Interface |
| **ASCII** | American Standard Code for Information Interchange |
| **BAPI** | Business Application Programming Interface |
| **BCT** | Business content |
| **BEx** | Business Explorer |
| **BI** | Business Intelligence |
| **BIA** | Business Intelligence Accelerator |
| **BSP** | Business Server Pages |
| **BW** | Business Information Warehouse |
| **CSV** | Comma separated value |
| **DDIC** | Data dictionary |
| **DIM ID** | Dimension Identification |
| **DWB** | Data Warehousing Workbench |
| **DWH** | Data warehouse |
| **EDW** | Enterprise Data Warehousing |
| **ETL** | Extraction, Transformation, and Load |
| **FOX** | Formula Extension |
| **GUI** | Graphical User Interface |
| **HKVK** | Full cost of goods manufactured |
| **HTML** | Hypertext Markup Language |
| **IDoc** | Intermediate Document |

| | |
|---|---|
| **LUW** | Logical Unit of Work |
| **ODBO** | OLE DB (Object Linking and Embedding Database) for OLAP |
| **ODS** | Operational Data Store |
| **OLAP** | Online Analytical Processing |
| **OLTP** | Online Transaction Processing |
| **RFC** | Remote Function Call |
| **RRI** | Report-report interface |
| **SAPI** | Service API |
| **SID** | Surrogate Identification |
| **SOAP** | Simple Object Access Protocol |
| **SQL** | Structured Query Language |
| **TCT** | Technical Content |
| **tRFC** | Transactional RFC |
| **SUn** | Sales Unit |
| **WAD** | Web Application Designer |
| **WAS** | Web Application Server |
| **WIB** | Web Interface Builder |
| **WYSIWYG** | What You See Is What You Get |
| **XML** | Extensible Markup Language |

# B    New Terminology

With SAP NetWeaver 2004s SAP introduced a number of new terms. The following lists provide an overview of the most important terminology changes in the warehouse management field.

## B.1    Replacements: old → new

| Old term | New term |
| --- | --- |
| Administrator Workbench | Data Warehousing Workbench |
| Monitor (for extraction) | Extraction monitor |
| OLAP statistics | BI Runtime Statistics |
| ODS object | DataStore object |
| RemoteCube | VirtualProvider |
| Reporting authorizations | Analysis authorizations (The term "standard authorizations" is used to differentiate the authorizations of the standard authorization concept in SAP NetWeaver from the analysis authorizations in BI.) |
| SAP RemoteCube | VirtualProvider |
| Tansactional InfoCube | Realtime InfoCube |
| Transactional ODS object | DataStore object for direct writing |
| Virtual InfoCube with services | VirtualProvider |

## B.2    Replacements: new → old

| New term | Old term |
| --- | --- |
| Analysis authorizations | Reporting authorizations |
| BI Runtime Statistics | OLAP statistics |
| DataStore object | ODS object |
| DataStore object for direct writing | Transactional ODS object |

| New term | Old term |
|----------|----------|
| Data Warehousing Workbench | Administrator Workbench |
| Extraction monitor | Monitor (for extraction) |
| Realtime InfoCube | Tansactional InfoCube |
| VirtualProvider | RemoteCube, SAP RemoteCube, and virtual InfoCube with services |

# C   Transaction Codes

## C.1   Transactions in the SAP BW System

| Transaction | Description |
|---|---|
| BAPI | BAPI Explorer |
| CMOD | Project Management of SAP Extensions |
| DB02 | |
| FILE | Maintenance of Logical File Paths |
| LISTCUBE | List Viewer for Data Targets (→ BasicCubes, ODS Objects, Characteristic InfoObjects) |
| LISTSCHEMA | Schema Viewer for BasicCubes (including Aggregates) |
| PFCG | Role Maintenance |
| REPORTING_ AGENT | Reporting Agent 3.x |
| RRC1, RRC2, RRC3 | Create/Modify/Display Definitions for Currency Translation |
| RRMX | Start BEx Analyzer |
| RS12 | Display and Delete Lock Entries (of Tables) |
| RS50 | Process Overview |
| RSA1 | Data Warehousing Workbench |
| RSA1OLD | BW Administrator Workbench (old) |
| RSA2 | OLTP Metadata Repository |
| RSA3 | Extractor Checker |
| RSA5 | Transfer DataSources from Business Content |
| RSA6 | Perform Follow-Up Work on DataSources and Application Component Hierarchy |
| RSA7 | Maintenance of Delta Queue |
| RSA9 | Transfer Application Components from Business Content |
| RSA10 | Real-Time Data Acquisition Test Interface |
| RSANWB | Analysis Process Designer |
| RSATTR | Attribute/Hierarchy Change Run |
| RSBBS | Report-Report Interface |

| Transaction | Description |
|---|---|
| RSCRT | Real-Time Data Acquisition Monitor |
| RSCUR | Currency Translation Type |
| RSCUSTV1 | Change Settings for Flat Files (→ Thousands, Decimal, and Field Separators; Field Delimiters) |
| RSCUSTV6 | Change Threshold Values for Data Loading (→ Package Size, PSA Partition Size, and IDoc Frequency Status) |
| RSCUSTV8 | Change Settings for Aggregate Change Run (→ Threshold Value for Restructuring and Block Size) |
| RSD1, RSD2, RSD3 | Maintenance of Characteristics/Key Figures/Units |
| RSD4, RSD5 | Editing of Technical Characteristics and Time Characteristics |
| RSDAB | Edit Data Archiving Process |
| RSDBC | DB Connect |
| RSDDBIAMON | BI Accelerator Maintenance Monitor |
| RSDDV | Maintenance of Aggregates/BIA Indices |
| RSDIOBC | Editing InfoObjectCatalogs |
| RSDMD | Maintenance of Master Data (for one Characteristic) |
| RSMO | Data Load Monitor |
| RSDMPROM | Editing MultiProviders |
| RSDMWB | Data Mining Workbench |
| RSDODS | Editing ODS Objects |
| RSDTP | DTP Maintenance |
| RSDV | Maintenance of Validity Slice |
| RSECADMIN | Management of Analysis Authorizations |
| RSFH | Test Tool for Extraction of Transaction Data |
| RSIMG | SAP BW Customizing Implementation Guide |
| RSISET | Maintenance of InfoSets |
| RSKC | Maintenance of Permitted Additional Characters in SAP BW |
| RSMD | Test Tool for Extraction of Master Data |
| RSMO | Monitor |

| Transaction | Description |
|---|---|
| RSMON | Administrator Workbench (→ Monitoring) |
| RSMONCOLOR | Valuation of Requests |
| RSO2 | Maintenance of Generic DataSources |
| RSO3 | Setup of Delta Extraction for Attributes and Texts |
| RSOR | Administrator Workbench (→ Metadata Repository) |
| RSORBCT | Administrator Workbench (→ Business Content) |
| RSPC | Maintenance of Process Chains |
| RSPLAN | BI-Integrated Planning |
| RSPRECADMIN | BW Excel Wokbook Precalculation Admin |
| RSRT | Query Monitor |
| RSRDA | Real-Time Data Acquisition Monitor |
| RSRTRACE | Query Trace |
| RSRV | Analysis and Repair of SAP BW Objects |
| RSSM | Maintenance of Reporting Authorization Objects |
| RSTT | RS Trace Tool Monitor |
| RSUOM | Definition of Quantity Conversion Type |
| RSU1/RSU2/RSU3 | Create/Modify/Display Update Rules (→ BasicCubes and ODS Objects) |
| SARA | Archive Administration |
| SBIW | Display of Implementation Guide (→ Customizing for Extractors) |
| SE03 | Transport Organizer Tools |
| SE09 | Transport Organizer |
| SE11 | ABAP Dictionary |
| SE16 | ABAP Data Browser |
| SE37 | Function Builder (→ Maintenance of Function Modules) |
| SE38 | ABAP Editor (→ Maintenance of ABAP Programs) |
| SE80 | Object Navigator |
| SICF | Maintenance of System Internet Communication Framework (ICF) |
| SM04 | User List |

| Transaction | Description |
|---|---|
| SM12 | Selection of Blocked Entries |
| SM21 | Online Analysis of System Log |
| SM37 | Job Overview |
| SM38 | Queue (Job) — Definition |
| SM50 | Process Overview |
| SM51 | List of SAP Systems |
| SM59 | Maintenance of RFC Connections |
| SM62 | Maintenance of Events |
| SM66 | Global Work Process Overview |
| SMX | System → Own Jobs |
| SPRO | Customizing Guidelines |
| SQ02 | Maintenance of SAP Query/InfoSets |
| SQ10 | Assignment of Query/InfoSets to User and Role |
| ST03N | SAP BW Statistics |
| ST05 | Performance Analysis (→ SQL Trace) |
| ST22 | ABAP Dump Analysis |
| SU01 | Maintenance of Users |
| SU24 | Maintenance of Role Templates |
| SU53 | Resolve Error Codes (at the Authorization Level) |
| TRSA | Test Tool for Service API |

## C.1.1    Transactions Relevant to Planning

Compared to other modules, the number of transactions used in the BW-BPS area is rather limited. The following table provides a brief overview of the most important transactions that are regularly used in planning projects.

| Transaction | Description |
|---|---|
| RSPLAN | Modeling BI-Integrated Planning |
| RSPLF1 | Start: Editing the Function Type |

| Transaction | Description |
|---|---|
| RSPLSA | BI Planning: Starter Settings |
| RSPLSE | BI Planning: Lock Management |

## C.2 SAP R/3 Transactions Relevant to SAP BW

| Transaction | Description |
|---|---|
| FD32 | Change Debtor Credit Management |
| FD33 | Display Debtor Credit Management |
| LBWE | Customizing Cockpit for Logistics Extract Structures |
| LBWQ | qRFC Monitor (Outbound Queue) |
| KEB0 | Create/Display/Delete CO-PA DataSource |
| RSA3 | Extractor Checker SAPI 3.0 |
| RSA5 | Transfer DataSources from Business Content |
| RSA6 | Perform Follow-Up Work on DataSources and Application Component Hierarchy |
| RSA7 | Maintenance of Delta Queue |
| RSA9 | Transfer Application Components from Business Content |
| RSO2 | Maintenance of Generic DataSources |
| RSO3 | Setup of Delta Extraction for Attributes and Texts |
| SBIW | Display of Implementation Guide ($\rightarrow$ Customizing for Extractors) |
| SMQ1 | qRFC Monitor (Outbound Queue) |
| TRSA | Test Tool for Service API |

# D   Literature

**Balanced Scorecard Institute:** *http://www.balancedscorecard.org.*

**Codd, Edgar Frank:** A Relational Model of Data For Large Shared Data Banks, Communications of the ACM 26, No. 1, January 1983.

**Codd, Edgar Frank et al.:** Providing OLAP (Online Analytical Processing) to User-Analysts: An IT Mandate, 1993. See also: *http://www. fpm.com/refer/codd.html.*

**Egger, Norbert:** SAP BW Professional, SAP PRESS 2004.

**Egger, Norbert; Fiechter, Jean-Marie R.; Rohlf, Jens:** SAP BW Data Modeling, SAP PRESS 2005.

**Egger, Norbert; Fiechter, Jean-Marie R.; Rohlf, Claudia; Rose, Jörg; Weber, Stephan:** SAP BW Planning and Simulation, SAP PRESS, 2005 (available only in German under the title *SAP BW – Planung und Simulation*).

**Egger, Norbert; Fiechter, Jean-Marie R.; Salzmann, Robert; Sawicki, Ralf Patrick; Thielen, Thomas:** SAP BW Data Retrieval, SAP PRESS, 2006.

**Egger, Norbert; Fiechter, Jean-Marie R.; Rohlf, Jens; Rose, Jens; Schrüffer, Oliver:** SAP BW Reporting and Analysis, SAP PRESS, 2006.

**Fischer, Roland:** Business Planning with SAP SEM, SAP PRESS 2005.

**Imhoff, Claudia; Galemmo, Nicholas; Geiger, Jonathan G.:** Mastering Data Warehouse Design: Relational and Dimensional Techniques, John Wiley, 2003.

**Inmon, William H.:** Building the Data Warehouse, John Wiley, 3rd edition 2002.

**Inmon, William H.; Imhoff, Claudia; Sousa, Ryan:** Corporate Information Factory, John Wiley, 2nd edition 2000.

**Kaplan, Robert S.; Norton, David P.:** The Balanced Scorecard. Translating Strategy Into Action, 1996.

**Kimball, Ralph; Merz, Richard:** The Data Warehouse Toolkit: Building the Web-Enabled Data Warehouse, John Wiley, 2000.

**Kimball, Ralph; Reeves, Laura; Ross, Margy; Thornthwaite, Warren:** The Data Warehouse Lifecycle Toolkit: Expert Methods for Designing, Developing, and Deploying Data Warehouses, John Wiley, 1998.

**Kimball, Ralph; Ross, Margy:** The Data Warehouse Toolkit: The Complete Guide to Dimensional Modeling, John Wiley, 2nd edition 2002.

**Pendse, Nigel:** The OLAP Report. What is OLAP? An analysis of what the increasingly misused OLAP term is supposed to mean, *http://www.olap report.com.*

**Pfläging, Niels:** Beyond Budgeting, Better Budgeting, Haufe Verlag, 2003.

**Rafanelli, Maurizio:** Multidimensional Databases: Problems and Solutions, Idea Group Publishing, 2003.

**Thomsen, Erik:** OLAP Solutions: Building Multidimensional Information Systems, John Wiley, 2nd edition 2002.

**Vesset, Dan:** Closed-Loop Business Analytics, IDC, 09.2003

# E    Authors

The authors are all acknowledged BI specialists of the **CubeServ Group** (*www.cubeserv.com*). The CubeServ Group (CubeServ AG, CubeServ GmbH, and CubeServ Technologies AG) specializes in Business Intelligence (BI) solutions and has practical experience with SAP BW dating back to 1998. It has already worked on hundreds of projects with SAP BW, SAP SEM, and SAP NetWeaver.

**Norbert Egger** is the Managing Director of the CubeServ Group, which specializes in BI solutions. In 1996, he established the world's first data warehouse based on SAP. Since then, he has implemented hundreds of projects with SAP BW and SAP SEM. He has many years of experience in the operation of SAP-based BI solutions.

Norbert Egger (*n.egger@cubeserv.com*) is the author of Chapter 3, *Data Modeling in the Administrator Workbench of SAP NetWeaver 2004s BI*, Chapter 4, *Data Retrieval*, Chapter 6, *Redesign Functions: Repartitioning and Remodeling*, Chapter 8, *Business Explorer Analyzer*, Chapter 10, *Report Designer*, and Chapter 12, *SAP Visual Composer*. He is the co-author of Chapter 5, *Performance Optimization with Aggregates and BI Accelerator*, and Chapter 7, *BEx Query Designer*.

**Dr. Jean-Marie R. Fiechter** has worked as a senior data warehousing consultant at CubeServ AG (Jona, Switzerland) since 2003 and is a certified SAP NetWeaver Business Intelligence consultant. He has international, practical experience in the areas of data warehousing, business intelligence, massively parallel processing, and management information systems (MIS). For the past several years, he has taught data warehousing at various universities and colleges. In addition, he works as a BI instructor on behalf of SAP.

Jean-Marie R. Fiechter (*j-m.fiechter@cubeserv.com*) is the author of Chapter 1, *Business Intelligence Concepts—Innovations*.

**Sebastian Kramer** has worked as an SAP BW consultant at CubeServ GmbH, Flörsheim, Germany, which specializes in business intelligence solutions. The main focus of his work lies on reporting, particularly web reporting. Sebastian Kramer graduated in business information systems technology at the technical college in Heidelberg, Germany. He has many years of experience with SAP Business Information Warehouse and SAP R/3 and has been involved in numerous national and international projects with well-known companies.

Sebastian Kramer (*s.kramer@cubeserv.com*) is the author of Chapter 7, *BEx Query Designer*, and Chapter 9, *BEx Web Application Designer*.

**Ralf Patrick Sawicki** is an SAP BW consultant at CubeServ GmbH (Flörsheim am Main, Germany), which specializes in business intelligence solutions. He has many years of experience with SAP Business Information Warehouse and SAP R/3 and has been involved in numerous national and international projects with well-known companies. Ralf Patrick Sawicki is a certified solution consultant for SAP NetWeaver Business Intelligence.

Ralf Patrick Sawicki (*rp.sawicki@cubeserv.com*) is the author of Chapter 2, *New Features of SAP NetWeaver 2004s—An Overview*.

**Peter Straub** is a member of the executive board at CubeServ Group, which specializes in business intelligence solutions. In 1994 he was in charge of establishing the SAP outsourcing area at Digital Equipment Corporation (DEC) in Switzerland and was jointly responsible for the GoLive of the first productive R/3 3.0 customer worldwide. Due to the constantly growing environment which has become increasingly complex the author had the opportunity to provide proof of his technical competencies in many global projects.

Peter Straub (*p.straub@cubeserv.com*) is the author of Chapter 5, *Performance Optimization with Aggregates and BI Accelerator*.

**Stephan Weber** is a senior consultant at CubeServ AG (Jona, Switzerland), which specializes in business intelligence solutions. After finishing his studies in business administration (with a focus on information management, production, and marketing) he first worked as an SAP consultant and project manager in the telecommunications, chemical, retail, and banking industries. In addition to his original R/3-related focus in the areas of accounting, controlling, and project system, has has also been involved in SAP BW and SAP SEM projects for several years.

Stephan Weber (*s.weber@cubeserv.com*) is the author of Chapter 11, *BI-Integrated Planning*.

**Wiebke Hübner** joined the CubeServ Group in 2004 as Project Manager for SAP publications. She has many years of experience in the preparation and communication of specialized topics. After graduating with a degree in Liberal Arts, she worked in project management for a cross-regional museum. In 2001, she became editor at Galileo Press (Bonn, Germany) for business-oriented SAP literature.

# Index